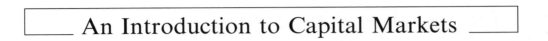

An Introduction to Capital Markets

Wiley Finance Series

An Introduction to Capital Markets

Products, Strategies, Participants

Andrew M. Chisholm

JOHN WILEY & SONS, LTD

Copyright © 2002 John Wiley & Sons, Ltd,
Baffins Lane, Chichester,
West Sussex PO19 1UD, UK

National   01243 779777
International   (+44) 1243 779777
e-mail (for orders and customer service enquiries): cs-books@wiley.co.uk
Visit our Home Page on http://www.wiley.co.uk

Other Wiley Editorial Offices

John Wiley & Sons, Inc., 605 Third Avenue,
New York, NY 10158-0012, USA

WILEY-VCH Verlag GmbH, Pappelallee 3,
D-69469 Weinheim, Germany

John Wiley & Sons Australia Ltd, 33 Park Road, Milton,
Queensland 4064, Australia

John Wiley & Sons (Asia) Pte Ltd, 2 Clementi Loop #02-01,
Jin Xing Distripark, Singapore 129809

John Wiley & Sons (Canada) Ltd, 22 Worcester Road,
Rexdale, Ontario M9W 1L1, Canada

British Library Cataloguing in Publication Data

A catalogue record for this book is available from the British Library

ISBN 0 471 49866 1

Typeset in 10/12pt Times from the author's disks by Dobbie Typesetting Limited, Tavistock, Devon
Printed and bound in Great Britain by Biddles Ltd, Guildford and Kings Lynn
This book is printed on acid-free paper responsibly manufactured from sustainable forestry,
in which at least two trees are planted for each one used for paper production.

Contents

Acknowledgements

I have learned a great deal about the capital markets and about how to teach the subject from Paul Roth. My regrets go to the family of the late Julian Walmsley, who commented on an earlier draft of this volume. I owe a tremendous debt of gratitude to my clients and to all the people who have attended my courses over the years and who have constantly challenged my thinking about the capital markets. They have helped me in countless ways. Any errors of omission or commission in this book remain of course my own responsibility. Special thanks to Pat Daly, Andrew Pullman, Lorna Byers, Amanda Whiteford and Sara Wiseman at Dresdner Kleinwort Wasserstein and to Brenda Hazelwood at JP Morgan Chase. Without Sam Whittaker at John Wiley & Sons I would never have taken up my word processor in the first place and I thank her for her help and encouragement. Above all this book is dedicated to my wife Sheila for her forbearance over my frequent withdrawals to my study and for her unfailing moral support in this as in all other areas of life.

1
Introduction:
The Market Context

Trade in general is built upon, and supported by two essential and principal foundations, viz., Money and Credit.

Daniel Defoe

In its broadest sense **capital** can be defined as accumulated wealth that is available to create further wealth. It is wealth that is engaged in a reproductive process. The capital markets are meeting places where those who require additional capital seek out others who wish to invest their excess. They are also places where risk can be distributed, shared and diversified — so that, for example, those with surplus wealth can spread their risk among a wider range of attractive investments. Originally the meeting places were physical spaces such as the forum of an ancient city or a coffee house or a stock exchange. In our day capital market participants may be located in different continents and conduct deals over the telephone or 'meet' in cyberspace via electronic mail and the internet.

Who exactly are the users of capital? In one sense we all are, at least part of the time. We borrow money to buy a house or a car so that we can live our lives, do our jobs, feed our families and make our own small contribution to the growing wealth of nations. We use our savings to pay school and university tuition fees and invest in the 'human capital' that will sustain the economic health of the country in future years. But capital is also used by corporations, by governments, by state and municipal authorities and by supranational agencies. When a company builds a factory or buys new equipment it is engaged in capital expenditure — using funds provided by the shareholders or lenders or set aside from past profits to purchase assets that are used to generate future cash flows. Governments use tax revenues to invest in major national infrastructure projects such as roads and subway systems and to invest in education and health and policing so that we can all go about our business and lead fulfilling lives. Agencies such as the World Bank and the European Bank for Reconstruction and Development inject funds into developing economies so that they have a basis for economic growth and future prosperity.

Who are the suppliers of capital? Again the answer is that we all are. Sometimes we do this directly by buying shares and bonds issued by corporations and debt securities issued by governments and their agencies. Sometimes we employ financial and other intermediaries to invest funds on our behalf. We deposit money in bank accounts, invest in mutual funds and set aside money in pension schemes for our retirement. We pay our taxes to the government and local authorities. We pay premiums to insurance companies who invest the proceeds against their future liabilities. Corporations themselves become sources of capital when they reinvest profits in their business rather than paying money out in the form of dividends to their shareholders.

1.1 FINANCIAL INTERMEDIATION AND RISK

This book is about the operation of the capital markets, the market participants, the role of the main financial intermediaries, and the products and techniques that are used to bring together the suppliers and the users of capital in the modern world. It is also to a very large extent about the management of risk. Risk takes many forms in the capital markets and financial institutions play a critical role in assessing, managing and distributing risk. For instance, a bank that lends money assumes a **credit risk** — the risk that the borrower might default on its payments. Bankers have developed techniques to analyse and mitigate such exposures over many centuries to help ensure that their shareholders and depositors do not face unacceptable losses.

Increasingly banks use their position as financial intermediaries to create loans and then 'package' them up and sell them off in the form of bond issues. This process is called **securitization**. The bond investors assume the credit risk on the loan book in return for a rate of interest greater than they could earn on government securities. The banks recycle the capital they were originally provided with by their shareholders and depositors so that they have funds available to create new loans. They analyse risk, manage risk and then distribute the risk through the public bond markets.

The boundaries between the different types of financial institutions are becoming increasingly blurred in the modern financial markets. Earlier in the last century the demarcation lines seemed rather more rigid. The Glass–Steagall Act of 1933, for example, created a firm distinction in the US between what became known as **investment banking** and **commercial banking**. Commercial banks took in deposits and made commercial loans. They assumed credit or default risk and contained this risk by carefully evaluating the creditworthiness of borrowers and by managing a diversified portfolio of loans. By contrast, investment banks underwrote new issues of securities and dealt in shares and bonds in the secondary markets. (A **primary** market is a market for creating or originating new financial instruments; a **secondary** market is a market for trading existing instruments.) They took **underwriting risk**. This arises when a bank or a syndicate of banks buys an issue of securities from the issuer at a fixed price and takes over the responsibility for selling or placing the stock into the capital markets.

At the time of Glass–Steagall the US Congress believed that a financial institution faced a conflict of interest if it operated as both an investment and a commercial bank, and duly passed the legislation. As a consequence the great banking house of Morgan split into two separate organizations. The commercial banking business later merged to form Morgan Guaranty Trust and is now part of the JP Morgan Chase Bank. The investment banking business was formed into Morgan Stanley which later combined with Dean Witter. By contrast, Merrill Lynch emerged from the securities broking and trading business in the US and only over time expanded its range of activities and its international reach to become a fully-fledged global investment bank.

In the UK similar divisions of responsibility used to apply until the barriers were progressively removed. After the Second World War and until the 1980s the new issue business in London was largely the province of so-called **merchant banks** who were members of the Accepting Houses Committee. Retail and corporate banking was dominated by the major clearing or 'money centre' banks such as Barclays and National Westminster Bank (now part of the Royal Bank of Scotland group). Trading and broking in UK and European shares and UK government bonds in London was conducted by a number of small partnership-based businesses with evocative names such as James Capel, Wedd Durlacher and Kleinwort Benson. The insurance companies were separate from the banks, and the world insurance market was dominated by Lloyds of London. These segregations have all since been swept away. Nowadays large UK financial institutions offer a very wide range of banking and investment products and services to corporate, institutional and retail clients.

In the US the constraints of Glass–Steagall were gradually lifted towards the end of the twentieth century. US commercial banks started to move back into the new issuance business both inside the US itself and through their overseas operations. One factor that spurred this development goes under the rather ungainly title of **bank disintermediation**. In the last decades of the twentieth century more and more corporate borrowers decided to raise funds directly from investors by issuing bonds (tradable debt securities) rather than by borrowing from a commercial bank or a syndicate of banks. This development was particularly marked amongst top-quality US borrowers with excellent credit ratings. In part the incentive was to cut out the margin charged by the commercial banks for their role as intermediaries between the ultimate suppliers of capital (depositors) and the ultimate users. In part it reflected the overall decline in the credit quality of the commercial banks themselves. Prime quality borrowers discovered that they could issue debt securities and fund their capital requirements at keener rates than the great majority of commercial banks. Disintermediation (cutting out the intermediation of the lending banks) developed apace in the US and then spread to other financial markets. Later on even lower credit quality borrowers discovered that they could raise funds very effectively through the public bond markets.

The advent of the new single European currency, the euro, has stimulated the same sort of process in continental Europe. Before the single currency Europe developed as a collection of relatively small and highly fragmented financial markets with many regional and local banks. Banks and corporations had very strong mutual relationships cemented by cross-shareholdings — in Germany the major banks and insurance companies owned large slices of the top industrial companies. Most corporate borrowing was conducted with the relationship bank. Shares and bonds were issued and traded primarily in domestic markets and in a range of domestic currencies. There were restrictions on the extent to which institutional investors could hold foreign currency assets. There was a general lack of understanding amongst investors of other European markets.

Now all this is being swept away, at great speed. Banks around Europe are consolidating and unwinding their cross-shareholdings to free up capital to invest in their own businesses. In Germany the government has promoted legislation to make this process more tax efficient. Borrowers are increasingly looking to the new issue markets to raise funds. Investors in Europe can now buy shares and bonds and other securities denominated in a single currency that are freely and actively traded across a whole continent. Stock and derivatives exchanges which originated in national markets are merging and re-inventing themselves as cross-border trading platforms.

1.2 THE EUROMARKETS

The modern capital markets have become truly global in their scale and their scope. Although New York is the biggest financial centre in the world, many of the developments that led to today's international marketplace for money actually originated in London. In the years immediately following the Second World War London had lost its traditional role as a place where capital could be raised for large-scale overseas investment projects. It shrank to a small domestic market centred around the issuance and trading of shares of UK companies and UK government bonds. Luckily for the many people who subsequently made their living there, the City of London rediscovered its birthright through the development of the so-called **Euromarkets**, starting in the 1950s and 1960s.

It all started with **Eurodollars**, which are dollars held in international accounts and outwith the direct regulatory control of the US Federal Reserve. The largest Eurodollar market is based in London, and from the 1950s banks from the US and around the world set up operations in London to capture a share of this lucrative business. The oil crisis of the early 1970s gave a tremendous boost to the Euromarkets. Huge quantities of so-called 'petro-dollars' from wealthy Arab countries found a home with the London-based banks. These dollars were recycled as loans to corporate and sovereign borrowers, and later through the creation of Eurodollar bonds which were sold to international investors searching for an attractive return on their surplus dollars.

The Eurobond market boomed in 1975, and the international market for securities has never looked back. The banks became ever more innovative in the financial instruments they created. A market developed in other so-called Eurocurrencies — Euromarks, Euroyen and so forth. The watchwords of the Euromarkets are innovation and self-regulation. The Bank of England and the UK government allowed the market to develop largely unhindered, and kept their main focus on the domestic sterling market and the UK banking system. Although London is the home of the Euromarkets there are also markets in other international centres, such as Singapore. The London market has been compared by some observers to the Wimbledon tennis tournament — it is staged in the UK but the most successful players are foreigners. This is not entirely fair (Barclays Capital is an obvious counter-example) but it is true that the large US, German and Swiss banks are major participants in the market.

Globalization, bank deregulation and the easing of constraints on capital flows around the world all led in the last decades of the twentieth century to the emerging belief that only a small number of so-called 'bulge bracket' investment banking firms would have the scale to operate on a truly international basis. The acknowledged market leaders were Goldman Sachs, Morgan Stanley and Merrill Lynch. These firms were able to offer the large multinational corporations that dominate the modern world the full range of services they needed, wherever and whenever they needed them. They could meet the burgeoning requirements of their institutional fund management clients for global research and investment ideas. They had the necessary expertise in complex structures and derivative products and they had made a huge investment in information technology. A consensus developed that the smaller merchant banks and securities houses would either be squeezed out or taken over. The more forward-thinking among the smaller firms might adapt and find some profitable niche business — perhaps exploiting their intimate knowledge of a local market, or strong client relationships, or a set of products that are not easy to replicate (or not worthwhile for the larger investment banks to offer).

Around the new millennium, though, a new paradigm emerged, and it is an open question at the time of writing where success will lie in the future. A round of banking mega-mergers created giant 'universal banks' combining very large scale commercial lending with global investment banking services. Chase Manhattan combined with JP Morgan, acquiring along the way the venerable house of Robert Fleming with its banking and portfolio management operations in the UK and the Far East. Citigroup acquired the famous trading firm of Salomon Brothers and in 2000 the investment banking division of Schroders.

In Europe the largest German bank, Deutsche Bank, decided that it could not sit back and rely on its domestic retail and commercial banking franchise, which would come under attack from the forces of disintermediation and from foreign competition. It acquired the UK house Morgan Grenfell in 1989 and built a global investment banking business both organically and later through the purchase of Bankers' Trust (which had previously absorbed the bulk of the equities business of National Westminster Bank). In response to all this frenetic activity Goldman Sachs floated as a public corporation in part so that it could raise the capital to compete in this world of banking monoliths. The head of Merrill Lynch openly raised the question of a possible merger with a global commercial banking group.

1.3   MODERN INVESTMENT BANKING

The term 'investment banking' tends to be used these days as something of an umbrella expression for a set of more-or-less related activities in the world of finance. We could classify firms such as Morgan Stanley or Goldman Sachs as 'pure' investment banks. Other organizations such as Citigroup and Deutsche Bank, Credit Suisse and JP Morgan Chase are universal banks with commercial and investment banking subsidiaries.

In some ways it is easier to explain what does *not* happen inside an investment bank these days than what does. For example, an investment bank will *not* operate a mass-market retail banking operation, which demands a completely different skill set. If an investment bank is a subsidiary of a large universal bank then retail banking will be located elsewhere in the group. On the other hand the investment banking operation *will* handle activities in the international wholesale capital markets and will also house the corporate advisory function. Typically it will also embrace participation in the new issues markets, securities research, securities trading and sales, links with institutional investors, expertise in derivatives and the ability to structure complex new financial products and to manage the risk on such products.

There is a more detailed list set out below of the activities that are typically carried out in an investment banking business, with a very brief description of what happens in each business area. Some large banking groups have also folded into their investment banking division the part of the operation that makes loans to major corporate clients. There is a view that large clients expect their relationship bank to 'put its balance sheet at their disposal' and that corporate lending, while not in itself highly profitable, will lead to lucrative investment banking mandates.

- **Corporate Finance or Advisory**
  Advising corporates on mergers, takeovers and acquisitions.
  Advice on strategic and financial restructuring.
  Advising governments on the privatization of state assets.

- **Debt Markets**
  Foreign exchange: research, trading, sales.
  Government bonds: research, trading, sales.
  Debt capital markets: managing new bond issues and underwriting issues for corporate and sovereign borrowers often operating as a member of a syndicate of banks.
  Corporate and emerging markets bonds: sales, trading, credit research (researching into the risk of changes in the credit quality of the bonds, which will affect their value).
  Credit derivatives (products that manage and re-distribute credit risk): research, trading and sales.
  'Flow' derivative products (standardized derivative products dealt in volume): research, trading, sales.
  Structured derivatives products (complex structures often devised with the needs of specific clients in mind).
- **Equity Capital Markets**
  Advising companies on initial public offerings of shares or subsequent offerings such as rights issues and private placements.
  Underwriting and syndicating new equity issues.
- **Equity Markets**
  Cash equities: research analysis, trading (market making), sales to institutional investors.
  Equity derivatives: equity swaps, options and structured products. Trading, sales, research. Clients will include institutional investors and corporations.

An investment banking business or subsidiary *may* also include:

- a custody business which holds securities on behalf of clients and manages cash;
- a private banking operation aimed at high net-worth individuals;
- an asset management business;
- a retail broking business which provides stockbroking services for private individuals rather than institutions;
- a private equity business which invests the bank's own capital and that of its clients in the shares of unlisted companies and companies listed on smaller stockmarkets.

It *will* include:

- operational staff who settle trades and handle payments (the so-called 'back office');
- risk management specialists and auditors and middle-office staff who monitor and measure risks and exposures and profits;
- information technology professionals who develop and manage the bank's computer systems;
- human resources and other support functions.

1.4   ABOUT THIS BOOK

This book is designed to provide a convenient one-volume introduction to the capital markets. The subject is of course a massive one and there will necessarily be topics which the reader will wish to explore later in much more detail. To help with this a list of suitable additional reading and useful internet sites is given at the end of the book. At the same time the aim of the current volume is to provide sufficient depth of explanation so that it is of practical use to people who are entering or planning to enter the capital markets business, or who are already working in the industry and who wish to improve their knowledge of specific areas of the markets.

The book describes how the key products and markets work, who the principal market participants are, and their overall goals and objectives. It includes a wide variety of examples and case studies designed to illustrate the application of the main capital markets products. One of the most daunting aspects of the financial markets is the sheer quantity of 'jargon' expressions that are used. Very frequently the same word is used with different meanings in different contexts. One aim of this book is to explain and illustrate these concepts as simply as possible, both in the text itself and also in the extensive Glossary at the end of the book.

Chapters 2 and 3 are concerned with two areas of the business that are intimately related, the market for short-term interest rate (STIR) products and the foreign exchange (FX) markets. In the past a bank dealing room handling such instruments would have been segregated into those desks handling 'spot market' products and others handling derivatives. The 'spot market' is the underlying market, in this instance for short-term loans and deposits and for spot foreign exchange transactions. A 'derivative' is anything whose value is derived from the underlying market, such as a currency forward or option contract.

Nowadays the spot and derivatives businesses are closely aligned and marketing staff are expected to have a wide knowledge of a range of products that provide solutions to the problems of the bank's corporate and institutional clients. The traders are also expected to have an understanding of the impact of events in other aspects of the business on the particular instruments they deal in. In Chapter 3 we explore the links between the short-term interest rate market and the foreign exchange market and between spot trades and forward foreign exchange deals. In later chapters we continue the theme of linking events in the underlying and the derivatives markets.

Corporations and governments raise funds through the issuance of a range of short-term debt instruments and also through longer-term notes and bonds. In Chapters 4–6 we look at the markets for government and corporate bonds, the issuers and the investors, and the role of the banks in bringing issues to the market and in trading bonds. Investors and traders in bonds have to understand how the securities are priced and how the returns and risks are evaluated. We consider a range of measures including yield to maturity (internal rate of return), duration, convexity, and their practical applications and limitations. The value of a financial asset such as a bond or a share (or indeed an entire company) is the present value of the expected future cash flows. The key to valuation is therefore an assessment of the likely future cash flows, and the application of the correct rate of discount with which to establish present value. Chapter 6 shows how to derive and apply discount rates and forward interest rates, absolutely essential tools in modern finance.

Corporations also raise funds through the issuance of equity securities or shares (known as common stock in the US). Chapter 7 describes the primary market for cash equities and the role of equity capital markets specialists within investment banks in the process of issuing new shares. The majority of shares in modern developed markets are held by investment management institutions managing money on behalf of pension funds, insurance companies and the individual investors who buy mutual funds. Many of these institutions are now divisions of larger banking groups, such as Merrill Lynch Asset Management, which in 1998 took over the assets of Mercury Asset Management, one of the largest UK managers. In Chapters 7–9 we explore equity investment styles and the secondary markets for trading shares once they are issued. We also consider how shares are valued in the market using multiples such as the price/earnings ratio and also using discounted cash flow methods.

As we noted previously, in the modern capital markets banks and securities houses not only bring together investors and corporations and governments looking to raise funds. They also play a critical role in the evaluation and management of risk. Chapters 10–13 explain key products that are used in the modern market to manage interest rate exposures and exposures to changes in bond values: forward rate agreements, interest rate futures, bond futures and interest rate swaps. Through a series of examples and case studies we show how these instruments are used in practice and how they can be priced using tools previously introduced in earlier chapters. Chapter 14 extends the concepts to the equity markets through a discussion on listed equity futures contracts and equity swap transactions.

One of the most remarkable features of the modern financial markets is the growth of financial options and structured products that are based on options. Sometimes the options are so deeply embedded in the structure of the instrument that it is not obvious to the untutored eye that they are there. In Chapter 15 we introduce fundamental option concepts and in Chapter 16 the principles underlying the pricing of options, including an explanation of how the famous Black–Scholes option pricing model, developed by Fischer Black, Robert Merton and Myron Scholes, can easily be set up on an Excel spreadsheet.

In Chapter 17 we consider the application of the pricing model in more detail. In particular we look at how the risks on option positions are measured and managed in practice. Chapter 18 explores some of the many applications of options in hedging and trading. Chapter 19 applies option concepts to currency and interest rate options, with a set of risk management cases and examples. It concludes with an explanation of how the standard pricing methodology can be adapted to value currency options and key interest rate option products such as caps, floors and swaptions.

It has become commonplace in the modern world to say that 'change is the only constant' and that the pace of change has accelerated over the past decades. (Although when we think about what our parents and grandparents lived through this is a very big claim.) In any event if this proposition applies anywhere it applies in the global financial markets. What seems like a revolutionary concept today becomes commonplace tomorrow. Products that seemed like the most arcane 'rocket science' 10 or so years ago, and which were regarded as almost impenetrably complex and only suitable for the most advanced professional user, now seem completely straightforward. We wonder what the fuss was about.

It is very dangerous to make forecasts in the capital markets business. But there is a good chance on current trends that many of the products and techniques which originated in the 'wholesale' capital markets business will be adapted for the retail market in the course of the following decades. Private investors can already buy structured products from banks and insurance companies that 'embed' quite complex derivatives. In the future we should see more of this type of financial engineering aimed at the individual rather than the corporation. We could see products that provide highly tailored investment solutions, and which also help individuals manage their exposures to a wide range of risks. Most people have exposures that they could at least consider hedging — to interest rates, house prices, currency rates, equity market prices, even the risk of a downturn in the industry they work in. In future, risk management tools such as those discussed in this volume may no longer belong just to the esoteric world of investment banking, they may form part of our everyday lives.

2
The Money Markets

We think in generalities but we live in details.
Alfred North Whitehead

2.1 CHAPTER OVERVIEW

In this chapter we consider the markets for borrowing and lending funds over the short term, traditionally known as the money markets. Borrowers include corporations, banks and governments. Investors include pension funds, insurance companies, corporations, governments and some retail investors. Money dealers working for major banks provide liquidity to the market by continuously taking in deposits and making loans (also known as 'placements'). Borrowers can also raise funds directly from investors by issuing short-term debt securities which are tradable in secondary markets. We look at key domestic money markets and also at the international market for funds, known as the Eurocurrency market. A domestic market is one in which funds are borrowed and lent in the domestic currency, subject to the authority of the central bank. The largest in the world is for deals made in US dollars contracted inside the United States. We consider the role of central banks such as the US Federal Reserve, the European Central Bank, the Bank of England and the Bank of Japan in the day-to-day operations of domestic money markets and in setting interest rates. We look at how governments borrow on a short-term basis by issuing Treasury bills, and their repo operations. The Eurocurrency market is an international wholesale market for borrowing and lending and is based in major international financial centres such as London. We explore some of the reasons for the growth of the Eurocurrency market and the major types of financial instruments used in the market, including Eurocurrency loans and deposits, certificates of deposit and Euro-commercial paper.

2.2 DOMESTIC MONEY MARKETS

The money markets are markets for borrowing and lending funds over the short term. 'Short term' is usually taken to mean a maturity of one year or less, although in practice some money market deals have maturities greater than one year. Major economies such as the US, Germany, France, the UK and Japan have highly developed **domestic money markets** in which short-term funds are borrowed and lent in the local currency, subject to the control of the regulatory authorities of that country, normally the central bank. These domestic money markets are quite distinct from the so-called **Eurocurrency market** which is an international market in which banks take deposits and make loans in a range of currencies outside the home country for those currencies and outwith the direct regulatory control of the central banks responsible for those currencies.

2.2.1 Market Participants

Borrowers using the money markets include:

- financial institutions such as commercial and investment banks;
- companies (often known as 'corporates' in the banking world);
- governments, their agencies, state and regional authorities.

The main investors are organizations (and some individuals) with surplus cash to invest, including:

- insurance companies, pension funds and mutual funds;
- the treasury departments of large multinational corporations;
- governments, their agencies, state and regional authorities.

Money dealers working for major investment banks and securities houses around the world bring borrowers and investors together by ensuring that there is an active and liquid market for money market instruments. Business is conducted by telephone and through computer screens rather than on a physical marketplace. At the simplest level, money dealers take in short-term deposits and make short-term loans (sometimes known as 'placements'). They may also trade a range of short-term interest rate products such as Treasury bills, commercial paper and certificates of deposit. These are described in detail in the current chapter.

Basis Points

Market participants often refer to interest rates in terms of **basis points**. One basis point is 0.01%. Therefore 100 basis points is 1%. If a central bank increases or lowers interest rates by 25 basis points this represents a change of 0.25%.

2.3 US DOMESTIC MARKETS

Activities in the US domestic money markets are dominated by the operations of the **Federal Reserve System**, the US central bank. The 'Fed' is increasingly used as a model for central banks around the world, and many of the features of the system appear in the new European System of Central Banks.

The Federal Reserve System was set up by Congress in 1913 and consists of 12 District Federal Reserve Banks and a Board of Governors appointed by the US President and confirmed by the Senate. Major policy decisions affecting the supply of credit and the cost of money in the US are taken by the **Federal Open Market Committee** (FOMC) which includes the Governors, the President of the New York Reserve Bank and the Presidents of four of the 11 other District Banks. Since 1980 the FOMC has held eight regularly scheduled meetings each year at intervals of five to eight weeks.

At its meetings the FOMC considers:

- the current and prospective business situation;
- conditions in the financial markets;

Federal Reserve Release

Press Release

Release Date: August 22, 2000

For immediate release

The Federal Open Market Committee at its meeting today decided to maintain the existing stance of monetary policy, keeping its target for the federal funds rate at 6-1/2 percent.

Recent data have indicated that the expansion of aggregate demand is moderating toward a pace closer to the rate of growth of the economy's potential to produce. The data also have indicated that more rapid advances in productivity have been raising that potential growth rate as well as containing costs and holding down underlying price pressures.

Nonetheless, the Committee remains concerned about the risk of a continuing gap between the growth of demand and potential supply at a time when the utilization of the pool of available workers remains at an unusually high level.

Against the background of its long-term goals of price stability and sustainable economic growth and of the information currently available, the Committee believes the risks continue to be weighted mainly toward conditions that may generate heightened inflation pressures in the foreseeable future.

Figure 2.1   FOMC announcement 22 August 2000
Source: US Federal Reserve.

- economic trends such as income, spending, money supply, business investment;
- the prospects for inflation in the United States.

2.3.1   FOMC Directives

The FOMC issues a directive at the end of a meeting to the Federal Reserve Bank of New York which carries out day-to-day open market operations. The Fed can inject cash into the banking system by buying back Treasury bills (short-term government debt securities) thereby increasing the supply of credit in the economy. Or it can seek to tighten credit and slow down economic growth by selling Treasury bills to the banking system, which reduces the supply of funds available for lending to companies and to individuals. See Figure 2.1.

In practice nowadays the Fed tends to perform its open market operations largely through so-called **repo** transactions rather than outright sales and purchases of Treasury bills. When the Fed conducts repo transactions it supplies funds to the banking system on a temporary basis and accepts Treasury bills as collateral against the loan. Repos are explained in more detail in the final sections of this chapter.

2.3.2   Federal Funds

The FOMC directives to the New York Federal Reserve Bank are designed to maintain the **Federal funds** rate at a certain target level. The Federal funds market is a market for interbank dollar lending inside the US and therefore operates under the supervision and control of the Fed in its capacity as central bank. The Fed funds market arises because banks in the US have to maintain minimum balances, called **reserves**, with the Federal Reserve in order to maintain the stability of the banking system. Banks have to maintain a minimum average balance over a period of two weeks based on the level of deposits that are taken in. A bank that has excess reserves can lend via the Fed funds market to another bank that is temporarily short of funds. The great bulk of lending is for overnight maturity, although longer-term loans are also contracted.

2.3.3   The Discount Window

In theory US banks that are short of cash can borrow money from the Fed through the so-called **discount window**. In practice this tends to be used these days in emergencies or as a last resort when no other sources of funds are available. The Fed operates under stringent rules to ensure that the facility is not used to shore up a non-viable financial institution.

2.4   EUROZONE MARKETS

The European System of Central Banks (ESCB) was established in 1998 and has many features in common with the US model. It is a system composed of the European Central Bank (ECB) plus the national central banks (NCBs) of the European Union countries. The **Governing Council** comprises the members of the Executive Board and the governors of the NCBs adopting the euro. The **Executive Board** comprises:

* the President;
* the Vice-President;
* four other members appointed by common accord of the governments of the member states.

The main responsibility of the Executive Board is to implement monetary policy in accordance with the guidelines laid down by the Governing Council, working through the NCBs.

2.4.1   ESCB Goals

The goal of the system was explicitly defined at its outset as the maintenance of **price stability**, that is, the control of inflation across the eurozone. It was established as a fully independent central bank. Members of the ECB and of NCBs are forbidden from taking instructions from any external body and member states may not seek to influence members of the ECB or NCBs in the performance of their duties. Indeed since the system was established by international treaty in one sense it is more independent than the central bank of a sovereign state — the system can only be changed by common agreement of all the member countries rather than by a single national legislature.

2.4.2   ESCB Regulation

Like the Fed, the ESCB imposes regulatory constraints on banks operating in its territory, which are required to maintain funds on reserve with the NCBs in proportion to their deposit base. The system of minimum reserve requirements is designed to prevent excessive lending by the banks and also to stabilize money market interest rates. Compliance with the requirement is based on average reserves over a period of one month.

The ESCB has taken the decision to pay interest on reserves, perhaps to ensure that money market activities in the euro do not move offshore where reserve requirements would not apply. The ESCB provides short-term borrowing and lending facilities to banks in the system and these rates establish minimum levels of interest rates throughout the eurozone. Finally, the ESCB conducts regular open market operations through the NCBs through which it provides funds to the markets, taking in return securities such as government bills and bonds as collateral.

2.5   STERLING MONEY MARKETS

The Bank of England (BoE) has had sole responsibility since 1998 for monetary policy in the UK. Decisions on interest rates are made by the Bank's **Monetary Policy Committee** (MPC). The Bank's monetary policy objective is to deliver price stability as defined by an inflation target set by the UK government. The MPC sets the short-term interest rate in pounds sterling and implements this rate through open market operations in the sterling money market. The Bank of England is therefore functionally independent of the UK central government. (Although in fact there is provision in the Act of Parliament for the British Chancellor of the Exchequer to issue directives on interest rates in an emergency.)

Transactions between banks in the UK are settled through accounts held with the Bank of England. The open market operations of the Bank of England ensure that the commercial banks have enough funds available to settle all transactions. The Bank lends funds against collateral consisting of high quality assets such as:

- Treasury bills;
- gilts (UK government bonds);
- certain eligible bank bills;
- securities issued by EU governments.

The rate of interest agreed in these transactions affects the overall level of interest rates in the UK economy.

2.5.1   Open Market Operations

The Bank of England's operations are conducted with a range of major financial institutions such as banks, building societies (mortgage lenders) and securities houses. Funds are lent with an average maturity of about two weeks. If the Bank believes that there are surplus funds available in the banking system and wishes to reduce the amount of money available for lending in the banking system, it can mop these up through outright sales of UK Treasury bills.

2.6   THE BANK OF JAPAN

The Bank of Japan (BOJ) was also restructured in 1998 to strengthen its independence from central government. The nine-member **Policy Board** which determines changes in the official discount rate consists of the Governor, the two Deputy Governors and six outside experts. The official **discount rate** is the interest rate charged by the BOJ on loans to financial institutions which have accounts at the Bank. The rate is applied when the BOJ buys commercial bills from financial institutions at a discount to their face or par value, and also when the BOJ lends money to such institutions against the collateral of qualified commercial bills.

Lender of Last Resort?

The BOJ is the **lender of last resort** for banks in Japan. However the BOJ is careful to clarify its role by saying that it will only consider lending to an insolvent financial institution when the problem poses a threat to the stability of the financial system. Central banks have to balance two concerns. One is that a bank failure may pose a **systemic risk**, the threat of a collapse in confidence in the whole financial system. However, a blanket guarantee of central bank support might create a **moral hazard** — banks may be tempted to take on ever greater risks in the expectation that the central bank will bail them out. The Bank of England drew an important line in 1995 when it declined to rescue Barings Bank from collapse as the result of speculative trading by Nick Leeson.

2.7 TREASURY BILLS

Treasury bills are short-term negotiable securities issued in their domestic money markets by governments such as the US, the UK, France and Germany. They are fully backed by the governments concerned and used as short-term funding instruments, in part to help smooth out the flow of cash from tax receipts but also, as we have seen, as instruments to control the supply of money in the banking system and hence the economy at large. The US Treasury regularly sells bills at auction (minimum denomination $1000) with maturities ranging from 4 to 52 weeks. The auction cycle is currently as follows.

- **One-Month Paper.** 4-week bills are offered each week. Except for holidays or special circumstances the offering is announced on Monday and the bills are auctioned on the following Tuesday and issued on the Thursday following the auction.
- **Three and Six-Month Paper.** 13-week and 26-week bills are offered each week. Except for holidays or special circumstances the offering is announced on Thursday and the bills are auctioned on the following Monday and issued on the Thursday following the auction.

The participants in the auction are major investment banks and security houses, other banks and institutional investors, and private investors. There are two types of bid that can be submitted. In a **non-competitive bid** the investor agrees to accept the rate determined by the auction. Most retail investors make non-competitive bids which can be submitted by telephone or nowadays via the internet. In a **competitive bid** the investor submits a rate to three decimal places in multiples of 0.005% (for example, 5.01%) and if the bid falls within the range accepted the investor will receive securities.

In the current system all successful bidders are awarded securities at the same rate, although a number of alternative systems have been tried over the years. Between auction and settlement the primary dealers make a market in **when-issued** bills — this allows traders to take a position in bills for future delivery and settlement.

2.8 DISCOUNTING TREASURY BILLS

US Treasury bills, also known as 'T-bills', do not pay interest as such. Instead they are issued and trade at a discount to their face or par value. The discount method, also used with UK T-bills, goes back to the early days of commercial banking and is sometimes known as the **bank discount** method, to differentiate it from modern discounted cash flow calculations. Financial instruments traded using the bank discount method are quoted in terms of a percentage discount from their face value rather than at their yield or rate of return.

Simple Example: Discounting Commercial Bills

An exporter agrees an export transaction with an importer and submits a bill for £1 million for the goods, payable in one year. The exporter needs to raise cash today and approaches a bank. The bank agrees to discount the bill at a rate of 10% and pays the exporter upfront £1 million less 10% of £1 million, which is £900,000. In one year the bank will collect the £1 million payment due from the importer for the goods.

In the above example the 10% discount from the £1 million par or face value of the bill charged by the bank is not in fact the yield or return it earns by discounting the bill. The bank pays out £900,000 today and will receive £1 million in one year. Its return on the original investment is:

$$\frac{£1,000,000 - £900,000}{£900,000} \times 100 = 11.11\%$$

Clearly the bank must be earning more than 10% on the deal. If it invested £900,000 at 10% for one year it would only have £990,000 at the end of the period. This is very satisfactory for the bank but not so pleasant for the exporter in the story. The exporter is effectively paying an interest rate of 11.11% to obtain money today rather than in one year, as opposed to what looks at first glance like a 10% charge.

2.8.1   Discount Formula

Of course not all discount securities mature in exactly one year. The general formula for calculating the settlement amount (dollar purchase price) of a US Treasury bill is as follows:

$$\text{Settlement Amount} = \text{Face Value} \times \left\{ 1 - \left(\frac{\text{Discount Rate}}{100} \times \frac{\text{Days to Maturity}}{360} \right) \right\}$$

The formula takes into account cases where there is less than one full year to the maturity of the instrument. It also uses the traditional US money market day counting convention known as **actual/360**. The discount rate is pro-rated by the actual number of calendar days to the maturity of the bill divided by a fixed 360-day year basis. The actual/360 convention has been adopted for Treasury bills issued in euros, the new European currency, by eurozone countries such as Germany, France and Italy and is widely used in money markets around the world. A notable exception is the case of UK Treasury bills where an **actual/365** day count convention applies.

US Treasury Bill Calculation

A dealer purchases a US Treasury bill with 40 days to maturity at a quoted discount rate of 5.5%. The face value is $100,000:

$$\text{Settlement Amount} = \$100,000 \times \left\{ 1 - \left(\frac{5.5}{100} \times \frac{40}{360} \right) \right\} = \$99,389$$

2.8.2 Yield or Return

The yield or return on an instrument such as a US Treasury bill that uses the bank discount method is always understated by the quoted discount rate. It can be calculated from the actual cash flows involved in buying the bill and holding it until maturity. In the above example the purchase price of the bill is $99,389. From this we can work out the percentage return on holding the paper until maturity and then annualize this figure to calculate a yield or return, on the assumption that the bill is held until maturity:

$$\text{Yield} = \frac{\$100,000 - \$99,389}{\$99,389} \times 100 \times \frac{360}{40} = 5.53\%$$

The rate of 5.53% can now be directly compared with money market instruments such as short-term bank deposits which are quoted in terms of the simple annualized rate of return on the investment, i.e. without compounding. The following explicit formula will calculate the yield on a Treasury bill directly. For UK Treasury bills substitute actual/365 for actual/360 in the formula:

$$\text{Yield} = \frac{\text{Quoted Discount Rate}/100}{1 - (\text{Days to Maturity}/360 \times \text{Quoted Discount Rate}/100)}$$

In our example:

$$\text{Yield} = \frac{0.055}{1 - (40/360 \times 0.055)} = 0.0553 \quad \text{or} \quad 5.53\%$$

2.8.3 UK Treasury Bills

The UK government also issues Treasury bills on a discount basis. These are fully backed by the UK government and effectively by the tax revenues of the country. The typical maturity is around three months and the maximum maturity is one year. On 3 April 2000 the Debt Management Office (DMO), an agency of the UK government, took over full responsibility for the weekly tender of T-bills from the Bank of England.

The formula for calculating the settlement amount (sterling purchase price) of a UK Treasury bill is:

$$\text{Face Value} \times \left\{ 1 - \left(\frac{\text{Discount Rate}}{100} \times \frac{\text{Days to Maturity}}{365} \right) \right\}$$

The day counting method is called actual/365.

2.8.4 The Risk-free Rate

The yield or return on Treasury bills issued by major economies such as the US, the UK, France and Germany is often taken to establish the **risk-free** rate of return available in that currency. The return is risk-free in the sense that the market assumes that these governments will never default on their short-term debt. It is also risk-free in the sense that a purchaser of a T-bill can effectively lock into a known and guaranteed rate of return until the maturity of the paper. This is because there are no interim interest payments to reinvest during the lifetime of a T-bill and therefore no uncertainty about future reinvestment rates.

Money market instruments issued by companies and banks offer an additional return over the risk-free return on T-bills. This **spread**, or additional yield over the T-bill rate, reflects the risk that the issuer might default on payments — in other words it represents additional return for taking on the additional credit risk.

2.9 US COMMERCIAL PAPER

Commercial paper (CP) is an unsecured promissory note (effectively an IOU) issued by:

- corporates;
- financial institutions;
- governments;
- supranational agencies.

Commercial paper originated in the US in the nineteenth century and the US commercial paper (USCP) market is the largest such market in the world. Originally CP offered a means by which large business enterprises such as the railroads could tap into sources of capital across the US continent and internationally, at a time when US banks were confined to single states and relatively small in terms of their capital base.

Classic commercial paper is unsecured and does not carry a bank guarantee. As a result (except in times of economic boom) it tends to be primarily a market for 'name' issuers with strong cash flows and a good credit rating. The average maturity of USCP is around 30 days, normally with a maximum of 270 days. The limit arises from the fact that paper issued with a maturity of more than 270 days requires registration with the US Securities & Exchange Commission (SEC) and this adds to issuance costs. In the case of a corporate borrower the funds are typically used to finance operating costs and working capital requirements.

USCP Quotation

USCP is quoted on a bank discount basis in the same way as US Treasury bills, so that the yield or return is understated by the quoted rate.

2.9.1   Settlement and Dealers

Settlement in the USCP market is normally the same day as purchase. Issuers often **roll over** USCP on maturity — that is, they issue new paper to redeem the maturing instruments. There is a risk that the new paper may not find enough buyers, so issuers can arrange a **standby credit line** with a bank so that the funds will always be available.

Large CP issuers such as General Electric Capital Corporation (GECC) place their paper directly with investors and employ teams of salespeople for this purpose. Issuance fees can be very low for a large and frequent borrower, as little as one or two basis points. However many issuers still operate through dealers who work for major Wall Street investment banks and securities houses. The dealers may agree to buy up and then resell the paper at a fixed price, or alternatively may agree simply to use their 'best endeavours' to find investors (the latter type of arrangement carries a lower fee). The denominations of bills are normally $100,000 and above.

Many top European names have set up USCP programmes, starting with Electricité de France in 1974, which used the proceeds to pay for its oil requirements in US dollars. Part of the reason for issuance in the USCP market is that domestic commercial paper markets in Europe are as yet relatively underdeveloped, although with the advent of the euro this may change in the years ahead.

2.10   CREDIT RISK ON USCP

Investors in USCP include:

- insurance companies;
- pension funds;
- governments;
- municipal authorities;
- corporates.

Generally speaking, investors buy commercial paper because they are looking for higher returns than they can achieve on Treasury bills. The spread over the risk-free rate is the number of basis points an issue of commercial paper pays above the rate on the Treasury bill with the nearest maturity. The spread will depend on the credit rating of the issuer — the greater the risk of default, the higher the spread over Treasuries. It will also depend on the market's general appetite for risk.

Most USCP is rated. The major US rating agencies, Standard and Poor's (S&P) and Moody's, use the rating scales set out in Table 2.1 for assessing default risk on short-term money market securities such as US commercial paper.

Table 2.1 Credit ratings for money market paper

S&P	Moody's
A1+	P1
A1	
A2	P2
A3	P3

Source: Ratings agencies.

The highest rated paper is at the top of the list, the lowest at the bottom. Because of the short-term nature of the securities being evaluated the agencies focus on assessing the cash flow-generating ability of the issuer — how likely or otherwise it is that the paper will be repaid at maturity in 30 or so days' time. The concern is normally not so much with the risk of outright bankruptcy as with liquidity risk — the danger that the issuer may not have enough cash to redeem all the paper at maturity. However when there is an economic downturn investors do start to have concerns about default, particularly about less well rated paper.

Flight to Quality

A US building materials company called Armstrong World Industries defaulted on its commercial paper in November 2000. In the aftermath the spread between A1/P1 paper and the riskier A2/P2 paper widened to over 100 basis points. The spread stood at only 15 basis points in the late 1990s. The market for lower-rated paper started to dry up as investors moved their money into lower risk, higher credit quality investments. Banks became reluctant to extend standby credit facilities. Some issuers switched to other sources of funds including asset-backed commercial paper which is secured or backed by specific revenue streams.

2.10.1 Advantages of USCP

For companies and institutions with a good credit rating USCP is an extremely cost-effective means of borrowing short-term funds, much cheaper than the traditional European method of borrowing short term via a bank on an overdraft facility. Top name A1/P1 borrowers can raise funds at a rate that is higher than the rate on US T-bills, but below the London Interbank Offered Rate and the rate payable on certificates of deposit issued in the Eurodollar market. In favourable market conditions lower quality A2/P2 issuers can also achieve keen funding rates. The secondary market for USCP is far less liquid than that for US Treasury bills and most paper is held by investors until maturity.

2.11 BANKERS' ACCEPTANCES

Bankers' acceptances (BAs) are trade-related negotiable bills issued by companies but **accepted** or guaranteed by a bank in return for a fee. They can be freely traded in the secondary market. In the US and UK BAs are issued at a discount to face value. The accepting bank guarantees that the face value of the bill will be paid at maturity. The goods involved in the underlying commercial trade also serve as collateral backing up the paper. BAs have declined in importance since the growth of the commercial paper market. Most BAs are backed by documentation such as invoices held by the accepting bank. The instrument traded in the secondary market will often simply be a note briefly describing the underlying commercial trade and specifying the name of the accepting bank.

2.11.1   Eligible Bills

In some domestic money markets there is a distinction between **eligible** and **ineligible** BAs. An eligible acceptance is essentially one which can be used by banks as collateral to borrow short-term funds from the central bank. The distinction grew up in the 1960s and 1970s when BAs were issued in the US and the UK as a means of avoiding tight credit restrictions rather than in support of trade-related activities. In an attempt to control the rising money supply the Fed and the Bank of England made such bills ineligible for rediscount with the central bank.

2.12   THE EUROCURRENCY MARKETS

The Eurocurrency markets have their origins in the 1950s and 1960s when substantial pools of US dollars were deposited with banks outside the US, mainly in London. The market received a major boost after the 1973–4 oil crisis when oil-producing states decided to place the bulk of their substantially increased dollar receipts in foreign centres such as London rather than in New York. London's main competitive advantage was that US dollar accounts held there were not subject to the regulatory regime of the Federal Reserve, in particular to reserve requirements and other laws in place at the time restricting the rate of interest that could be paid on dollar deposits in the US domestic market. The London-based banks recycled the money by making loans to major corporations and governments, and the so-called Eurodollar market was born. The prefix 'Euro' in this context is an historical accident and is **not** related to the new European currency called 'the euro' (symbol €).

Eurocurrency Definition

A **Eurocurrency** is essentially a currency borrowed and lent outside the domestic money market for that currency and therefore outwith the direct regulatory control of the domestic central bank. A dollar borrowed or lent inside the US and subject to reserve requirements imposed by the Federal Reserve is a domestic money market transaction. A dollar borrowed or lent outside the US is a Eurodollar (the transaction does not have to take place in Europe). Following the lead set by the dollar, international markets later developed in Euromarks and Euroyen.

2.13   EUROCURRENCY LOANS AND DEPOSITS

The Eurocurrency markets are primarily wholesale markets in which the main participants are international corporations, institutional investors, commercial banks and global investment banks. In London the main players include the major American, German and Swiss banks, names such as Citigroup, Deutsche Bank and Union Bank of Switzerland. Most Eurocurrency money market deals are term deposits and loans with a maturity of one year or less, with the majority of deals around the three to six-month maturity range. Money dealers at the major banks stand ready to quote their **offer** (lending) rates and **bid** (borrowing) rates for a range of Eurocurrencies and a range of maturities from overnight out to one year and beyond.

2.13.1 Term or Time Deposits

In the case of **overnight** deals the funds are delivered on the day the deal is arranged and repaid with interest on the next business day. Unless agreed otherwise, in the case of a **term or time** deposit for longer periods such as three months the funds are actually delivered two business days after the deal is arranged. This is called **spot delivery**, or a deal agreed 'for value spot'. The funds are then repaid with interest at maturity three calendar months (or whatever the agreed term of the deal is) after the spot value date. This aligns the Eurocurrency market with the foreign exchange (FX) market in which the bulk of trades are for value spot, i.e. two currencies are exchanged two business days after a deal is agreed. (See Chapter 3 for details on the currency markets.)

2.13.2 LIBOR

The key reference rate in London, the largest Eurocurrency market in the world, is the **London Interbank Offered Rate (LIBOR)**. LIBOR is calculated and broadcast on electronic news services at 11:00 a.m. London time by the British Bankers' Association. It is an average of the offer (lending) rates for short-term interbank loans between major banks in the London market. There is a separate LIBOR rate for each currency and for a range of maturities. Table 2.2 shows LIBOR rates for 23 August 2000 for one-week, one-month, three-month, six-month and 12-month loans.

For example, in Table 2.2 the three-month dollar LIBOR rate is 6.69% per annum. This is based on the average interbank offered rates quoted by a panel of 16 major banks and is a rate for spot delivery of funds (in two business days' time). Principal plus interest is paid at the maturity of the loan three months after spot.

The final column in the table shows the euro LIBOR rates, the BBA calculated rates for lending in the euro (the new European currency) for maturity one week, one month, three months, six months and 12 months after spot, also based on a sample of 16 banks

Table 2.2   BBA LIBOR rates 23 August 2000

CCY	USD	GBP	CHF	JPY	EUR
1WK	6.57625	5.9375	3.20500	0.33000	4.55125
1MO	6.62000	6.05625	3.25000	0.34375	4.67250
3MO	6.69000	6.21594	3.48167	0.37125	4.77913
6MO	6.83250	6.32656	3.75833	0.42000	5.08063
12MO	6.97938	6.51375	3.96000	0.46250	5.31375

Source: Bloomberg.

in the London market. The rival reference rate to euro LIBOR is **euribor** which is calculated by the European Banking Federation in Brussels from the spot lending rates in the euro posted by a group of 57 banks based in the eurozone. (The sterling rates in Table 2.2 are in fact the exception in that they are quoted for delivery of funds on the day of the quotation rather than for value spot.)

2.13.3   Applications of LIBOR

LIBOR is frequently used in the financial markets as a benchmark or reference point for establishing payments. In the **syndicated loan** market the rate of interest paid by a borrower to the syndicate of lending banks is often reset every three or six months according to the LIBOR rate for the period, plus a spread in basis points based on the relative creditworthiness of the borrower. For instance, the rate might be fixed at the three-month dollar LIBOR for an interest period plus 80 basis points (0.8%).

In the interest rate derivatives market the payments due on many products are based on LIBOR. Less frequently mentioned is LIBID — the rate top banks in London pay to borrow funds from other banks — and LIMEAN which is mid-way between LIBOR and LIBID. In Section 2.3 we encountered the Fed Funds rate; it is an interbank dollar lending rate for dollar loans made inside the US and is therefore the domestic equivalent of the international dollar interbank lending rate established by dollar LIBOR.

2.14   EUROCURRENCY RATE QUOTATIONS

Money market dealers in London traditionally quote Eurodollar rates in fractions, to the nearest 1/16% or 1/32%. The interest rates on most other currencies are quoted in decimal format to two decimal places, that is, to the nearest basis point. London money traders quote their offer (lending) rate first then their bid (borrowing) rate second. In other financial centres the rates are normally quoted bid then offer. Interest on deposits and loans up to one year is normally paid at maturity along with the repayment of the principal. This type of repayment structure is sometimes known as a **bullet**. Deposits with more than one year to maturity usually pay interest on an annual or six-monthly basis.

Interest Calculation

Interest on Eurodollar and most other Eurocurrency deals is calculated using the actual/360 day count convention. Suppose a bank borrows $10 million for three months at 6.7% per annum from a money dealer. The value date, when the funds are actually received, is spot, two working days after the deal is agreed. The actual calendar number of days from spot to maturity is calculated as 93 days. The interest due at the maturity of the loan is therefore $10 million$\times$0.067$\times$93/360 = $173,083. Sterling uses an actual/365 convention.

The actual/360 convention has some interesting side effects. For example, suppose a bank decides to borrow $10 million for a full year (365 days) at a rate of (say) 7%. The interest due at maturity would be more than $700,000:

$$\text{Interest Due} = \$10 \text{ million} \times 0.07 \times 365/360 = \$709,722$$

The borrower has to pay an extra five days in interest (\$9722) because of the day count convention. Put another way, the effective rate of interest is higher than the rate quoted by the dealer:

$$\text{Effective Rate} = 7\% \times 365/360 = 7.0972\%$$

The key formulae for Eurodollar deposits and loans with one year or less to maturity are as follows:

$$\text{Interest Accrued} = \text{Principal} \times \frac{\text{Interest Rate}}{100} \times \frac{\text{Actual Days}}{360}$$

$$\text{Principal} + \text{Interest} = \text{Principal} \times \left\{ 1 + \left(\frac{\text{Interest Rate}}{100} \times \frac{\text{Actual Days}}{360} \right) \right\}$$

Interest in all these formulae is calculated on a **simple interest** basis, i.e. without compounding.

2.15   EUROCURRENCY CERTIFICATES OF DEPOSIT

A Eurocurrency certificate of deposit (CD) is created when funds are deposited with a bank. Unlike a regular term deposit, however, the CD can be freely traded and the holder can sell the paper for cash in the secondary market. In practice the liquidity of CDs in the secondary market will depend on the credit standing of the issuing bank. In the Eurocurrency markets CDs are normally issued in **bearer** form, which means that the holder of the physical certificate has sole title to the principal and interest on the underlying bank deposit due to be paid at maturity. This facilitates trading and maintains anonymity of ownership.

2.15.1   CD Definition

A CD is simply a title to a known future cash flow of principal plus interest. The rate of interest is sometimes called the **coupon rate**. The **future value** of a Eurodollar CD at maturity is calculated using the same formula that we used for Eurodollar deposits. It is the principal amount deposited, also known as the present value (PV), plus interest at maturity:

$$\text{Future Value at Maturity (FV)} = \text{PV} \times \left\{ 1 + \left(\frac{\text{Coupon Rate}}{100} \times \frac{\text{Actual Days}}{\text{Year Basis}} \right) \right\}$$

2.15.2   Eurodollar CD: Example

A Eurodollar CD was issued on 1 March 2000 for maturity 1 June 2000. The principal is \$1 million and the coupon (fixed interest rate) is 5.5%. The calendar tells us that there are 92 actual days from issue until maturity. Therefore:

$$\text{Future Value} = \$1 \text{ million} \times [1 + (0.055 \times 92/360)] = \$1,014,056$$

Suppose however we buy the CD not when it was issued, but for settlement (delivery) on 3 April 2000. What is the fair value of the instrument—in other words, how much should we pay for it on that date? There are now only 59 days remaining until maturity. We notice from the money market rates screen that the rate for two-month money is currently 5.25%. By rearranging the formula for calculating future value we can derive a formula for working out the value today of a sum of money to be received in the future—its present value. The formula becomes:

$$\text{Present Value} = \frac{\text{Future Value}}{1 + (\text{Interest Rate}/100 \times \text{Actual Days}/\text{Year Basis})}$$

The future value at maturity of the Eurodollar CD in 59 days in our example is $1,014,056. The present value of this fixed sum discounted back to 3 April 2000 at a rate of 5.25% is therefore:

$$\text{Present Value} = \frac{\$1,014,056}{1 + (0.0525 \times 59/360)} = \$1,005,405$$

2.16   CD YIELD TO MATURITY

Dealers normally quote CDs not in money terms but in terms of the rate of discount used to calculate present value. This rate is also known as the CD's **yield to maturity**. In the previous example if we bought the CD for $1,005,405, held it to maturity and received from the issuer principal plus interest of $1,014,056 the total annualized return on our initial investment is 5.25%. This is exactly the yield or return we would achieve by placing the funds on a two-month Eurodollar money market deposit. Quoting CDs in terms of the discount rate allows traders and investors to compare the returns available on these negotiable instruments with those available on Eurocurrency deposits.

Suppose we could buy the CD more cheaply in the market from another dealer, at a dollar price of only $1,005,000. By rearranging the formula for calculating the present value of the CD we can calculate the yield to maturity we would achieve by buying the paper at that price. The formula becomes:

$$\text{Yield} = \frac{FV - PV}{PV} \times \frac{\text{Year Basis}}{\text{Days to Maturity}} \times 100$$

In our example the values to insert into the formula are:

Future value = $1,014,056
Present value = $1,005,000
Days to maturity = 59 (actual days)
Year basis = 360

Therefore:

$$\text{Yield} = \frac{\$1,014,056 - \$1,005,000}{\$1,005,000} \times \frac{360}{59} \times 100 = 5.50\%$$

If we could buy the CD for only $1,005,000 the annualized return from holding the instrument until maturity is 5.50%. Effectively the formula works out the percentage return on our initial investment then annualizes the result based on the number of days from purchase to maturity. Again, this is a simple interest calculation with no compounding. To compare the return on the CD with the return on an instrument which uses a simple interest calculation but an actual year basis rather than a 360-day year we simply multiply 5.50% by 365/360, or in a leap year 366/360.

2.17   EURO-COMMERCIAL PAPER

Euro-commercial paper (ECP) is issued in the international Euromarkets (primarily in London) rather than in a domestic money market such as the US. ECP issues are short-term, unsecured, bearer securities sold by major corporations with maturities ranging from one week to one year. The market took off in London in the 1980s. It is now a substantial and active market. The main buyers are institutional investors seeking higher returns than they can achieve on Treasury bills, through a flexible investment that is available with a variety of maturities. For a well-known borrower a Euro-CP issue permits access to a global pool of investors; and an issuance programme is fairly inexpensive to set up. Unlike USCP, Euro-CP can be actively traded in the secondary market.

2.17.1   Quotation Method

The key difference between Euro-CP and USCP is that Euro-CP is normally quoted on a yield basis and not using the traditional bank discount method employed for US T-bills and USCP. Deals are normally also for spot rather than same-day settlement.

Euro-CP Calculation

We buy a Euro-CP issue maturing in 30 days. The face value is $1 million and the yield quoted by the dealer is 5.5%:

$$\text{Purchase Price} = \frac{\text{Face Value}}{1 + (\text{Yield}/100 \times \text{Days to Maturity}/360)}$$

$$= \frac{\$1 \text{ million}}{1 + (0.055 \times 30/360)}$$

$$= \$995,438$$

2.18   REPOS AND REVERSES

The expression 'repo' is shorthand for **sale and repurchase agreement**. In a classic repo transaction:

- a security is sold for cash to a counterparty;
- with a simultaneous agreement that it will be repurchased on an agreed date in the future at the same price.

A classic repo deal involves drawing up a legal contract signed by both parties, although in developed markets the terms and conditions are often highly standardized. The repo market developed in the US but repos have become extremely common in financial markets around the world. They are used by traders and investors holding positions in securities who wish to raise short-term funds by using the securities as collateral.

The securities are often safe investments such as Treasury bills or Treasury bonds (longer-dated government debt securities; see Chapter 4). This makes repo a cheaper form of borrowing compared to borrowing without collateral. Repos are widely used by fixed-income operations to fund their trading activities. In addition, investors such as pension fund managers can put their securities out on repo and reinvest the funds raised at higher returns.

2.18.1   The Repo Rate

The **repo rate** is the rate of interest charged by the lender of funds to the borrower, who supplies collateral. A classic repo transaction has two legs. In leg one the collateral (the securities) is sold by the borrower to the supplier of funds. In leg two the sum borrowed against the collateral is returned to the supplier of funds plus interest calculated according to the agreed repo rate, and the collateral is sold back to the original owner.

2.19   REPO: CASE STUDY

A trader holds a €10 million nominal or face value position in bunds, German government bonds. The bonds can be sold in the market for a total settlement price of €101.8417 per €100. (The total settlement amount is called the **dirty price** in the bond market; see Chapter 4 for more information on bond quotations.) On a €10 million nominal holding the bonds are therefore worth €10 million $\times 1.018417 =$ €10,184,170. The trader decides to repo the bonds out to a repo dealer for a term of one week. The repo rate is 4.5% per annum. The transaction has two legs.

- **Leg 1.** In the first leg of the repo the trader sells the bonds to the repo dealer and receives the current settlement value of €10,184,170.
- **Leg 2.** In the second leg of the repo in seven days the repo dealer returns the bonds to the trader (the original owner) and the trader pays back €10,184,170 plus interest at 4.5% per annum.

$$\text{Interest Due} = \text{€10,184,170} \times 0.045 \times 7/360 = \text{€8911}$$
$$\text{Total Repayment} = \text{€10,184,170} + \text{€8911} = \text{€10,193,081}$$

The cash flows on the repo transaction are illustrated in Figure 2.2.

2.20   OTHER FEATURES OF REPOS

In a classic repo if there is an interest payment due on the securities during the term of the repo this is paid over to the original owner, on the payment date. In effect the party 'repo-ing' out the collateral maintains the same economic exposure to the securities as if

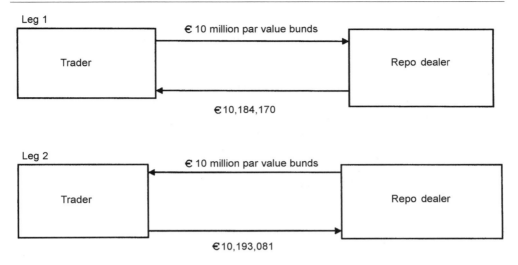

Figure 2.2   Repo transaction

they retained ownership. The lender or supplier of funds in a classic repo transaction is sometimes described as having carried out a **reverse** or reverse repo transaction.

Reverses are often used by short sellers or 'shorts' who need to borrow securities temporarily to cover a position in which they have sold stock they do not own, in anticipation of a price fall. In leg 1 of the repo the short acquires the securities and can then sell them into the market at their current market value. In leg 2 of the repo the short has to return the securities and will receive back the original amount lent against them, plus interest at the repo rate. The short will make a profit if the securities can be bought back cheaply in the cash market in order to return them to the original owner.

As we have seen, many central banks use repo as a tool to inject or to drain liquidity on a short-term basis from the market. In their open market operations they take in T-bills or quality commercial bills in return for cash, or sell bills to take cash out of the banking system.

Haircuts

In a repo the sum borrowed against the collateral may be less than its current market value. For example, the lender may only be prepared to lend $9.5 million in cash against a receipt of collateral currently worth $10 million on the market. The discount (here $0.5 million) is sometimes called a **haircut**. In practice the size of the haircut will depend on how much the collateral fluctuates in value in the market. It will be small for Treasury bills, but very substantial if highly volatile securities are offered as collateral against a loan.

2.20.1   Sell/Buy-backs

A sell/buy-back agreement is very similar to a classic repo except that it is structured in a slightly different way. It is a cash sale of bonds with a separate agreement to buy the bonds back on a forward (i.e. later) date at a higher price. The rate of interest charged on the loan is not explicitly stated; it is implied in the fact that the repurchase price on the forward date is higher than the cash sale price. Any coupon payments due on the collateral are not paid over separately; they are incorporated into the forward price and therefore paid at the termination of the agreement rather than on the actual coupon dates.

2.21   CHAPTER SUMMARY

The money markets are markets for short-term borrowing and lending of funds for maturities up to one year. Domestic markets are regulated by central banks such as the Federal Reserve in the US, the European Central Bank in the eurozone and the Bank of England in the UK. Governments issue short-term funding instruments called Treasury bills in their domestic money markets. The central banks act to control the amount of credit in the banking system by setting short-term interest rates and by conducting open market operations such as lending funds against collateral to commercial banks. In the US many large corporations and financial institutions raise short-term funds by issuing US commercial paper, which unlike US T-bills carry default or credit risk. The Eurocurrency market is an international market for funds based in major global centres such as London. The majority of deals are in US dollars and the banks can borrow and lend Eurocurrencies without being subject to regulation by the central bank of the currency in question. The main participants are commercial banks, securities houses, international corporations and investing institutions such as pension funds and insurance companies. Eurocurrency deposits and loans are made for a specific term such as three months or six months. Investors can also buy a range of negotiable (freely tradable) money market securities such as Eurocurrency certificates of deposit and Euro-commercial paper.

3
The Foreign Exchange Market

Money speaks a language all nations understand.
Aphra Behn

3.1 CHAPTER OVERVIEW

The foreign exchange market is a global, technology-based marketplace in which banks, corporations, governments and institutional investors trade currencies around the clock. In this chapter we explore the structure of the market and the role of foreign exchange (FX) dealers and brokers in sustaining liquidity. We consider the changing role of central banks in a world largely based on freely floating exchange rates. We look at how a spot FX dealer makes two-way quotations and assesses the profitability of deals. We consider the different types of risks that have to be managed in the FX dealing room, such as **market risk** and **settlement risk**, and the factors that determine FX rates between currencies. Although the bulk of FX deals are still settled two business days after the deal is agreed (spot transactions) there is also a highly active market in forward FX transactions. We look at the application of products such as **outright forward FX** deals and **FX swaps** in managing currency risks, in matching expected future cash flows and in switching investments into foreign currency assets.

3.2 MARKET STRUCTURE

In the millennium year 2000 average daily volumes in FX trading around the world exceeded $1.5 trillion for the first time. However, according to the Bank for International Settlements (BIS), import and export transactions between countries accounted for only around 3% of these trades. The bulk of FX deals are made by commercial banks including giants such as JP Morgan Chase, Citigroup and Deutsche Bank which together take almost one-third of the market share. The banks facilitate the trading and investment activities of their corporate and institutional clients by standing ready to lend or exchange a wide range of currencies, and in turn make markets in currencies amongst themselves.

Activities of the Banks

Some of the FX deals made by banks are purely speculative. Others are contracted as a means of 'laying off' risk acquired through transactions made with their clients and with FX dealers at other banks. Increasingly, the service that banks provide for their clients involves assembling and marketing complex FX derivative products that provide currency risk management solutions, rather than the straightforward exchange of one currency for another.

Traditionally, flows of money between currencies were largely determined by import and export transactions. As currency restrictions were gradually lifted in the decades after the Second World War, and especially when the era of floating exchange rates between major currencies opened in 1973, speculative currency trading began to assume considerable importance in the FX markets. In recent years the effects of investment flows between countries have become increasingly apparent. Institutional investors such as pension funds, insurance companies and mutual funds invest in shares, bonds and money market securities on a global basis and have to enter the foreign exchange markets to buy and sell currencies. In addition, major international corporations making direct investments in their foreign subsidiaries or completing cross-border takeovers of foreign companies generate substantial requirements for foreign exchange.

3.2.1 The Central Banks

In major economies such as the US, Europe, the UK and Japan there is no longer an official rate of exchange and the national currency floats freely against other currencies in response to supply and demand factors in the international markets. The central bank plays two main roles:

- it supervises the market;
- it maintains control over the supply of money and domestic interest rates, which will influence the attractiveness of the currency to foreign investors.

The central bank may seek to smooth out fluctuations in currency movements by buying and selling currency in the markets, often working in consort with other central banks around the world. In countries where there are still exchange controls the central bank fixes the official rates of exchange and may also act as the central counterparty in all FX transactions.

3.3 FX DEALERS AND BROKERS

FX dealers working for banks tend to specialize in one or more of a small group of closely related currency pairs. The most actively traded markets in the world are for deals in major currencies such as the US dollar, the euro, the Swiss franc, the Japanese yen and the pound sterling. Because of the advent of the euro, trading in formerly active currency pairs such as the Deutschemark against the French franc has ended. Some of the slack has been taken up by trading in emerging markets currencies such as the Polish zloty and the South African rand.

The professional FX market is an **over-the-counter** market. In other words, deals are made directly between market participants over the telephone or using electronic networks such as the Reuters system, and there is no physical marketplace or exchange. The currencies involved, deal sizes, value dates and rates of exchange are all negotiable. However FX dealers post indication rates for standard deal types on information services such as Reuters and Telerate. In a highly developed FX market such as the London market traders are linked by brokers who relay the best quotes currently available. Traditional brokers send prices to their clients through voice systems but increasingly brokers are connected to clients through electronic networks such as the Reuters Instinet system.

Role of the Brokers

Broking firms do not quote FX rates on their own account or take positions in currencies. They operate on a commission basis and the commission is normally related to the amount, size and complexity of the deal required. Brokers do not discuss the name of the banks quoting or accepting rates until the deal has been agreed. This can be valuable when a dealer wants to make a trade without revealing his or her current position to the market.

3.4 SPOT FOREIGN EXCHANGE DEALS

A spot FX transaction is a deal in which one currency is exchanged for another for **spot delivery** which (in the case of major currency pairs) is two business days after the trade is agreed. The details of the trade—currencies, amounts, exchange rate, payments information—are agreed by the counterparties on the trade date and the two currencies are exchanged on the spot date. In the FX markets the day when currencies are actually exchanged is called the **value date** and so a spot deal is 'for value spot'. In the interbank FX market the currencies are actually exchanged by funds transfer through the SWIFT system (Society for Worldwide Interbank Financial Telecommunications).

On request via the telephone or the Reuters network, a spot FX dealer will quote a **two-way** rate to fellow market professionals; that is, a bid (buy) rate followed by an offer or ask (sell) rate. The first step in interpreting an interbank FX quote is to determine which is the **base currency** and which is the **counter-currency** (the other currency involved in the quotation). The quote is expressed in terms of so many units of the counter-currency per single unit of the base currency. The dealer making the quote buys the base currency at his or her bid rate, the lower of the two numbers, and sells the base currency at the offer rate, the higher of the two numbers.

Example Spot FX Quotation

A spot FX trader quotes the following rates:

USD:CHF   1.7574/84

The base currency is the US dollar and the counter-currency is the Swiss franc. The dealer buys one unit of the base currency, the US dollar, at the left-hand (bid) rate and pays 1.7574 Swiss francs. The dealer sells one unit of the base currency at the right-hand (offer) rate and asks in return 1.7584 Swiss francs.

The currency pair in the example, USD:CHF, is quoted to four decimal places. The first part of the rate, in this case 1.75, is sometimes known as the **big figure**. The last two digits are known in the London market as the **pips**. Notice that in the example the dealer has quoted only the pips for the offer side of the quotation. The full rate is 1.7584. Professional dealers sometimes quote rates to each other using just the last two decimal places—for example '74/84'. However at the end of the conversation the two parties must confirm the trade details in full, using the full exchange rate.

3.4.1   The Dealer's Spread

The dealer's spread in the example quotation is CHF 0.0010 or 10 pips. The spread represents the risk the dealer takes in pricing the exchange of two currencies at a given moment in time. Suppose a counterparty 'hits' the dealer's bid rate and the trade amount is $10 million. In two business days' time the dealer will receive $10 million from the counterparty and will have to pay in return a fixed amount of Swiss francs:

> Receive $10 million
>
> Pay 10,000,000 × 1.7574 = CHF 17,574,000

The dealer therefore has a **long position** in dollars (and at the same time a short position in Swiss francs) for value spot. If the dollar weakens the dealer will lose out on the position, since to unwind the original trade the dealer will have to sell dollars and buy Swiss francs. For example, suppose that later in the same trading day the spot rate falls to USD:CHF 1.7500 and the trader enters a second offsetting spot deal at that rate. On the second deal the cash flows on the spot value date are:

> Pay $10 million
>
> Receive 10,000,000 × 1.7500 = CHF 17,500,000

The loss on the two deals combined is CHF 74,000, equivalent to $42,286 at a spot rate of 1.7500.

3.5   STERLING AND EURO QUOTATIONS

In the interbank FX market the dollar is normally the base currency. The main exceptions are where the dollar is traded against the British pound and against the euro, in which cases the dollar becomes the counter-currency. A two-way quotation of GBP:USD 1.5955/61 means that:

- the dealer bids for one pound and pays $1.5955 in return;
- the dealer offers one pound and charges $1.5961.

A two-way quotation of EUR:USD 0.9544/49 means that:

- the trader buys one euro and pays in return $0.9544;
- the trader sells one euro and asks in return $0.9549.

Of course if a client of the bank wishes to have the quotation expressed with the dollar as the base currency it is easy to make the conversion. If one euro is worth $0.9549 on the offer side of the quote then one dollar is worth 1/0.9549 or 1.0472 euros.

3.6   FACTORS AFFECTING SPOT FX RATES

At any given time some market participants wish to buy a currency and others wish to sell. The rate of exchange is the price of the base currency expressed in units of counter-currency that matches supply and demand. Behind supply and demand lie a range of economic factors, or **fundamentals** as they are sometimes known in the capital markets industry.

Key Economic Fundamentals

- Trade balance
- Interest rates
- Money supply
- Inflation
- Government fiscal policy — its spending and tax policy

3.6.1   The Trade Balance

The trade balance represents the difference between a country's exports and imports of goods and services. Importers are buyers and exporters are sellers of foreign currency. An excess of imports over exports will tend to bring downward pressure on the domestic currency. However, this effect is balanced by the fact that in modern global markets currency flows are strongly influenced by international investment, both direct investment (buying foreign companies) and indirect investment (buying financial assets such as bonds and shares denominated in foreign currencies).

In recent years the United States has run a substantial current account deficit with its trading partners, reaching $339 billion in 1999. This means that US importers have to sell dollars to buy foreign currency such as yen and euros. As noted above, this exerts a downward pressure on the dollar. However foreign investors, particularly in Japan where interest rates are extremely low, have been strong buyers of dollars to purchase dollar-denominated assets such as US Treasury bonds and US equities. European companies have been stepping up their direct investment in the US through acquisitions of US-based companies completed in US dollars.

Table 3.1 shows purchases of US assets (bonds and shares) by foreign investors between 1995 and 1999. The capital inflows in 1999 (in millions of dollars) included $200,506 from Europe and $43,366 from Japan.

A similar picture is revealed when we look at dollar reserves held by foreign countries over a similar period. Table 3.2 shows changes in official foreign exchange reserves held

Table 3.1   Net foreign purchases of US long-term securities 1995–99 in millions of US dollars

	Government bonds	Corporate bonds	Shares	Total
1995	162,844	57,853	11,240	231,937
1996	273,964	83,743	12,511	370,218
1997	234,024	84,358	69,597	387,979
1998	105,841	121,930	50,020	277,791
1999	84,205	160,537	107,522	352,264

Source: US Department of Treasury.

Table 3.2 Changes in dollar and non-dollar reserves 1996–99 ($bn)

	Dollar reserves	Non-dollar reserves	Total
1996	+161.7	+38.7	+200.3
1997	+87.6	+33.7	+121.2
1998	+40.2	−19.2	+21.0
1999	+191.1	−31.7	+159.4
Total outstanding at end-1999	1358.9	387.1	1746.0

Source: IMF.

in dollars and in other currencies between 1996 and 1999. The non-dollar reserves are translated to US dollar equivalents at the year-end exchange rate.

3.6.2 Interest Rates and Fiscal Policy

Higher interest rates can make a currency more attractive to international investors, at least over the short term, and increase demand for the currency. In practice the relationship between interest rates and currency rates is rather more complex. High rates of interest tend to occur at times of inflation. Accelerating inflation and money supply growth may be taken as signs that a currency may lose its value relative to other currencies and will tend to weaken the currency.

Finally, the government's fiscal stance will have a significant effect on the international standing of the currency. If the government runs a budget deficit by spending more than it collects in tax revenues the difference is made good by borrowing on the domestic or international capital markets. Too much spending can lead to excess growth in the money supply and inflation, which erodes the value of the currency. Too much borrowing can lead to rising interest rates, which slows down economic growth and tends to adversely affect the market values of investment assets such as fixed income bonds and equities, making the currency less attractive as an investment vehicle.

3.6.3 Release of Statistics

Statistics on the trade balance, money supply growth, Gross Domestic Product (GDP), tax receipts and other **economic indicators** are reported on a regular basis. The dates and times of release of the key numbers are well known to the market and are avidly followed. Many of the indicators are influenced directly or indirectly by the activities of the central bank and other government agencies. Currency analysts, dealers, economists, investment strategy advisors and corporate treasurers use the indicators to assess the next moves of the authorities. If for example the growth rate in the economy slows down sharply (as occurred in the United States in the first months of 2001) this may be taken by the market as a sign that the central bank will cut interest rates to stimulate growth and avert recession.

3.7 SPOT FX TRADING

Spot FX traders may adjust or **shade** their two-way quotations according to their current position and their future expectations on where currency rates are moving. For

Table 3.3   A trader's spot position in EUR:CHF

CHF bought (+)/sold (−)	Rate	EUR bought (+)/sold (−)
−31,550,000	1.5775	+20,000,000

example, suppose that a trader has the position shown in Table 3.3 in a EUR:CHF spot trading book (the base currency is the euro and the counter-currency the Swiss franc).

The trader has made spot FX deals which result in a 31.55 million short position in Swiss francs and a 20 million long position in euros for spot delivery. The deals will settle in two business days' time, and the dealer will have to pay a net 31.55 million Swiss francs and receive in return a net 20 million euros. If the euro weakens against the Swiss franc the dealer will make a loss on the position. The trader could take that risk and wait for the deals to settle, although it will be important to ensure that adequate funds are available to cover the net CHF payments. Alternatively, the dealer might decide to **close the position** through an offsetting spot FX trade (or a number of trades).

3.7.1   Shading the Rates

The trader in the example could call another dealer for a quotation, but the disadvantage of this approach is that the counterparty would gain the benefit of the bid/offer spread. Instead, the trader could quote a two-way EUR:CHF rate into the market in such a way that it would make it attractive for counterparties to sell Swiss francs to the trader in return for euros.

Assume that the current market rates are now EUR:CHF 1.5770/80. The trader could quote EUR:CHF 1.5769/79.

- **Bid Rate.** On the bid side the trader is bidding to buy one euro and pay only CHF 1.5769, so this is unattractive.
- **Offer Rate.** But on the offer side the trader is offering to sell one euro and asks in return only CHF 1.5779, a better rate than the current market level.

Suppose the trader contracts a spot EUR:CHF deal to sell €20 million to a counterparty at 1.5779 and receive in return CHF 31.558 million. In two business days' time the net cash flows in euros will now be zero but the trader will be left with a net surplus of CHF 8000 on the Swiss franc account. This is illustrated in Table 3.4.

The net profit in Swiss francs can easily be calculated. It is the difference between the rates at which the euros were sold and bought applied to the €20 million position:

$$\text{Net Profit} = (1.5779 - 1.5775) \times 20 \text{ million} = \text{CHF } 8000$$

Table 3.4   An offsetting EUR:CHF deal

CHF bought (+)/sold (−)	Rate	EUR bought (+)/sold (−)
−31,550,000	1.5775	+20,000,000
+31,558,000	1.5779	−20,000,000

The profit is given in Swiss francs because the exchange rates are expressed in terms of CHF per EUR. Normally traders convert profits and losses (P&Ls) into their home currency at the current market rate, often mid-way between the bid and the offer rate on the market. If the trader's home currency is euros then the P&L at the current market mid-rate of 1.5775 is calculated as follows:

$$\text{Net Profit} = \frac{8000}{1.5775} = €5071$$

Rules for Shading Spot FX Rates

A trader who wishes to make a competitive quotation to sell the base currency should lower the offer rate. A trader who wishes to make a competitive quotation to buy the base currency should raise the bid rate.

Suppose the market rate is EUR:CHF 1.5770/80 and a trader wishes to buy rather than sell euros; then an appropriate two-way quotation to make might be EUR:CHF 1.5771/81:

- the trader buys one euro and pays 1.5771 Swiss francs, more than the market;
- the trader sells one euro and charges 1.5781 Swiss francs, a less attractive offer rate than the market, which will discourage buyers of euros.

3.8   SPOT POSITION KEEPING

A spot FX trader keeps a manual or electronic **deal blotter** which lists:

- all the trades that have been made;
- the amounts;
- the rates;
- the deal counterparties involved.

Table 3.5 shows a typical spot trading blotter for a spot GBP:USD trader. Deals in the pound sterling against the dollar are often called **cable** trades in the market, after the trans-Atlantic cable formerly used to conduct and settle deals.

The first column shows the counterparty the trade was made with. The second column shows the counter-currency (US dollar) amount in full. The third column shows

Table 3.5   Spot GBP:USD deal blotter

(1) CPTY	(2) USD bought (+)/ sold (−)	(3) Deal rate	(4) GBP sold (−)/ bought (+)	(5) Net GBP position
ABN-AMRO	−14,723,000	1.4723	+10	+10
MERRILL	−7,362,500	1.4725	+5	+15
BARCLAYS	+14,727,000	1.4727	−10	+5
HSBC	+14,724,000	1.4724	−10	−5

the deal rate; the fourth the base currency amount in millions of British pounds. The final column shows the trader's net sterling position for spot delivery, a running total of the numbers in column four.

The first trade listed was with ABN-AMRO. The details are as follows:

- the trader bought GBP 10 million ('ten pounds' in the jargon of the markets) for spot delivery;
- the exchange rate is GBP:USD 1.4723;
- the dealer will pay in return for the pounds $14,723,000.

In the second trade the trader bought five million pounds at a rate of 1.4725. By the third trade the trader was starting to unwind the 'long' sterling position by selling pounds. By the fourth trade the rate had started to weaken and the trader had established a net short position of five million pounds, possibly in anticipation of a further weakening in the pound. To close out this overall position the trader would have to enter into a spot GBP:USD deal buying five million pounds and selling dollars.

3.8.1 Revaluation

How profitable has the cable dealer's trading campaign been so far? One way to work this out is to match off all deals in which the trader bought pounds with deals in which the trader sold pounds and check the rates at which the deals were entered into. If the trader buys pounds at a low rate and sells them at a high rate the trading campaign is profitable.

In practice this can be a very laborious way to calculate profits and losses because a spot trader in an active currency pair may have many individual trades listed in the blotter, and the trade sizes do not exactly match on a deal-by-deal basis. In addition, the trader will often have a net open position at the end, which was the case in the example shown in Table 3.5 — the trader has sold a total of 20 million pounds for value spot but has bought only 15 million pounds.

A common methodology is to take a revaluation or mark-to-market rate from the market (often the mid-rate, half-way between the bid and the offer rates) and apply it to each trade individually to calculate the P&L on that trade. For illustration we will take a revaluation rate of 1.4690 and apply this to the trader's blotter, as shown in Table 3.6.

In the first deal the trader bought GBP 10 million at 1.4723. The 'reval' rate is 1.4690. This is a loss:

$$\text{Loss (dollars)} = 10,000,000 \times (1.4690 - 1.4723) = \text{USD} -33,000$$

We then translate this into pounds at the revaluation rate:

$$\text{Loss (pounds)} = \frac{33,000}{1.4690} = -\text{GBP } 22,464$$

In the final deal the trader sold GBP 10 million at 1.4724. At the revaluation rate of 1.4690 this represents a profit:

$$\text{Profit (dollars)} = 10,000,000 \times (1.4724 - 1.4690) = \text{USD } 34,000$$

$$\text{Profit (pounds)} = \frac{34,000}{1.4690} = \text{GBP } 23,145$$

Table 3.6 Revaluation profits and losses

CPTY	USD bought (+)/sold (−)	Deal rate	GBP sold (−)/ bought (+)	P&L USD	P&L GBP
ABN-AMRO	−14,723,000	1.4723	+10	−33,000	−22,464
MERRILL	−7,362,500	1.4725	+5	−17,500	−11,913
BARCLAYS	+14,727,000	1.4727	−10	+37,000	+25,187
HSBC	+14,724,000	1.4724	−10	+34,000	+23,145
Totals	+7,365,500		−5	+20,500	+13,955

The rule is simple — if the trader buys above the 'reval' rate, mark in a loss; if the trader sells above the revaluation rate, mark in a profit.

3.8.2 Average Deal Rate

The net total P&L from all four trades is $20,500, which is equivalent to GBP 13,995 at the GBP:USD 1.4690 revaluation rate. We can cross-check the result by calculating the average rate at which the trades were created and comparing it with the revaluation rate:

$$\text{Total Net USD Bought} = \text{USD } 7,365,500$$
$$\text{Total Net GBP Sold} = \text{GBP } 5,000,000$$
$$\text{Average Deal Rate} = \frac{7,365,500}{5,000,000} = 1.4731$$
$$\text{Revaluation Rate} = 1.4690$$
$$\text{Net P\&L} = 5,000,000 \times (1.4731 - 1.4690) = \text{USD } 20,500$$

A net five million pounds was sold at a rate of 1.4731. It could be bought at a lower revaluation rate (1.4690) so the position is in profit. The $20,500 profit would only be realized in full if the trader does an offsetting trade to buy GBP 5 million for value spot.

3.9 FX RISK CONTROL

In a modern dealing room spot FX traders can enter trades directly into electronic deal capture systems which will maintain the blotter and calculate the revaluation profit or loss on the book based on the current market exchange rate. In addition, at the end of the trading day, a check will be made on the trader's book by the middle office or risk control department to assess the trader's position and to carry out an independent revaluation of the trading book based on current market rates. This shows not only how much realized profit or loss has been made but also the profit or loss that would result from closing any open positions. If it appears that the risks are too high the positions may be reduced or cut altogether.

3.9.1 Market Risk

The main risk in an FX dealing room is **market risk** — the risk that arises from running long or short positions in currencies that might weaken or strengthen. To control market risk traders are set limits on the size of positions they can maintain. Also, as we have noted, traders' positions are revalued or marked-to-market at the end of the day by financial or risk control specialists to assess the level of risk.

FX trading is carried out in international centres such as London, New York and Hong Kong and nowadays is a 24-hour business. A spot trader in London running an FX book with an open position overnight in (say) dollar/yen could find the rate has moved adversely by the time he or she returns to monitor the position on the next morning. One solution to this problem of **overnight risk** is to close the position at the end of the London trading day. Another is to place an order with a New York bank or with a colleague based in New York to make a deal on the trader's behalf, closing the position if the dollar/yen rate moves beyond a certain level. This is known as a **stop-loss** (or stop-profit) order.

Global Trading

In the modern global markets the solution to overnight risk in a large bank is for the FX trading book to be passed around the world, from London, to New York, to the bank's Far Eastern centre, and then back to London. The book is traded 24 hours a day.

3.9.2 Settlement Risk

FX deals give rise to settlement risk of three main types:

- operational failure;
- replacement risk;
- Herstatt risk.

The first type of risk results from simple operational failures, often known as 'trade fails'. It arises, for example, when payment instructions are incorrectly made and the currency that should be credited to a counterparty's bank account is sent to the wrong place. The bank may have to pay interest to its counterparty if this happens. Simple trade 'fails' of this kind can result in significant losses by the end of the year.

The second type of risk is that the counterparty may cease to trade before the deal is actually settled. The bank may have agreed the trade at a rate that is advantageous in comparison with current exchange rates, and replacing the trade with a new counterparty might result in a loss or a reduced level of profit. This is often referred to as **replacement risk**. The third and most dangerous type of settlement problem sometimes goes under the title of **Herstatt risk**. It is the risk that a bank might make the payment for its side of the deal but the counterparty might not reciprocate.

Herstatt Bank

Herstatt Bank was a German bank that failed in 1974 as a result of over-trading. Because of time differences, payments on a large number of FX deals in Deutschemarks were made to Herstatt Bank, but it closed operations and never made the return dollar payments to New York. The resulting legal actions spent many years in the German courts.

To reduce the risk of settlement problems and to cut back-office costs, banks are increasingly turning to technology-based solutions. The focus is on electronic deal capture rather than manual deal tickets and straight-through deal processing by computer. Human intervention is made on an exceptional basis, to rectify problems, to make sure that trade details are properly set up before the value date, and to establish procedures for handling more complex trades which will not automatically settle through the computer systems.

One potential trend for the future, perhaps, is for banks to outsource more of their back-office arrangements to specialist firms who can invest in the technology and spread the investment costs across a wider number of clients. Banks are also increasingly making 'netting' agreements with their counterparties. This means that trades are not settled individually, only the net payments due to either side are made.

Nostro and Vostro

These are terms frequently heard in FX settlements. A bank's payment account with another bank is called a **Nostro account**, from the Latin word meaning 'our'. For example, if the Royal Bank of Scotland has a dollar account with Bank of America in New York for dollar receipts on FX transactions this is a Nostro account for the Royal Bank. If Bank of America had a sterling account with the Royal Bank of Scotland then for the Royal Bank this would be a **Vostro account**, meaning 'your account with us'.

3.10   CROSS-CURRENCY RATES

A cross rate is an FX rate established between two currencies using their exchange rate against a common currency, typically the US dollar. The method of calculation depends on whether or not the common currency is the base in both cases.

3.10.1   Common Base Currency

Suppose that a corporate client wants a quotation from a bank to sell Swiss francs to the bank for value spot and to buy in return Japanese yen. The bank's spot rates against the US dollar are as follows:

$$\text{USD:CHF} \quad 1.6345/56$$
$$\text{USD:JPY} \quad 105.660/710$$

The bank's task is to quote a spot rate CHF:JPY to the client by 'going through the dollar':

- the bank would sell one dollar to the client and ask in return CHF 1.6356;
- the bank would buy that dollar back from the client and give in return JPY 105.660.

The bank's spot rate CHF:JPY is therefore:

$$\frac{105.660}{1.6356} = 64.6001$$

Since 1.6356 Swiss francs will buy 105.66 yen it follows that one Swiss franc will buy 64.6001 yen. In practice of course the bank's actual quotation may differ slightly from this theoretical number. Note that this is the bank's **bid rate** — the rate at which it buys the base currency CHF. Using the same logic we can calculate that the offer rate is CHF:JPY 64.6742.

In the above example the two cross-currencies share the same base currency, the US dollar.

Rule: Common Base Currency

The rule for calculating the bid and offer cross rates when the base currency is the same is to divide bid/offer and then offer/bid:

$$\text{Bid/Offer} = 105.660/1.6356 = 64.6001 \text{ (Bid)}$$
$$\text{Offer/Bid} = 105.710/1.6345 = 64.6742 \text{ (Offer)}$$

3.10.2 Different Base Currency

What happens when the two cross-currencies have a different base? Suppose that a UK fund manager wishes to shift funds to the Japanese market to take advantage of rising equity prices. She wishes to buy Japanese yen and to sell British pounds and contacts a bank. The bank's spot rates against the US dollar are currently as follows:

$$\text{GBP:USD} \quad 1.5965/75$$
$$\text{USD:JPY} \quad 105.660/710$$

The bank is asked to quote a cross rate GBP:JPY for the client:

- the bank would sell $1.5965 to the client and ask in return one pound sterling;
- the bank would buy $1.5965 back from the client and give in return 105.660× 1.5965 = 168.6862 Japanese yen.

Therefore the cross rate GBP:JPY is 168.6862. Note that this is the bank's rate for buying pounds (selling yen), i.e. its GBP:JPY bid rate. The bank's offer rate would be GBP:JPY 168.8717.

Rule: Different Base Currency

The rule for calculating the bid and offer cross rates when the base currency is different is very simple. It is to multiply the two bid rates and the two offer rates:

$$\text{Bid} \times \text{Bid} = 1.5965 \times 105.660 = 168.6862 \text{ (Bid)}$$
$$\text{Offer} \times \text{Offer} = 1.5975 \times 105.710 = 168.8717 \text{ (Offer)}$$

3.11 OUTRIGHT FORWARD FX DEALS

An **outright forward** foreign exchange deal is:

- a firm and binding commitment between two parties;
- to exchange two currencies;
- at an agreed rate;
- on a future value date that is later than spot.

The two currencies are not exchanged until the value date is reached, but the rate is agreed on the trade date. Outright forward deals are commonly used by companies that have known cash flows in foreign currencies that are payable or receivable on specific dates in the future. They can enter into contracts with a bank that will lock them into a known exchange rate and eliminate the risk of losses resulting from adverse foreign exchange rate fluctuations. The other side of the coin, of course, is that the contract must be honoured even if the company could obtain a better rate in the spot market. The company surrenders any potential gains resulting from favourable movements in FX rates in return for certainty.

3.11.1 Hedging with FX Forwards

The outright forward exchange rates quoted by banks are determined by the relative interest rates in the two currencies. Traders sometimes talk about this in terms of the relative **carry cost** of holding positions in the two currencies. In effect, as the following example illustrates, the forward FX rate is established through a hedging or arbitrage argument — what it would cost a bank to hedge against the risks involved in entering into an outright forward FX deal. If the rates are out of alignment then there is potential for a risk-free or 'arbitrage' profit.

3.12 FORWARD FX HEDGE: CASE STUDY

A Swiss company HELCO has exported goods to the US. The payment due is $10 million. The current spot rate is USD:CHF 1.6416/25. If the invoice was due for immediate settlement then HELCO would receive CHF 16.416 million from the bank in exchange for the dollars. However in this case the payment is actually due in three months' time, 91 days after spot. If the dollar weakens over that period then HELCO will find itself receiving fewer Swiss francs for the dollars, perhaps eliminating its profit margin from the export transaction.

By way of illustration, if the FX rate had moved to (say) USD:CHF 1.6000 when HELCO comes to sell its dollars, it would receive only CHF 16 million as a result of its export transaction. Of course a strengthening dollar would result in greater Swiss franc receipts, but HELCO may not be prepared to accept the currency risk, on the assumption that it has to pay its own suppliers and workers in its home currency, the Swiss franc.

Alternatively, HELCO could approach its relationship bankers at BIGBANK and enter into an outright forward FX deal in which HELCO would pay over the $10 million in three months' time and receive in return a fixed amount of Swiss francs. But how could BIGBANK establish a fair forward FX rate for the deal? It could base the rate on its estimate of what it believes the USD:CHF rate will be in three months. But unless it puts a hedge or protective device in place this could be a very risky transaction — the bank might make money on the deal but it might also lose substantial amounts of money, depending on what happens to FX rates in the meantime. An alternative is for BIGBANK to base the forward FX rate it quotes to HELCO on the cost of hedging the position created through the forward FX contract. In fact the simplest type of hedge in this case is to use borrowing and lending in the money markets.

3.12.1   Hedging the Bank's Risks

If it enters a forward FX deal with HELCO then BIGBANK will agree to receive $10 million in three months' time, 91 days after spot, and pay to HELCO in return a fixed amount of Swiss francs. BIGBANK could manage this exposure through the following transactions for value spot:

- borrow the present value of $10 million and agree to repay this with interest in three months' time;
- sell the dollars that are borrowed for Swiss francs;
- deposit these Swiss francs with a money dealer for three months.

In three months' time (91 days after spot) BIGBANK will have to repay $10 million on its dollar borrowing. However this will be covered by the receipt of $10 million from HELCO on the outright forward FX contract. The CHF deposited on the money market by BIGBANK (plus interest) will be available to pay Swiss francs over to HELCO in return for the $10 million.

3.12.2   Calculating the Payments

Suppose that BIGBANK can borrow dollars for three months at 6 9/32% per annum (6.28125% in decimal format). The present value of $10 million is:

$$\frac{\$10 \text{ million}}{1 + (0.0628125 \times 91/360)} = \$9,843,706$$

If BIGBANK borrows $9,843,706 for spot delivery it will have to repay exactly $10 million in three months, which will be covered by the dollars received from HELCO on the forward FX deal.

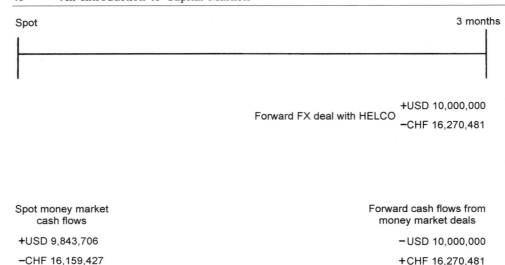

Figure 3.1   BIGBANK's total cash flows

BIGBANK then converts this \$9,843,706 into CHF 16,159,427 at a spot rate of USD:CHF 1.6416. Next, it deposits the Swiss francs in the money markets for three months. Suppose the CHF money market rate is 2 23/32% (2.71875% in decimal format). Then BIGBANK will have in three months' time principal plus interest of CHF 16,270,481. This is calculated as follows:

$$\text{CHF } 16,159,427 \times [1 + (0.0271875 \times 91/360)] = \text{CHF } 16,270,481$$

If BIGBANK agrees to pay over to HELCO in three months' time exactly CHF 16,270,481 it will have covered all the cash flows on the forward FX deal without taking any risk on FX movements. (Of course in practice the bank will want to make some profit on the deal and also to cover remaining risks such as settlement risk.) BIGBANK's cash flows from the forward FX deal with HELCO and from the covering money market deals are illustrated in Figure 3.1.

   The three-month outright forward rate achieved by HELCO is calculated as follows:

$$\text{Outright Forward Rate} = \frac{16,270,481}{10,000,000} = \text{USD:CHF } 1.6270$$

3.13   FORWARD FX FORMULA

The forward rate can be calculated directly using the following formula. Note that in the formula interest rates are entered as decimals:

Forward FX Rate =

$$\text{Spot Rate} \times \left[\frac{1 + \{\text{Counter-Currency Interest Rate} \times (\text{Days}/\text{Year Base})\}}{1 + \{\text{Base Currency Interest Rate} \times (\text{Days}/\text{Year Base})\}} \right]$$

In our example:

Spot rate $= 1.6416$
Counter-currency (CHF) interest rate $= 2.71875\%$
Base currency (USD) interest rate $= 6.28125\%$
Days $= 91$
Day counting for both currencies $=$ actual/360

Therefore:

$$\text{Forward FX Rate} = 1.6416 \times \left[\frac{1 + \{0.0271875 \times (91/360)\}}{1 + \{0.0628125 \times (91/360)\}} \right]$$
$$= 1.6270$$

In the formula the spot rate is adjusted by a factor (in large brackets) that is determined by the relative interest rates in the two currencies. In the HELCO example the base currency USD interest rate is higher than the counter-currency CHF interest rate. The adjustment factor is therefore less than one (in fact it is 0.9911) and so the dollar buys fewer Swiss francs for forward delivery compared to spot delivery.

Intuitively, the higher dollar interest rate builds in a higher inflation expectation than the Swiss franc interest rate and in these circumstances it makes sense that the dollar should be worth less in CHF terms for forward delivery than it is at the moment. If the counter-currency interest rate were higher than the base currency interest rate then in that case the base currency would buy more units of the counter-currency for forward delivery compared to spot delivery.

3.14 FX OR FORWARD SWAPS

A forward FX trader will have numbers of deals on the book and a proportion of the FX risks will cancel out. If there are residual FX exposures on forward dates the trader could cover this by borrowing and lending in the money markets as outlined in Section 3.12. In practice, however, this is a little messy since it involves using the bank's balance sheet to borrow and lend money and it could involve substantial counterparty risk.

Let us return to the HELCO example and assume that BIGBANK has just entered into a three-month outright forward FX deal with HELCO at a rate of exactly USD:CHF 1.6270. The bank's cash flows arising from this deal are illustrated again in Figure 3.2.

As it stands BIGBANK is exposed to a weakening US dollar — if the USD:CHF rate falls to (say) 1.6000 the bank will be able to sell the $10 million due from HELCO for only CHF 16 million while at the same time paying HELCO 16.27 million on the outright forward deal. We saw before that BIGBANK could cover this risk through borrowing and lending in the money markets.

As an alternative it could cover at least part of its FX risk by simply entering into an FX spot deal in which it sells dollars and buys Swiss francs. Then if the dollar weakens

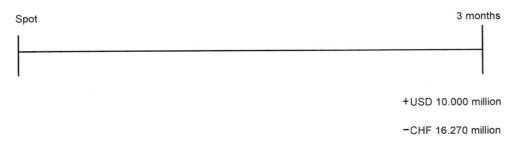

+USD 10.000 million

−CHF 16.270 million

Figure 3.2 BIGBANK's cash flows from the forward FX deal

it will be losing on the outright forward deal with HELCO but making a profit on the spot deal in which it is short dollars. The spot USD:CHF rate is 1.6416 so the combination position for BIGBANK (outright forward with HELCO, covering spot FX deal) is shown in Figure 3.3.

The problem of course is that the spot deal will settle in two business days' time, while the outright forward is for value three months after spot. Put another way, there is a time lag between the two deals. This can be handled using a product called an FX swap.

FX or Forward Swap Definition

An FX swap is the exchange of one currency for another on one date (normally spot) combined with a reverse exchange of the two currencies on a later date.

To manage the time gap shown in Figure 3.3 BIGBANK has to enter into an FX swap deal to buy dollars (sell Swiss francs) spot. The forward leg of the swap would consist of selling dollars (buying back Swiss francs) for value three months after spot.

−USD 10.000 million   +USD 10.000 million

+CHF 16.416 million   −CHF 16.270 million

Figure 3.3 BIGBANK's cash flows covering with a spot deal

3.15 FX SWAP QUOTATIONS

Forward FX traders tend to quote FX swap rates in terms of **forward points** rather than outright rates. These are subtracted from or added to the rate for the spot leg of the swap to establish the rate for the forward leg of the swap for the re-exchange of the two currencies. Suppose that BIGBANK receives a quotation for the FX swap deal of 146/135 and the rate for the spot leg of a swap is agreed at 1.6416. The rules for interpreting an FX swap quotation are odd at first sight but the good news is that they are always the same.

- **High–Low.** If the points are quoted with the numerically larger number first ('high–low') then they are **subtracted** from the rate for the spot leg of the swap to establish the rate for the forward leg of the swap. The points in fact are **negative**, although the sign is not normally shown.
- **Low–High.** If the points are quoted with the numerically smaller number first ('low–high') then they are **added** to the rate for the spot leg of the swap to establish the rate for the forward leg of the swap. The points in fact are **positive**, although the sign is not usually shown.
- **Left-hand Rate.** The trader making the quotation sells the base currency spot and buys it back forward at the left-hand number.
- **Right-hand Rate.** The trader making the quotation buys the base currency spot and sells it back forward at the right-hand number.

In the BIGBANK case USD is the base currency and the spot rate is to be USD:CHF 1.6416. BIGBANK needs to buy dollars in the spot leg of the swap and sell dollars in the forward leg of the swap. So the swap trader making the quote to BIGBANK will be selling dollars to BIGBANK for value spot and buying dollars back in three months' time. The trader will do that at the left-hand number in his two-way quotation of 146/135 which is 146 points or CHF 0.0146 per dollar.

But what does this mean?

- **Spot Leg.** The FX swap dealer will sell one dollar for value date spot and ask in return the agreed spot rate CHF 1.6416.
- **Forward Leg.** On the forward leg of the swap in three months' time the dealer will receive back one dollar and pay in return only CHF $1.6416 - 0.0146 = $ CHF 1.6270.

The reason the dealer pays back a smaller amount of Swiss francs is connected with the relative interest rates in the two currencies. In the swap the dealer is moving out of the dollar (the high yield currency) and into the Swiss franc (the low yield currency) for a period of three months. The dealer is compensated for this, by paying back fewer Swiss francs on the forward leg of the swap than he received on the spot leg. In effect the 146 points represent the interest rate differential between the two currencies expressed in currency terms. The dealer is paid 146 points, or in the jargon of the forward FX markets, receives 146 points 'in his favour'.

3.15.1 Using an FX Swap to Manage the Time Gap

We return to the story of BIGBANK. BIGBANK agrees to enter into an FX swap deal with the swap dealer in which BIGBANK will buy $10 million spot and pay in return

Figure 3.4   BIGBANK's cash flows covering the outright forward with a spot deal and with an FX swap

CHF 16.416 million at a rate of CHF 1.6416. This matches the cash flows on the spot deal that was transacted to cover the FX risk on the original outright forward transaction with HELCO.

On the forward leg of the swap BIGBANK will return the $10 million to the swap dealer but this time receive back Swiss francs at a lower rate of $1.6416-0.0146 = 1.6270$. So BIGBANK will receive back only CHF 16.270 million on the forward leg of the swap. BIGBANK's cash flow diagram now is shown in Figure 3.4.

Now all BIGBANK's cash flows and the FX exposures arising from the original outright forward deal with HELCO have been matched. Of course in practice it would be better to achieve this while locking in a profit from the various transactions! In effect BIGBANK has used the FX swap as a way of managing the time gap between the three-month outright forward deal and the covering spot FX deal.

3.15.2   The FX Swap as Borrowing and Lending

Looked at another way, the FX swap could be considered as a means by which BIGBANK borrows US dollars for three months combined with placing out CHF 16.416 million for the same time period. However the FX swap is structured as an exchange of two currencies for value date spot combined with an agreement to re-exchange the two currencies on a forward date. The relative interest rates between the two currencies are expressed in terms of forward points. This has the advantage that the deal is **off balance sheet** — legally it is simply a contract between two parties which combines a spot with a forward FX transaction made at two different rates.

3.16   INTERPRETING FORWARD POINTS

In the BIGBANK example the FX swap dealer's two-way quotation was 146/135. The left-hand number 146 means that:

- the dealer will sell the base currency (the US dollar) spot and buy it back forward at 146 points;
- on the forward leg of the swap the dealer will receive back dollars but return the Swiss francs at the rate for the spot leg of the swap minus 146 points, i.e. CHF 0.0146 per dollar.

What does the right-hand number 135 mean? It means that:

- the dealer will buy the base currency (the US dollar) spot and sell it back forward at 135 points;
- on the forward leg of the swap the dealer will return the dollars and receive back Swiss francs at the rate agreed for the spot leg of the swap minus 135 points, i.e. CHF 0.0135 per dollar.

In the second case the dealer, via the swap, is moving into the high yield currency (the USD dollar) for the period of the swap and has to pay points to the counterparty in compensation. The dealer pays 135 points. That is, the dealer receives back his Swiss francs on the forward leg of the swap at the spot rate less CHF 0.0135 per dollar.

3.16.1   Base Currency Rate is Lower

Of course it is not always the case that the base currency interest rate is higher than the counter-currency interest rate. For example, an FX swap dealer might quote a rate for a 12-month EUR:GBP FX swap of 134/144. In this case the rates are quoted **low–high**, which means that they are **added** to the rate for the spot leg of a swap to establish the rate for the forward leg. This tells us that the base currency euro is a lower interest rate currency than the British pound and buys more pounds for forward delivery than for spot delivery.

Suppose the EUR:GBP spot rate is 0.6062. Then the dealer sells one euro spot in return for GBP 0.6062 and buys back one euro in 12 months' time. The dealer will repay:

$$GBP\ 0.6062 + 0.0134 = GBP\ 0.6196$$

The dealer pays 134 points to move into the high yield currency and out of euros.

On the other side of the quotation the dealer buys one euro spot at GBP 0.6062 and returns the euro in 12 months' time. The dealer will receive back in return:

$$GBP\ 0.6062 + 0.0144 = GBP\ 0.6206$$

Dealer's FX Swap Quotes

In general, if you take FX swap rates from a forward dealer as a market user you will pay the bigger of the two numbers (forward points) and earn the lower of the two numbers. You will pay points to move into the higher yielding currency via the FX swap and you will receive points if you move into the lower yielding currency for the duration of the FX swap.

In practice FX swap dealers may transact the spot leg of a swap at a rate mid-way between the bid and the offer spot rate, although there is a certain amount of flexibility in this since whatever spot rate is chosen for the spot leg of the swap is simply applied to the forward points to calculate the forward leg of the swap.

3.16.2   Covered Foreign Currency Investments

It can very often appear attractive for an investor to switch funds into a foreign currency that offers better returns. However the investor also acquires foreign exchange risk in the process, if we assume that the foreign currency proceeds have to be converted back into the home currency at some future date. An FX swap can be used to manage the currency risk. The investor uses the spot leg of the swap to transfer funds into the foreign currency to buy assets denominated in that currency. The forward leg ensures that funds are translated back into the home currency at a known exchange rate.

3.17   CHAPTER SUMMARY

Foreign exchange trading is dominated by interbank deals, although underpinning such deals are currency transactions made by importers and exporters and by institutional investors such as mutual funds and insurance companies. In developed economies nowadays currencies are free floating and FX rates are largely driven by demand and supply factors. The central banks in these countries seek to influence the FX markets through regulation, monetary policy and occasional direct intervention. The FX market is a 24-hour global marketplace in which dealers working for major banks are connected by telephone and computer screens. Most deals are for spot delivery, which in the case of major currency pairs means delivery two business days after the trade is agreed. Settlement in the interbank market is normally made through the SWIFT system. Spot FX dealers maintain a list of all their deals on a deal blotter and also assess the revaluation profit and loss on their positions in order to measure returns and contain risks. An outright forward FX transaction is a deal in which two currencies are exchanged for a value date later than spot. The exchange rate is agreed at the time the deal is made. Corporates and institutions use forward FX deals to manage currency risk. In the interbank market most forward deals are not made in the form of outright forward transactions but are FX or forward swaps. An FX swap is an agreement to exchange one currency for another and to re-exchange the currencies on a later date. Dealers normally quote swap rates in the form of forward points which are subtracted from or added to the rate for the spot leg of the swap to establish the rate for the forward leg. FX swaps are used to manage the risk on outright forward deals with clients, to manage time gaps between currency cash flows and generally to switch from one currency to another for a specific period of time, perhaps to take advantage of higher interest rates or asset returns.

4

Bond Markets

Is it so nominated in the bond?
William Shakespeare

4.1 CHAPTER OVERVIEW

In this chapter we explore the markets for government and corporate bonds. We look at issuance procedures and at trading methods in the secondary markets. The largest government bond market in the world is the market for US government debt, and many of the conventions from the US Treasury market are being exported around the world. For example, UK government bonds (gilts) and government bonds issued in the eurozone now use the day counting convention developed in the US market. We look at how bonds are quoted and valued using discounted cash flow techniques. Two measures of yield or return are introduced: current or interest yield and yield to maturity. Investors cannot entirely ignore the possibility that governments may default on debt obligations (or order a restructuring of their debt) so we consider the rating of sovereign debt by the major rating agencies. Corporate borrowers can issue bonds in a **domestic** market or in the international **Eurobond** market which is based in major centres such as London. We consider the structure of corporate bonds and issuance procedures. Credit or default risk is a significant issue when analysing corporate bonds. We look at how credit risk is measured by the ratings agencies and the relationship between credit risk and the yield or return on corporate bonds. In an Appendix to the chapter there are details of Japanese government bonds (JGBs) and government bonds in the eurozone.

4.2 GOVERNMENT BOND MARKETS

Bonds are long-term negotiable debt securities issued by governments, government agencies, financial institutions and corporations in order to raise debt capital. The majority of bonds are **straight** or 'plain vanilla' bonds which:

- pay fixed interest amounts — known as **coupons** — on regular dates;
- have a fixed maturity or **redemption** date, at which point the bond's par or face value is repaid to the bond investors.

Governments around the world raise long-term debt by issuing bonds to finance budget deficits, the difference between government spending and the amount of money raised in taxation. If a government begins to run a budget surplus, as has happened in developed economies in recent years, it may start to buy bonds back through outright purchases in the open market or via 'reverse auctions' in which it bids for securities held by dealers and investors.

4.2.1 Trading Methods

In some markets such as the UK, France and Germany government bonds are listed on the local **stock exchange**. However in these and most countries including the US government bonds are traded mainly on **over-the-counter** (OTC) markets through dealers who work for the large banks and security houses. Dealers support the liquidity of the market by making bid (buy) and offer or ask (sell) prices. Their prices are displayed on screen-based information services such as Bloomberg and deals are contracted over the telephone or by electronic communication.

Brokers

In some government bond markets such as the US there is a system of **interdealer brokers** who further enhance the liquidity of the market by helping traders find the best available bid (buy) or offer (sell) price at any point in time. Brokers also help to maintain anonymity since the names of the dealing counterparties are not revealed until the trade is agreed. This can be helpful if a trader has a large buy or sell order to contract and does not want to alert the market to their position.

4.2.2 Market Sizes

At the time of writing the largest government bond market in the world is the market for US government debt, followed by the government bond markets in Japan, Italy and Germany. Table 4.1 shows the relative size of each market in US dollar equivalents. The table also shows in each case the annual turnover in the cash market (that is, the market for trading the underlying government bonds) combined with trading in futures contracts on those bonds. The latter are contracts to exchange bonds on future dates traded on major derivatives exchanges such as the Chicago Board of Trade (CBOT), Eurex, the combined German–Swiss futures and options exchange, and the London International Financial Futures Exchange (LIFFE). Chapter 11 has further details on bond futures.

Table 4.1 Size and liquidity of government bond markets end-1997. Nominal values $bn

Country	Outstanding central government debt	Yearly cash and futures turnover
United States	2741	103,829
Japan	1855	31,735
Italy	971	10,455
Germany	653	6600
France	484	18,634
United Kingdom	459	6516
Canada	210	6428
Belgium	191	975
Netherlands	168	450
Sweden	102	4763
Switzerland	27	215

Source: BIS. Reproduced by permission of the Bank for International Settlements.

4.3 SOVEREIGN RISK

In the major industrial countries government bonds issued in the domestic currency represent the lowest credit risk of any borrower in that currency. Historically they have set the reference or benchmark interest rate for any given maturity. The return or yield on US Treasuries, for example, will establish a minimum or benchmark rate of return that any other dollar borrower, whether sovereign, corporate or financial, will have to pay to attract investors. The benchmark for borrowing in Japanese yen is established through the yield or return on Japanese government bonds. The benchmark for borrowing in euros is normally set by German government bonds, although in some cases French government bonds may be used as an alternative benchmark (particularly around the five-year maturity, where they are highly liquid). By contrast, in a developing country it is possible for a major corporation owning significant assets — particularly natural resources such as oil or minerals — to borrow more cheaply than the government of that country. The major rating agencies now allow for this possibility in their published credit ratings.

4.3.1 Sovereign Debt Ratings

The fact that there is a risk of default on government debt, particularly debt issued in foreign currencies by developing countries, has led the rating agencies such as Fitch, Standard and Poor's and Moody's to institute **sovereign debt ratings**. The longer-term debt of the United States is, not surprisingly, awarded the highest available AAA rating by Standard and Poor's with a 'stable' outlook on this rating — that is, it is unlikely to be put under review. In its 1999 report on US government debt Standard and Poor's cited the following reasons for its decision:

- the US is the world's largest and most diversified economy (21% of world GDP in 1999);
- high per capital income ($33,000 in 1999);
- the key role the US dollar plays in world trade and finance;
- the independence of the Federal Reserve and its success since the 1990s in containing inflation;
- a moderate net general government debt burden, only 58% of GDP in 1999;
- the stability of the political system, the power of US armed forces and the diplomatic influence of the United States.

In February 2001, by contrast, Standard and Poor's rated the local currency longer-term debt of the Islamic Republic of Pakistan at B+ stable. The foreign currency debt was rated B— stable. According to the agency the rating was constrained by the relatively high level of public debt in Pakistan (about 105% of GDP, consuming some 45% of general public revenues) and high levels of expenditure on defence. The ratings were supported by a well-developed and efficient system for funding government debt and the government's cautious monetary policy. Standard and Poor's cited as a positive factor the fact that Pakistan had a long-term trend rate of inflation of 10% which compared favourably with other countries in similar rating bands.

Investment banks and securities firms have separate dealing desks or business units responsible for trading government bonds issued by the major industrial nations such as the G7 or G10 countries. The dealers focus primarily on the effects on bond prices of changes in interest rates and currency rates, driven largely by inflation expectations. Bonds issued by less well-developed emerging nations are traded on other desks, which focus to a large extent on the dangers of sovereign default and on possible debt restructuring programmes. They can also take a positive view of a country and its debt if it seems likely to strengthen its economic performance.

The G10

The major economies are often taken to be those in the so-called Paris Club or **Group of 10 (G10)**, plus Switzerland. The G10 nations are those that in 1962 agreed to lend money to the International Monetary Fund (IMF). They are Belgium, Canada, France, Italy, Japan, the Netherlands, Sweden, Germany, the UK and the USA.

4.4 US GOVERNMENT BONDS

US government debt securities are obligations of the US government issued by the US Department of Treasury and backed, ultimately, by the tax-raising powers of the US government. There are three main types of security issued: Treasury bills, Treasury notes and Treasury bonds (Table 4.2).

4.4.1 Issuance Procedures

US Treasury notes and bonds are sold at auction in regular cycles. The current cycle is as follows.

- **Two-Year Notes.** These are issued once a month. The notes are generally announced near the middle of each month and auctioned one week later. They are usually issued on the last day of each month or, if it is a non-business day, on the following business day.

Table 4.2 US government securities

Treasury bills	Short-term paper with maturities up to and including one year, issued at a discount to face value. T-bills are quoted in terms of the discount rate (see Chapter 2 for more details).
Treasury notes	Medium-term debt securities with maturities greater than one year and up to 10 years. Interest is paid semi-annually and the securities are redeemable at par. Notes are quoted per $100 nominal or par value.
Treasury bonds	Long-term debt securities with maturities from 10 to 30 years. Interest is paid semi-annually and the securities are redeemable at par. Bonds are quoted per $100 nominal or par value.

- **Five-Year Notes.** These are usually announced on the first Wednesday of February, May, August and November. They are generally auctioned on the second week of February, May, August and November and are issued on the 15th of the same month or, if it is a non-business day, on the following business day. (Formerly five-year notes were issued on a monthly cycle.)
- **10-Year Bonds.** Auctions are usually announced on the first Wednesday of February, May, August and November. They are generally auctioned during the second week of February, May, August and September and are issued on the 15th of the same month or, if it is a non-business day, on the following business day.
- **30-Year Bonds.** The US Treasury announced in 2001 that it was ending sales of its 30-year bond after 24 years of regular auctions. The decision was made in the light of reduced borrowing requirements and the relatively high interest rates at this maturity. Some market commentators argued that the Treasury may have to re-introduce sales of the long bond at a later date if the economy falls into recession and tax receipts dry up.

The US Treasury also auctions inflation-linked notes, generally during the second week of January and July. Two types of bid can be submitted in a Treasury auction. In a **non-competitive bid** the investor agrees to accept the rate determined by the auction and in return is guaranteed securities. In a **competitive bid** the investor submits a yield to three decimal places (for example, 6.254%) and if the bid falls within the range accepted the investor will receive securities. In the current (2001) US auction system all securities are sold at the same price, the price equivalent to the highest yield of accepted competitive tenders.

Maximum Bid Size

A bid cannot exceed (currently) 35% of the issue size. This was instituted in response to an auction in 1991 in which Salomon Brothers submitted unauthorized orders on behalf of clients and took control of almost 90% of the issue.

4.4.2   When-issued and Secondary Market

Initially only the size of the issue and the maturity of the bond is announced. The notes or bonds are traded for a time in the **when-issued** market on an estimated yield for a bond of that maturity. Effectively this is a forward market in which deals are settled after the issue of the bonds. The most recently issued note or bond with a coupon that is representative of the current interest rate environment becomes the benchmark or **on-the-run** security for that maturity. Many investors and traders focus on the on-the-run note or bond, which becomes highly liquid and often pays a lower yield or return when compared with US Treasuries with a similar maturity.

Daily average trading volumes in the secondary market for US Treasuries exceed $120 billion. It is an over-the-counter market based on telephones and screens with a large number of dealers. The primary dealers (large investment banks and securities firms) play a special role in the market since they deal directly with the Federal Reserve in its open market operations.

4.5   US TREASURY QUOTATIONS

US Treasury notes and bonds pay fixed coupons or interest payments on regular dates throughout their life. In addition, the principal or par or redemption value of the bond (these terms all mean the same thing) is repaid at maturity. The coupon on a US Treasury note or bond is paid in two semi-annual instalments.

Coupon Payments

A US Treasury with a coupon rate of 5.00% and a par value of $100 would pay two six-monthly interest instalments each of $2.50 per annum.

US Treasury notes and bonds are quoted by dealers as a percentage of their face or par value on a **clean price** basis, that is, net of coupon interest that has accrued but has not yet been paid out by the US government since the last coupon date. A bond trading at par is trading at exactly $100. Quotes are given in fractions, normally to the nearest 1/32% although sometimes to the nearest half of 1/32% or 1/64%. The sign '+' or sometimes 'H' is used to indicate 1/64%.

US Treasury Bond Quotation

On 25 July 2001 the 5.00% US Treasury bond maturing on 15 February 2011 was trading at an offer or ask price of 99-6+. Dealers were selling the bond at 99 6/32% plus 1/64%. This is equivalent to $99 13/64 or $99.203125 per $100 par value. The settlement date—when the bonds are delivered and cash payment made—is one day after the trade date (known as '$T+1$'). In this case the price was for settlement 26 July 2001.

4.5.1   Accrued Interest and Dirty Price

The 99-6+ price quoted in the above example is a **clean price**. It is net of interest that has accrued but not been paid on the settlement date. The bond's coupon rate is 5.00% payable semi-annually. The day counting convention for calculating accrued interest on US Treasury notes and bonds is called **actual/actual**. To calculate the accrued interest in this system we need to know how many days there are in the current semi-annual coupon period and how many days have elapsed from the last coupon date to the settlement date.

The relevant dates in our example are as follows:

Last coupon date: 15 February 2001
Settlement date: 26 July 2001
Next coupon date: 15 August 2001

The calendar tells us that there are 181 actual calendar days in the current semi-annual coupon period (from 15 February to 15 August 2001) and 161 days have elapsed from the last coupon date to the settlement date.

$$\text{Accrued Interest per } \$100 = \frac{\text{Annual Coupon per } \$100}{2}$$
$$\times \frac{\text{Days Elapsed Since Last Coupon}}{\text{Days in Current Coupon Period}}$$
$$= \frac{\$5.00}{2} \times \frac{161}{181} = \$2.223757$$

The accrued interest calculation is based on the actual number of days that have elapsed since the last coupon period divided by the actual number of days in the semi-annual period. This ratio is multiplied by the semi-annual coupon due in that period.

The actual settlement price for a US Treasury note or bond is the clean price plus interest accrued to the settlement date. This is also known as the bond's **dirty price**. In our example:

$$\text{Dirty Price} = \$99.203125 + 2.223757$$
$$= \$101.426882 \text{ per } \$100 \text{ nominal}$$

4.5.2 The Coupon Cycle

Given that the actual price paid for a Treasury bond is the dirty price, why is it that traders quote the prices on a clean price basis? In fact the standard bond pricing model (discussed later in this chapter) calculates the bond's dirty price, and this is the amount actually paid for the bond. Dealers have to calculate the accrued, then subtract it from the dirty price to establish the clean price. Then when the deal is done the accrued has to be added back again! It seems that it would save time and effort if prices were simply quoted on a dirty price basis in the first place.

To see why prices are quoted clean, Figure 4.1 shows the clean price and the dirty price of a semi-annual bond during two complete coupon cycles. The coupon dates are 1 January and 1 July. The bond has a 6% coupon and is priced to yield 6% on a range of dates over the course of the year. The clean price throughout is at or just under par.

The graph shows that the dirty price increases in a straight-line fashion as interest accrues, but when the coupon is paid out the dirty price falls back to the clean price (in this case to par). This phenomenon makes it difficult to see how a bond is being affected by factors such as changes in market interest rates. In effect the clean price is the underlying value of the bond, with the 'noise' factor caused by the daily accrual of interest removed. Using dirty prices also makes it very difficult to compare the relative values of different bonds that have different coupon cycles — a bond that has just paid a coupon will have very little accrued interest compared with a bond that is a long way into its coupon cycle.

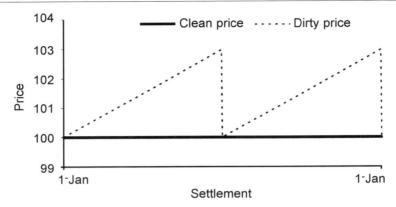

Figure 4.1   Clean and dirty prices during the coupon cycle

4.6   US TREASURY STRIPS

STRIPS stands for Separate Trading of Registered Interest and Principal Securities. They are zero coupon debt obligations of the US Treasury. They differ from straight notes and bonds in that they do not pay any interest and therefore always trade below par. STRIPS are now directly created by the US Treasury. Originally they were created by permitted financial institutions which sold off the individual cash flows on straight coupon-paying bonds in the form of zero coupon securities.

There is a ready market for STRIPS amongst institutional investors. Some financial institutions are also permitted to reconstitute a coupon-paying bond from the individual STRIPS. The concept originated in 1982 when a number of US banks started stripping US Treasuries and found they could earn more from the constituent parts than they paid for the bonds. The resulting instruments were given acronyms based on animal names, such as Merrill Lynch's TIGRs, Salomon Brothers' CATS and Lehman Brothers' LIONs.

4.7   BOND PRICING

Notes and bonds are priced by applying discounted cash flow techniques. However since they have maturities of more than a year when issued, the calculations are a little different to those we used in Chapter 2 when we looked at the money markets. They take into account the effects of compounding, or interest on interest.

Compound Interest Calculation

We invest $100 for two years at 10.00% p.a. and interest is compounded at the end of each year. Call the $100 the present value, or PV. At the end of year one there is $100 \times 1.1 = \$110$ in our account. To work out principal plus interest at the end of year two multiply this by 1.1 again. Call this the future value, or FV:

$$FV = 100 \times 1.1 \times 1.1 = 100 \times 1.1^2 = 121$$

The effect of compounding means that in the example we have interest of $21 at the end of two years. The first year's interest was $10. The second year's interest is $11. In addition to interest on the original principal of $100, we have earned $1 interest on interest. The general formula is:

$$FV = PV \times (1 + r)^n$$

where:

n = number of compounding periods
r = interest rate as a decimal for each compounding period

In the example interest is compounded only once a year and it is a two-year deposit, so $n = 2$. The interest rate is the rate per annum, so $r = 0.10$.

The present value of a future cash flow discounted using this method is calculated by solving for PV in the formula:

$$PV = \frac{FV}{(1 + r)^n}$$

4.7.1   The Standard Bond Pricing Model

In essence a straight bond is simply a title to a series of future cash flows — the coupons plus the principal amount payable at maturity. This is illustrated in Table 4.3. In the table C is a coupon payment, R is the par value and n is the time to maturity in coupon periods.

The fair value of a bond is simply the sum of the present values of all its cash flows. In the traditional bond pricing model each of the bond's cash flows is discounted at exactly the same discount rate r. The present value of the bond is therefore given by the following formula:

$$PV = \frac{C}{(1 + r)^1} + \frac{C}{(1 + r)^2} + \ldots + \frac{C + R}{(1 + r)^n}$$

where:

r = discount rate for each coupon period as a decimal
C = regular coupon payment
R = par or redemption value
n = number of coupon periods to the maturity of the bond

Table 4.3   Cash flows on a straight bond

Time period	1	2	...	n
Cash flow	C	C	...	$C + R$

4.8 PRICING COUPON BONDS: EXAMPLES

A bond pays an annual coupon of 10% and has exactly four years to maturity. The discount rate — the required rate of return on the bond — is 11%. In practice the discount rate can be established from the return that is currently available on investments with a similar risk profile. The present values of the bond's cash flows are shown in Table 4.4.

Table 4.4 PV calculation for an annual coupon bond

Time (coupon periods)	1	2	3	4
Cash flow	$10	$10	$10	$110
PV calculation	$10/1.11^1$	$10/1.11^2$	$10/1.11^3$	$110/1.11^4$
PV	$9.01	$8.12	$7.31	$72.46

$$\text{Bond Value} = \text{Sum of PVs} = \$9.01 + \$8.12 + \$7.31 + \$72.46$$
$$= \$96.90 \text{ per } \$100 \text{ nominal}$$

The present value of $96.90 is the **dirty price** of the bond, which in this particular case is the same as the clean price since we are exactly one coupon period away from the next coupon date.

Note that the value of the bond is less than its par value of $100. This illustrates a basic law of fixed income securities such as bonds — the value of such instruments moves **inversely** with current market interest rates. The bond in our example was issued with a coupon rate of 10%, the going rate for investments of this kind at the time of issue. However time has passed and the current going rate of return for such an investment is now 11%. The coupon rate on the bond is fixed at an unfavourable 10% so its price adjusts downwards.

Supply and Demand

Considered in terms of simple supply and demand, we could say that a 10% coupon bond will become less attractive to investors at a time when they can achieve 11% elsewhere on similar investments, and its price will fall to compensate for this.

4.8.1 Pricing a Semi-annual Coupon Bond

The standard pricing model applied to a semi-annual bond discounts each six-monthly cash flow at half the annual discount rate. The dirty price of the bond is the sum of the present values.

Consider the case of a semi-annual bond with exactly two years to maturity and a coupon rate of 10% per annum. The discount rate is 8% per annum. The present values of the individual cash flows are shown in Table 4.5.

Table 4.5 PV calculation for a semi-annual bond

Time (coupon periods)	1	2	3	4
Cash flow	$5	$5	$5	$105
PV calculation	$5/1.04^1	$5/1.04^2	$5/1.04^3	$105/1.04^4
PV	$4.81	$4.62	$4.45	$89.75

$$\text{Total Present Value} = \$4.81 + \$4.62 + \$4.45 + \$89.75 = \$103.63$$

Note that in this calculation the life of the bond is cut into four semi-annual coupon periods.

- The cash flows consist of a series of $5 semi-annual coupons plus the par value at redemption.
- Each cash flow is discounted at half the annual discount rate. The first $5 coupon is discounted back at 4% for one semi-annual period, the second $5 coupon at 4% for two semi-annual periods and so on.
- The bond's present value is the sum of the PVs, which is $103.63.

The bond is trading above par because the discount rate (its required rate of return in current market circumstances) is less than the fixed coupon rate on the bond. In other words, the bond pays an attractive coupon in current market circumstances and trades at a premium to its par value.

4.9   DETAILED BOND VALUATION: US TREASURY

What we looked at in the last section were in fact somewhat simplified applications of the traditional bond pricing model. This is because we priced the bonds at the very start of a coupon period. We have to make some adjustments when this is not the case, as the following example shows. This example uses the appropriate market conventions for US Treasury notes and bonds. As we saw before the day counting method (now also adopted for UK gilts and government bonds in the eurozone) is called actual/actual.

Example

We want to price a US Treasury bond for settlement 3 July 2001 that matures on 15 November 2002. The coupon rate is 8% paid semi-annually and the discount rate for valuing the bond is 6%.

- **Step 1.** Calculate the number of days in the current semi-annual coupon period. The last coupon would have been paid on 15 May 2001 and the next is due on 15 November 2001. So the current coupon period has 184 days.
- **Step 2.** Calculate the number of days from the settlement date 3 July 2001 to the next coupon date 15 November 2001. It is 135 days.

- **Step 3.** Divide the answer to Step 2 by the answer to Step 1 to get the number of days remaining to the next coupon as a fraction of the current coupon period. It is 135/184 or 0.7337. In other words the first cash flow is due in 0.7337 of a coupon period, the one after that is due in 1.7337 coupon periods, and so on.
- **Step 4.** Discount the cash flows on the bond as illustrated in Table 4.6.

Table 4.6   PV calculation for a US Treasury bond

Coupon date	15 Nov 01	15 May 02	15 Nov 02
Coupon periods	0.7337	1.7337	2.7337
Cash flow	$4	$4	$104
PV calculation	$4/1.03^{0.7337}	$4/1.03^{1.7337}	$104/1.03^{2.7337}
PV	$3.91	$3.80	$95.93

Key features of Table 4.6:

- the six-monthly cash flows are present valued by discounting at 3% which is half the annual 6% discount rate;
- the first $4 cash flow would be discounted at 1.03^1 if it were due in exactly one coupon period's time. In this example we discount at $1.03^{0.7337}$ to take into account the fact that only a proportion of the coupon period remains.

The total present value of the bond at a discount rate of 6% is the sum of the individual present values in Table 4.6:

$$\text{Present Value} = \$3.91 + \$3.80 + \$95.93 = \$103.64 \text{ per } \$100 \text{ par or nominal}$$

4.9.1   The Clean Price

The present value of $103.64 is a dirty price, which differs from the clean price in this particular example since settlement is part way through a coupon period. The accrued interest and hence the clean price can be calculated as follows. The current coupon period has 184 days and 49 days has elapsed since the last coupon paid on 15 May 2001:

$$\text{Accrued Interest} = \frac{\$8}{2} \times \frac{49}{184} = \$1.0652$$
$$\text{Dirty Price} = \$103.64$$
$$\text{Clean Price} = \$102.58$$

4.10   BOND YIELD

The discount rate used to price a bond is equivalent to the required return on the bond given the riskiness of the cash flows. In the case of US Treasuries we can assume that there is virtually no risk of default, which is why the return on US Treasuries forms the benchmark or reference rate for dollar investors and borrowers. A corporate or an emerging market country issuing a dollar bond pays the return on Treasuries plus a spread in basis points which represents the additional risk of default.

It is also possible to measure the return that would be achieved on a bond if it was purchased at a given price. We saw before that the value of a four-year annual 10% coupon bond at an 11% discount rate can be established through a present value calculation:

$$PV = \frac{\$10}{1.11^1} + \frac{\$10}{1.11^2} + \frac{\$10}{1.11^3} + \frac{\$110}{1.11^4} = \$96.90$$

Equivalently, if the bond is bought for $96.90 and held to maturity the annualized yield or return on this investment is 11% per annum. But what if the bond is bought at a different price, say $96.50? What is the yield in this case? A simple approximation is to calculate the bond's so-called **current** or running yield (also known in the market as flat or interest yield). This is calculated as follows:

$$Current\ Yield = \frac{Annual\ Coupon\ Payment}{Market\ Clean\ Price} \times 100$$

$$= \frac{\$10}{\$96.50} = 10.36\%$$

Intuitively, the formula says that the lower the purchase price of the bond the higher the yield or effective return on that investment. If the bond was trading at par the current yield would be 10%, exactly the same as the coupon rate. Since it is trading below par the current yield is higher than the coupon rate.

4.10.1   Limitations of Current Yield

Current yield is very easy to calculate but unfortunately does not capture all the returns on a bond investment. In our example if the bond is held until maturity the principal repayment is the par value of $100 whereas the bond can be purchased below par. The bond will 'pull to par' as it approaches maturity and a capital gain will result which is not captured in the current yield calculation. If the bond was trading at a premium to par there would be a capital loss to take into account in measuring the total return on the investment. Secondly, the current yield calculation does not take into account the time value of money: 'a dollar today is worth more than a dollar in the future'. The cash outflow on the bond today cannot be directly compared with the future inflows of coupons and the redemption payment. Finally, the current yield number also ignores a further source of income from buying a bond, the income that results from reinvesting coupons as they are received.

4.10.2   Yield to Maturity

The bond market commonly uses a measure of bond return known as **yield to maturity** (YTM) or redemption yield. Mathematically, yield to maturity is the single discount rate that equates the market's dirty price of a bond with its present value. It is an internal rate of return calculation. Yield to maturity is the total annualized return earned on a bond assuming that:

Table 4.7   YTM as a constant discount rate that equates market price with present value

Time	1	2	3	4
Cash flow	$10	$10	$10	$110
PV calculation	$10/1.1113^1	$10/1.1113^2	$10/1.1113^3	$110/1.1113^4
PV	$8.999	$8.097	$7.286	$72.122

- the bond is bought at its current market dirty price;
- it is held until maturity and all the future cash flows are received;
- the coupons are reinvested at a constant rate in the market — in fact at a rate equivalent to the calculated yield to maturity.

What is the yield to maturity on the annual 10% coupon bond if purchased at a total settlement price of $96.50 with exactly four years remaining to maturity? The answer is established through iteration (trial and error) by searching for a single discount rate that generates a total PV for the bond of exactly $96.50. In Table 4.7 we discount all the cash flows at a rate of 11.13%.

$$\text{Total Present Value} = \$8.999 + \$8.097 + \$7.286 + \$72.122 = \$96.50$$

At an 11.13% discount rate the PV of the bond is approximately the same as the purchase price of $96.50. The yield therefore is 11.13%. Note that the yield to maturity is higher than the 10.6% current yield previously calculated, primarily because of the capital gain that would result from buying the bond below par and holding it until maturity.

4.11   REINVESTMENT ASSUMPTIONS

The yield to maturity on a coupon bond is in fact a rather tricky measure, since it makes the simplifying assumption that all the coupons on the bond are reinvested at a constant rate — in fact at the yield to maturity! This assumption is integral to the standard bond pricing model which uses a constant discount rate to price bonds, or establishes the yield on the bond as the single discount rate that equates the present value with the bond's market dirty price. In practice of course this is just a simplifying assumption, which means that the actual return on a bond may be higher or lower than the yield to maturity depending on what happens to reinvestment rates in the future.

4.11.1   Horizon Return

Yield to maturity also assumes that the bond is held to maturity and that all the expected future cash flows on the bond are received. If the issuer defaults on the bond or if it is called back early by the issuer then the actual returns achieved may be significantly lower than those forecast by yield to maturity.

   If the instrument is sold before maturity the actual annualized return on the investment will depend on the sale price. It is possible to calculate a **horizon return** based on three assumptions:

- an assumption about how long the bond will be held;
- the price (or yield) at which it will be sold in the future;
- the rate at which intervening coupons can be reinvested.

4.12 ANNUAL AND SEMI-ANNUAL BOND YIELDS

There is a further practical difficulty with the traditional yield to maturity measure used in the bond market. Let us compare two bonds both with 10% coupons with exactly two years to maturity and both trading at par. Assume that the issuers of the bonds are identical in terms of credit quality. The key difference between the two bonds is that bond A is an annual bond and bond B is a semi-annual investment.

Most people would quickly opt for bond B. Both instruments are trading at par but in the case of bond B half the annual coupon will be received half-way through the year. Basic time value of money precepts tell us that it is better to receive money sooner rather than later, since it can be reinvested in the market. But what is the yield to maturity of bond A and of bond B?

In the case of bond A it is fairly obvious that the yield must be 10% — the same as the annual coupon rate — since the bond is trading at par. How do we calculate the yield of bond B? Recall that yield to maturity is simply the single annualized discount rate that equates the market dirty price of the bond with the total PV of the bond at that discount rate. As Table 4.8 shows, the discount rate that calculates a PV of exactly $100 is 5% on a six-monthly basis.

Table 4.8 PV calculation for bond B

Coupon period	1	2	3	4
Cash flow	$5	$5	$5	$105
PV calculation	$5/1.05^1	$5/1.05^2	$5/1.05^3	$105/1.05^4
PV	$4.76	$4.54	$4.32	$86.38

Total PV of bond B $= \$4.76 + \$4.54 + \$4.32 + 86.38 = \$100$

Note that in the calculation the life of the bond is divided into four semi-annual coupon periods and the coupon payment in each period is $5. The single discount rate that produces a total PV of $100 is as we noted 5%. But this is a rate for each six-monthly period. The convention in the market is simply to double this number to annualize it, which means that the annual return on bond B is exactly 10%. In many ways this seems an odd result since the return on bond A was also 10% and yet most people would prefer bond B to bond A as an investment.

4.12.1 Annual Equivalent Yield

This result tells us that the traditional yield to maturity calculation is rather crude in that it fails to discriminate properly between bonds with different coupon frequencies. Put another way, it is not possible to directly compare the yield on an annual coupon bond such as bond A with the yield on a semi-annual bond such as bond B. The problem arises from the fact that to annualize the 5% discount rate applied in the case of bond B we simply doubled the number to obtain a yield of 10%.

A return of 10% paid semi-annually actually equates to a higher return on an annual investment. If we assume that interim cash flows can be reinvested at 10% per annum then the annual equivalent (r_{ann}) of the 10% semi-annual rate can be established as follows:

$$(1 + 0.10/2)^2 = (1 + r_{ann})$$

$$\text{Annual Equivalent Rate } r_{ann} = 0.1025 = 10.25\%$$

Although bond B pays a 10% yield on a semi-annual basis this equates to 10.25% on an annual equivalent basis. So effectively bond B *is* a higher return investment than bond A although it does not look like it at first glance.

4.12.2 Yield Conversions

To compare the return on a dollar corporate bond that pays annual coupons with the return on a US Treasury note or bond it is necessary first to convert the semi-annual yield on Treasuries to an annual basis or (this is more common) to convert the annual yield on the corporate bond to a semi-annual equivalent. The semi-annual equivalent of an annual yield is always lower — for example, the semi-annual equivalent of an annual 10.25% rate is 10%. The semi-annual equivalent (r_{sa}) of an annual rate of 10% can be calculated as follows:

$$\left(1 + \frac{r_{sa}}{2}\right)^2 = 1 + 0.10$$

$$\text{Semi-annual Equivalent Yield } r_{sa} = 9.76\%$$

4.13   UK GOVERNMENT BONDS

UK government bonds (known as gilts or gilt-edged securities) are issued via the Debt Management Office (DMO), an agency of the British government. The DMO took over this responsibility from the Bank of England in 1998. Coupons on standard gilts (sometimes in the UK called **dividends**) are paid semi-annually and the day count convention is actual/actual as with US Treasuries. Settlement is on the next business day after the trade date and prices are quoted per £100 nominal or par value in fractions, normally to two decimal places. Dealers quote prices on a clean price basis but the settlement price takes into account accrued interest. Most gilts are straight bonds which pay regular semi-annual coupons and have a fixed maturity date. However there are a number of non-standard bonds currently on issue.

- **Undated Bonds.** There is no fixed maturity date so they could pay coupons in perpetuity. An example is 3.5% War Loan. The yield on a perpetual bond is simply its current or running yield. For example, if 3.5% War Loan is offered at £77.24 then the yield on the bonds is £3.5/£77.24 = 4.53%.

- **Index-Linked Bonds.** Bonds whose payments are linked to the UK retail inflation rate, the Retail Price Index (RPI).
- **Split Maturity Dates.** Bonds which have a range of dates during which they will mature, at the option of the UK government, rather than a single maturity date.
- **Strips.** Zero coupon bonds which pay no coupons during their life, only the par value at maturity, and which therefore always trade below par. Zero coupon bonds are very popular with investment managers in institutions such as insurance companies and pension funds since the one-off cash flows from the bonds can be accurately matched with future liabilities.

4.13.1 Ex-dividend Dates

The key difference between gilts and US Treasuries is that US Treasuries are always traded on a **cum-dividend** basis, that is, the buyer of a bond will always receive the next coupon from the US Treasury regardless of the settlement date. Gilts trade cum-dividend except for a short period of time leading up to a coupon payment when they trade **ex-dividend**. During the ex-dividend period the seller of the bond will retain the right to receive the next coupon if the bond is sold within that period. When a bond is sold ex-dividend the seller has to pay 'negative' accrued interest over to the buyer, so reducing the settlement price. The accrued is calculated from the settlement date to the date of the forthcoming coupon.

Example Gilt Quotation

For settlement 24 August 2000 the UK 5.75% coupon gilt maturing 7 December 2010 was trading at 103.13/103.19. Dealers were bidding for (buying) the bonds at £103.13 and offering (selling) the bonds at £103.19 per £100 nominal.

The prices quoted in the above example are clean prices. There were 183 days in the coupon period and 78 days had elapsed since the last coupon was paid:

$$\text{Accrued Interest} = \frac{£5.75}{2} \times \frac{78}{183} = £1.2254$$

$$\text{Dirty Price (offer side)} = £103.19 + £1.2254 = £104.4154$$

The next ex-dividend date was 29 November 2000 after which time a buyer would be compensated for the loss of accrued interest from the settlement date up until the next coupon due on 7 December 2000.

4.14 CORPORATE BONDS

Increasingly companies raise debt through issuing bonds in the capital markets rather than bank loans. The issuer of the bonds (the borrower) can eliminate the fees and spreads on loans charged by the commercial bank by tapping the capital markets directly. The investor buys a debt security that is tradable on the secondary market and which will pay a higher return than Treasury bonds. Corporate bond issuance is particularly attractive to large blue chip companies with strong credit ratings. Many of these borrowers have higher credit ratings than the commercial banks and can borrow more cheaply by accessing the bond markets than they could by borrowing directly from a bank.

The change in corporate borrowing habits has spread from the United States around the world. In June 2001 the value of non-government sterling bonds outstanding rose to just under £246 billion, overtaking gilts for the first time since the Second World War.

4.14.1   Credit Risk

A dollar bond issued by a corporate carries credit or default risk, unlike a US Treasury. Therefore investors will demand extra return or yield for holding a corporate bond with a given maturity over and above the yield on the Treasury with the nearest maturity. This excess yield is called a **credit spread**. The more credit risk there is on the issuer, the higher the credit spread. Some professional traders refer to corporate bonds and other bonds that carry credit risk as 'credit spreads'. Credit risk is not in any way a theoretical problem. In 2000 a total of 106 US companies defaulted on bonds worth $33.4 billion.

Some corporate bonds are secured on collateral such as land, property or other fixed assets. In the UK **debenture** bonds are secured on specific assets. In US parlance, debentures are not secured on any specific assets but have a general claim on the assets of the company and have to be paid before the ordinary shareholders. **Subordinated** bonds rank behind secured debt for payment. They are higher risk securities, paying higher returns. Underlying a corporate bond is a set of legal documentation that makes it clear where the investor ranks for payment and also what legal protection he or she may have against activities of the issuer that might be prejudicial. These are known as **covenants**. They may for example place restrictions on:

- the amount of additional debt the issuer can raise;
- sales of assets;
- levels of additional capital expenditure;
- the minimum amount of cash and liquid assets the company must hold.

Credit risk may also be contained by the existence of a **sinking fund**. The issuer redeems a set proportion of bonds each year to ensure that it does not have a large principal repayment bill to meet at maturity.

4.15   CREDIT DERIVATIVES

Credit risk can also be managed through a new generation of derivative products called credit derivatives. The simplest such product is called a **credit default swap**. Essentially it is a form of insurance policy. In return for a premium which is either paid upfront or in instalments a bank or insurance company (the 'protection seller') will agree to compensate a bond investor in the event that the issuer defaults on its debt or suffers some other form of financial distress. The compensation amount may be a fixed amount

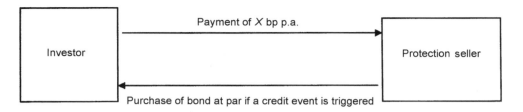

Figure 4.2   Credit default swap

or an estimate of how much of the face value of the bond can be recovered from the issuer. Alternatively the investor may have the right to sell the bond to the protection seller at a fixed price.

Figure 4.2 shows the structure of a typical transaction. In return for a fee of X basis points per annum the protection seller agrees to buy the bond at par from the investor if a defined 'credit event' occurs, for example, if the bond issuer defaults on interest payments or is put into liquidation.

4.16   CREDIT RATINGS

Many investors do not have the resources available to carry out detailed credit risk analysis and rely on the work of the independent ratings agencies. Two of the most important agencies are Standard and Poor's (S&P) and Moody's Investor Services. Borrowers raising funds through the issuance of bonds normally require a credit rating to attract investors, and pay the rating agencies to carry out an analysis. Their ratings scales are set out in Table 4.9.

The ratings range from top quality AAA or Aaa paper to speculative bonds where there is a much higher risk of default. Issues rated below BBB− are often referred to as 'below investment grade'. Many institutional investors such as fund managers are restricted to investment grade paper. Non-rated bonds tend to be the province of specialist investors.

4.17   OTHER CORPORATE BOND FEATURES

Bonds may have a **call feature**, which allows the issuer to redeem the bond early at a specified price and on specified dates. The call price is often at a small premium to the par value. This is of little comfort to investors normally, because the issuer will call the bonds back when interest rates fall and when it can refinance debt at a lower rate. A corporate bond may have a **put feature** which allows the investor to retire the bond early at a specified price and on specified dates. This is an advantage to the bond investor. He or she can put the bond back to the issuer if interest rates rise and higher coupon investments are now available on the market.

Table 4.9 Credit ratings

S&P	Moody's	Quality
AAA	Aaa	Highest quality, extremely strong
AA+	Aa1	
AA	Aa2	High quality, very strong
AA−	Aa3	
A+	A1	
A	A2	Upper medium quality
A−	A3	
BBB+	Baa1	
BBB	Baa2	Medium quality, adequate protection
BBB−	Baa3	
BB+	Ba1	
BB	Ba2	Speculative elements, very moderate protection
BB−	Ba3	
B+	B1	
B	B2	Speculative and vulnerable
B−	B3	
C	C	Highly speculative, major risk of non-payment
D	D	In default

Source: Ratings agencies. Reproduced with permission.

- A bond with a call feature should offer a higher coupon than the equivalent 'straight' bond from the same issuer without the call feature.
- A bond with a put feature should offer a lower coupon than the equivalent 'straight' bond from the same issuer without the put feature.

4.17.1   Other Non-straight Corporate Bonds

There are some other variants on the 'straight' bond formula.

- **Convertible Bonds (CBs)**. The investor has the option to convert the bond into a fixed number of ordinary shares of the company that issued the bond.
- **Exchangeable Bonds**. The investor can exchange the bond for a fixed number of shares in a company other than the issuer of the bond.
- **Floating Rate Notes (FRNs)**. These pay a coupon based on a set spread over the LIBOR rate for the coupon period. For example, an FRN might pay a coupon every three months of dollar LIBOR plus 80 basis points. The coupon rate for a given period will be set at the three-month LIBOR rate for that period plus 0.80% p.a.

4.18   SECURITIZATION

One of the most significant developments in the bond markets in recent years has been the growth of **securitization**. Essentially it is the process by which liquid and attractive bonds are created from future cash flow streams. Mortgage-backed securities (MBS) are based on a pool of mortgage loans. The bonds may be simple **pass-through** structures, which means that the cash flows from the loans are passed through on a pro-rata basis to make the principal and interest payments to the bondholders. A **collateralized mortgage obligation** (CMO) by contrast is a debt security based on the cash flows from a pool of mortgage loans, but where different categories or 'tranches' of securities with different risk/return characteristics are sold to investors. The securitization process that creates CMOs converts illiquid mortgage loans into liquid market assets.

Bowie Bonds

Investment bankers have become increasingly ingenious in the types of securitization deals on offer. Bonds have been issued based on the cash flows due from credit card and auto loans, trade receivables, commercial banking loans, even unpaid tax due to the Italian government. As long as a reasonably predictable stream of future cash flows can be isolated it seems that bonds can be sold and capital raised from investors against the projected cash flows. In 1997 the so-called **Bowie bonds** took the market into a new sphere. $55 million was raised by selling 7.9% coupon bonds against the future royalties due to the rock singer David Bowie from 25 albums. Since then the back-catalogues of artists such as James Brown and Marvin Gaye have been used to launch bond issues.

4.19   EUROBONDS

Corporate bonds may be issued by companies in domestic bond markets or in the international Eurobond market. The largest Eurobond market is in London and the majority of issues are in US dollars. A Eurodollar bond issued in London is offered to international investors and is not subject to US domestic regulation. The prefix 'Euro' in this context is historical and does not refer to the new European single currency. Eurobonds are also issued by sovereign borrowers. Eurobonds have other features in common:

- they are bearer instruments, the physical certificate is the sole title to ownership;
- interest is paid gross and free from any withholding tax;
- straight Eurobonds are normally issued at or slightly below par and redeemed at par;
- coupons are normally paid annually although semi-annual instruments are issued from time to time.

There has been discussion in the European Union in recent years about imposing a withholding tax on Eurobonds. So far this has been successfully blocked by the UK government, which argues that such an imposition would simply drive the market offshore. It has argued instead for better sharing of tax records between governments.

4.19.1   Primary and Secondary Markets

Eurobonds (also known as international bonds) are issued by:

- governments;
- government agencies;

- states and regional authorities;
- international bodies such as the World Bank;
- corporations;
- banks and financial institutions.

The market is dominated by major borrowers with credit ratings from the ratings agencies. Issue sizes can exceed $1 billion in the case of the largest borrowers. A key feature of the Eurobond market is that issuers can tap into funds provided by investors and investing institutions from around the world.

New issues are brought to the market by the lead-manager investment bank. Normally the lead forms a **syndicate** of co-managers who share in the underwriting and assist in the distribution of the bonds. The role of the syndicate in a bond issue is to place the bonds with buyers using their sales and distribution networks. For the bond issuer, underwriting means that it is guaranteed to raise the required capital. The underwriters earn their fees from the difference between the price paid to the issuer for the bonds and the price at which they are re-offered to investors.

Eurobond trades in the secondary market are settled through the clearing systems Euroclear and Clearstream (previously known as Cedel). Settlement takes place three business days after the date of the trade. Most bonds are in bearer form but the actual certificates are normally held by safekeeping banks on behalf of investors. The clearing systems arrange for coupon and redemption payments so that investors do not have to present physical certificates for payment. Secondary market trading is regulated by ISMA, the International Securities Market Association based in Zurich.

4.20 PRICING EUROBONDS AT ISSUE

A straight Eurobond will normally be priced close to or slightly below par and pay an annual coupon rate that is designed to attract investors in the current market conditions, whilst minimizing the cost of borrowing to the issuer. A Eurodollar bond will offer a yield or return that is some number of basis points over the yield on the US Treasury bond with the nearest maturity. The **spread over Treasuries** is required by investors because a Eurodollar bond issued by a corporation, an emerging market nation or even an institution such as the World Bank will carry some measure of credit or default risk, whereas to all intents and purposes US Treasuries are free of default risk. The spread is partly determined by the credit rating, partly by the appetite of the market for the paper in current market circumstances.

Spread Over Treasuries: An Example

A Japanese corporate issues a five-year annual Eurobond denominated in US dollars in the London market. The bond is issued at par and the coupon rate is 6.50%. So it is issued at a yield to maturity of 6.50% on an annual basis. The par US Treasury with a maturity closest to five years is yielding 5.50%. However this is a semi-annual yield. The semi-annual equivalent of the 6.50% yield on the Eurobond is 6.40%. So the Eurobond was issued at 90 basis points over the yield on the reference Treasury.

Bonds denominated in euros are normally priced to yield a spread over the most liquid French or German government bond with the nearest maturity. There has been a trend in recent years towards using swap rates as the benchmark rather than government bond yields, occasioned by the lack of supply of Treasuries at certain maturities and the resulting distortions in price and yield. (For details of swap rates see Chapter 12.)

4.20.1 Liquidity

The liquidity of the secondary market will also be a factor in determining the price investors are prepared to pay for a bond. Generally speaking, the larger the issue size the more actively traded a bond is likely to be in the secondary market.

4.20.2 Day Count Conventions

Most though not all Eurobonds carry annual coupons. New issues now use the actual/actual day count method. Some older issues still in circulation use a day count method known as 30/360 or sometimes '30E/360'. The letter 'E' here is to differentiate the method from a very similar but marginally different day counting convention used in the US domestic market. Essentially the convention assumes that each month has 30 days and each year has 360 days. It dates back to the early days of the market and was originally adopted to simplify day counting.

30/360 Accrued Interest Example

We want to calculate the accrued interest on an 8.00% Eurobond for settlement 3 June 2000. The bond matures on 15 December 2002. The last coupon was paid on 15 December 1999. The days that have elapsed since then are:

15 days remaining in December 1999 +
30 days × 5 months January 2000–May 2000 +
3 days in June 2000

Total days since last coupon = 168 days
Accrued interest per $100 par = $8 × 168/360 = $3.7333

4.21 CHAPTER SUMMARY

Governments around the world issue medium and long-term debt securities. The largest government bond market in the world is in the US. US Treasury notes and bonds are regularly auctioned at a single price that clears all the available securities. The secondary market is an over-the-counter market in which dealers make bid and offer (ask) prices. The notes and bonds are quoted as a percentage of par on a clean price basis. The settlement price on a deal is the dirty price, i.e. the clean price plus interest that has accrued since the last coupon period. The traditional way to price a bond is to present value the cash flows at a single discount rate. This is convenient but makes the simplifying assumption that coupons are reinvested at a constant rate. The current yield of a bond is simply the annual coupon payment divided by the clean price. The yield to maturity is the single discount rate that equates the market dirty price of the bond with the present value of the bond at that discount rate. Government bonds issued by the major industrial countries such as the G10 nations in their home currency establish the minimum rate of return demanded by investors in that currency. The ratings agencies use sovereign ratings to assess the likelihood of default on government bonds. UK government bonds are called gilts. The benchmark instruments issued in the eurozone are bonds issued by the German government, and on occasions those of the French government.

Corporate bonds are issued in domestic markets and in the international Eurobond market. Because it carries the risk of default, a corporate bond issued in a major currency will pay a higher yield or return than the Treasury with the nearest maturity. The spread over Treasuries depends on the creditworthiness of the borrower, which is assessed by the ratings agencies. Spreads are also affected by the general market outlook and by the liquidity of the issue. Products such as credit default swaps can be used to manage credit risk. Securitization is the process of creating bonds backed by asset pools and future revenue streams. Eurobonds are issued in major markets such as London through syndicates of underwriting banks and are bought by international investors. Issuers include corporates, financial institutions and sovereign states and their agencies. Eurobonds are normally bearer securities and coupons are paid gross.

APPENDIX: OTHER MAJOR GOVERNMENT BOND MARKETS

The Japanese government bond (JGB) market is at the time of writing the second largest government bond market in the world, after the US Treasury market. JGBs are debt obligations of the Japanese government. There are three main types of instrument.

- **Treasury Bills.** Maturities up to one year. These are issued at a discount to face value and quoted on a yield basis using an actual/365 convention.
- **Medium-term Bonds.** Maturities of between two and six years. These are predominantly coupon-bearing securities although some are zero coupon.
- **Long-term Bonds.** Coupon bonds with maturities of between 10 and 30 years.

Fixed coupon bonds are semi-annual and yield is normally quoted on a simple yield basis (not yield to maturity). The day counting convention is actual/365. Bonds always trade cum-dividend. Bonds are issued via a combination of bank underwriters and a competitive auction. Historically there is a substantial retail market for JGBs as well as institutional buyers. However liquidity in the secondary market can be limited except in the case of the most recently issued 10-year benchmark bond whose coupon tends to reflect the current market interest rate environment.

Eurozone Government Bonds

The German government issues bonds with maturities ranging from six to 30 years, although the most popular instrument is the 10-year **bund**. The majority of bonds are issued via an auction to a group of banks and securities houses called the Bund Issues Auction Group (which includes foreign firms) who then resell the bonds. Interest is paid annually and the day count convention is actual/actual. There is no ex-dividend trading. The Bundesbank also regularly auctions five-year notes called Bundesobliga-tionen (Bobls).

The French government auctions **OATs** (Obligations Assimilable du Trésor) with maturities up to 30 years. OATs are listed on the Paris Stock Exchange although most deals are contracted on an over-the-counter basis. The day count is actual/actual and coupons are paid annually. The French government also sells medium-term notes called **BTANs** (Bons du Trésor à Taux Fixe et à Intérêts Annuel) with maturities of two and five years, as well as Treasury bills called **BTFs** (Bons du Trésor à Taux Fixe et à Intérêts précompté) with a maximum maturity of one year.

At the time of writing the Italian government bond market is the third largest in the world. About one-third of issues are **BTPs** (Buoni del Tresoro Poliennali) with maturities 3, 5, 10 and 30 years. Coupons are semi-annual and the day count method is actual/actual, in line with modern eurozone practice. The Italian government also regularly auctions Treasury bills called **BOTs** (Buoni Ordinari del Tresoro) at a discount, which use the actual/360 convention.

5
Bond Price Sensitivity

When you can measure what you are talking about and express it in numbers, you know what you are talking about.

Lord Kelvin

5.1 CHAPTER OVERVIEW

We have seen that bond prices move inversely with market interest rates. In this chapter we explore the sensitivity of bond prices to changes in yields. Key terms are defined such as Macaulay's duration, modified or adjusted duration, and the price value of a basis point (PVBP). We look at how to calculate these measures and their inter-relationships. Duration measures are approximations, and for large changes in market yields they become increasingly inaccurate. This is because the relationship between bond price and yield is not linear. In the case of a straight bond with no call features the graph of the price/yield curve is convex. Various methods of estimating this convexity effect are illustrated as well as how to use duration and convexity combined to produce a more accurate estimation of the change in the price of a bond for a significant yield change. Finally, we explore practical applications of duration in portfolio management. We look at how it can be used to create a portfolio of bonds that matches future payment obligations, and how to construct a duration-based hedge against the effects of changes in interest rates on a bond portfolio.

5.2 BOND MARKET LAWS

The bond pricing model introduced in Chapter 4 shows us that the price of a bond changes inversely with its yield. This arises from the fact that the bond's cash flows are discounted more or less heavily depending on current market interest rates. It does not follow, however, that all bonds change in value at the same rate for a given change in interest rates.

Consider the two bonds in Table 5.1. Both have a coupon rate of 10% (paid semi-annually) but the first bond has a maturity of five years and the second of 20 years. Both bonds are trading at par so they yield 10%. The current bond prices and yield are shown in bold. The table also shows the values of the bonds for a range of different yields around 10%.

Table 5.1 demonstrates some important results:

- the change in price for a given change in yield is not the same for the two bonds;
- the longer maturity bond is more sensitive to changes in yield than the shorter maturity bond.

The phenomenon can be explained intuitively, in terms of interest rate exposures. If interest rates rise the values of both bonds will drop because the coupon rates are now

Table 5.1   Comparing the interest rate sensitivity of two bonds

Yield	10% 5 years PV	10% 20 years PV
9.96%	100.1546	100.3441
9.97%	100.1159	100.2579
9.98%	100.0773	100.1718
9.99%	100.0386	100.0859
10.00%	**100.0000**	**100.0000**
10.01%	99.9614	99.9143
10.02%	99.9228	99.8286
10.03%	99.8843	99.7431
10.04%	99.8457	99.6578

less attractive. However the longer maturity bond falls more sharply in value because cash is tied up in the investment for a much longer period of time. On the other hand, if rates fall the longer maturity bond will be paying a more attractive coupon for 20 years compared to only five years on the other bond, and its price will rise more sharply. The exposure to changes in interest rates is much greater in the case of the 20-year bond.

5.2.1   The Price/Yield Relationship

Table 5.1 also shows other key relationships:

- for small changes in yield (such as one basis point) the percentage change in a bond price is roughly the same whether the yield is increased or decreased;
- for a larger change in yield the percentage rise in the bond price if the yield is decreased is greater than the percentage fall in the bond price if the yield is increased.

For example, for a one basis point rise/fall in yield the price of the five-year bond falls/rises by 0.0386%. For a four basis point change the fall is only −0.1543% but the rise is 0.1546%. For even larger changes in yield the difference is more exaggerated.

If the numbers for one of the bonds in Table 5.1 were plotted on a graph this would show that the relationship between the price of a bond and its yield is in fact non-linear. The shape of the price/yield curve for straight bonds without embedded options is **convex**. This is illustrated in Figure 5.1.

The fact that the price/yield relationship is convex tells us that if yields rise by a large amount the fall in the bond price is less pronounced than it would be if the relationship between yield and price were linear. On the other hand if yields fall the rise in the bond price is more pronounced than it would be if the relationship between price and yield were linear. Convexity has the effect of accelerating the rise in the bond price as yields fall, but slowing down the fall in the bond price as yields rise.

5.3   OTHER FACTORS AFFECTING PRICE SENSITIVITY

It can also be shown that bond price sensitivity is related to coupon rate:

- the lower the coupon on a bond, the more sensitive it is to changes in market interest rates—the bigger its percentage price change for a given change in yield.

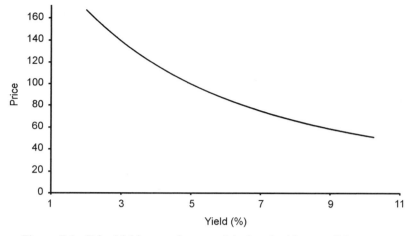

Figure 5.1 Price/yield curve for a straight bond without call features

The effect is most exaggerated with a zero coupon bond: if yields rise the increase in the discount rate used to present value the single future cash flow due on the bond is magnified by the time to the receipt of that cash flow, and the bond price falls sharply. Put another way, with a zero there are no intervening coupons to reinvest to help offset the effect of rising yields. By contrast, the holders of coupon bonds have the compensation of being able to reinvest the coupons at higher interest rates, which will serve to cushion the fall in the price of the bonds. This reduces their effective exposure to interest rate rises. On the other hand if market yields fall, zero coupon bonds will tend to do better than coupon bonds with the same maturity. Investors in the zeros are locked into a fixed return whereas holders of coupon bonds will suffer because the coupons will now be reinvested at lower interest rates.

5.3.1   The Interest Rate Environment

One further conclusion can be drawn by inspecting the price/yield curve in Figure 5.1:

- in a low interest rate environment a given change in yield produces a larger change in the price of a bond than in a high interest rate environment.

In fact this is a very straightforward effect. A 100 basis point increase in yield from 1% to 2% will have a much larger effect on the price of a bond than an increase from 10% to 11%. The absolute yield change in both cases is the same, but the proportional change is very different.

5.4   MACAULAY'S DURATION

Consider the following securities:

- a 5% coupon bond maturing in 15 years;
- a 10% coupon bond maturing in 30 years.

It is not easy to tell by simple inspection which of the two bonds is likely to be more sensitive to changes in yields. The first bond has a lower coupon, but the second bond has a longer term to maturity. We need a measurement that allows us to combine both factors. This measurement is known as **duration**.

The earliest measure of duration was formulated by Frederick Macaulay in 1938. **Macaulay's duration** is the weighted average life of a bond's cash flows, where each cash flow is weighted by its present value as a proportion of the bond's total present value. Macaulay's duration is a measure of a bond investor's effective exposure to interest rate changes. It blends the bond's term to maturity with the size of its coupon payments. The longer the term to maturity and the lower the coupon, the higher the duration of a bond — the more sensitive it is to changes in market yields.

Definition

Macaulay's duration is the weighted average life of a bond. The weights are the PVs of the cash flows to be received at each time period as a proportion of the total PV of the bond.

5.5   CALCULATING MACAULAY'S DURATION

To illustrate the method we will take a three-year annual coupon bond trading at par. The coupon rate is 10%, the yield is 10% and there are exactly three years until maturity. There are three cash flows due on the bond:

1 year	$10 coupon
2 years	$10 coupon
3 years	$10 coupon + $100 principal

The full calculation of Macaulay's duration for this bond is set out in Table 5.2:

Column (1) is the year when a cash flow is received.
Column (2) is the size of the cash flow.
Column (3) is the present value of the cash flow discounted at 10% (the bond's yield).
Column (4) is the present value in column (3) divided by the bond's total present value ($100).
Column (5) is column (4) multiplied by column (1), the time when the cash flow is received.

Table 5.2   Duration calculation for three-year 10% coupon bond

(1) Year	(2) Cash flow	(3) PV at 10%	(4) PV/total PV	(5) (PV/total PV)×time
1	$10	9.09	0.0909	0.0909
2	$10	8.26	0.0826	0.1653
3	$110	82.64	0.8264	2.4793
	Total PV = 100.00			Duration = 2.7355 years

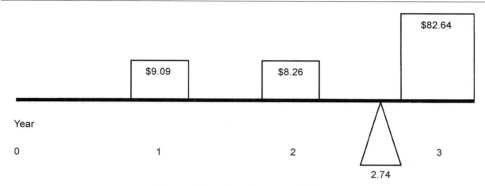

Figure 5.2   Duration as a balance

Macaulay's duration is the sum of the column (5) figures. In this example it is approximately 2.74 years.

5.5.1   Interpreting Macaulay's Duration

What does it mean? Although the bond in our example has three years to maturity, its sensitivity to interest rate changes is a little less than that might suggest, because of the interim coupon payments. The fact that coupons are paid and can be reinvested at current market interest rates reduces the effective life of the investment and the exposure to interest rate changes. The larger the coupons, all other things being equal, the lower the duration.

The duration calculation can be visualized as a balance, as shown in Figure 5.2. The bond's cash flows (actually their present values) are the weights placed on the balance. The duration — the effective life of the bond — is the balancing point measured in years.

5.6   DURATION OF A ZERO

To help understand the duration measure a little more clearly, we will calculate the Macaulay's duration of a three-year zero coupon bond. The calculation is set out in Table 5.3.

The three-year zero coupon bond has a Macaulay's duration of exactly three years. If interest rates rise the price of the zero coupon bond will fall more sharply in percentage terms than the price of a three-year coupon bond. The one and only cash flow that is

Table 5.3   Duration of three-year zero coupon bond

Year	Cash flow	PV at 10%	PV/total PV	(PV/total PV)×time
1	$0	0	0	0
2	$0	0	0	0
3	$100	75.1315	1	3
	Total PV = 75.1315			MAC = 3 years

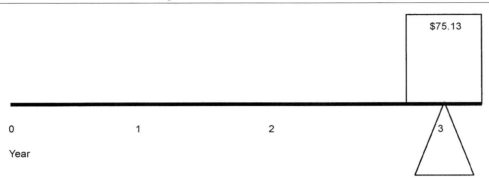

Figure 5.3   Three-year zero balancing point

due on the zero bond will be received in three years, and the investor is missing out on higher interest rates in the meantime.

The three-year 10% coupon bond has a Macaulay's duration of less than three years. The fact that coupons are paid and can be reinvested at current market interest rates reduces the effective life of the investment and the exposure to interest rate changes. In fact a three-year 10% coupon bond yielding 10% with a duration of 2.74 years will have the same sensitivity to (small) changes in interest rates as a 2.74-year zero coupon bond also yielding 10%.

Figure 5.3 shows the balancing point for the three-year zero coupon bond. It is exactly three years.

The Macaulay's duration of a zero coupon bond is always the same as its maturity. An investor receives only one cash flow on the bond and if interest rates rise in the meantime the investor has nothing to reinvest and is exposed for the full maturity of the bond. The price of the bond will fall sharply. The process works in reverse, though. If an investor buys a zero bond and rates fall the investor is locked in at a higher yield; the investor will not suffer from falling reinvestment rates because there are no intervening coupons to reinvest. The price of the bond will rise sharply, more than a coupon bond which will suffer from falling reinvestment rates.

5.6.1   Duration of Money Market Investments

At the other extreme, the Macaulay's duration of cash is zero. If interest rates change an investor holding cash can invest immediately at the new market interest rates and is not locked in for any period of time. The exposure to changes in market interest rates is zero. The duration of a one-week money market term deposit placed today is exactly one week. The funds will be repaid in seven days and can be reinvested at whatever the prevailing LIBOR rate happens to be then. The duration of a newly issued floating rate note with a coupon that re-fixes in three months' time is three months.

5.7   MODIFIED DURATION

The most commonly used measure of the sensitivity of the price of a bond to changes in interest rates is **modified duration**, also known as adjusted duration or Macaulay modified duration.

> **Definition**
>
> Modified duration is the percentage change in the dirty price of a bond for a 1% change in yield. It assumes that market yields or interest rates increase or decrease by the same amount at all maturities.

Modified duration assumes that the cash flows on a bond are not affected by changes in yields. This is a reasonable assumption for straight bonds paying regular coupons on regular dates with a fixed maturity date. It may not be the case with callable and putable bonds. If yields fall it becomes more probable that callable bonds will be redeemed early by the issuer and less likely that putable bonds will be retired early by investors. There is also a problem with high-yield corporate bonds. Rises in interest rates may make it more difficult for the issuer to meet interest payments and the risk of default on the payment of coupons and principal may increase.

5.7.1   Calculating Modified Duration

Modified duration can be derived from Macaulay's duration (hence the name). It is simply Macaulay's duration discounted at the bond's yield to maturity. In the case of the three-year 10% coupon bond we calculated Macaulay's duration at 2.7355 years. Therefore:

$$\text{Modified Duration} = \frac{2.7355}{1 + 0.1} = 2.4868\%$$

Note that if the bond pays a semi-annual coupon and its Macaulay's duration is expressed in years the yield in the denominator must be divided by two to derive the modified duration.

5.7.2   Estimating Modified Duration

Modified duration is sometimes estimated using a bond calculator or on a spreadsheet, using the following steps.

- **Step 1**. Work out the change in the dollar price of the bond for a one basis point rise in yield.
- **Step 2**. Work out the change in the dollar price of the bond for a one basis point fall in yield.
- **Step 3**. Average the results from Steps 1 and 2. An average is necessary because Steps 1 and 2 will not produce exactly the same result due to the convex price/yield relationship.
- **Step 4**. Calculate the answer to Step 3 as a percentage of the starting price of the bond.
- **Step 5**. Multiply the answer to Step 4 by 100 to approximate the percentage price change for a 100 basis point change in yield.

5.8   PRICE VALUE OF A BASIS POINT

From modified duration it is easy to estimate the profit or loss on a bond in cash terms for a given change in yield. The normal market convention is to measure the profit or loss for a one basis point change, that is 0.01%. This is known as the **price value of a basis point** (PVBP). It is also sometimes called basis point value and (for US bonds) the dollar value of an 01, where '01' represents a one basis change in yield.

In the case of the three-year 10% annual bond the starting bond price was $100 and modified duration is 2.4868%. Therefore:

$$PVBP = \frac{\$100 \times 0.024868}{100} = \$0.024868$$

The change in the bond price per $100 nominal for a one basis point change in yield is roughly two and a half cents. In the calculation we divide by 100 to adjust for the fact that modified duration is the change in price for a 100 basis point change in yield. Note that modified duration is the percentage change in the *dirty price* of a bond. If it is used to estimate PVBP it must be applied to the dirty price not the clean price (unless there is no accrued in which case the clean and dirty prices are the same).

5.9   CONVEXITY

Duration can be used to estimate the change in the price of a bond regardless of whether yields rise or fall. However this can only be an approximate estimation. This is because measures such as duration and PVBP assume that the relationship between bond price and yield is linear. In fact the actual relationship, as shown in Figure 5.1, is non-linear and (for a straight bond with no call features) convex.

PVBP is the slope or tangent on the bond price curve at a given yield, and Figure 5.1 shows that PVBP is not a constant. In practical terms this means that the actual change in the price of a straight bond for a 10 or a 50 basis point yield change is not simply PVBP times 10 or 50. Because of the curvature in the bond price/yield relationship the greater the yield change the less accurate PVBP will be in predicting the actual change in the bond price.

5.9.1   Testing Modified Duration

Recall that the three-year 10% bond trading at par had a modified duration of 2.4868%. This suggests that the percentage change in the dirty price of the bond for a 100 basis point yield change is 2.4868%. In fact checking the *actual* change in the price by revaluing the bond at different yields reveals that it is not completely accurate:

- the percentage rise in the price of the bond for a 100 point fall in yield is actually 2.5313%, which is 0.0445% more than predicted by modified duration;
- the percentage fall in the price of the bond for the same level of increase in yield is actually only 2.4437%, which is 0.0431% less than predicted by modified duration.

Duration is a first approximation and is good only for small changes in interest rates. (Mathematically it is the first derivative of the bond pricing model.) It can be improved

Table 5.4   First stages of convexity calculation

(1) Year	(2) Cash flow	(3) PV at 10%	(4) PV/TPV	(5) (PV/TPV)×time×(time+1)
1	$10	$9.09	0.0909	0.1818
2	$10	$8.26	0.0826	0.4959
3	$110	$82.64	0.8264	9.9174
		Total = $100.00		Total = 10.5951

by taking into account the effects of the curvature in the price/yield relationship, which is known as **convexity**. A normal straight bond with no call features is said to have positive convexity. In fact for the purchaser of a bond positive convexity is a benefit — the bond falls by less in price and rises by more in price for a given yield change than predicted by duration on its own.

5.10   MEASURING CONVEXITY

Convexity can be measured in a similar way to Macaulay's duration. Table 5.4 shows the first stages of the calculation for the 10% coupon three-year annual bond trading at par. In columns (4) and (5) 'TPV' stands for total present value, the sum of the present values in column (3). In this example TPV is $100. The bond is trading at par and the yield is the same as the 10% coupon rate.

The final step is:

$$\text{Convexity} = \frac{10.5951}{(1 + \text{YTM})^2} = \frac{10.5951}{(1.1)^2} = 8.7563$$

The convexity measure can easily be converted to work out the approximate percentage change in a bond's price for a given change in yield that is caused by convexity. The formula is:

$$0.5 \times \text{Yield Change}^2 \times \text{Convexity} \times 100$$

For a 100 basis point change in yield (the assumption used in calculating modified duration) the result for our bond is:

$$0.5 \times 0.01^2 \times 8.7563 \times 100 = 0.0438\%$$

In this calculation 0.01 is simply 100 basis points (1%) expressed as a decimal. For a 1% fall in yield the predicted rise in the price of the bond is:

Modified duration	2.4868%
+ Percentage convexity	0.0438%
= Total % change in price	2.5306%

Given some rounding errors this is much closer to the actual result — a change of 2.5313% — than is suggested by modified duration alone. For a 1% rise in yield the predicted fall in the price of the bond is:

Modified duration	−2.4868%
+ Percentage convexity	+0.0438%
= Total % change in price	−2.4430%

The actual fall in price as calculated by the bond pricing model is −2.4437%. Note that convexity for a straight bond is additive: it boosts the rise in the bond price as yields fall and reduces the decline in the price as yields rise.

5.10.1 Estimating Convexity from Yield Changes

Convexity is sometimes roughly approximated from the discrepancy between the percentage change in the price of a bond for a given fall in yield and the percentage change in the bond price for an equal rise in yield. By discounting the cash flows at different yields we can work out the following data for the three-year 10% bond:

PV of bond at 10% yield = $100 ('starting bond price')

PV of bond at 9% yield = $102.5313. Change = 2.5313%
PV of bond at 11% yield = $97.5563. Change = 2.4437%
Discrepancy = 2.5313% − 2.4437% = 0.0876%

Percentage convexity ≅ 0.0876%/2 = 0.0438%

5.11   CONVEXITY BEHAVIOUR

Table 5.5 shows a sample of annual bonds, all yielding 10%. In each case modified duration (MOD) and convexity (CNX) are calculated in percentage terms based on a 1% change in yield.

Modified duration is higher the lower the coupon and the longer the term to maturity. The table also shows that convexity obeys the same rules. The graph in Figure 5.4 shows the price/yield curves for two of the bonds considered in Table 5.5: a five-year 15% coupon bond and a 15-year zero coupon bond. The modified duration of a short maturity high coupon bond is low. The exposure to interest rate changes is only a little greater than that of holding cash and a change in yield has relatively little effect on this position. Furthermore, the bond's present value changes in a fairly linear fashion in response to yield changes. At the other extreme, the modified duration of a

Table 5.5   MOD and CNX for different bonds

Coupon	Maturity	MOD (%)	CNX (%)
0%	5	4.5455	0.1240
0%	10	9.0909	0.4545
0%	15	13.6364	0.9917
10%	5	3.7908	0.0968
10%	10	6.1446	0.2640
10%	15	7.6061	0.4342
15%	5	3.5938	0.0898
15%	10	5.7101	0.2359
15%	15	7.0832	0.3858

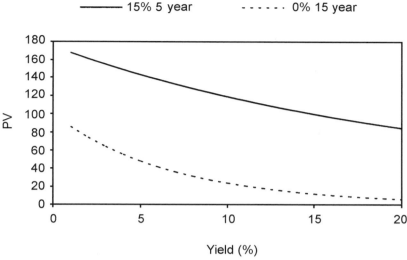

Figure 5.4   Convexity of a coupon bond and a zero bond

long maturity zero coupon bond is high and the change in the bond price in response to a change in yield is far less linear — it is a more convex investment.

As we noted before, positive convexity is in itself a 'good thing'. If yields fall the percentage rise in the bond price is greater than that predicted by modified duration. If yields rise the percentage fall in the bond's price is less than that predicted by duration. We would therefore expect that if two bonds have the same credit risk and time to maturity then the more convex bond would offer a slightly lower return than the less convex bond.

5.12   PORTFOLIO DURATION

The duration of a portfolio is the weighted average duration of the bonds in the portfolio. The weights are established by the market value (dirty price) of each bond divided by the total market value of the portfolio. For example, take a portfolio consisting of the three annual coupon bonds shown in Table 5.6.

The total par value of the portfolio is $100 million, made up of:

$30 million par value of the 10% three-year bond;
$50 million par value of the 7% 10-year bond;
$20 million par value of the 14% 13-year bond.

Table 5.6   Portfolio of three annual coupon bonds

Bond	PV	YTM (%)	MOD (%)
10% 3 year	$100.0000	10.00	2.4869
7% 10 year	$81.5662	10.00	6.5624
14% 13 year	$128.4134	10.00	6.6779

Table 5.7   Market value of the bond portfolio in $ millions

Bond	Par×PV	=	Market value
10% 3 year	$30×100%		$30
7% 10 year	$50×81.5662%		$40.7831
14% 13 year	$20×128.4134%		$25.6827
			Total = $96.4658

The total market value of the portfolio is shown in Table 5.7. Amounts are in $ millions.

The modified duration of the portfolio is:

$$[30/96.4658 \times 2.4869\%] + [40.7831/96.4658 \times 6.5624\%]$$
$$+ [25.6827/96.4658 \times 6.6779\%] = 5.3257\%$$

The modified duration measure means that for a 1% change in the yield of all three bonds the market value of the portfolio will change by approximately 5.3257%. The PVBP of the portfolio is:

$$\$96.4658 \text{ million} \times \frac{0.053257}{100} = \$51,375$$

In fact the actual change in the portfolio value for a one basis point rise and fall in yield averages out at exactly $51,375. However the actual percentage rise in the portfolio value for a 1% fall in yield is 5.5593%. The discrepancy compared to the modified duration estimate of 5.3257% is caused by the convexity of the portfolio.

5.13   DEDICATION

The sum of money achieved at the maturity of an investment in a coupon bond will depend to some extent on the actual rate at which coupons are reinvested over the life of the bond. This contrasts with a zero coupon bond, where a sum of money can be invested and a known future cash flow achieved. If the zero is a 'strip' (see Chapter 4) issued by a major government such as the US government then the future value is guaranteed. This explains why zeros are so highly regarded in fixed income portfolio management. The future cash inflows can be matched off against the projected future cash outflows from an insurance company or a pension fund. This strategy is known as **dedication**.

Dedication

A fund has a liability of $100 million that must be paid in exactly four years. Annually compounded interest rates are currently 10% p.a. The fund's portfolio manager buys a four-year zero coupon bond. If the yield is 10% then the purchase price with annual compounding is $100 million/$1.1^4$ = $68.3013 million. The maturity value is exactly $100 million. The portfolio manager has locked into a 10% per annum return over the desired investment horizon.

Table 5.8   Value at maturity with coupons reinvested at 10% p.a.

Year	Cash flow	Maturity value reinvested at 10.00%
1	6.8301	9.0909
2	6.8301	8.2645
3	6.8301	7.5131
4	75.1315	75.1315
		Total = 100.000

5.13.1   Dedication with a Coupon Bond

But what if no such zero bond exists or the fund's portfolio manager does not like the zeros that are on offer—perhaps because the prices are too high, or because they are not sufficiently liquid? An alternative approach is to buy a four-year coupon bond. Suppose there is such a bond with annual coupons trading at par and yielding exactly 10%. On the assumption that coupons are reinvested at 10% the portfolio manager needs to buy bonds costing $68.3013 million. Since it is a par bond the nominal value is also $68.3013 million so annual coupons will be:

$$\$68.3013 \text{ million} \times 10\% = \$6.8301 \text{ million}$$

The first coupon payment due in one year can be reinvested for a further three years at (on our assumption) 10% per annum. This will grow to become:

$$\$6.8301 \times 1.1^3 = \$9.0909 \text{ million}$$

The total cash generated by the bond at maturity is shown in Table 5.8. Amounts are in $ millions.

   The problem with this strategy is that it assumes coupons can always be reinvested at 10%, which may or may not turn out to be true. Suppose that immediately after the portfolio manager invested in the bond yields fell to 8% and stayed at that level for the remaining four years. The total cash generated by the bond at maturity in this case is recalculated in Table 5.9.

   The annualized return actually achieved in this second scenario is:

$$\sqrt[4]{\frac{\$99.0787}{\$68.3013}} - 1 = 9.75\%$$

Table 5.9   Value at maturity with coupons reinvested at 8% p.a.

Year	Cash flow	Value at maturity reinvested at 8.00%
1	6.8301	8.6040
2	6.8301	7.9667
3	6.8301	7.3765
4	75.1315	75.1315
		Total = 99.0787

This demonstrates that if reinvestment rates fall the portfolio manager will fail to achieve the expected rate of return and the target cash flow at maturity. On the other hand the manager will exceed the target return and future value if rates rise.

5.14   IMMUNIZATION

Another alternative for the portfolio manager is to buy a bond with a maturity greater than four years. When rates fall reinvestment income will also fall. However the portfolio manager has a shorter investment horizon than the maturity of the bond and will be able to sell the bond after four years at a favourable price that reflects falling interest rates.

If rates increase then interest on interest arising from the reinvestment of coupons will be higher, but the bond has to be sold before its maturity at a higher yield. These two factors — the reinvestment effect and the proceeds from the sale of the bond before maturity — offset each other when the Macaulay's duration of the assets matches the desired investment horizon. The process of constructing such a portfolio is known as **immunization**. The purpose is to lock into a required rate of return at the time of purchase of the bonds regardless of what happens subsequently to interest rates.

5.14.1   Immunization: Example

The story as before is that the portfolio manager is trying to match a $100 million liability due in four years. Suppose there exists in the market a suitable five-year annual bond with a coupon of 13.75% yielding 10%. The present value of the bond is $114.2155 per $100 and its Macaulay's duration is approximately four years. To generate the required cash flow, bonds should be bought with a total purchase price of $68.3013 million. The par value will therefore be:

$$\frac{\$68.3013 \text{ million}}{1.142155} = \$59.8004 \text{ million}$$

The annual coupons received will be:

$$\$59.8004 \times 13.75\% = \$8.2226 \text{ million}$$

Table 5.10 shows the value of the coupons generated and reinvested at the end of four years if the reinvestment rate is 8%. Amounts are in $ millions.

Table 5.10   Value of reinvested coupons from the five-year bond in four years reinvested at 8.00% p.a.

Time	Coupon	Value after four years reinvested at 8.00%
1	8.2226	10.3581
2	8.2226	9.5908
3	8.2226	8.8804
4	8.2226	8.2226
		Total = 37.0519

However, on the assumption that the yield on the bond is still 8% with one year remaining to maturity we can also work out its sale price at the end of the four-year investment horizon. At maturity the bond will pay a final coupon of $8.2226 million plus the par value of $59.8004 million, a total of $68.023 million. Therefore the sale price with one year to maturity at an 8% yield is:

$$\frac{\$68.023}{1.08} = \$62.9843 \text{ million}$$

Add this to the cash flow from the reinvested coupons of $37.0519 and the total cash generated at the end of the four-year investment horizon is $100.0362 million. The return achieved over the four-year investment horizon is calculated as follows:

$$\sqrt[4]{\frac{\$100.0362}{\$68.3013}} - 1 = 10.0\%$$

5.14.2 Cash Flows if Interest Rates Rise

What happens if the portfolio manager buys the five-year bond and rates rise, let us say to 12%? As Table 5.11 shows, the total cash generated by reinvesting coupons after four years would increase to $39.2984 million.

However the sale value of the bond at a 12% yield is less than at an 8% yield:

$$\frac{\$68.0230}{1.12} = \$60.7348 \text{ million}$$

The total cash due in four years in this scenario is $100.0332 million and the return achieved over the investment period is again 10.0%.

It seems that whether interest rates rise or fall the portfolio manager will achieve the required return and the required future cash flow. The reason this works is because the five-year bond in our example has a Macaulay's duration of four years and behaves rather like a four-year zero. The problem with the strategy in practice is that the composition of the portfolio may have to be adjusted periodically to match the duration of the liabilities.

Table 5.11 Value of reinvested coupons from the five-year bond in four years reinvested at 12.00% p.a.

Time	Coupon	Value after four years reinvested at 12.00%
1	8.2226	11.5521
2	8.2226	10.3144
3	8.2226	9.2093
4	8.2226	8.2226
		Total = 39.2984

5.15   DURATION-BASED HEDGES

When constructing a hedge against the fall in the price of a bond portfolio due to changes in yield the appropriate measure to use is PVBP rather than Macaulay's or modified duration. The strategy is to select a hedging vehicle whose change in dollar value for a given yield change offsets that of the bond portfolio to be hedged.

Hedge Example

A trader holds $10 million nominal value of an annual 8% coupon 10-year bond trading at par. The PVBP of the bond is $0.06710 per $100 nominal. The trader wants to hedge against the risk that interest rates will rise.

The total profit/loss on the portfolio of 8% bonds for a one basis point yield change is $6710:

$$\frac{\$0.06710}{100} \times \$10 \text{ million} = \$6710$$

Since the trader owns the bonds, in market jargon this is a 'long position'. The trader will make money if the bond price rises (yields fall) and will lose money if the bond price falls (yields rise). The trader decides to hedge against the risk of rising interest rates by shorting a 14% coupon annual bond with a 10-year maturity also yielding 8%. Then if yields rise the trader can buy the short bond back more cheaply at a profit, reducing or cancelling out the loss on the long position. The present value of the 14% bond to be shorted is $140.2605 per $100. The PVBP of this second bond is $0.08526 per $100 nominal. Clearly the trader does not need to short $10 million par value of the higher coupon bond to implement the hedge.

The profit/loss on the 14% coupon bond for a one basis point yield change on a $10 million nominal position would be:

$$\frac{\$0.08526}{100} \times \$10 \text{ million} = \$8526$$

This is greater than the profit and loss (P&L) on the long bond to be hedged and the position is over-hedged. The problem is clearly that the short bond will generate a greater P&L for a one basis point yield change than the long bond. The amount sold has to be reduced in proportion. The hedge ratio calculation is:

$$\frac{\text{PVBP of Bond to be Hedged}}{\text{PVBP of Hedging Vehicle}} = \frac{\$0.06710}{\$0.08526} = 78.7\%$$

The amount of the hedging bond to be shorted is approximately:

$$\$10 \text{ million} \times 0.787 = \$7.87 \text{ million par value}$$

Then for a one basis point yield change the profit/loss on these bonds would be:

$$\frac{\$0.08526}{100} \times \$7.87 \text{ million} = \$6710$$

This matches the expected P&L on the 8% coupon bond owned by the trader.

5.16   CONVEXITY EFFECTS ON DURATION HEDGES

In practice the hedge we have just assembled would rarely work exactly, especially for large movements in yields. This is not simply because of rounding in the calculation of PVBP and the hedge ratio.

Consider Table 5.12. This shows the P&L on the 8% coupon bond for a 1% and a 2% rise and fall in yields. It then shows the P&L on the 14% coupon bond shorted by the trader as a hedge, using the same yield change assumptions. Note that the trader has a $10 million long position in the first bond but shorted only $7.87 million par value of the second bond.

For small movements in yields the P&Ls will more or less cancel out. The trader has successfully hedged against losses on the long bond position, at the expense of not being able to make a profit if the bond rises in price—any profits will be offset by losses on the bonds that are shorted. However for larger movements in yields it appears that the trader always makes a (small) profit.

The reason is convexity. The long 8% bond has greater convexity (0.3%) compared to the short bond (0.26%) because it has a lower coupon rate. This has implications:

- for large falls in yield the trader will make more money on the long bond compared to losses on the short bond, because convexity gives the rise in value of the long bond a greater 'boost';
- for large rises in yield the trader will lose less money on the long bond compared to profits on the short bond, because convexity holds up the fall in value of the long bond.

In this example both the bonds have 10 years to maturity. However suppose the trader had hedged the exposure on the 10-year bond by shorting the appropriate amount of (say) a five-year bond, calculated using the hedge ratio method we employed before. Then there is an additional risk. As long as yields change by the same amount and in the same direction at the five and at the 10-year points then the profits and losses on the two bonds would more or less cancel out. In practice this may well not happen. In

Table 5.12   P&Ls on the long and on the short bond

Yield	Long 8% coupon 10-year bond: P&L on $10 million	Short 14% coupon 10-year bond: P&L on $7.87 million	Net P&L
6%	$1,472,017	−$1,465,410	$6607
7%	$702,358	−$700,792	$1566
8%	$0	$0	$0
9%	−$641,766	$643,152	$1386
10%	−$1,228,913	$1,234,189	$5276

Chapter 6 we discuss in detail the concept of a **yield curve**, a graph showing the yields on a given class of bonds (such as government bonds) against their time to maturity. The yield curve is in fact subject to non-parallel shifts. It is possible, for example, for yields to rise at the 10-year point but at the same time fall at the five-year maturity, so that the trader in our example could actually lose on both the long and the short position. This is sometimes known as **curve risk**.

5.17   CHAPTER SUMMARY

The price of low coupon, long maturity bonds is highly sensitive to changes in market yields. This is because most of the cash flows occur far out into the future and cannot be reinvested at new levels of interest rates for a long time. The effective life of a bond investment is measured by Macaulay's duration. A zero coupon bond has a Macaulay's duration equal to its maturity. The duration of a coupon bond and its effective exposure to interest rate changes are less than its maturity because the coupons can be reinvested at the prevailing market rate. Modified duration is a related measure which shows the percentage change in the dirty price of a bond for a 1% change in yield. It can be used to estimate the change in the money value of the bond for a 0.01% yield change. This is known as the price value of a basis point or basis point value. Duration can be used to put together a portfolio of bonds which matches expected future cash flows. This technique is called immunization. Duration can also be used to construct a hedge against the fall in the value of a bond portfolio. Duration is only an approximate measure because the relationship between the price of a bond and its yield is non-linear. Convexity is a measure of this curvature. It can be used to provide a better estimate of the actual change in the price of a bond for a substantial yield change.

6
The Yield Curve

A man has one pair of rabbits at a certain place entirely surrounded by a wall. We wish to know how many pairs will be bred from it in one year, if the nature of these rabbits is such that they breed every month one other pair and begin to breed in the second month after their birth...

Fibonacci

6.1 CHAPTER OVERVIEW

In Chapter 4 we looked at the bond markets and at the traditional measure of return on bonds: yield to maturity, or internal rate of return. This chapter extends the discussion and explores the relationship between bond yield and time to maturity. We review the components of a quoted or nominal interest rate, and the concept of annual equivalent rate. We then move on to the yield curve itself and prevalent theories about the shape of the curve. Most investors and traders agree that the curve builds in expectations of future interest rates, although others believe that there may be other factors at work such as the preference investors have to 'keep their options open' by favouring short-dated securities. We consider the different yield curves for government bonds and corporate bonds. We then look at how to extract future interest rates from the yield curve. To do this we first use a methodology called 'bootstrapping' to derive zero coupon or spot rates from the yields on coupon bonds trading at par. We then derive future interest rates from the spot rate curve and relate the results back to the expectations theory of yield curves. Finally, we show how to derive discount factors which can be applied directly to future cash flows to calculate their present values, without making reinvestment assumptions, and show how discount factors and forward interest rates are related.

6.2 REAL AND NOMINAL INTEREST RATES

The cost of borrowing money for a period of time (its time value) is measured by the interest rate for the period. Interest rates and bond yields are usually quoted on a nominal basis. A nominal interest rate has two components.

- **Inflation Rate**. This compensates the lender for the assumed erosion in the value of the money over the time period.
- **Real Rate**. This compensates the lender for the use of the funds over the time period.

The relationship can be expressed in a formula:

$$(1 + \text{Nominal Rate}) = (1 + \text{Inflation Rate}) \times (1 + \text{Real Rate})$$

It therefore follows that:

$$\text{Real Rate} = \left[\frac{1 + \text{Nominal Rate}}{1 + \text{Inflation Rate}}\right] - 1$$

If the nominal interest rate for one-year money is 10% with annual compounding and the assumed rate of inflation over the period is 5% then the real interest rate can be calculated as follows:

$$\text{Real Rate} = \left[\frac{1.10}{1.05}\right] - 1 = 4.76\%$$

6.2.1   Volatility of Interest Rates

Inflation rates and market expectations about inflation rates are usually more volatile than real interest rates, which are determined by fundamental factors such as the supply and demand for credit in the economy. Short-term interest rates in major economies are strongly influenced by the activities of the central bank, which drives the rate up or down depending on whether it wishes to dampen down the economy and reign in inflation, or to stimulate the economy. To a large extent long-term interest rates are determined by bond prices and bond yields, which build in a market consensus expectation about inflation and the likely direction of interest rates.

6.3   COMPOUNDING PERIODS

We saw in Chapter 4 that some bonds pay coupons annually and others semi-annually. The traditional method of calculating the yield on a bond is to find the single discount rate that equates the market dirty price of the bond with the present value of the bond at that discount rate. This is an internal rate of return calculation. If the bond is a semi-annual bond then the calculated discount rate is annualized by simply doubling the figure. One problem with this convention is that the yield on a semi-annual bond is not directly comparable with the yield on a bond that pays annual coupons. The general formula for calculating the effective annual interest rate or yield when interest is compounded n times per annum is as follows:

$$r_{\text{ann}} = \left\{1 + \left(\frac{r}{n}\right)\right\}^n - 1$$

where:

r_{ann} = effective annual equivalent rate as a decimal
r = quoted rate as a decimal
n = number of compounding periods per annum

Example

A quoted 10% per annum rate with semi-annual compounding is equivalent to 10.25% per annum with annual compounding:

$$r_{\text{ann}} = 1.05^2 - 1 = 0.1025 = 10.25\%$$

Table 6.1 Annual equivalent rates

Quoted rate	Compounding frequency	Annual equivalent rate
10% p.a.	Annually	10.0000% p.a.
10% p.a.	Semi-annually	10.2500% p.a.
10% p.a.	Quarterly	10.3813% p.a.
10% p.a.	Daily	10.5156% p.a.

A par bond that yields 10% on a semi-annual basis has the same effective return as a bond with annual coupons that yields 10.25% on an annual basis. Table 6.1 shows what happens to the annual equivalent rate as interest is compounded semi-annually, quarterly and daily.

As interest is compounded more and more frequently the effective annual rate approaches a limit. This limit is defined by what is known as **continuous compounding**, a method of calculating interest commonly used in the derivatives markets. The effective annual equivalent rate where interest is compounded continuously can be calculated as follows:

$$r_{ann} = e^{r_{cont}} - 1$$

where:

r_{cont} = quoted annual rate of interest with continuous compounding
e = base of natural logarithms $\cong 2.71828$

Example

A quoted 10% per annum rate with continuous compounding is equivalent to approximately 10.5171% per annum with annual compounding:

$$r_{ann} = e^{0.1} - 1 = 0.105171 = 10.5171\%$$

6.4 THE YIELD CURVE DEFINED

The yield curve is a graph plotting the yield to maturity of a set of debt securities against time to maturity. The securities are selected to be comparable in all respects apart from their term to maturity. There is a separate yield curve for US government bonds, government agencies, municipal authorities, AAA rated corporates and so on. The US Treasury curve shows the yields on dollar investments for a range of maturities that carry (in effect) no credit risk. The curve is normally constructed from the yields on bonds trading at or around par.

6.4.1 Shape of the Yield Curve

The shape of the yield curve varies over time. There are four main types of curve (see Figure 6.1).

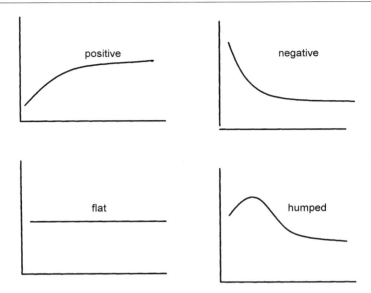

Figure 6.1 Basic yield curve shapes

- A **positive** or upward sloping or 'normal' curve occurs when yields on longer maturity securities are higher than those on shorter maturities. It tends to occur when short-term interest rates have been cut to relatively low levels.
- A **negative** or downward sloping or inverted curve occurs when yields on shorter maturity securities are higher than those on longer maturities. It tends to occur when short-term interest rates have been raised to relatively high levels.
- A **flat** yield curve occurs when yields on short and long maturity securities are roughly equal.
- A **humped** curve occurs when yields rise gradually from short to medium-term securities but then fall off in the case of longer maturities.

The slope of the yield curve tends to level off after 15 or so years. The market tends to lump longer maturities together and sees little distinction between (for example) 20 and 30-year bonds. There are many variations on the four basic types. For example, the curve may develop a 'kink' within a certain maturity range rather than describing a smooth curve.

6.5   THEORIES OF YIELD CURVES

Many theories have been promoted to explain why yield curves take the shapes they do. The most popular are:

- market expectations theory;
- liquidity preference theory;
- preferred habitat or institutional theory.

The following discussion is based on the curve for government securities such as US Treasuries. This eliminates, for the moment, issues concerning default risk, which we consider later. The main risk on an investment in US government bonds is market or price risk—the risk of making a loss because of changes in the market price/yield of the securities as a result of changes in general market conditions, such as a rise in interest rates.

6.5.1 Market Expectations Theory

Market expectations theory is the most widely held view. It says that a positive yield curve is a sign that the market expects rises in interest rates. Intuitively, if interest rates are rising investors in short-term investments will be paid back sooner and will be able to reinvest the proceeds at the new higher rates of interest. On the other hand investors buying longer-dated investments are locking their money away for longer time periods and will not be able to take advantage of reinvesting at the new higher interest rates to the same extent. They will demand a higher yield or return on their investment in compensation.

Conversely, a negative yield curve is held to be a sign of falling interest rates. In a declining interest rate environment holders of longer-term paper are content to lock in at relatively low yields because they think that yields on short-term paper are currently at a high level and are due to fall. In this environment investors who buy short-term debt securities would suffer from falling reinvestment rates.

6.5.2 Empirical Evidence

Negative yield curves often occur in circumstances in which short-term interest rates have been raised to relatively high levels by the central bank in order to control inflation. Market expectations theory holds that the yield curve is negative in this environment because investors believe the medicine will work and rates will eventually fall.

Empirical evidence suggests that the yield curve is not in fact a particularly good predictor of future interest rates. Proponents of the expectations theory will argue that this is not especially relevant. The market's expectation on future interest rates is an unbiased consensus view based on all the currently available information. This information will change over time and is necessarily always incomplete. At any one moment our view is based on the facts at hand. If the yield curve shows the current market consensus on the direction of interest rates then at least it allows market participants to decide whether or not they agree with the consensus—and act accordingly.

In recent years the yield curve for US Treasury bonds and UK gilts has been negative for prolonged periods of time. Most market practitioners accept that this had little to do with expectations of interest rates and was mainly caused by the lack of supply of long-dated Treasuries. As governments acted to buy back longer maturity bonds in the secondary market this caused prices to rise and yields to fall below those of shorter maturity bonds.

6.5.3 Liquidity Preference Theory

This theory argues that since the price or market risk of a bond increases with the term to maturity investors will demand a risk premium for holding longer maturities.

Longer-duration bonds are more sensitive to changes in interest rates than shorter-duration bonds. All other things being equal, investors prefer to have their money in short-term securities so they can quickly respond to changes in market interest rates.

If this theory was interpreted simplistically it would imply that yield curves should always be positive, which is clearly not the case. In fact adherents tend to argue that the yield curve should incorporate both interest rate expectations and a risk premium for holding longer-term bonds. This means that a positive curve *may* incorporate expectations of rises in interest rates. Alternatively, there may be no such expectation in the market and the upward slope is explained purely by the liquidity risk premium effect.

Liquidity Premium

Pure expectations theory would suggest that an investor who agrees with the market consensus on the direction of interest rates should not demand a liquidity premium. Such an investor would be indifferent between investing in a one-year Treasury bill and investing in a 30-year Treasury bond with the intention of selling it after one year. This is because future interest rate expectations and hence future bond prices can be predicted from the current shape of the yield curve. We will explain the method later in the present chapter.

6.5.4 Preferred Habitat Theory

This theory accepts the view that the term structure reflects the expectation of future interest rates and also includes a risk premium. However proponents deny that the risk premium is due to a preference for shorter maturity securities. They argue that investors and borrowers have preferences for particular maturities. If there is an excess of demand for funds at a given maturity additional investors can only be attracted out of their 'preferred habitat' by offering a risk premium. If there is an over-supply of funds further borrowers can only be attracted by lowering interest rates.

6.6   YIELD CURVES AND CREDIT RISK

The discussion on the shape of yield curves so far was based on government bonds that carry no credit risk. At every maturity an investor will demand a risk premium for holding corporate bonds and other bonds that carry default risk. The size of the risk premium will depend on the credit rating of the issuer. Figure 6.2 shows the sort of graph we would expect to see in a positive yield curve environment. The yield curve for AAA rated dollar bonds sits above that for US Treasuries. Yields on AA rated bonds at all maturities are higher still.

Normally the spread over Treasuries will increase with time to maturity. There is a higher risk that a corporate issuer will default over 10 years than over one year and investors will demand an increased risk premium. An additional factor that will determine the spread over Treasuries is the **liquidity** of a corporate bond, which in this context means how actively it is traded. When an illiquid bond is traded in any size it

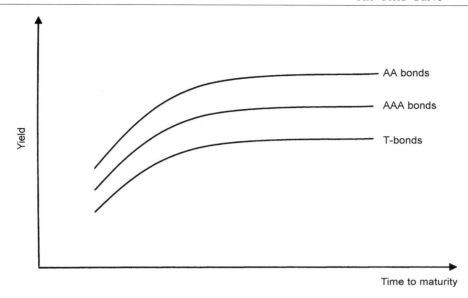

Figure 6.2   The Treasury curve and credit spreads

can have an effect on the price. All other things being equal, a less liquid security should pay a higher rate of interest than a more liquid security.

6.7   ZERO COUPON OR SPOT RATES

All the theories discussed in the last section agree that the yield curve incorporates market expectations about future or 'forward' interest rates. In fact using a simple arbitrage argument it is possible to derive interest rates for future time periods from the yield curve for government bonds. These are called **implied forward rates**. The curve for government bonds such as US Treasuries is used because this eliminates credit risk issues.

Unfortunately the yields on coupon bonds cannot be used directly to establish forward rates, since they actually assume that coupon payments can be reinvested for all future periods at a constant rate. To help explore the difficulties with yields on coupon bonds we will consider a yield curve based on one, two and three-year annual coupon bonds trading at par. This is known as a **par yield curve**. The rates are set out in Table 6.2. The bonds in this example are presumed to be free of credit risk.

Table 6.2   Par yield curve for annual coupon bonds

Maturity	Coupon rate	Yield to maturity
1 year	8%	8%
2 years	9%	9%
3 years	10%	10%

6.7.1 Coupon Stripping

We will carry out the following strategy today.

- **Step 1**. Buy $100 of the two-year 9% coupon bond trading at par.
- **Step 2**. Sell off the title to the first $9 coupon on this bond due in one year's time to another investor.

Effectively we have 'stripped' out the first coupon and created a one-year zero coupon bond with a future value of $9. Since the yield on one-year maturity annual bonds is 8% it seems reasonable that we should sell off this $9 future cash flow at a yield of 8%. The present value received from selling the bond is:

$$\frac{\$9}{1.08} = \$8.3333$$

- **Step 3**. Next, we sell off the title to the final coupon and the par value of the 9% coupon bond both due in two years' time.

Now we have 'stripped' out the final cash flow on the 9% coupon bond and created a two-year zero coupon bond with a future value of $109. The yield to maturity on two-year coupon bonds is currently 9% (from Table 6.2). Assuming that we sell off the $109 cash flow at a 9% yield the present value received from the investor is:

$$\frac{\$109}{1.09^2} = \$91.7431$$

To summarize the position:

- we have bought a two-year 9% coupon bond for $100;
- sold the title to the first $9 cash flow from the bond for $8.3333;
- sold off the title to the second and final $109 cash flow from the bond for $91.7431;
- our outgoings today are $100 and our receipts are $100.076.

If we carry this 'coupon stripping' exercise out on millions of dollars' worth of bonds we are going to make a great deal of free money!

6.7.2 Calculating the Two-Year Spot Rate

Since we have made a risk-free or arbitrage profit here something must be wrong with the calculations. We discounted the first $9 cash flow at a yield of 8% and this is correct because 8% is the yield on one-year annual bonds which have no intervening coupons. The problem arose over discounting the second cash flow of $109 using the 9% yield on two-year coupon bonds. This yield measure assumes that the interim $9 coupon is received and reinvested for a further year at 9% and then that $109 is received at maturity. It cannot be used to price the year two cash flow on the bond when it is sold off separately without receiving and reinvesting the intervening coupon.

From the data we are given it is possible to calculate the appropriate discount rate at which the year two $9 cash flow should be sold off today such that there are no arbitrage profits available. Recall that:

- we have paid $100 for the two-year 9% coupon bond;
- we have sold the title to the first $9 coupon at the one-year yield of 8% for a present value of $8.3333.

There are no intervening coupons to reinvest on a one-year annual bond so this 8% rate can be applied directly to present value any one-off risk-free dollar cash flow due in one year. It is the one-year zero coupon rate, also known as the **spot rate** for the period. We will call it z_1. In our example, $z_1 = 8\%$.

The question to be resolved is how much we would have to receive today for the title to the year two cash flow of $109 such that we exactly break even on stripping the bond:

- cost of two-year 9% coupon bond today $= \$100$;
- received for title to year one cash flow at $z_1(8\%) = \$8.3333$;
- required for title to year two cash flow to break even $= \$100 - \$8.3333 = \$91.6667$.

If we are to just break even on the coupon stripping exercise we will be paid $91.6667 for the year two cash flow of $109. The yield on this investment is the two-year zero coupon or spot rate, which we will call z_2. How do we calculate this rate? The present value formula used in bond markets is as follows:

$$PV = \frac{FV}{(1 + r)^n}$$

where:

FV = future value
PV = present value
r = discount rate per compounding period as a decimal
n = number of compounding periods

We can shuffle this formula around and solve for r:

$$r = \left\{ \sqrt[n]{\left(\frac{FV}{PV} \right)} \right\} - 1$$

In our example the future value is $109, the present value is $91.6667 and the investment period is two years. The two-year zero coupon yield z_2 is therefore calculated as follows:

$$z_2 = \left\{ \sqrt[2]{\left(\frac{109}{91.6667} \right)} \right\} - 1 = 0.090454 = 9.0454\%$$

6.8   BOOTSTRAPPING

The lesson from the previous section's exercise is that the 9% yield on two-year coupon bonds cannot be used directly to present value a one-off cash flow due in two years' time with no intervening coupon to reinvest. For this we need to use z_2, the two-year zero coupon or spot rate. If zero coupon bonds exist in the market then the yields on

Table 6.3   Par yields and spot rates

Maturity	Par yield	Spot rate
1 year	8%	8%
2 years	9%	9.0454%
3 years	10%	

such bonds can be observed directly and used as spot rates. Otherwise, spot rates can be extracted from the yields on coupon bonds trading at par using the methodology we employed to calculate the two-year spot rate z_2.

This methodology is often called **bootstrapping** in the capital markets. To see why, recall that we started by assuming the one-year yield on annual coupon bonds establishes z_1, the one-year spot rate. We then used this to calculate z_2, the two-year spot rate. We can extend this methodology one step further and use z_1 and z_2 to calculate z_3, the three-year spot rate. We 'pull ourselves up by our own bootstraps'. Table 6.3 sets out again the yields for one, two and three-year coupon bonds trading at par. It also shows the one and two-year spot rates we have calculated.

6.8.1   Calculating the Three-Year Spot Rate

The methodology is the same as we used before to calculate the two-year spot rate.

- Assume we buy a three-year 10% coupon bond for $100.
- Sell off the one-year $10 coupon at the one-year spot rate $z_1 = 8\%$:

$$\text{Present Value} = \frac{\$10}{1.08} = \$9.2593$$

- Sell off the two-year $10 coupon at the two-year spot rate $z_2 = 9.0454\%$:

$$\text{Present Value} = \frac{\$10}{1.090454^2} = \$8.4098$$

- Calculate how much we would have to receive for the title to the three-year cash flow of $110 to exactly break even on the exercise:

$$\text{Break-even Price} = \$100 - \$9.2593 - \$8.4098 = \$82.3309$$

- Calculate z_3 the yield that an investor would make on this year three cash flow if purchased at our break-even price of $82.3309:

$$z_3 = \left\{ \sqrt[3]{\left(\frac{110}{82.3309} \right)} \right\} - 1 = 10.1395\%$$

The complete set of par yields and spot rates is shown in Table 6.4.

6.9   RELATIONSHIP WITH THE PAR CURVE

There is a clear relationship in the example we have worked through between the par yield curve and the spot rates:

Table 6.4   Complete table of par yields and spot rates

Maturity	Yield to maturity	Spot rate
1 year	8%	8%
2 years	9%	9.0454%
3 years	10%	10.1395%

- the two-year spot rate is higher than the yield on two-year coupon bonds trading at par;
- the three-year spot rate is higher than the yield on three-year coupon bonds trading at par.

The result can be explained intuitively in terms of the expectations theory of yield curves. The par yield curve in our example is positive or upward sloping — three-year yields are higher than two-year yields, which are higher than one-year yields. This builds in an expectation of future increases in interest rates. An investor who buys a two-year or three-year zero coupon bond will miss out on the ability to reinvest interim cash flows at rising interest rates. The investor has to be compensated through a higher yield than is available on coupon bonds with the same maturity.

Negative Curve

If the yield curve for par bonds is inverted or downward sloping zero coupon yields will be below the yields on par coupon bonds. A negative curve builds in expectations of falling reinvestment rates. Intuitively, investors in zero coupon bonds will not suffer from this since they have no interim coupons to reinvest, unlike investors in coupon bonds; to compensate they earn lower returns.

6.10   PRICING MODELS USING SPOT RATES

Traditionally, as we saw in Chapter 4, bonds are valued by discounting each cash flow at exactly the same discount rate. This is equivalent to assuming a constant reinvestment rate for future cash flows. However this is a simplifying assumption and applying the yield to maturity on coupon bonds to present value one-off future cash flows such as cash flows from zero coupon bonds produces inaccuracies. More sophisticated pricing models in the capital markets employ spot rates. A financial instrument is broken down into its individual cash flows and each cash flow is discounted at the specific spot rate for the period of time to the receipt of the cash flow. No assumption need be made about reinvestment rates. If there is a risk that a cash flow may not be received it can be discounted at the spot rate for Treasuries plus a credit spread.

6.10.1   Outright Risk and Curve Risk

Duration measures use the traditional bond pricing model, which is based on constant reinvestment rates. They assume implicitly that the yield curve moves in parallel shifts.

Modified duration can be used to measure what is sometimes known as **outright risk** — the profits and losses that result from parallel movements in the yield curve. However bond traders also have to take into account the profits and losses that might result from 'twists' in the shape of the curve. This is sometimes called **curve risk**. For example, a positive curve might shift upwards but also flatten, such that short-term interest rates rise more sharply than long-term interest rates. (This is a common phenomenon.)

The advantage of breaking a security down into its component cash flows and discounting each cash flow at the spot rate is that potential profits and losses can be calculated for non-parallel movements in the curve. For example, it might be assumed that one-year spot rates increase by 50 basis points but 10-year rates by only 25 basis points, flattening a positive curve.

6.11   FORWARD RATES

In the previous sections we started with a par yield curve and calculated the spot rates for each time period using the bootstrapping methodology. It is also possible to calculate the forward interest rates implied in the par yield curve between two time periods.

To do this we employ an arbitrage argument using the rates in Table 6.4. (This example ignores spreads on borrowing and lending rates which would apply in practice.) Let us assume that we are able to borrow \$1 for two years at the two-year spot rate z_2 which is 9.0454%. At maturity we would have to repay the future value:

$$\text{Future Value} = \$1 \times (1.090454)^2 = \$1.1891$$

Next, we invest the \$1 today for one year at z_1, the one-year spot rate, which is 8%. The future value in one year will be \$1.08. Finally, we arrange to reinvest the \$1.08 proceeds due to be received in one year for a further year at a fixed rate of interest. We will call this rate f_{1v2} because it is a forward rate of interest for investing money in one year for one year. The investment will mature two years from today.

If we can earn more on the two investments combined than the \$1.1891 we have to repay in two years on our borrowings then there would be an arbitrage opportunity available. We will assume that no arbitrage opportunity exists (if it did traders would no doubt soon exploit it and it would disappear). In that case the cash flow we will receive in two years from the two investments will exactly match the repayment amount due on our borrowings. The cash flows involved in this example are set out in Figure 6.3. The first line shows the cash flows from our two-year borrowing. The second line shows the \$1 invested for one year at z_1 and then reinvested for a further year at f_{1v2}.

For no arbitrage profits to be available it must be the case that:

$$\$(1 + z_2)^2 = \$(1 + z_1) \times (1 + f_{1v2})$$

To put this equation into words, the repayment amount due on the \$1 borrowing for two years at z_2 must equal the proceeds from investing the money for one year at z_1 and reinvesting for a further year at the forward rate f_{1v2}.

- We already know that the repayment amount on our borrowing $\$(1 + z_2)^2$ equals \$1.1891.

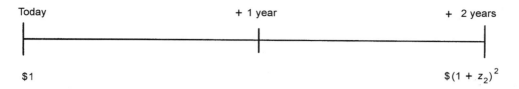

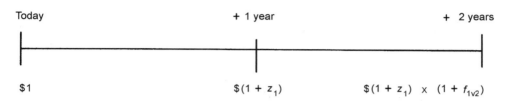

Figure 6.3   Cash flows for the forward rate calculation

- We also know that the future value of the $1 invested for the first year $(1+z_1)$ is $1.08.

We also have the equation:
$$(1 + z_2)^2 = (1 + z_1) \times (1 + f_{1v2})$$

By turning this equation round we can solve for f_{1v2} by inserting the values for z_1 and z_2:

$$f_{1v2} = \left[\frac{(1 + z_2)^2}{(1 + z_1)} \right] - 1$$

$$= \left[\frac{1.090454^2}{1.08} \right] - 1$$

$$= 10.1009\%$$

6.11.1   Explaining the Result

Again, the result can be explained in terms of expectations theory. The par yield curve is positive or upward sloping so the one-year forward rate is higher than the rate for investing today for one year, the cash market rate of 8%. The curve builds in expectations of future rises in interest rates.

6.11.2   Extending the Argument

The forward rate f_{2v3} for a one-year period starting in two years can be calculated from the spot rates using the same methodology.

- We borrow $1 for three years at the three-year spot rate z_3 which is 10.1395%. The repayment amount in three years will be $1.3361.
- We invest the $1 for two years at the two-year spot rate z_2 which is 9.0454%. The future value in two years will be $1.1891.
- We calculate f_{2v3} as the rate for reinvesting money in two years for a further year such that we exactly break even on all the transactions. In this example f_{2v3} equals 12.3607%.

6.11.3 Consistency Check

If we have calculated the spot and forward rates correctly the future value from the following two investment strategies should be consistent.

1. Invest $1 for three years at $z_3 = 10.1395\%$.
2. Invest $1 for one year at $z_1 = 8\%$:
    - roll over the proceeds for a second year at $f_{1v2} = 10.1009\%$;
    - roll over the proceeds for a third year at $f_{2v3} = 12.3607\%$.

The future value from strategy 1 is $\$1 \times 1.101395^3 = \$1.3361$. The future value from strategy 2 is $\$1 \times 1.08 \times 1.101009 \times 1.123607 = \$1.3361$.

6.12 DISCOUNT FACTORS

Market professionals often prefer to work with discount factors rather than spot rates. This is really a matter of convenience since a discount factor is simply the present value of $1 discounted at the spot rate for a given future date.

For example, if the one-year spot rate z_1 is 8% then the one-year discount factor DF_1 is calculated as follows:

$$DF_1 = \frac{\$1}{1.08} = 0.9259$$

If the two-year spot rate z_2 is 9.0454% then the two-year discount factor DF_2 is given by:

$$DF_2 = \frac{\$1}{1.090454^2} = 0.8410$$

The discount factor can be applied directly to a future cash flow to establish its present value. For example, if we know that we are entitled to receive a cash flow of $5 million in two years' time and the spot rate for that time period is 9.0454% then the present value of the cash flow is given by:

$$\text{Future Value} \times DF_2 = \$5 \text{ million} \times 0.8410 = \$4.205 \text{ million}$$

6.12.1 Discount Factors and Forward Rates

Table 6.5 summarizes the par, spot and forward rates and discount factors used in the examples in this chapter.

Table 6.5   Spot and forward rates and discount factors

Maturity	Par yield	Spot rate	Forward rate	Discount factor
1 year	8%	8%		0.9259
2 years	9%	9.0454%	10.1009%	0.8410
3 years	10%	10.1395%	12.3607%	0.7485

There is an important relationship between discount factors and forward interest rates:

$$\text{Period Discount Factor} = \frac{\text{Discount Factor for the Previous Period}}{1 + (\text{Forward Rate between the Two Periods})}$$

For example:

$$DF_2 = \frac{DF_1}{1 + f_{1v2}} = \frac{0.9259}{1.101009} = 0.8410$$

This relationship can be very useful in practice. For example if we know that DF_2 is 0.8410 and we can establish that the forward rate of interest between years two and three, f_{2v3}, is 12.3607% then we can calculate the year three discount factor DF_3:

$$DF_3 = \frac{DF_2}{1 + f_{2v3}} = \frac{0.8410}{1.123607} = 0.7485$$

This produces the same result as we obtain by deriving DF_3 from the three-year spot rate:

$$DF_3 = \frac{\$1}{(1 + z_3)^3} = \frac{\$1}{(1.101395)^3} = 0.7485$$

The relationship is useful since in major currencies forward interest rates can be observed directly because of the existence of derivative products such as forward rate agreements and interest rate futures (see Chapter 10). We will also use the relationship when pricing interest rate swaps in Chapter 13. Note that when using discount factors in practice it is usually necessary to use around six to eight decimal places to obtain accurate results.

6.13   CHAPTER SUMMARY

Interest rates and bond yields are normally quoted on a nominal basis which includes inflation expectations. The real rate of interest is the nominal rate adjusted for the inflation assumption. Bond yields quoted on an annual and on a semi-annual basis cannot be compared directly. Instead, the semi-annual yield has to be converted to an annual equivalent yield (or vice versa). In the derivatives market interest is often compounded on a continuous basis. The yield curve is a graph based on a certain class of bonds which plots bond yield against maturity. There is a yield curve for government bonds and yield curves for bonds that carry credit or default risk. At all maturities investors will demand a higher yield for taking on a greater degree of credit risk.

Default risk tends to increase with time. The expectations theory of yield curves holds that a positive or upward sloping curve builds in expectations of rising interest rates. A negative or downward sloping curve anticipates falling interest rates. The par yield curve is the curve for coupon bonds trading at par. Using arbitrage arguments it is possible to extract from the par curve zero coupon or spot rates and forward interest rates. Deriving the spot rates is called bootstrapping. Spot rates can be applied directly to present value future cash flows since they make no reinvestment assumptions. The spot rate derived from government bonds will have to be adjusted if the cash flow carries credit risk. A discount factor is the present value of $1 at the spot rate for the time period. Discount factors can also be derived from observed forward interest rates in the market.

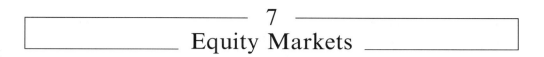

7
Equity Markets

Cecily, you will read your Political Economy in my absence. The Chapter on the Fall of the Rupee you may omit. It is somewhat too sensational.

Oscar Wilde

7.1 CHAPTER OVERVIEW

Previously we have considered short and long-term debt securities. In this chapter we set the scene for later discussions by exploring the operations of equity markets. We review the factors that make debt securities and equity securities (shares or 'common stock' in the US) different for issuers and for investors. In developed markets most shares are held by institutional investors such as pension funds, insurance companies and mutual funds. We consider the legal structure of mutual funds, and different equity portfolio management styles. One of the most hotly debated subjects in finance is the extent to which markets are efficient. The practical implications of this debate for equity traders and investors are assessed. We consider the key stages of an initial public offering (IPO) of new shares and look at how further shares are issued through rights issues or general cash offers. Unlike bond markets, most share trading around the world is conducted on organized stock exchanges. We look at quote-driven markets based on dealers, and order-driven markets in which buy and sell orders are directly matched. Market operations are illustrated by looking at the New York Stock Exchange and the London Stock Exchange. The remaining sections of this chapter explore the markets for depository receipts, stock borrowing and lending, and portfolio trading.

7.2 DEBT AND EQUITY

Most companies are funded through a mixture of debt capital and share or equity capital. Debt capital is provided by a bank or by investors who buy bonds issued by the company, or by trade suppliers who offer terms of credit. Equity capital is provided by the company's **ordinary shareholders** who are part-owners of the business. In the US, ordinary shares are known as common stock.

7.2.1 Features of Debt Capital

- Providers of debt normally demand lower returns than the ordinary shareholders.
- Debt is lower risk for an investor than equity. The company has a legal obligation to repay interest and the loan principal at maturity. It does not have to pay dividends on shares.
- Debt may be secured on assets such as land and property, further reducing risk to the lenders.

- A company with a substantial proportion of debt is said to have high **leverage** (US) or **gearing** (UK). Leverage is a double-edged sword. If a company borrows money and uses it effectively it will have more than enough funds to pay the interest, and the profits belong to the ordinary shareholders. If the company performs badly it still has to pay the interest. Increased leverage increases the risk of **financial distress** — action by creditors to recover money owed, or outright bankruptcy.
- In most countries interest payments are tax deductible, unlike dividends on ordinary shares.
- There are limits on how much debt a company can raise — either imposed by the existing providers of debt through legal covenants, or by the external market which will stop lending beyond a certain level as the risk of financial distress increases.

7.2.2   Features of Equity Capital

- Ordinary shareholders — common stockholders — are part-owners of the business and (usually) have voting rights.
- Equity is risk capital. The ordinary shareholders have the lowest ranking in the capital structure, which means that other investors must be paid out first. Equity is a residual claim on the assets of the company — if a company is put into liquidation the ordinary shareholders are paid last.
- A company is not obliged to pay dividends. It must pay interest.
- Equity investors benefit from the growth in the value of the company through an increasing share price and/or a rising dividend stream.
- Equity is (normally) more expensive for a company to service than debt, because investors demand higher returns to compensate for higher risk. On the other hand, if it gets into difficulties, a company can cut or miss a dividend.
- Start-up companies are normally funded largely through equity since shareholders are prepared to wait for their return on capital, perhaps by selling their stake later on in a public offering.
- Some companies (especially in Continental Europe) have a class of non-voting ordinary shares. Often these are issued by family-owned businesses that want to raise cash without diluting the family's control over business direction. The regulators and authorities in the US and the UK are proponents of **shareholder democracy** and non-voting shares have been phased out over the years.

7.2.3   Limited Liability

A limited company is defined in law as a 'legal person' separate from the shareholders who own the company. The company can enter contracts and litigate in its own right. The shareholders have the advantage of **limited liability**. If the company fails the most they can lose is their equity stake. Shareholders are not liable to further compensate the company's creditors out of their own personal resources.

7.3   ADDITIONAL FEATURES OF EQUITY

When shares are first issued they may be given a nominal or par value. However, the market value of most shares bears no relationship to the nominal value. The **market capitalization** of a company is the total value of the company's shares on the market:

$$\text{Market Capitalization} = \text{Ordinary Shares Issued} \times \text{Current Share Price}$$

In practice, stock analysts often calculate market capitalization on a **fully diluted** basis. This means that they take into account not just the shares that have actually been issued but also those that would be created through, for example, the exercise of stock options and convertible bonds:

$$\text{Fully Diluted Market Capitalization} = \text{Actual and Potential Shares Issued}$$
$$\times \text{Current Share Price}$$

7.3.1 Share Capital and Dividends

A share may be **partly paid**. When the share was issued a proportion of the price was paid to the company, and the company has the right to call in the remainder from the shareholder on a set date or dates. Publicly-owned businesses in the UK have often been privatized through share issues in which the full price was payable in a number of instalments. In its **Memorandum of Association** a UK company will set out its authorized share capital, the maximum number of shares it can issue.

7.3.2 Dividends

The Board of Directors may decide to pay interim dividends during a company's financial year, followed by a final dividend at the end of the year. Most UK companies pay only one interim dividend, except for those also listed on a US exchange. When a share is trading **ex-dividend** (xd) a buyer is not entitled to receive the next dividend payment — it will go to the seller. A share 'goes xd' a few weeks before the dividend payment. During this period it would be difficult for the company to change the share register in time to reflect the new ownership, so the forthcoming dividend is paid to the original owner. A share bought **cum-dividend** (cd) carries entitlement to the next dividend payment.

7.4 HYBRID SECURITIES

Some securities are 'hybrids' between debt and equity. They are designed to appeal to different categories of investors.

- **Preference Share (Preference Stock in the US)**. Holders must receive their (normally fixed) dividend before the ordinary shareholders are paid. 'Prefs' rank above ordinary shares in the event of liquidation. They are like fixed income securities, but with no maturity date.
- **Cumulative Preference Share**. If the dividend is not paid one year, it must be paid in the following year or whenever the company generates sufficient profits. The arrears must be paid off before any dividend is paid on the ordinary shares or on other preference shares with a lower ranking.
- **Convertible Preference Share**. A preference share that can be converted into ordinary shares. Before conversion they are lower risk than the ordinary shares because they have higher ranking and (normally) pay a fixed dividend.

- **Convertible Bond**. A bond that can be converted into a fixed number of (normally) ordinary shares at the option of the holder on or before a fixed date.

7.5   INSTITUTIONAL INVESTORS

Shares are bought by individual investors, corporations and governments, and by large investing institutions such as pension funds, insurance companies and mutual funds. These days most shares in developed markets are bought and sold by institutions. Mutual funds are collective investment vehicles which invest in shares, bonds and other assets. The portfolios of assets are run by professional managers, for a commission fee. There are three main types of legal structure.

- **Open-ended Fund**. These are known in the UK as unit trusts. Units are bought from and sold to the fund manager. There is no limit on the amount of money that can be invested and units in the fund created. There is a spread between the fund manager's buy price and sell price.
- **Closed-ended Fund**. An investment company with a fixed amount of capital. Investors buy and sell shares in the company on an exchange. These are known in the UK as investment trusts.
- **Open-ended Investment Company (OEIC)**. An investment company listed on an exchange which can issue new shares according to demand. Shares are bought and sold at a single price, which is a feature designed to appeal to retail investors. These are common elsewhere in the world but have only recently been introduced into the UK.

7.6   EQUITY INVESTMENT STYLES

Fund managers are sometimes known as the 'buy side' of the market. Securities trading and broking operations are the 'sell side' because they provide investment ideas and transact orders for institutional investors. Traditional fund managers such as those managing the assets of pension funds are said to run **long-only** funds. This means that unlike hedge funds (see below) they do not run short positions. There are two principal approaches to running a 'long-only' fund: passive style and active style management.

- **Passive Management.** The fund manager seeks to track a benchmark market index. These are also known as index tracker funds. Because it is expensive in terms of transaction costs to buy all the shares in the index the manager may use a 'sampling' methodology and buy a subset of shares in the index. If so, the manager runs the risk of making a **tracking error**.
- **Active Management.** The fund manager seeks to outperform a benchmark index. This could be a country-specific index such as the S&P 500, or a global index. The benchmark normally represents a highly diversified portfolio of securities.

Active managers use a wide variety of investment styles to try to beat their benchmark index. Two widely followed approaches are **growth** investment and **value** investment.

- **Growth Investment.** Buying shares in high-growth businesses such as technology companies, and companies whose growth prospects are reckoned to be underestimated by the market. Profits are realized primarily through capital gains on the stocks.

- **Value Investment.** Buying shares in companies that are reckoned to be undervalued by the market. Profits are realized through capital gains and/or high dividends.

On top of this, many fund management operations place a great deal of emphasis on their **asset allocation** process. In this system the fund is firstly apportioned between different asset classes (e.g. bonds, shares, cash), different geographical locations (e.g. the US, Europe, the Far East) and different business sectors (e.g. pharmaceuticals, manufacturing, retail). After the allocation process is completed, decisions are taken on which securities in each category to buy. The allocation weightings are adjusted from time to time in line with economic and market forecasts.

Asset Allocation: An Example

The asset allocation committee of a global equity fund decides to 'go overweight' the US market for the next quarter. The benchmark weighting is 40%. This means that the US equity market is currently 40% by market capitalization of the global index. The committee increases the proportion of the fund's assets to be invested in the US market to 50%. The actual decisions on which shares to buy are taken by the team of fund managers that specializes in US equities.

A fund manager which operates an asset allocation process is sometimes said to use a **top-down** methodology. By contrast, a **bottom-up** fund manager starts with individual stock selections and builds the fund up from there. The essence of successful asset allocation is timing. Top-down funds seek to add value by being in the right market at the right time as well as picking the right stocks at the right time.

Chinese Walls

Fund management businesses that form part of an investment bank must be separated from the rest of the bank by a so-called **Chinese Wall**. This is a set of arrangements to ensure that the fund managers act on behalf of their investing clients and that their decisions are not influenced by any of the other activities of the parent bank (in particular, the broking, trading and new issuance operations).

7.7   EFFICIENT MARKETS

In part the movement towards passive or index-tracking funds in the US and UK has been fuelled by an increasing recognition that it is very difficult to outperform the market benchmark on a consistent basis. Even when it seems that an active fund has outperformed for a number of years this may be no more than a random result. In fact there is a tendency for funds that have outperformed in recent times to underperform over the next few years — which may simply be because their long-term performance is reverting to the market average, or because a style of investment that works well in one set of market conditions works less well when circumstances change.

The argument about the merits or otherwise of active portfolio management turns on whether or not the market is efficient, and if so how efficient. Broadly speaking, an **efficient market** is one in which information is already fully reflected in share prices. E.F. Fama and others have categorized three levels of market efficiency.

- **Weak Form.** The past history of the shares is fully reflected in current prices.
- **Semi-strong Form.** All publicly available information is already reflected in share prices.
- **Strong Form.** All information including information that is not publicly available is already reflected in share prices.

This is one of the most controversial subjects in finance, and one where the opinions of market practitioners and academics have tended to diverge sharply in the past. If a share price accurately reflects all available information then the only thing that can move the price is some new piece of information. By definition this is unknowable, it could equally be 'good news' or 'bad news' for the share. Therefore the next movement in the share price is random and there is nothing we can do with the existing information we have available to predict that movement with any accuracy. Share prices will follow a so-called **random walk**.

7.7.1   Practical Consequences

There are real-world implications of the efficient market debate.

- **Technical Analysis**. If share prices follow a random path then it is not possible to predict future price movements consistently by analysing historical data. Many traders believe that there are clearly discernible patterns in historical share price charts that will recur in the future. Exploring such patterns is known as technical analysis or 'chartism' in the capital markets.
- **Fundamental Analysis**. If a market is semi-strong efficient then it should not be possible to identify on a consistent, non-random basis stocks that are under- or overpriced through the analysis of financial statements or any publicly available information. All of this information should already be built into the current share price. In practice stock analysts and investment managers do believe that they can still find shares that are trading on prices that do not accurately reflect 'the fundamentals' — perhaps because of panic selling, or over-exuberant buying.
- **Insider Dealing**. If the strong form theory were true then even inside traders could not profit from their activities. The information they have is already reflected in the share price.

7.7.2   Research on Market Efficiency

Few if any people believe in strong form efficiency. But even if the semi-strong form is true it should be impossible to develop a technique that would consistently outperform a market index such as the S&P 500 or the FT-SE 100. A strategy that involves picking potential 'winners' and 'losers' amongst the constituent shares could only succeed for a time through sheer good luck. Research is focusing these days on exactly how efficient different types of market are. It may be that the prices of major blue-chips accurately reflect all available information, but it is far less certain that this is the case with smaller capitalization companies. If this is indeed true then there are implications for how funds are operated. The proportion of a fund earmarked to buy large blue-chips should perhaps be put into a tracker fund with transaction costs kept to a minimum. The proportion allocated to 'small cap' companies should be given to an active fund manager who can exploit market inefficiencies and 'beat the index'. There has been a trend in this direction, especially in the US, although some commentators argue that active managers of blue-chip funds will come back into their own in a falling market when tracker funds by definition are losing money.

7.8   HEDGE FUNDS

Wealthy individuals interested in speculative investments may pool their cash with other like-minded investors into so-called **hedge funds**. The name can be something of a misnomer. Some hedge funds are actually extremely risky investments seeking well above average returns. For example, they may speculate on currencies, interest rates or commodity prices, or on corporate takeovers. A **macro fund** is one that focuses on large-scale macro-economic events such as a currency crisis. The most famous is the Quantum Fund run by George Soros which speculated successfully against the British pound in September 1992 and helped to break its link with the Deutschemark established through the Exchange Rate Mechanism (ERM). The Quantum Fund made over $1 billion on that occasion.

LTCM

The near collapse of the Long-Term Capital Management (LTCM) hedge fund in 1998 shocked the market. It had been assumed that most of the risks on the fund were hedged out, and that it was exploiting price anomalies through a range of complex derivatives trades based on its mathematical models. In fact the fund had huge exposures to yield spreads in the fixed income markets and to stock market volatility, magnified by its highly leveraged structure. In September 1998 the Federal Reserve organized a $3.625 billion bail-out from a consortium of major banks, leaving the original investors with only 10% of the fund.

7.8.1   Long–Short Hedge Funds

A long–short hedge fund can take short as well as long positions in securities or whole markets. For example, the fund might decide to short the euro or the Japanese equity market or a particular share that is under pressure at the moment. Or it may try to exploit anomalies in the relative market prices of two assets. At the time of writing a large number of these funds are being launched aimed primarily at high net-worth individuals. A long–short fund holds out the prospect of absolute returns even in a bear market. Traditional 'long-only' funds tend to lose money in bear markets, unless the fund manager is extremely skilful (or lucky) in being able to pick stocks that perform well when prices generally are falling. On the other hand hedge funds charge larger management fees and can take as much as 20% of annual profits on the fund in performance bonuses.

7.9   PRIMARY MARKETS

A primary market is one in which securities are sold to investors for the first time. A secondary market is one in which existing securities are traded (such as a stock exchange).

An **initial public offering** (IPO) is an offer to sell shares in a company to the investing public for the first time. The shares may be existing shares owned by the founders of the business who wish to realize profits from their investment, or new shares issued to raise additional capital for the company. Often both are involved at the same time. The company is normally advised on its IPO by an investment bank. The business unit that works on IPOs and other new share issues in an investment bank is usually known as the Equity Capital Markets (ECM) group.

7.9.1   Issuance Methods

Perhaps the simplest way for a company to issue its shares would be to fix a price and offer the shares to potential investors at that price. If there is any uncertainty about the pricing, the shares might be auctioned (in the UK this is known as a **tender issue**). The danger with a fixed price offer is that the price may be set too high (there is insufficient demand) or too low (the company raises less capital than it should). The potential danger with an auction is that the bids might come in too low, or investors may be unclear about what to bid and may stay out of the bidding process altogether. This may be a particular concern in the case of retail investors. Perhaps for this reason tender issues are unusual in the UK, although they have been more common in France.

These days many IPOs around the world tend to be conducted using a modification to a straightforward fixed price offering. The investment bank advising the issuer values the business and puts out a price range. The actual issue price is set towards the end of the process, after having established the level of demand for the shares. In practice it is very difficult to value many companies in the modern world, since their main assets are intangible — brands, patents, the skills of the workforce, client relationships and so on. It is wise to test a theoretical valuation against the opinions of investors and general market sentiment before finally fixing the issue price.

7.9.2   Stages in an IPO

A modern IPO will tend to follow a number of stages.

- **Lead Manager(s).** The company appoints an investment bank (sometimes more than one) as lead manager or bookrunner of the issue. The lead investment bank has primary responsibility for the whole IPO process, working with other advisors such as auditors, lawyers, registrars, brokers, investor relations specialists and so on. The lead bank will also deal with the regulators and the exchange(s) on which the shares are to be listed.

- **Syndication.** In a larger issue the lead manager(s) will assemble a syndicate of banks which help in the process of selling and distributing the shares. Typically the syndicate will also **underwrite** the issue, which guarantees the issuer will raise the capital it needs. The underwriters take on the risk that they may be left holding the shares. Their fee is the difference between the issue price and the price paid to the company for the shares. If the issue is especially risky the lead investment bank may decline to underwrite it and agree only to use its best endeavours to sell the shares.
- **Valuation.** The company will be valued for the IPO using a range of techniques — assessing its assets, sales and profits; looking at the valuations of similar businesses; forecasting and discounting future cash flows. A price range is set and this is used to assess demand for the shares.
- **Initial Prospectus.** A document is drawn up and issued setting out details of the company, its financial statements, information about the management, its business plan, trading history and the purpose for which it needs to raise funds. In the US the initial prospectus is sometimes known as a **red herring** because it has still to be fully cleared by the Securities & Exchange Commission (SEC) and traditionally has to carry a warning red banner.
- **Bookbuilding.** Investor roadshows are run to publicize the issue and the underwriters assess demand for the shares at a range of different prices. Sometimes the feedback suggests that the whole price range has to be reviewed. A fixed issue price is set and an allocation procedure determined that will clear the available shares.
- **Greenshoe Option.** The underwriters often try to sell more shares than are actually being offered in the 'basic' deal. A greenshoe is an option for the underwriters to purchase additional shares in order to satisfy excess demand. The maximum greenshoe in the US is 15% of the announced issue size. If the option is exercised either the company issues more shares, or the extra shares are sold by the existing shareholders. (The strange name comes from the flotation of the Green Shoe Manufacturing Company, where the technique originated.)
- **Aftermarket.** The underwriters usually provide support after the shares have been issued by acting as market makers, quoting bid and offer prices to the market for the shares. This helps reassure investors that there will be an active and liquid market.

New issues may be traded in the **grey market** before the official launch on the secondary market. An investor who sells in the grey market is effectively selling short, since if he or she does not receive the expected allocation the shares will have to be bought in the secondary market to complete the sale, potentially at a higher price.

Private Placement

A cheaper alternative to a full IPO is for the issuer's investment bank to place the shares directly with major institutional investors. This procedure may be used with smaller issues. The costs are appreciably lower than with a full public offering. In the height of the internet boom there were a number of IPOs in which shares were sold to the public directly through the web. It seems unlikely that this will supplant the traditional method except in very unusual cases.

7.10 SUBSEQUENT ISSUES

A company that has already issued shares can raise further equity capital through a **rights issue**. The full legal name is 'pre-emption rights'. In a rights issue additional shares are offered to existing shareholders in proportion to their current holdings, normally at a discount to the current market price. Shareholders can take up their rights or sell them on to another investor. Rights issues are the standard method in the UK and in most of Europe for a company to raise new share capital. By contrast they are uncommon in the US. A US company that wishes to sell new stock normally makes a **general cash offer** to existing and new shareholders alike via underwriters.

The fact that a rights issue is made at a discount to the current share price has an effect on the value of the company's shares, as the following example illustrates. The example also shows a simple and widely used method for valuing the rights if an existing investor decides to sell rather than take up the rights.

7.11 RIGHTS ISSUE: EXAMPLE

Dilution Ltd. has one million shares on issue currently worth £5 each. The company as a whole is therefore worth £5 million. Dilution Ltd. needs £1 million to invest in a new project. It does this through a rights issue. The terms are as follows.

Terms: 1 for 4 (one new share offered for each four already owned)
Rights price for new share: £4 per share

- Since one million shares are currently on issue, the rights issue creates a further 250,000 shares, making a total of 1.25 million.
- If we assume that after the rights issue, which raises £1 million in cash, the company is worth £6 million then the value of each share is now £4.80:

$$\frac{£6 \text{ million}}{1.25 \text{ million}} = £4.80$$

- The value of the rights is £0.80 per share. An investor who decides to take up the rights will pay £4.00 for a new share that (in theory) will be worth £4.80 after the rights issue.

7.11.1 Investor Choices

Take the case of an investor who owns a portfolio consisting of 100 Dilution shares worth £500 plus £100 in cash before the rights issue is announced. Table 7.1 shows the position if the investor decides to take up the rights. Table 7.2 shows the position if the investor decides to sell the rights at £0.80 per share.

Before the rights the investor had 100 shares worth £500 plus £100 in cash. The position is not affected whichever approach is taken to the rights offer.

- **Take up Rights.** The investor now owns 125 shares worth £600.
- **Sell Rights.** The investor now owns 100 shares worth £480, plus £20 in cash for the sale of the rights, plus the initial £100 in cash.

Table 7.1   Investor takes up the rights

Portfolio value before rights	£500 shares + £100 cash = £600
Rights entitlement (1 for 4)	25
Payment for new shares at £4 per share	£100
Share value after rights	£4.80
New shares in portfolio	125
New portfolio value	£600 shares + £0 cash = £600

Table 7.2   Investor sells the rights

Portfolio value before rights	£500 shares + £100 cash = £600
Rights entitlement (1 for 4)	25
Sell rights at £0.80 per share	£20
Share value after rights	£4.80
New shares in portfolio	100
New portfolio value	£480 shares + £120 cash = £600

This is a theoretical valuation. In practice, the value of the company after the rights depends on how well the market believes the cash raised will be used and on the future prospects for the company. It is the present value of the company's anticipated future cash flows.

7.12   OTHER NEW SHARE ISSUES

A **stock split** (bonus or capitalization issue in the UK) occurs when the share price becomes too high and unwieldy. For example, a company whose share price is currently £100 might decide to issue 100 new shares for every one existing share. Unlike a rights issue, the company is not raising any new equity capital and in theory the price of each new share after the split should settle at £1. The purpose is to increase the attractiveness of the stock to investors and the number of shares traded. An active or liquid market in a share is an advantage for a shareholder. It is easier to buy and sell the stock without affecting the price.

In a **scrip dividend** the dividend is paid out in the form of new shares rather than cash. In some countries there is a tax benefit since a cash dividend would be taxed as income tax while a profit on the new shares would only be realized and taxed when they are sold. In the UK there is actually a tax disadvantage for ordinary investors, since scrip dividends are taxed exactly as if the cash dividend had been received. The only remaining benefit is a lower level of transaction costs to acquire new shares.

7.13   THE LONDON STOCK EXCHANGE

A **secondary market** is one in which existing securities created through a primary market can be traded. The simplest type of market is based on deals made directly between two parties. The origins of the London Stock Exchange (LSE) can be traced back to such informal trading activities, based in a number of coffee shops around

Change Alley in eighteenth century London. In 1773 the Exchange established its own building in Threadneedle Street in the heart of the modern financial district, and developed into an organized marketplace with a famous motto 'my word is my bond'. One of the traders on the early London Stock Exchange was Abraham Ricardo the father of David the famous economist. David Ricardo had his own views about the operations of the market (quoted in David Kynaston, *The City of London Volume 1*, Pimlico, 1995):

> *The Stock Exchange is chiefly attended by persons who are unremittingly attentive to their business, and are well acquainted with its details; but there are very few in number who have much knowledge of political economy, and consequently they pay little attention to finance, as a subject of science. They consider more, the immediate effect of passing events, rather than their distant consequences.*

7.13.1   The LSE and the 'Big Bang'

The London Stock Exchange was reformed in the 1986 'Big Bang' which swept away some of the traditional features of the market.

- **Dual Capacity.** Member firms were permitted to act as market makers (traders) buying and selling shares on their own account, as well as brokers transacting orders for their clients.
- **Commissions.** The old system of fixed minimum commissions was abolished and member firms began to compete on transaction costs.
- **Wider Membership.** Membership of the Exchange was opened up to the major US and foreign banks.

Traditionally, the LSE was a **quote-driven** market. Brokers acting on behalf of individual or institutional investors would contact market makers (called 'jobbers' in the pre-Big Bang world) to transact orders. The market makers acted as principals buying and selling shares on their own account. They quoted a buy (bid) price and a sell (offer) price and made their profits through buying and selling shares at different prices. The brokers earned commissions from their clients. The Big Bang broadly retained the quote-driven method but allowed member firms to act as both market makers and brokers. It also introduced a new quote-display system called SEAQ, which quickly led to the demise of the physical trading floor.

SEAQ

Stock Exchange Automated Quotations. Market makers enter their competing bid and offer prices for the shares in which they are authorized to trade into the system. The quotations are sent out electronically to investors and other member firms. The so-called 'yellow strip' shows the best (highest) bid and the best (lowest) offer for a share at any one moment in time. Market makers are obliged to quote continuous bid and offer prices to other members of the Exchange in their authorized stocks.

7.13.2   Liquidity

A quote-driven market based on competing market makers means that there is always a liquid market in shares. (The NASDAQ market in the US also uses market makers.) Traders have to quote both buy and sell prices to other members of the Exchange. And the Exchange regulates the market to ensure that the spreads — the difference between the market makers' buy and sell prices — are not too wide. This means that even in extreme market conditions such as the October 1987 crash an investor can always find a price at which to sell their shares. In a pure order-matching market this might not be the case — there may not be any buyers at all in a crash and the whole market might simply dry up. (The main practical difficulty in the 1987 crash was getting through to the market makers on the telephone.) Market making is a potentially dangerous business and the traders maintain their bid–offer spreads as a means of protecting themselves against losses, as well as generating trading profits.

7.13.3   Trading Activities

In London the share traders work for the Equity Markets divisions of major investment banks and securities houses. In practice trading operations tend to mix two sorts of activities: flow trading and proprietary trading (position taking).

- **Flow Trading.** The firm's analysts and equity salespeople generate buy and sell orders from institutional investors. Traders facilitate these orders by buying and selling lines of stock, often in substantial 'size', and offload positions with other traders and with institutional investors.
- **Proprietary Trading.** Traders may also take positions in shares (up to specified dealing limits) and seek to profit from short-term changes in the share prices. They may take straightforward long or short positions in shares, or set up a 'pairs' trade in which they buy one share and sell a second share in the expectation that the spread (difference) between the two share prices will narrow or widen.

Equity market professionals often take the view that while 'flow' business may not in itself always be highly profitable, it builds valuable knowledge of what is happening in the market. It keeps them 'in the flow'.

7.14   STOCK EXCHANGE TRADING SYSTEM (SETS)

In 1997 the LSE introduced a new electronic order-matching system called SETS. Buyers and sellers place their orders on the system (via a broker if they are not members of the Exchange) and these are directly matched by the SETS computer system. There are no intervening market makers. SETS was introduced initially for the top 100 shares, but has been extended to around 200 UK shares and at the time of writing is being extended to international stocks. For the moment the traditional quote-driven system based on market makers and the order-matching SETS system continue to operate in tandem. Each method has its own particular features.

- **Market makers** provide liquidity and will take large 'block' trades at an agreed price. However they take a bid–offer spread.

- **Order-matching** by computer is fast and efficient, designed to cut dealing spreads, and prices are established in an open and transparent market. However there is a risk of illiquidity particularly in smaller stocks and in extreme market conditions — it may be difficult to find a match for a buy or sell order except by making a significant change to the price.

7.14.1 Central Counterparty

In 2001 the London Clearing House (LCH) was appointed as the central counterparty for trades on the London Stock Exchange. This will effectively eliminate settlement risk, since all transactions will be cleared through the clearing house which guarantees that sellers will receive their cash and buyers their shares. It also means that trades can be anonymous. Buyers and sellers on SETS settle through the clearing house and need not know the name of their trade counterparty.

7.15   THE NEW YORK STOCK EXCHANGE

The New York Stock Exchange (NYSE) originated with the share deals made around the famous buttonwood tree in lower Manhattan. The NYSE still operates a physical trading floor located in Wall Street. Orders are routed to the exchange by telephone and electronic links from all over the world. Apart from exchange staff there are two main types of market participants on the NYSE trading floor: brokers and specialists.

- **Floor Brokers.** These act on behalf of clients, for a commission fee, transacting buy and sell orders. A broker with a buy (sell) order takes it to the trading pitch handling that stock and tries to match the order at the best available price with a broker acting on behalf of a seller (buyer).
- **Specialists.** These are responsible for ensuring that the auction process runs smoothly and that orders are properly matched. If a broker cannot find another broker willing to take the other side of the deal then the specialist will buy or sell the shares on his or her firm's own account, acting as a principal.

On the NYSE the floor brokers are agents, operating on behalf of their clients. Primarily, it is an order-driven system in which buy and sell orders are directly matched. The main responsibility of the specialist is to ensure an orderly market. However, specialists also act as 'emergency' market makers in order to provide liquidity in the market. This is a comfort to investors who know that in all market conditions there is always a buy price and a sell price available in a stock.

7.16   DEPOSITORY RECEIPTS

Depository receipts (DRs) are receipts issued by a bank in local currency for a deposit of shares in a foreign company. They allow companies to tap a pool of international capital, and to increase liquidity in their shares. From a local investor's perspective, depository receipts provide a relatively simple means of investing in foreign securities, bypassing the need for global custodian services and using local settlement procedures. In addition, they are quoted in a familiar currency. Table 7.3 shows the volume of listed depository receipts from 1996 to 2000.

Table 7.3   Volume of listed depository receipt programmes 1996–2000

Year	Volume ($bn)
1996	341
1997	503
1998	563
1999	667
2000	1352 (forecast)

Source: Bank of New York reproduced with permission.

7.16.1   ADRs

The biggest market is for **American depository receipts** (ADRs). ADRs were first introduced in 1927 to bypass restrictions preventing UK companies from registering shares abroad. US investors could invest in the UK market by lodging shares with the London branch of a US bank that would then issue ADRs in the US. Since then exchange-listed ADRs have become extremely popular in the US. The main advantage these days for a US-based investor is that ADRs provide a relatively simple means of investing in foreign shares. ADRs:

- are traded in US dollars;
- pay dividends in dollars;
- settle locally in the US.

Table 7.4 shows the top five most widely held ADRs at June 2000 (the Shell figure is at September 2000).

A global depository receipt (GDR) is a receipt for a package of shares of a foreign company normally based in a developing country. The first GDR was issued in 1994 in London for East India hotels.

7.17   STOCK LENDING

The stock lending market allows holders of assets, such as portfolio managers or traders, to make extra returns by lending their shares to a borrower for a fee. An intermediary may bring the lender and borrower together. The borrower of the stock might be:

Table 7.4   The top five most widely held ADRs at June 2000 (Shell figures at September 2000)

Company	Country	Shares held through ADRs	Value ($bn)
Nokia	Finland	1,205,511,808	60.03
Royal Dutch/Shell	Netherlands	588,484,416	36.17
BP Amoco	UK	598,840,960	33.82
Vodafone	UK	557,304,768	23.00

Source: JP Morgan.

- a trader or other market participant who has agreed to sell the shares but for some reason is unable to obtain them;
- a trader who is running a short position — selling a share he or she does not own in the expectation of buying it back later at a cheaper price. The short seller has to borrow the shares and replace them later;
- an option trader who needs to hedge their book by taking short positions in the underlying shares.

The fees paid to the lender of shares will depend on the type and quantity of shares borrowed, supply and demand for the shares in the market, and the term of the loan. The term may be a fixed period, or the loan may be rolled over on a daily basis.

7.17.1   Collateral

Lenders of shares demand **collateral** to guarantee that the borrower will return the shares or compensate them in cash. Collateral may be in the form of cash, or securities such as government bills or bonds. Where securities are used as collateral they may be valued at some discount to their actual market value — this is sometimes known as a **haircut**. In addition, if the shares that are borrowed rise in value during the loan the lender may require additional collateral. If the collateral posted is cash the lender of shares will pay the borrower of the shares some rate of interest that reflects current money market rates, less the lender's fee. If the collateral is in the form of securities the lender's fee may be quoted as a percentage of the market value of the shares lent.

7.17.2   Termination and Ownership

The borrower or lender of shares can normally terminate the arrangement early. The borrower might do this when the shares become available to purchase or when he or she decides to close a short position or hedge. The lender might choose to terminate the loan in order to sell the shares. Once the shares are returned to the lender (the original owner) the borrower's collateral is returned and any outstanding lending fees are paid.

7.17.3   Manufactured Dividends

When shares are loaned out the actual ownership is transferred to the buyer, so the buyer can sell them on to another party. The borrower agrees to compensate the lender for any dividends paid on the shares during the loan — this is sometimes called a **manufactured dividend**. Similarly, if the company whose shares have been loaned out launches a rights issue the borrower must take the rights up on behalf of the lender or reimburse the lender for the value of the rights.

7.18   PORTFOLIO TRADING

Portfolio trading specialists help institutional clients to analyse and execute buy and sell orders on large portfolios of shares. Portfolio trades are implemented in two main ways: on a risk basis and on an agency basis.

- **Principal/Risk Basis**. The broker/dealer quotes a firm price for the portfolio to the institution and takes the risk that it may make a loss on dealing at that price.
- **Agency Basis**. The broker acts as an agent for the institution for a commission fee and seeks to transact the order at the best available price(s) in the market.

Currently most portfolio trades in the UK are transacted on a principal basis. This reflects the quote-driven traditions of the London share market. Principal trades can be advantageous to the broker/dealer firm since they create substantial deal flows for the trading book.

The model in Continental Europe is almost the exact opposite, with the great majority of trades conducted on an agency basis. In some of these cases the broker is set a target to execute the portfolio trade at or around the **volume weighted average price** (VWAP) for the day the trade was executed. VWAP is believed by many to be a better benchmark indication of where a share was actually trading on a given day than the closing price or the simple arithmetical average of the trade prices that day. If a portfolio trader executes a trade at or around VWAP this is a sign that they have handled the deal effectively and minimized the market impact of dealing in volume.

Some market practitioners believe that the agency model will spread in the UK, although others feel that since principal trades are conducted at such keen prices at the moment, institutions will continue to prefer passing the principal risk on to the portfolio trading firms. In some cases a hybrid arrangement is agreed under which the portfolio trading firm and the institutional investor share the price risk on executing the trade.

7.18.1 Implementing Portfolio Trades

Portfolio traders use a number of strategies to help implement orders. For example, they may be able to arrange a **cross** by looking for buyers and sellers amongst their client base rather than dealing on the open market. When they deal in the open market, portfolio traders often analyse dealing patterns to assess when the shares are most actively traded and when the majority of orders are likely to be brought to the market.

Institutional clients look for a number of features when they select a portfolio trading firm:

- competitive commissions on agency deals;
- keen pricing on principal deals;
- the ability to handle the market impact of large trades;
- speed of execution;
- efficient back-office processing.

7.18.2 Market Trends

There are a number of current market developments that are impacting on the portfolio trading business in the US and in Europe.

- **Technology**. The portfolio trading business is increasingly technology-driven, with a focus on straight-through deal processing wherever possible.

- **Switching**. Trustees of funds tend to switch asset managers more frequently nowadays. A significant change in the investment style will mean that major portfolio trades will have to be executed.
- **Liquidity**. Some commentators are concerned that liquidity in shares is increasingly being spread between different exchanges and trading platforms and this will impact on the ability of portfolio traders to handle large deals. Leading shares nowadays are often traded on a number of major exchanges, and electronic communications networks (ECNs) for share trading have been springing up as rivals to the traditional exchanges. Institutions are also trading directly between themselves through 'crossing' networks.
- **Performance Measurement**. Institutional clients have become more rigorous about measuring the performance of brokers executing portfolio trades on their behalf against trading benchmarks such as VWAP. In North America consulting actuaries are sometimes hired to help analyse execution performance.
- **Use of Derivatives**. Funds can now use products such as index futures and equity swaps to quickly change their asset allocation profile. They can then conduct the necessary portfolio trades over a period of time to replace the derivatives with positions in the underlying shares. (See Chapter 14.)

7.19   CHAPTER SUMMARY

Ordinary shares (common stock in the US) differ from debt securities in that the holder is a part-owner and benefits from the growth of the business. However, there is no requirement to pay dividends and ordinary shares have the lowest ranking in the capital structure. Shareholders in public companies benefit from limited liability. In developed countries most shares are held by institutions such as pension funds and insurance companies (and sometimes banks). Investors pool their savings into collective investment vehicles called mutual funds whose assets are managed by professional portfolio managers. Some funds (closed-ended) have a fixed amount of capital and others (open-ended) can easily increase their capital base. A passive fund seeks to track an index and an active fund to outperform the market. Many active portfolio managers operate an asset allocation process and switch resources between broad asset classes and locations. If a market is perfectly efficient it should not be possible to consistently outperform the market by picking stocks that appear to be mispriced. Hedge funds differ from traditional fund management in taking short positions and sometimes in the degree of risk they are prepared to accept.

Shares are firstly made available to the general public through initial public offerings. In most IPOs a lead manager investment bank manages the whole process and underwrites the issue, often with a syndicate of sub-underwriters. Some issues are directly placed with investors. In the UK and Continental Europe companies raise additional equity capital mainly through rights issues. New shares are offered to existing shareholders at a discount, in proportion to their current holdings. In the US the new shares are usually made available to all investors. After they are issued shares are traded on exchanges such as the NYSE and the London Stock Exchange. In an order-driven market buy and sell orders are directly matched. In a quote-driven market deals are transacted with traders (market makers) who provide liquidity. A depository receipt is a receipt for a deposit of shares in a foreign company held by a bank. They make it easier for domestic investors to gain access to foreign equity markets. Shares are borrowed and lent through the stock lending markets. Borrowers include traders taking short positions (selling shares short in the expectation of buying them back more cheaply later on) and option traders hedging their books. Portfolio traders carry out trades in large portfolios of shares for institutional investors. They operate on a risk basis by quoting fixed prices for the shares; or act as an agent for the institution using their market knowledge to buy and sell shares at the right time with minimum impact on the price.

APPENDIX: EQUITY MARKETS STATISTICS

Table 7.5 shows the size of the major global stock exchanges by market capitalization of domestic listed companies (excluding closed-ended funds) as at 30 November 2000.

Table 7.6 shows details of UK share trading on the London Stock Exchange between 1997 and 2000.

In the year 2000 the value of UK shares traded on the LSE reached a record of nearly £1900 billion, an increase of about 35% from 1999. Turnover in international equities was over £3500 billion. Deutsche Börse reported a 20% rise in the value of shares traded in 2000 to €6100 billion compared with €5100 billion in 1999. Frankfurt accounted for over 80% of trading on German exchanges.

Table 7.5   Stock exchanges by market capitalization

Exchange at 30 November 2000	Market capitalization of domestic listed companies ($trn)
NYSE	11.1
NASDAQ	3.6
Tokyo	3.4
London	2.4
Germany	1.2
All exchanges	30.5

Source: NYSE.

Table 7.6   UK equity trading on the London Stock Exchange

Year	Shares traded (m)	Value (£m)
1997	280,255	1,012,535
1998	259,371	1,037,137
1999	335,459	1,410,590
2000	472,734	1,895,534

Source: LSE.

8
Equity Analysis and Valuation

No fixed capital can yield any revenue but by means of a circulating capital. The most useful machines and instruments of trade will produce nothing without the circulating capital which affords the materials they are employed upon, and the maintenance of the workmen who employ them.

Adam Smith

8.1 CHAPTER OVERVIEW

When assessing the current condition and future prospects of a company investors and analysts tend to start with the information contained in the annual report and accounts. In this chapter we look at the main financial statements contained in the annual report. We define the key items in the balance sheet and the profit and loss account. We set out the balance sheet equation and explain the concepts of accruals accounting and accounting for assets at their historic cost rather than at current market value. We explore what is meant by equity as it appears in a balance sheet and compare it with market capitalization. In order to make the discussion more concrete we apply the concepts to two well-known UK retailing businesses, Tesco plc and J Sainsbury plc. We compare and contrast the information contained in their accounts. Equity analysts use a range of financial ratios to extract information about a company from its financial statements. We define the main types of ratios and apply these measures to figures extracted from the accounts of the two retailers and compare their relative performance. Traditional equity valuation involves the use of multiples. We look at the most widely used of these, the price/earnings ratio, and explore the applications and limitations of the measure. Finally we consider some alternative valuation measures including the price/book ratio and a measure that is now widely used by professional analysts, the firm value/EBITDA multiple. All of these multiples are based on accounting numbers, although EBITDA is close to cash flow. In the following Chapter 9 we consider equity valuation methodologies based on discounted cash flow techniques.

8.2 VALUATION PRINCIPLES

Ordinary shares (common stock) provide an investor with a share in the total net assets (total assets minus total liabilities) of a company plus the right to receive any dividends that are distributed. Unlike a fixed income security such as a bond there is no pre-determined return on an investment in a share. Nor is there a fixed redemption date. This makes the valuation of shares a complex and uncertain process. There are many factors to take into account:

- the value of the company's assets including intangible (non-physical) assets such as brands, patents, reputation and client relationships;
- its laibilities including bank loans and money owed to trade creditors;
- forecasts of future sales, costs, profits and dividends;

- the company's business strategy, its sources of competitive advantage, its order book, the quality of its management and workforce;
- the nature of the business sector in which it operates, the levels of competition and profitability in the sector, and the scope for future revenue growth.

8.3 THE MAIN FINANCIAL STATEMENTS

The starting point for information about a company for many investors is the annual report and accounts. In this chapter we focus on two of the main financial statements to be found in the annual report: the balance sheet and the profit and loss account (known in the US as the income statement). We then explore the key financial ratios commonly used to analyse the health and prospects of the business.

- **Balance Sheet.** The balance sheet shows the financial position of the company at a particular moment in time. It lists the assets of the company then its liabilities and its equity. Total net assets — total assets less total liabilities — equals equity.
- **Profit and Loss Account.** The profit and loss account shows the company's income and expenditures over a period of time. The latest annual report will have the figures for trading activity in the last financial year although companies listed on stock exchanges also issue interim financial statements during the course of the year.

The annual report of a listed company will also contain a **cash flow statement**. This is similar to the profit and loss account in the sense that it deals with trading activities over a period of time. The difference is that it shows how cash has been generated and spent by the company. Some items in the profit and loss account, such as the depreciation of fixed assets, are internal book entries and do not represent actual cash flows. The company will explain in a note to the cash flow statement how the operating profit (the profit arising from normal trading activities) shown in the profit and loss account is reconciled with the net cash flow generated from operating activities.

8.4 THE BALANCE SHEET EQUATION

The basic balance sheet equation tells us that:

$$\text{Assets} = \text{Liabilities} + \text{Equity}$$

The assets of the company are divided into **fixed assets** and **current assets**. Fixed assets are longer-term assets for use in the company's business operations rather than for resale. They are further divided into tangible and intangible fixed assets.

- **Tangible Assets.** This will include land and building, plant and machinery, motor vehicles. The assets are normally shown at their original cost less depreciation to date. In the UK some accounts may show land and property at a market value based on a revaluation rather than at historic cost. Depreciation is a charge for the use of an asset over its useful life.
- **Intangible Assets.** It is common international practice now that companies do not try to place a value on internally generated intangible assets unless a clear value can be established. However if a company takes over another business it will often have to pay something for the goodwill of the target as well as for the physical assets. This will

be shown on the acquiring company's balance sheet and in many countries is amortized (written off) over a period of time through a series of charges to the profit and loss account. In the past a number of UK companies tried to place a value on their internally developed brands on the balance sheet but this proved highly controversial.

The balance sheet may also list under fixed assets long-term investments in other businesses.

Current assets are short-term assets used in the operation of the business, including:

- cash;
- stock;
- debtors (called in the US accounts receivable);
- short-term investments such as Treasury bills.

8.4.1 Sources of Funds: Liabilities and Equity

A company has two main sources of funds to purchase assets: liabilities (debt) and equity. In a set of accounts liabilities is normally divided into two broad categories:

- current or short-term liabilities;
- creditors falling due after one year (long-term liabilities).

Current liabilities includes short-term debt such as bank overdrafts and money owed to trade creditors (in US accounting parlance creditors are listed under the heading 'accounts payable'). Creditors falling due after one year includes longer-term bank loans and bond issues.

Equity is known in the UK as **equity shareholders' funds**. Essentially it consists of the funds paid by investors to buy ordinary shares in the company, plus **retained earnings**. Earnings is the profit after tax that is available to be paid out to the ordinary shareholders. Earnings not paid out in the form of dividends is recorded in the balance sheet as retained earnings and added to equity shareholders' funds. Effectively, when a portion of earnings is not paid out in dividends it is reinvested in the business and helps to increase the value of the company and the value of a stake in the company.

8.4.2 Equity as Risk Capital

The balance sheet equation reminds us that equity is **risk capital** in the sense that it is a residual claim on the assets of the business. If the company is put into liquidation and broken up then the assets are used in the first instance to pay off liabilities such as money owed to trade creditors and lenders, and then the preference shareholders. Anything that remains (if there is anything) belongs to the ordinary shareholders.

8.4.3 The Balance Sheet Equation Illustrated

Figure 8.1 illustrates the idea of the basic balance sheet equation. Current and long-term liabilities comprise the debt capital used to operate the business. Together with shareholders' funds they form the total capital base of the company, debt plus equity, which equals total assets. (Here we have included preference shares as part of long-term liabilities since in the main they are effectively debt-like securities.)

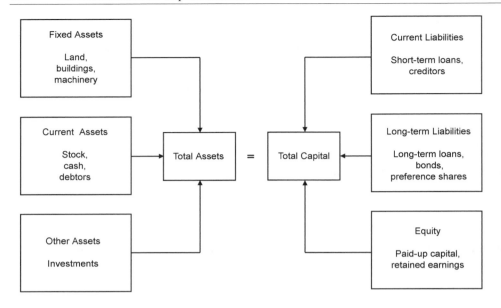

Figure 8.1   The basic balance sheet equation

8.5   THE PROFIT AND LOSS ACCOUNT

The profit and loss account (the income statement in the US) shows how a company has performed over a specific period of time. It lists the company's sales and costs and the profit (or loss) generated over that period of time. The key concept in the profit and loss account is the concept of **accruals accounting**. This says that revenues and costs are accounted for in the period in which the revenue is earned or the cost is incurred. For example, if a company sells goods worth £1000 in the financial year ended 31 December 2001 and is paid a deposit of £200 for the goods the transaction is recorded in that year's accounts, even if the remaining £800 is not received until the next financial year. In most accounting systems cash-based accounting (recording sales and costs only when the cash actually changes hands) is not permitted.

8.6   UK FOOD RETAILING: CASE STUDY

For the remainder of this chapter we will explore some key financial ratios that are widely used to analyse and interpret financial statements. The analysis is based on two of the main companies in the UK food retailing sector, Tesco plc and J Sainsbury plc. We start with some background information about the sector.

8.6.1   The Market Environment

The UK food retailing sector is highly competitive. The main participants such as Tesco, J Sainsbury, Safeway, Waitrose and Morrison fight aggressively for market share. The US giant Wal-Mart has joined the fray with the purchase of ASDA in 1998. Low cost bulk retailers compete on price. Other companies such as Marks & Spencer have focused on the top-end of the market by selling delicatessen-style prepared foods to achieve higher profit margins. This is still a profitable business for Marks & Spencer although it faces stiff competition now from the supermarket chains.

UK supermarkets have become increasingly diverse. Many now house cafes, pharmacies and dry cleaners alongside an expanding array of food and non-food items branded and own-label. Tesco has led the move into selling well-known clothing brands. By 2001 total food grocery sales in the UK will reach over £80 billion of which £75 billion will be accounted for by supermarkets and superstores. The smaller grocery operations are unable to compete on price and have been progressively squeezed out. One constraint on the growth of the market has been the reluctance of the local and central government authorities in the UK to grant planning permission for more out-of-town hypermarkets. The chains have moved back into the centres of towns and cities through initiatives such as the Tesco Metro stores, which are popular with busy urban professionals.

8.6.2   Tesco and J Sainsbury

Tesco plc is the acknowledged UK market leader. It increased its market share in its core UK business to 15.5% in the financial year 2000. It opened 38 new stores and increased market share in non-food items to 3%. Tesco grocery home shopping became the largest internet grocery business in the world with annualized sales of £125 million. It accelerated its international expansion which is targeted at key markets in Central Europe and the Far East rather than wholesale expansion. Overseas space reached 30% of total space in the year 2000. The goal of Tesco is to become an international retailer with the scale to tackle major global players such as Wal-Mart and Carrefour, the French retailer. Retail analysts in 2000 rated the management highly on strategy and in the day-to-day operation of the business. Tesco also operates a joint banking venture with the Royal Bank of Scotland.

J Sainsbury lost its position as the number one UK food retailer to Tesco in the 1990s. It came under attack from Tesco and other competitors intent on building market share. In the financial year 2000 the new senior management launched a 'back to basics' strategy focused on the food retailing business in the UK. Their objective was to open up a quality gap with competitors while tightening the grip on costs and remaining price competitive. The company launched a programme to re-engineer its information technology systems and distribution networks and upgraded its home delivery business. It later sold its DIY business, closed loss-making overseas operations and opened new format food retailing outlets including convenience stores and stores selling a higher volume of fresh produce. It runs a banking business called Sainsbury's Bank.

8.7   BALANCE SHEETS

The balance sheets for the two companies for the financial years ending in 2000 are set out (slightly simplified) in Table 8.1.

Table 8.1 Tesco and Sainsbury balance sheets

Balance sheets 2000 (£m)	Tesco	Sainsbury
Fixed assets		
Tangible assets	8140	6563
Intangible assets	136	316
Investments	251	98
	8527	**6977**
Current assets		
Stock	744	986
Debtors	252	320
Investments	258	18
Bank current assets	0	1718
Cash	88	533
	1342	**3575**
Total assets	**9869**	**10,552**
Current liabilities		
Bank current liabilities	0	(1607)
Other creditors due within one year	(3487)	(3113)
	(3487)	**(4720)**
Total assets less current liabilities	6382	5832
Creditors due after one year	(1565)	(993)
Provisions and charges	(19)	(48)
Total net assets	**4798**	**4791**
Equity shareholders' funds	4769	4742
Equity minority interests	29	49
	4798	**4791**

Source: Company annual reports.

8.7.1 Notes on the Balance Sheets

Assets are items owned by the business and available for its future use.

- **Tangible Fixed Assets.** The value of land, buildings, fixtures and fittings, motor vehicles less depreciation to date. The Sainsbury figure takes into account revaluations of the property portfolio in 1973 and 1992. The company's current policy is not to update the valuations. The Tesco figure is at cost less depreciation.
- **Intangible Fixed Assets.** Both companies list goodwill on their balance sheets. This is amortized by making a charge against the profit and loss account each year. The Tesco figure includes goodwill paid in the financial year to buy businesses in South Korea and Thailand. This will be written off over 20 years. The Sainsbury figure includes goodwill arising from the purchase of three businesses also to be amortized over 20 years, and goodwill paid for pharmacy licenses to be amortized over 15 years. The amortization period is chosen to represent the economic life of the asset.

- **Fixed Asset Investments.** In both cases this item is concerned with long-term investments in joint venture operations.
- **Current Assets.** The current assets of the supermarket chains consist primarily of their stocks of food and other goods for sale plus debtors, cash, bank deposits and other short-term investments.

Sainsbury has set up a banking operation called Sainsbury's Bank. The £1178 million in current assets we have listed as 'bank current assets' includes £684 million in customer loans, £542 million in loans made to banks, plus sundry other assets such as the bank's holdings of Treasury bills.

8.8 LIABILITIES

Balance sheets used to be set out in horizontal format with assets on the left and liabilities and equity on the right. These days they are normally set out in vertical format. From total assets is subtracted, firstly, short-term liabilities, and then long-term liabilities. What remains (after a few minor adjustments) is equity shareholders' funds.

- **Current Liabilities.** Debts payable within one year of the balance sheet date. The main short-term liabilities are money owed to trade creditors, short-term debt and the provisions made for corporation tax and dividend payments. Sainsbury also lists an item for £1607 million under 'Sainsbury's Bank' which primarily consists of the cash it holds on account for the clients of its banking business.
- **Long-term Liabilities.** Longer-term debt such as bonds, obligations under financial leases and other long-term liabilities.
- **Provisions and Charges.** Includes any other provisions made by the accountants against potential liabilities.

8.9 EQUITY

Tesco and Sainsbury operate businesses in which others have an equity stake. The portion of total net assets (total assets less total liabilities) that belongs to the minority interests is listed separately in the balance sheets. For example, Tesco's total net assets is listed as £4798 million of which £29 million belongs to the minority interests. Tesco's equity shareholders' funds is therefore £4798−£29 = £4769 million.

Total assets	9869
Less liabilities:	
Current liabilities	(3487)
Long-term liabilities	(1565)
Provisions	(19)
Equals:	
Total net assets	4798
Less:	
Minority interests	(29)
Equals:	
Equity shareholders' funds	4769

If a company makes a loss on the profit and loss account the loss is deducted from retained earnings and so reduces shareholders' funds. When a company trades profitably it normally pays dividends, in which case the cash paid out to shareholders is subtracted from current assets. It can also retain money for reinvestment. The accounting entry here is to transfer the profits belonging to the ordinary shareholders from the profit and loss account into shareholders' funds under the retained earnings heading.

8.10   PROFIT AND LOSS ACCOUNTS

Table 8.2 sets out the profit and loss accounts for Tesco and J Sainsbury in their financial year 2000 accounts.

8.10.1   Notes on the P&L Accounts

- **Sales.** The sales figures include cash sales and sales on credit made in the financial year. The figures are net of VAT.
- **Gross Profit.** This is sales less the direct cost of sales — wages, salaries, payments made to suppliers, store operating and distribution costs.
- **Operating Profit.** Gross profit less administration costs such as the cost of running the head office.
- **Profit before Interest and Tax (PBIT).** This is operating profit plus profits and losses arising from other sources such as disposals and joint ventures.
- **Earnings.** Also known as profit attributable to the ordinary shareholders. It is profit after interest, tax, payments to minority interests, extraordinary items and preference share dividends. Extraordinary items are non-recurring items. UK accounting standards say that they have to be clearly labelled as such in the profit and loss account so that investors and analysts can identify them.
- **Non-cash Items.** Earnings is not cash flow. The profit figures for both companies are arrived at after deducting expenses incurred in the financial year including non-cash items such as depreciation and goodwill amortization.

Table 8.2   Profit and loss accounts

Profit and loss accounts 2000	Tesco	Sainsbury
Sales ex VAT	18,796	16,271
Cost of sales	(17,365)	(15,201)
Gross profit	1431	1070
Administration expenses	(401)	(542)
Operating profit	1030	528
Profit before interest and tax	1032	581
Earnings	674	349
Dividends	(302)	(274)
Retained earnings	372	75

Source: Company annual reports.

- **Retained Earnings**. A proportion of earnings is paid out in dividends. The rest is reinvested in the business. In accounting terms, it is added to equity shareholders' funds in the balance sheet.

8.11   EARNINGS PER SHARE

Earnings per share (EPS) is total earnings divided by the number of ordinary shares. It measures the profit from that year's trading activities attributable to each ordinary share. The figures from the Tesco and Sainsbury 2000 accounts are set out in Table 8.3 (the numbers are shown in pence per share).

The Tesco EPS figure is based on the weighted average number of shares on issue during the financial year, which amounted to approximately 6693 million shares:

$$\frac{\text{Earnings}}{\text{Shares Issued}} = \frac{£674 \text{ million}}{6693 \text{ million}} = 10.1 \text{ pence}$$

Earnings per share is a very important measure in equity valuation. It shows the earnings power of an individual share. Shareholders and analysts look for rising EPS numbers year-on-year, reflecting continued success and growth in the company's business activities.

8.11.1   Diluted Earnings per Share

The 10.1 pence figure for Tesco could be considered as incomplete because it is based on the actual number of shares on issue during the financial year. Tesco also had share options outstanding which if exercised would have added a further 124 million shares. A measure called **diluted earnings per share** takes into account not just the actual number of shares on issue but also the potential new shares that would be created through the exercise of stock options and similar instruments. The actual and potential number of shares is:

$$6693 + 124 = 6817 \text{ million}$$

Therefore Tesco's diluted earnings per share is:

$$\frac{£674 \text{ million}}{6817 \text{ million}} = 9.9 \text{ pence}$$

Table 8.3   Earnings and dividends 2000

	Tesco	Sainsbury
Earnings per share (pence)	10.1	18.3
Dividend per share (pence)	4.48	14.3

Source: Annual reports.

8.11.2 Adjusted Earnings per Share

Equity analysts normally adjust the 'headline' earnings numbers to add back exceptional items such as non-recurring restructuring costs and profits or losses arising from the disposal of assets. This makes it easier to compare the underlying performance of the company from one year to another, and also to compare different companies in the same sector. If we add back integration costs, loss on disposals and goodwill amortization, the Tesco undiluted earnings per share for 2000 was 10.4 pence. On a fully diluted basis the figure is 10.2 pence per share. Note that different analysts and investors have their own method for adjusting earnings to reflect what they believe is the underlying position of the company. For example, analysts may differ on exactly what constitutes a non-recurring profit or loss.

In the larger share-broking firms a rule book sets out the 'house' method for adjusting or 'normalizing' earnings per share figures to reflect the underlying health of the business and to capture the underlying trends. Clients of the firm studying its research notes will then know that earnings figures are calculated on a consistent basis.

8.12 DIVIDEND PER SHARE

Dividend per share is a similar measure to EPS except that it is based only on the proportion of earnings paid out in the form of dividends. During the financial year 2000 Tesco plc paid an interim dividend of 1.34 pence and a final dividend of 3.14 pence, a total of 4.48 pence per share. The adjusted diluted earnings was 10.2 pence per share.

The **dividend payout** ratio measures the proportion of earnings paid out in dividends. Its reciprocal **dividend cover** measures the number of times the company could have paid the dividend out of that year's earnings. The financial year 2000 numbers for Tesco were as follows:

$$\text{Dividend Payout Ratio} = \frac{4.48}{10.2} = 43.9\%$$

$$\text{Dividend Cover} = \frac{10.2}{4.48} = 2.3\times$$

Tesco could have paid the dividend more than twice over from the earnings it generated that year. Sainsbury had less of a comfort margin. Its year 2000 dividend was covered 1.4 times by earnings.

8.12.1 Dividend Policy

In theory companies pay dividends that vary according to their profits. In practice this is not necessarily true. Shareholders generally like to see steadily rising dividend payments, smoothing out the effects of economic booms and downturns on the company's earnings. Many companies operate a dividend policy to meet this requirement. Even if a company fails to make a profit in a given year the directors are likely to maintain or even increase the dividend, paid out of earnings retained from previous years' trading activity. Of course this cannot be sustained indefinitely. One of the UK's major retailers Marks & Spencer was forced to cut the dividend in its financial year 2000 to nine pence per share as a result of declining profits. Even so it had to pay out 100% of that year's earnings to cover the dividend.

8.13 ACCOUNTING RATIOS

The balance sheet and profit and loss account are valuable sources of information about the past performance of a company, and a starting point for forecasts of future performance. The base case for a forecast of next year's expected earnings per share is the historical EPS and the historical growth rate in EPS. This has, of course, to be balanced against what is known about changes in the company and the environment in which it operates, which could affect expectations of future growth rates.

Equity analysts use a number of financial ratios when assessing the information contained in company accounts:

- **liquidity ratios** measure the ability of the company to raise cash when it has to make payments to its creditors;
- **profitability ratios** measure profit margins and returns on capital invested;
- **gearing (leverage) ratios** measure the proportion of debt and equity in the business and the ability of the company to pay its interest bill.

In the following sections we will look at each of these measures in turn for Tesco and J Sainsbury for the financial year 2000.

8.14 LIQUIDITY RATIOS

The key liquidity measures are the **current ratio** and the **quick ratio**, also known as the acid ratio:

$$\text{Current Ratio} = \frac{\text{Current Assets}}{\text{Current Liabilities}}$$

$$\text{Quick Ratio} = \frac{\text{Current Assets} - \text{Stock}}{\text{Current Liabilities}}$$

These ratios provide an idea of how easy it is for the company to clear its most immediate liabilities with the assets it can most easily raise money on. A current ratio of one means that current liabilities are exactly matched by current assets. If there is a trend for the current ratio to decrease consistently over a period of time this would set alarm bells ringing. The quick ratio (sometimes known as the acid test) is a more rigorous measure since it excludes stock, which in some industries may not be all that readily turned into cash to pay off creditors.

8.14.1 Ratios for Tesco and Sainsbury

The ratios for the two supermarket chains based on the financial year 2000 balance sheets are set out in Table 8.4.

A current ratio of less than one means that current liabilities exceeds current assets. In some industries such as heavy engineering this would be a major cause for concern. A company in this sector might struggle to sell off its stock of work in progress or

Table 8.4   Liquidity ratios 2000

	Tesco	Sainsbury
Current ratio	0.38	0.76
Quick ratio	0.17	0.55

Source: Annual reports.

finished goods quickly enough to pay off its short-term creditors in a hurry. In a fast turnover retail business, however, a current ratio figure of less than one is not something that causes too many concerns; it may actually be a sign of efficiency. Stock can be purchased on trade credit terms from suppliers. Provided the stock moves off the shelves and is quickly turned into cash the suppliers can be paid. This minimizes the amount of capital the retailer has tied up in running the business, and boosts its profitability.

8.14.2   Interpreting the Ratios

The Sainsbury figures are not directly comparable with Tesco since they include the current assets and liabilities of the banking business. However even if we net these out and focus just on retailing the Sainsbury current ratio is still higher at 0.60 compared to the Tesco figure of 0.38. Sainsbury had £986 million tied up in stock in the financial year, compared with only £744 million for Tesco. An analyst would want to look a little further into why this was so — it might be a reflection on purchasing policy, a tendency to carry lines of stock that stay on the shelves too long; it may be a reflection of how well suppliers and the distribution network are managed.

8.15   PROFITABILITY RATIOS

The main ratios used to measure a company's profitability and efficiency are:

- net profit margin;
- return on equity (ROE);
- return on capital employed (ROCE);
- return on total assets.

The first two ratios are usually calculated as follows:

$$\text{Net Profit Margin} = \frac{\text{Profit before Interest and Tax}}{\text{Sales}} \times 100$$

$$\text{ROE} = \frac{\text{Profit after Tax and Minority Interests}}{\text{Equity Shareholders' Funds}} \times 100$$

Net profit margin measures the profits extracted from each £1 of sales. A high figure means that the company is able to charge relatively high prices in relation to the costs of running the business. In some industries such as luxury goods and perfumes the profit margins are extremely high. In other sectors such as food retailing intense competition keeps the margins down. The large retailers fight back through aggressive cost containment measures, including sourcing from a large number of suppliers and using the scale advantages of their huge purchasing power. They also seek to boost profit margins by selling own-brand labels and selling higher margin items such as wine and prepared foodstuffs.

Some analysts prefer to measure **operating profit margin**, which is calculated by dividing operating profit by sales. This excludes profits and losses from activities not related to the day-to-day operation of the business.

8.15.1   Return on Equity

Return on equity is, obviously, a measure of the returns made by the ordinary shareholders from a given year's trading activities. It is, however, an accounting measure and is not based on actual cash flows; as a result it cannot be compared directly with returns on investments in gilts or money market deposits. The numerator is profit attributable to the ordinary shareholders, which is calculated after the deduction of non-tax items such as depreciation and goodwill amortization. The denominator is the value of the equity as it appears on the balance sheet, and not the actual market value of the equity on the stock exchange. In the next chapter we explore how the returns on shares can be measured in cash flow rather than accounting terms.

8.15.2   Return on Capital and Return on Total Assets

There is no one agreed definition of return on capital employed, although the following calculation is widely used:

$$\text{ROCE} = \frac{\text{Profit before Interest and Tax}}{\text{Capital Employed}} \times 100$$

where:

$$\text{Capital Employed} = \text{Total Assets} - \text{Current Liabilities}$$

In this definition, capital employed is classified as shareholders' funds plus the stakes of the minority interests in the business plus long-term liabilities. It excludes short-term borrowings such as overdrafts.

Return on total assets is a related measure calculated using total assets and without excluding current liabilities. In effect, it treats items such as overdrafts and money owed to creditors as part of the ongoing capital base of the business (which in many cases is not unreasonable):

$$\text{Return on Total Assets} = \frac{\text{Profit before Interest and Tax}}{\text{Total Assets}}$$

8.15.3   Profitability Ratios for Tesco and Sainsbury

Table 8.5 shows profit margin and return figures for Tesco and Sainsbury for the financial year 2000.

Table 8.5   Profitability ratios

	Tesco	Sainsbury
Net profit margin	5.49%	3.57%
ROE	14.13%	7.36%
ROCE	16.17%	9.96%
Return on total assets	10.46%	5.51%

Source: Annual reports.

The profit margin figures measure the net profits generated by each £1 of sales. Tesco's superior performance in 2000 is a reflection of its ability to generate higher levels of sales and profits from its cost base.

8.16   COMPOSITION OF RETURN ON ASSETS

To see such effects in a little more detail it is helpful to calculate a ratio called **asset turnover**. It can be measured in various ways, but if we base the calculation on total assets it is calculated as follows:

$$\text{Asset Turnover} = \frac{\text{Sales}}{\text{Total Assets}}$$

Asset turnover measures the quantity of sales a company extracts from each £1 of total assets tied up in the business. It is a measure of how efficiently the assets are put to use. If one supermarket can generate more sales per square metre of floor space than another then it will have a higher asset turnover. We have already calculated return on total assets:

$$\text{Return on Total Assets} = \frac{\text{Profit before Interest and Tax}}{\text{Total Assets}}$$

It therefore follows that:

$$\text{Return on Total Assets} = \frac{\text{Sales}}{\text{Total Assets}} \times \frac{\text{Profit before Interest and Tax}}{\text{Sales}}$$

This equation tells us that return on total assets equals asset turnover times net profit margin. Table 8.6 shows the components of return on total assets for the two supermarket chains in the financial year 2000.

Table 8.6   Components of return on assets

	Tesco	Sainsbury
Net profit margin	5.49%	3.57%
Asset turnover	1.9045×	1.542×
Return on total assets	10.46%	5.51%

This shows that Tesco's superior return on assets is determined by:

- its ability to achieve higher profit margins;
- its ability to generate a higher level of sales for each £1 of assets tied up in the business.

8.16.1 Return on Total Capital

Since total assets equals total capital (liabilities and shareholders' funds) it follows that return on total assets also measures the return on the total amount of capital tied up in the business, including short-term liabilities. This tells us that a superior return on capital is the result of two factors:

- achieving high profit margins (which in turn means selling goods that people want to buy, while containing costs);
- generating the maximum amount of sales for every £1 tied up in the assets of the business (which in turn means converting stock into cash as quickly as possible, and not carrying stock on the shelves for too long).

Return on equity and return on capital are important comparative numbers. A company that consistently makes higher returns on each £1 of equity tied up in the business than the sector average has some source of competitive advantage that is sustainable over time — and which makes it an attractive investment for shareholders. Stock analysts look at the historical trends in the return on equity and return on capital figures to help forecast future sales and profits.

8.17   GEARING/LEVERAGE RATIOS

These ratios measure the proportion of debt used to fund the business and the ability of the company to service that debt (leverage is the US term). Gearing can be calculated in a number of ways. Most analysts base the calculation on long-term debt and exclude current liabilities. Gross gearing is long-term liabilities divided by equity. Net gearing nets out cash held by the company from its liabilities:

$$\text{Gross Gearing (Leverage)} = \frac{\text{Long-term Debt}}{\text{Equity}}$$

$$\text{Net Gearing (Leverage)} = \frac{\text{Long-term Debt} - \text{Cash Held}}{\text{Equity}}$$

8.17.1 Measuring Gearing

The gross gearing figures for Tesco and Sainsbury in the financial year 2000 were respectively 32.82% and 20.94%. Gearing may also be calculated as the proportion of debt to total capital, that is, debt plus equity. A further variant is to include current liabilities in the calculation. Calculated in this way gearing measures the proportion of the firm's total assets owned by long and short-term creditors. Note that all the above measures are accounting numbers, since they are based on the book value of the equity and of the debt. The value of a company's debt is normally a smaller proportion of the market value of the equity (the market capitalization).

8.17.2 Effects of Gearing

The impact of gearing on the ordinary shareholder is on the risk profile of their investment. On average it is cheaper for a company to raise money through debt because equity holders demand higher returns to compensate them for taking on additional risks. Furthermore, interest payments are tax deductible while dividend payments are not.

If a highly geared company puts its borrowings to good use, therefore, it will generate enough cash not only to pay the interest on the debt but also to boost earnings. However if the company gets into difficulties and profits fall it still has to make the interest payments. There may be little or no money left over for the ordinary share-holders. Shares of highly geared companies are a riskier investment in the sense that the returns are more variable. In the extreme, there is a greater chance that the company may be forced into liquidation.

8.17.3 Interest Cover

Analysts measure the ability of a company to pay its interest bill using a measure called interest cover:

$$\text{Interest Cover} = \frac{\text{Profit before Interest and Tax}}{\text{Gross Annual Interest Payment}}$$

The figures for Tesco and Sainsbury for the financial year 2000 were respectively 6.66 and 5.38 times. Tesco could have paid its interest bill almost seven times over out of pre-tax profits, which is a comfortable margin. Interest coverage is closely related to the willingness of lenders to supply additional funds, and to the credit ratings published by the major ratings agencies.

8.18 INVESTOR RATIOS AND VALUATION

The information from the financial statements must be looked at in the context of the current market price of a share. An investor has to decide whether the stock is undervalued or whether it is the right time to sell out. Two of the main ratios used by analysts and investors searching for value in shares are the price/earnings ratio and the dividend yield:

$$\text{Price/Earnings Ratio} = \frac{\text{Market Price per Share}}{\text{Earnings per Share}}$$

$$\text{Dividend Yield} = \frac{\text{Dividend per Share}}{\text{Market Price per Share}} \times 100$$

Both ratios can be calculated on a **historic** basis, based on last year's EPS and dividends; or on a **prospective** basis, based on estimates of future earnings and dividends.

8.18.1 The Price/Earnings Ratio

The price/earnings ratio is used to rate which shares in a given sector are 'cheap' and 'dear' relative to each other. Effectively, the p/e ratio is a payback measure. If a share has an historic p/e of 20 then the current share price is 20 times last year's earnings per share — it would take 20 years of earnings at that level to recoup the purchase price. It is relatively more expensive than a share with a price only 15 times earnings.

It makes sense to compare the p/e ratios of two similar companies. They are in the same line of business and their performance is affected by the same kinds of factors. If one is rated more highly than the other in p/e terms it is usually because the market sees it as more likely to generate higher future earnings, or as a lower risk, or both. Price/earnings ratios are also determined by the general level of interest rates. For a given set of earnings assumptions, as interest rates fall p/e ratios in the market will generally tend to rise. In practice, though, changes in interest rates will also tend to have an effect on corporate earnings.

8.18.2   Dividend Yield

The dividend yield measures the income return from a share, which can be compared to the general level of deposit rates in the money markets. It does not take into account returns arising from the growth in the share price. Often high growth stocks have high p/e ratios (building in expectations of strong future earnings growth) and low dividend yields (the dividend is low in comparison to the high share price). Many growth companies pay no dividends at all — shareholders expect to achieve their returns from the growth in the share price.

8.19   TESCO AND SAINSBURY INVESTOR RATIOS

Table 8.7 shows Tesco and Sainsbury share prices at mid-January 2001. It then measures the price/earnings ratios based on these share prices and the financial year 2000 earnings per share figures.

Clearly, at that point the market was expecting higher future earnings growth from Tesco. However there were also signs that the market felt there was a good recovery story for Sainsbury. The gap between the prospective p/e ratios was narrower. At the time analysts were forecasting 2001 earnings per share of around 11.5 pence for Tesco and 20 pence for Sainsbury. On these forecasts the prospective p/e ratios were as follows:

$$\text{Tesco} = \frac{264}{11.5} = 23\times$$

$$\text{Sainsbury} = \frac{380}{20} = 19\times$$

Table 8.7   Price/earnings ratios at mid-January 2001

	Tesco	Sainsbury
Adjusted diluted EPS	10.2 pence	20.5 pence
Share price	264 pence	380 pence
Historic p/e ratio	25.9×	18.5×

By mid-June 2001 the recovery story for Sainsbury was coming to be more widely recognized. The share price had accelerated to 415 pence. Analysts were forecasting 2002 earnings per share at around 21.5 pence. On this forecast the share was trading at 19.3 times prospective 2002 earnings. By comparison Tesco was trading at 20.8 times prospective 2002 earnings (based on an average of brokers' forecasts at mid-June 2001).

8.20 APPLYING VALUATION MULTIPLES

The price/earnings ratio is the most widely mentioned valuation multiple in the equity markets. It is commonly used by analysts and by investment banks pricing new shares in an initial public offering. When valuing a company for sale using a p/e multiple two numbers are required:

- a figure for earnings;
- an earnings multiple, normally established by taking the average multiple for similar businesses that are already publicly traded.

Let us suppose that Flotation plc is expected to make £10 earnings per share next year, based on recent results. The average prospective p/e multiple for similar businesses is 20 times. Therefore the theoretical value of one Flotation share is calculated as follows:

$$\text{Value of Flotation plc share} = \text{£}10 \times 20 = \text{£}200$$

8.20.1 Practical Difficulties with p/e Valuation

Valuing a company for IPO using an average p/e multiple is very simple in theory, but in practice there are often difficulties in its application.

- **Comparability.** It is important to ensure that the earnings figures for the different companies are directly comparable. For example, different companies may use different methodologies for depreciation of fixed assets and amortization of goodwill.
- **Sample Group.** The sample group used to establish the average p/e multiple must be engaged in similar business activities and have similar growth prospects and risk characteristics.
- **Fair Value.** The shares in the sample group must also be trading at a fair value otherwise their p/e ratios are distorted.
- **Negative Earnings.** The p/e multiple approach is of little use when the company to be valued has negative earnings.

8.20.2 P/e Multiples and Relative Value

The price/earnings multiple is also used as a measure of relative value when comparing listed companies. The fact that Sainsbury was trading at a lower p/e compared to Tesco in early January 2001 might have been an indication that it represented good value. However it has to be remembered that p/e ratios build in consensus expectations about future earnings growth. Logically, the only reason for buying Sainsbury shares at the time was if one believed in the recovery story for the company and felt that growth prospects were in fact better than suggested by the relatively low p/e ratio. (By mid-2001 that was beginning to look like a well-argued proposition.)

8.21 OTHER VALUATION MULTIPLES

One way to ensure comparability of earnings between companies is to adjust the stated after-tax profit figures to a common basis. Another is to base the company valuation on a different measure of earnings, known as EBITDA.

EBITDA

Earnings before interest, tax, depreciation and amortization. EBITDA permits a more transparent comparison between the profitability of different firms because it is not distorted by factors such as differing depreciation policies. It is more akin to actual cash flow.

It is important to realize, however, that EBITDA is a stream of earnings that is used to make interest and principal repayments on debt, as well as to reward the ordinary shareholders. Therefore the appropriate valuation measure is not EBITDA as a multiple of equity, but EBITDA as a multiple of equity and debt combined — the total value of the firm (also known as **enterprise value**):

Firm or Enterprise Value = Market Value of Debt + Market Value of Equity

The market value of the equity is simply market capitalization. In theory the debt ought to be valued at current market interest rates, although if the rate of interest on the debt is close to current market interest rate levels, the par value will be a close approximation.

The EBITDA multiple is therefore calculated as:

$$\frac{\text{Firm Value}}{\text{Earnings before Interest, Tax, Depreciation and Amortization}}$$

8.21.1 Valuing Firms with no Earnings

There are other multiples that can be used to value a company which is not currently making a profit. Two of the most common are:

- the price/sales ratio;
- the price/book ratio.

Applying a price/sales ratio involves finding a sample group of similar firms, calculating the average multiple of total sales to market capitalization, then applying this multiple to the company to be valued. As with the p/e ratio, it is critically important that the sample group is comparable.

The price/book ratio compares the market capitalization of the company with the book value of the equity — that is, to total assets minus total liabilities. The market capitalization is based on forecast sales and profits, whereas the book value of the equity is based on the historic cost of the assets less depreciation and total liabilities. The price/book ratio has some advantages as a valuation tool:

- it is intuitive and easy to work with;
- it is reasonably stable over time;
- it can be used to price a company with negative earnings.

The ratio is however based on the accounting measurement of net assets. When it is used to compare the valuation of different companies care has to be taken to ensure that adjustments are made for factors such as different depreciation policies. A variant is to use the **replacement** rather than the book value of the assets, reflecting what it would actually cost in current market conditions to establish the assets of the business. This approach derives from the work of the economist James Tobin.

8.22   CHAPTER SUMMARY

Forecasts of a company's future profits and cash flows normally start with the historical information contained in the financial statements. The main financial statements are the balance sheet, the profit and loss account and the cash flow statement. The balance sheet lists assets owned by the company, its liabilities and equity. Equity is total net assets, that is, total assets minus total liabilities. Assets is divided into fixed assets such as property and plant and current assets such as cash and debtors. Liabilities is divided into short-term liabilities such as creditors and long-term liabilities such as bond issues. The profit and loss account shows income and expenditures over a period of time. Sales are recorded when they are made and expenses when they are incurred. Profit after interest, tax and payments due to minority stakeholders is known as earnings or profit attributable to the ordinary shareholders. It is paid out as dividends or added to equity shareholders' funds in the balance sheet. Earnings per share is a measure of the earnings attributable to each ordinary share. It may be adjusted for non-recurring items.

The price/earnings ratio is a key valuation tool in the equity markets. On a historic basis it is the current share price divided by last year's earnings per share. It can also be based on forecast earnings. The p/e ratio is used as a measure of value to compare different businesses in the same sector. A high p/e indicates that the market as a whole expects significant future growth in earnings. If an investor believes that the growth prospects are overstated then the share can be judged as overpriced. Analysts apply a range of other ratios to assess the health and prospects of a company. Liquidity ratios measure the ability of the firm to pay its short-term creditors. Profitability ratios measure profit margins, cost efficiency, capital efficiency and return on capital. Gearing or leverage ratios give an indication of the amount of debt in the business and whether the company may have difficulties in meeting interest payments. EBITDA measures earnings before interest, tax, depreciation and amortization. Firm value is the total value of a firm, debt plus equity. Measures such as the p/e ratio and the firm value/ EBITDA ratio are based on accounting measures of earnings (although EBITDA is closer to actual cash flows). In the next chapter we consider equity valuation methods based on discounting expected future cash flows.

9
Cash Flow Models in Equity Valuation

On two occasions I have been asked [by Members of Parliament], pray, Mr Babbage, if you put into the machine wrong numbers, will the right answers come out?

Charles Babbage

9.1 CHAPTER OVERVIEW

A widely used method of valuing shares involves the use of multiples such as the price/earnings ratio. This is a relative valuation method. In an initial public offer the shares are often valued using the average price/earnings ratio for similar firms. This assumes that the sample is comparable and that the share prices of the companies in the sample are fairly valued. An alternative is to value shares using discounted cash flow methods. In this chapter we investigate models in which the expected dividend stream from a share is discounted in order to establish fair value. We explore a version in which dividends continue to grow at a constant rate in perpetuity, and practical issues with applying such models. The links between dividend discount models and key ratios such as the price/earnings ratio and dividend yield are investigated. We consider briefly the concept of the equity risk premium and the implications for stock market value. We then look at how to estimate firm or enterprise value by forecasting and discounting free cash flows. Firm value is the total value of a company, debt plus equity. Discounted cash flow models require a discount rate, which is the required return on the cash flows given the degree of risk. We explore an industry standard model for establishing the discount rate and links between this model, portfolio theory and the optimal levels of debt and equity in a firm.

9.2 THE BASIC DIVIDEND DISCOUNT MODEL

The return to a shareholder from owning a share consists of dividends plus capital gains or losses. Suppose, for example, that an investor buys a share costing £100, holds it for a period of one year, earns a £10 dividend and then sells it for £110. The holding period return on the equity investment r_e is calculated as follows:

$$r_e = \left[\frac{£10 + £110}{£100} \right] - 1 = 0.20 = 20\%$$

The investment return consists of 10% income plus 10% capital gains. Suppose, however, the investor is content to earn a 15% return on this particular investment. Then the spot price S_0 the investor should pay for the share can be calculated by rearranging the formula and inserting the required 15% return into the equation:

$$0.15 = \left[\frac{£10 + £110}{S_0}\right] - 1$$

$$S_0 = \frac{£10 + £110}{1.15} = £104.35$$

This is a present value calculation. £104.35 is the present value of £120 due in one year at a 15% discount rate. It establishes a fair value for the share on the assumption that the one-year cash flow will be £120 and the appropriate rate of return for an investment of that type is 15%. The general formula is as follows:

$$S_0 = \frac{d_1 + S_1}{1 + r_e}$$

where:

S_0 = spot value of the share
S_1 = value of the share in one year
d_1 = expected dividend due in one year
r_e = required return on the share as a decimal

9.2.1 Extending the Basic Model

The formula can easily be extended to cope with situations in which cash flows are due in more than one year. For example, if the holding period is two years then the fair spot value S_0 is calculated as follows:

$$S_0 = \frac{d_1}{1 + r_e} + \frac{d_2 + S_2}{(1 + r_e)^2}$$

where:

d_2 = expected dividend due in two years
S_2 = value of the share in two years

This approach can be extended indefinitely by taking longer and longer holding periods. If the holding period has no limit then the fair value of the share can be calculated as the present value of the expected dividend stream extending to infinity:

$$S_0 = \frac{d_1}{1 + r_e} + \frac{d_2}{(1 + r_e)^2} + \frac{d_3}{(1 + r_e)^3} + \dots$$

The formula says, in effect, that a share price discounts all known information about future dividends. It is also consistent with the idea that valuing the equity in a firm as a whole should involve the same method used to value all the individual projects making up the company. The individual projects are valued by discounting their anticipated future cash flows. The equity is valued by discounting expected future dividend payments that are generated by the sum of the company's investment projects.

9.3   CONSTANT DIVIDEND GROWTH MODELS

The first version of the dividend discount model we developed requires an estimation of the resale value of the share at the end of the holding period. In some ways this seems unrealistic — if we know the value of the share in the future why don't we know its value today? The second version of the model avoids this criticism, but at the expense of requiring us to estimate dividends in perpetuity (or at least for a long time to come). Most equity analysts are prepared to forecast earnings and dividends for one or two years ahead but beyond that point the exercise becomes increasingly speculative.

9.3.1   Perpetuity Formula

Luckily there is a simple solution. The formula for valuing a perpetuity with constant cash flows is as follows (this version of the formula assumes the next cash flow is due in exactly one year):

$$PV_0 = \frac{CF_1}{r}$$

where:

PV_0 = present value of the perpetuity
CF_1 = cash flow due in one year (the same for all subsequent years)
r = annualized required return on the investment as a decimal

The formula can be used to value a perpetual bond. For example the British government currently has an 'undated' (perpetual) gilt-edged security on issue with a 2.5% coupon. If the required return on the bond in current market circumstances is 4.78% then its price is given by the perpetuity formula:

$$PV_0 = \frac{£2.50}{0.0478} = £52.30$$

If the bond is trading at £52.30 it has a current or income yield of 4.78%. Intuitively what is happening in the perpetuity formula is that the far-dated cash flows are discounted more and more heavily and cease to have any meaningful impact on the present value calculation. In this way the calculation can be 'collapsed' into the simple formula.

9.3.2   Constant Dividend Growth

If we assume that the dividends on a share are not constant but grow at a constant rate g then the perpetuity formula can easily be modified. It becomes:

$$S_0 = \frac{d_1}{r_e - g}$$

where:

d_1 = next year's expected dividend
r_e = required return on the share as a decimal
g = constant annual growth rate in dividends as a decimal

Next year's expected dividend d_1 can be calculated from last year's dividend payment d_0 and the expected dividend growth rate. In symbols:

$$d_1 = d_0 \times (1 + g)$$

9.3.3 Constant Dividend Growth Model: Example

DDM Ltd. paid a dividend last year of £5 on earnings per share of £10, representing a 50% dividend payout ratio. It is expected that earnings will grow at 8% per annum and that the company will maintain the same payout ratio in future. The required return on equity is 12% per annum. The fair value of the company's shares, S_0, is calculated as follows:

$$S_0 = \frac{£5 \times 1.08}{0.12 - 0.08} = £135$$

If we are an equity trader the decision rule is a simple one. If the share is trading below £135 it should be bought, and if it is trading above £135 it should be sold. Note that if earnings grow at a constant 8% and the payout ratio is constant it follows that dividends will also grow at 8% in perpetuity.

9.4   THE IMPLIED RETURN ON A SHARE

All dividend discount models require a decision to be made on the required return on the share. One answer is provided by the Capital Asset Pricing Model (CAPM) which is explored in a subsequent section of this chapter. An alternative approach is to turn the constant growth formula around. Rather than calculating the fair value of the share from a known discount rate, we can work out the rate of return implied in buying the share at its actual market value and receiving the predicted dividend stream. If MV_0 is the market value of the share today then the formula becomes:

$$r_e = \frac{d_1}{MV_0} + g$$

For example, suppose it were possible to buy DDM Ltd. shares at less than our estimate for fair value, say at only £120 each. Then assuming we agree on the 8% constant dividend growth rate the return on equity is calculated as follows:

Next year's forecast dividend d_1 = £5 × 1.08 = £5.4
Current share price MV_0 = £120
Constant dividend growth g = 8%

Therefore:

$$r_e = \frac{£5.4}{£120} + 0.08 = 12.5\%$$

The expected return on the share is higher than our estimate for the required return on equity. Some equity analysts rank companies in the same sector or country by their returns calculated in this fashion. Companies that return above the sector or market average are classified as potential buys. Companies that return below the average are classified as potential sells. This methodology cannot be applied in an indiscriminate fashion, however. There may be a good reason why investors demand a higher return from one share rather than another. Typically it is because the future cash flows are more uncertain and the stock bears higher risks. However the analysis may reveal possible pricing anomalies in the market that bear further investigation.

9.5   REQUIRED RETURN AND DIVIDEND YIELD

In the model we developed in the previous section (derived from the constant growth dividend discount model) two terms are required to calculate the required return on a share:

$$r_e = \frac{d_1}{MV_0} + g$$

The first term is simply the share's prospective dividend yield based on next year's forecast dividend and the current market value of the share. The second term is the constant dividend growth rate. Effectively, the formula says that the required return on a share is its prospective dividend yield plus the expected growth rate in dividends. Reshuffling the formula also reveals the following expression:

$$\frac{d_1}{MV_0} = r_e - g$$

This says that a share's prospective dividend yield is its required rate of return less the expected growth rate in dividends. A growth stock may have a high expected overall return but the prospective dividend yield is restrained by the fact that dividends are expected to grow at a fast rate. A high dividend yield income stock such as a utility with a low dividend growth rate but also has a low required return (reflecting a lower degree of risk).

9.5.1   Deriving Dividend Growth Rates

The constant growth model also reveals the expression:

$$g = r_e - \frac{d_1}{MV_0}$$

This formula says that the market's expectations on dividend growth rates can be deduced from a share's required return and its prospective dividend yield. Take the case of DDM Ltd. Assuming that the share is trading at £135, the required return is 12% and next year's forecast dividend is £5.40, then:

$$\text{Forecast Dividend Yield} = \frac{£5.40}{£135} = 0.04 = 4\%$$

$$\text{Constant Dividend Growth Rate} = 12\% - 4\% = 8\%$$

A trader or investor using the constant growth model and considering an investment in the shares would have to decide whether it is likely that the dividend growth rate could continue at 8% in perpetuity. If not (and assuming the other inputs to the model are agreed) then the share may be overpriced. Suppose that a trader decides the constant dividend growth rate is more likely to be 7.52%. Then the share should actually trade at only £120 on a fair value basis:

$$\text{Fair Value } S_0 = \frac{£5 \times 1.0752}{0.12 - 0.0752} = £120$$

9.6 PRICE/EARNINGS RATIO

The constant growth dividend discount model also offers valuable insights into the meaning and interpretation of price/earnings ratios. The model says that:

$$S_0 = \frac{d_1}{r_e - g}$$

Let b be the share's dividend payout ratio. Then next year's dividend d_1 must be next year's earnings e_1 times the dividend payout ratio:

$$d_1 = b \times e_1$$

Substituting the right-hand part of this equation for d_1 in the constant growth model we have:

$$S_0 = \frac{b \times e_1}{r_e - g}$$

This can be rearranged as follows:

$$\frac{S_0}{e_1} = \frac{b}{r_e - g}$$

This equation calculates the share's prospective price/earnings ratio — the current share price divided by next year's forecast earnings per share. According to the constant growth model it is equal to the dividend payout ratio divided by the difference between the required return on the share and the constant dividend growth rate.

9.6.1 Price/Earnings Ratio Calculation

We can check the result for DDM Ltd. using the original values we inserted into the constant growth model:

Fair value of the share = £135
Growth rate in dividends = 8% per annum
Last year's earnings per share = £10.0
Forecast earnings per share = £10.8
Dividend payout ratio = 50%
Required return on equity = 12% per annum

The £135 share value is 12.5 times next year's forecast earnings per share of £10.8. It is also the dividend payout ratio divided by the required return on equity less the growth rate in dividends:

$$\frac{£135}{£10.80} = \frac{0.5}{0.12 - 0.08} = 12.5\times$$

9.6.2   Reinvestment Rates

The formula for the price/earnings ratio we have just derived might seem a little odd at first sight, since it appears that a company could boost its price/earnings ratio at a stroke by simply increasing the dividend payout ratio. However this would reduce the proportion of earnings reinvested and would in all probability impact on the future rate of growth in earnings and dividends.

In fact the critical issue here is the rate at which a company can reinvest retained earnings. All other things being equal, the higher the reinvestment rate on earnings the higher the price/earnings ratio. High internal rates of return, over and above the required return on equity, lead to rapid earnings growth and a high price/earnings ratio. If the reinvestment rate is above the required return on equity then cutting the dividend payout ratio can boost the share's price/earnings ratio. Since investors are benefiting from internal rates of return above that which can be achieved on similar stocks in the market they should be content to have a large proportion of earnings reinvested in the firm rather than having the money paid out in dividends.

The price/earnings formula also suggests that, all other things being equal, the lower the required rate of return on a share the higher its price/earnings ratio. Intuitively, future cash flows will be discounted less heavily and the stock's fair value and hence its price/earnings ratio will increase. If market interest rates fall then the required returns on shares will also fall and price/earnings ratios generally will tend to rise.

9.7   STAGE DIVIDEND DISCOUNT MODELS

The constant growth model works fairly well for utilities which tend to pay a steadily rising dividend stream (assuming they are not attacked by the government or the courts). In other cases it is simply not realistic to assume that a share's earnings and dividends can increase at a constant rate indefinitely. A new company can achieve phenomenal growth rates for a number of years. However, the growth often tends to slow down over time and revert to a rate nearer to the sector or economy average. In fact if a company continued to grow at a rate that is much faster than the economy average in perpetuity sooner or later it would actually become the entire economy! To cope with this problem some analysts use **two-stage** dividend discount models. The stages are typically as follows.

- **Stage One.** The company's earnings per share and dividend per share are forecast for a set number of years ahead. This can be done by assuming a constant growth rate over the period or by making an explicit forecast for each year, in which case the growth rate does not have to be regular. Forecast dividends are then discounted to a present value at the required return on equity.

- **Stage Two.** The terminal or continuing value of the share at the end of the forecast period is calculated and discounted back to a present value. This is added to the present value of the forecast dividends calculated in stage one, to establish the fair value of the share today. Terminal value can be calculated by assuming a constant growth rate in dividends from that point on and valuing this cash flow stream as a perpetuity.

9.8   TWO-STAGE MODEL: EXAMPLE

Recall the case of DDM Ltd. which paid a dividend last year of £5. It was initially expected that dividends would grow at 8% per annum in perpetuity. The required return on equity is 12% per annum. On this basis we calculated the fair value of the company's shares at £135.

Suppose, however, that the average growth rate in earnings in the sector is only 6%. A more conservative approach would be to assume that DDM's growth rate will converge towards the sector mean or average after some period of time. Existing competitors may start to fight back, perhaps cutting prices and reducing profit margins in the sector, or new players may enter the sector attracted by the high earnings and erode DDM's market share. Assume that DDM can sustain its 8% growth rate for five years but that growth will reduce to 6% after that point and stay at that level in perpetuity. The present value of the first five years' dividend stream is shown in Table 9.1.

Assuming that the company will continue to trade after five years it will have a continuing or residual value at that point. If dividends grow at 6% per annum in perpetuity the value of the share S_5 at year five can be calculated using the constant growth perpetuity formula:

$$S_5 = \frac{£7.35 \times 1.06}{0.12 - 0.06}$$

$$= £129.85$$

This is the residual value per share at year five. The value today is the future value discounted at the 12% required return on equity:

$$\frac{£129.85}{1.12^5} = £73.68$$

The total value of a share today is therefore:

$$£22.44 + £73.68 = £96.12$$

Table 9.1   Present value of five years' forecast dividends

Year	Forecast dividend	PV at 12%
1	£5.40	£4.82
2	£5.83	£4.65
3	£6.30	£4.48
4	£6.80	£4.32
5	£7.35	£4.17
	Total =	£22.44

9.8.1 Multi-stage Models

Some equity analysts use three and even four-stage dividend discount models. In practice this involves making a series of different assumptions about dividend growth rates over time. For example, it might be assumed that DDM Ltd. can sustain an 8% growth rate for five years, a 7% growth rate for a further five years and only then will the growth rate revert to the 6% sector average. For the record, this analysis would produce a fair value for DDM of £99.27. A more complex alternative is to assume that the company's growth rate will steadily revert to the sector average and then subsequently to the total economy growth rate over some period of time rather than in a sudden movement.

9.9 THE CAPITAL ASSET PRICING MODEL

Models such as the dividend discount model require a discount rate to present value future cash flows. Intuitively, the discount rate should be appropriate to the riskiness of the future cash flows. If a company operates in a relatively safe sector then the required return on equity and the discount rate should be substantially less than that for a company operating in a highly cyclical industry with considerable variance in earnings. An example of the first type of company is a utility; the second might be a high-technology firm.

Many capital market practitioners establish a discount rate (required return on equity) by using the CAPM developed by William Sharpe and others in the 1960s. CAPM starts with the intuition that the returns on shares (dividends plus capital gains) are normally higher, but also subject to more variation, than those achieved on government bonds. The minimum return that investors will demand in a major currency such as the US dollar is established through the yield or return on government securities. This is the **risk-free** rate of return. Investors will demand an additional **risk premium** to invest in other securities. The market risk premium is the additional return over the risk-free rate demanded by investors to hold a highly diversified portfolio of securities. If an individual share has exactly the same risk profile as the market as a whole then the required return on that share is exactly the same as the market portfolio return. If a share is more or less risky than the market its return is adjusted by a factor known as beta (Greek letter β).

9.9.1 CAPM

CAPM says that the required return r_a on a risky asset is the risk-free rate plus a risk premium which is the market risk premium times the beta of the asset. In symbols:

$$r_a = r_f + [\beta \times (r_m - r_f)]$$

where:

r_a = expected return on the security
r_f = risk-free rate for the expected holding period of the asset
β = the security's beta, a measure of how risky its returns are relative to the risk on the market portfolio

r_m = return on a diversified market portfolio
$r_m - r_f$ = the difference between the market portfolio return and the risk-free rate, i.e. the market risk premium.

9.10 BETA

Beta is the percentage change in the price of a security for a 1% move in the market portfolio. It can be estimated statistically from historical price data, as shown later in this chapter. If a share has a beta of one, this means that for a 1% movement in the whole market it will also tend to move by 1%. In other words, the share tends to move in line with the market.

Consider the following market data:

$$r_f = 6\%$$

$$r_m = 10\%$$

In this case the market risk premium $r_m - r_f = 4\%$.

According to CAPM the required return on a security with a beta of one is calculated as follows:

$$6\% + [1 \times (10\% - 6\%)] = 10\%$$

This is exactly the same as the market return. Blue-chip shares that are very representative of the economy as a whole tend to have betas around one. The events that move the equity market as a whole—changes in interest rates, oil prices, foreign exchange rates and so on—tend on average to affect their prices to more or less the same extent as they affect the market. Since it has the same risk profile as the market, the required return on a share with a beta of one is the market return.

9.10.1 High and Low Beta Shares

On the other hand a share with a beta of two is twice as risky as the market portfolio. A 1% move in the market should be associated with a 2% move in the value of the share. Using a 6% risk-free rate and a 4% market risk premium the required rate of return on a share with a beta of two would be:

$$6\% + [2 \times (10\% - 6\%)] = 14\%$$

This is higher than the expected return from the market portfolio. Adding such a share to a market portfolio increases risk. By comparison, the required return on a share with a beta of less than one would be less than the market return. Adding such a share to a diversified portfolio actually reduces the overall risk on the portfolio. In practice, high beta shares tend to be the shares of companies operating in volatile or cyclical sectors such as technology and construction. Low beta securities include utility shares and investment grade corporate bonds.

9.11   MARKET RETURN AND THE RISK PREMIUM

How can we establish the market return and therefore the market risk premium that is required by the CAPM? One approach is to compare the actual returns achieved on a diversified portfolio of securities with the returns achieved on Treasury bills or bonds over a historical time period and measure the average excess returns on the former.

In theory the market portfolio used in this calculation should include investments in all available securities including equities and bonds weighted by their market capitalization. In practice it is common to use an equity index and calculate the average returns achieved on the stock market over a long period of time with those on Treasury bills or bonds. This will calculate an **equity risk premium** — the additional returns achieved on a diversified portfolio of shares compared to risk-free returns. This premium can then be added to the current nominal yield on Treasuries to establish the required return on the stock market (the nominal Treasury yield builds in current inflation expectations). To establish the required return on an individual share the equity risk premium is adjusted by the beta of the share.

9.12   THE EQUITY RISK PREMIUM CONTROVERSY

In practice the historical equity risk premium calculation is extremely tricky and the subject of great controversy. The risk premium for the US based on data available from 1926 to the mid-1990s tends to come out at around 7%–8% (excess arithmetical average returns over Treasury bonds). However data from the last years of the twentieth century suggests a smaller figure. Some analysts argue that the market risk premium derived from such calculations is excessive. It is based on a period of unparalleled growth in the US economy in a country which did not suffer the interruptions to financial markets endured by countries such as France, Germany and Japan. In short, the figure may represent a (fortunate) historical aberration and we have no reason to expect similar returns on equities in the future.

9.12.1   Deriving the Equity Risk Premium

As an alternative to the historical method we can derive an equity risk premium from the dividend discount model. For simplicity here we will use the constant growth version, although it is probably better to use a stage model which can capture expected changes in future dividend growth rates.

The required return on a portfolio of shares such as that represented by the FT-SE 100 index is the yield on gilts plus an equity risk premium — the additional return demanded by investors to tempt them out of gilts and into the stock market, given the greater degree of risk. We will call the required return on the stock market as a whole r_m. The equity risk premium is simply the difference between the risk-free rate r_f and r_m, the required return on the market. The nominal risk-free rate is composed of a real rate of return plus expected inflation. From the constant growth model we can derive an expression for r_m:

$$r_m = \frac{d_1}{MV_0} + g$$

where:

r_m = required return on a market portfolio
d_1 = next year's forecast dividends
MV_0 = current market value
g = expected growth rate in dividends

This equation tells us that the required return on the market is its prospective dividend yield plus the expected dividend growth rate. At the time of writing (mid-2001) the forecast UK inflation rate is about 2.5% and the nominal yield on long-dated gilts is approximately 5.0%. The prospective dividend yield on the FT-SE 100 index is around 2.5%. Suppose that dividends are expected to grow at 4.5% per annum in perpetuity (a real growth rate of about 2% per annum). Then the constant growth formula tells us that:

$$\text{Required Market Return} = 2.5\% + 4.5\% = 7\%$$

If this is true then the UK equity risk premium is only $7\% - 5\% = 2\%$. This is well below figures derived from the excess historical returns on UK shares over gilts. If the equity risk premium was actually 4% then the required return on the market would be 9%. This implies a constant dividend growth rate of 6.5%, a real growth rate of approximately 4%. Given that the long-run real growth rate in the UK economy is likely to be very much lower than this (probably much closer to 2%) the figure is implausible. Company dividends cannot keep taking a larger and larger share of the output of the economy in perpetuity.

9.12.2   Changes in the Equity Risk Premium

One possible conclusion we could draw from this analysis is that the UK equity market was overpriced at mid-2001 (although a more sophisticated stage dividend discount model might refine our conclusions). Another possibility is that the equity risk premium has indeed declined over the years and that market price levels were broadly sustainable. A number of possible explanations have been advanced for a decline in the risk premium:

- investors have more opportunities these days to diversify their portfolios both domestically and internationally, which reduces the risks on share portfolios;
- the transaction and other costs associated with domestic and international diversification have fallen sharply;
- the very high historical equity risk premium over the twentieth century was a one-off which will not recur in the future;
- increased participation in the equity markets means that shares are more liquid and more fairly priced than they were historically.

9.13   CAPM AND PORTFOLIO THEORY

The CAPM analysis is closely related to portfolio theory developed by Harry Markowitz in the early 1950s. This says that the total risk on a portfolio as measured by the variation in its returns is less than the weighted average risk of the constituent securities. Intuitively, this is because market events that are bad for some stocks are beneficial for others, so the overall volatility of the returns on the portfolio is reduced. The principle holds true provided the stocks in the portfolio do not exactly move in line with each other. In the real world there are 'offsetting' effects in a portfolio of securities, and hence total risk is reduced through diversification. The annualized standard deviation of returns on an index such as the FT-SE 100 tends to be around 20%, whereas the standard deviation of returns on the more volatile constituent shares can be 35% and higher.

9.13.1 Diversifiable Risk

The risk that can be reduced and potentially eliminated through diversification is called **diversifiable** or specific or unsystematic risk. In practice it is possible to greatly reduce the variation of returns in a portfolio by choosing between 10 and 20 securities at random. Thereafter the effect tends to level off. The risk that remains in a fully-diversified portfolio is known as undiversifiable, market or **systematic** risk. CAPM makes the assumption that a rational investor holds a fully-diversified portfolio and is not rewarded for diversifiable risk. Therefore it is not the total variation in the returns of a security that explains its expected return, only that element which cannot be diversified away, and that is measured by beta. Beta measures how much risk a security contributes when added to the market portfolio.

9.13.2 Calculating Beta

Beta is estimated by comparing the percentage return on a share against the return on a suitable market index on a monthly, weekly or daily basis over a period of time (some analysts use five years, others two years or less). If the stock pays a dividend then the yield is added to the return for that period. To illustrate the general method, Table 9.2 shows the returns on a share and on the market index for 10 time periods.

Table 9.2 Market return and share return

Time period	Market return	Share return
1	3%	6%
2	2%	3%
3	−2%	−4%
4	3%	5%
5	−5%	−4%
6	1%	2%
7	−3%	1%
8	2%	3%
9	5%	4%
10	−1%	−3%
Average	0.50%	1.30%

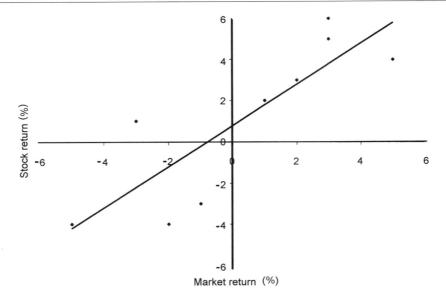

Figure 9.1 'Best fit' straight line

The graph in Figure 9.1 plots the data from Table 9.2. It shows the stock return for each time period on the x-axis, against the market return on the y-axis. A 'best fit' straight line has been drawn as closely as possible to the plotted points using the statistical technique of regression analysis.

9.13.3 Beta and Alpha

The slope or tangent of the straight line is one. This is the beta of the share. It means that if the market return is 1% we expect the stock also to return 1%. Note that the line does not exactly pass through the origin. The 'intercept' where the line passes through the y-axis in this example is 0.8%. This is known as the security's **alpha.** It is the rate of return achieved by holders of the stock historically when investors in the market as a whole earned nothing. This reminds us that we calculated beta using historical returns. CAPM holds that expected future returns are entirely explained by beta and that there is no reason to assume that the alpha figure will tell us anything about the future returns on the share.

9.13.4 Statistical Relationship

Some commercially available beta estimates also calculate a number called r^2. This is a statistical measurement of the extent of the relationship between the two factors in a regression analysis. It is also known as the 'coefficient of determination'. In the case of a beta calculation r^2 measures the proportion of the total variance in the returns on the share that can be explained by changes in the market index. In the example in Table 9.2 the r^2 is 71.31%. This means that 71.31% of the total variance in returns on the share is accounted for by changes in the index. It tells us the impact on the security's returns of market or undiversifiable risk, as measured by beta and captured by the straight line on the graph. The remaining 28.69% is not explained by market risk and is due to specific or diversifiable risk.

In practice r^2 can turn out to be surprisingly low, sometimes 20% or less. This implies that only a small proportion of the stock's variation in returns is explained by market movements. CAPM proponents say this simply means that the bulk of the risk on the stock is diversifiable. Critics say that CAPM does not capture the whole story about the relationship between risk and return and that beta is not a reliable measure of risk.

9.14 FREE CASH FLOW VALUATION

Many analysts value companies by discounting free cash flows rather than dividends. Partly this is because dividends are less important as a proportion of the total returns on shares than they were historically. Companies that do not pay dividends often have positive free cash flows, or at least will start to generate positive free cash flows over a forecast time period.

Free Cash Flow

Free cash flow for a given year is earnings before interest, tax, depreciation and amortization (EBITDA), less any net investments in fixed assets or changes in working capital and less cash tax payments made in that year.

The company's fair value can be established by discounting its projected free cash flows back to a net present value. If free cash flow is negative for a given year it means that the providers of capital are putting money into the company that year. If it is positive it means that free cash is available to be paid out to the investors from that year's trading (even though it may actually be retained in the business).

9.14.1 Debt and Equity Streams

If a company is entirely funded by equity capital then positive free cash flows are available to the ordinary shareholders. If a company is funded through a mixture of equity and debt then it splits its free cash flows into two streams. One is a relatively safe stream of interest and principal payments due to the debt holders. The other is a more risky cash flow stream available to the ordinary shareholders. The net present value of free cash flows therefore measures the total value of the firm, the present value of the equity plus the present value of the debt. It is **firm value**, also known as enterprise value.

Equity Value

The value of the equity is simply firm value less the value of the debt, which can be measured by present valuing the future payments on the debt at current market interest rates. For ease of calculation the value of the debt is sometimes taken simply as the book value or the face value of the debt.

9.14.2   Forecasting Free Cash Flows

Forecasting free cash flows is of course the key to the whole exercise. It is a lengthy process, if the company to be valued is of any size. Typically the analyst builds a spreadsheet with forecasts of sales, direct and overhead costs, capital expenditures and working capital requirements for a number of years ahead. The forecast free cash flows for each year are then discounted at the required return on capital and summed to establish enterprise value. In practice it is an iterative process. The result from the model is checked against valuations using other methods such as price/earnings multiples, and the sensitivity of the model to changes in the input values is investigated.

9.15   WEIGHTED AVERAGE COST OF CAPITAL (WACC)

Calculating the present value of free cash flows requires a discount rate. To see how we could establish the discount rate we will consider this time the case of a company funded through a mixture of equity and debt. We have the following information available about the company:

Required return on equity $=$ 16%
Required return on debt $=$ 8%
Debt/(debt + equity) $=$ 30%
Equity/(debt + equity) $=$ 70%
Tax rate on profits $=$ 33%

The required return on equity can be established using the CAPM. This means that we need a beta for the company's equity. If the shares have little or no trading history with which to establish a beta then we have to use a proxy — in other words, take the beta for a listed company which operates in a similar business sector and which has similar risk characteristics. The return on debt can be established by taking the yield on Treasuries with a maturity date closest to the maturity of the company's debt and adding a credit spread depending on the credit rating of the company's debt.

The problem in this case is that the company is funded through a mixture of debt and equity. Discounting the company's free cash flows at the 8% cost of debt to establish the present value would not fully take into account the risks faced by the equity investors, and would overstate the company's value. On the other hand using a 16% discount rate (the required return on equity) would understate the company's true value since the company is not entirely funded by equity. The debt holders are taking lower risks and require lower returns.

9.15.1   Calculating WACC

A common solution to this problem is to discount the free cash flows at the company's **weighted average cost of capital** (WACC). This is an average of the cost of equity and the cost of debt weighted by the proportions of equity and debt in the business. A slight complication is that interest payments are tax deductible (assuming that the company pays tax) and hence the effective cost of debt to the firm is somewhat less than the gross

8% actually paid to debt holders. On the assumption that interest payments can be fully offset against tax at 33% the effective cost of debt is calculated as follows:

$$\text{Effective Cost of Debt} = 8\% \times (1 - 0.33) = 5.36\%$$

WACC, as we have seen, is simply the weighted average of the required return on debt (taking into account any tax benefits) and the required return on equity. The weights are the proportions of debt and equity capital in the firm. In our example WACC is calculated as follows:

$$\text{WACC} = [0.3 \times 8\% \times (1 - 0.33)] + [0.7 \times 16\%] = 12.8\%$$

The weights should be established by the market values of the debt and of the equity. The market value of equity can be taken as the company's market capitalization, total shares issued times the current market price of the shares. As we have seen, the market value of debt can be established by present valuing the future stream of interest and principal payments at the current yield to maturity for debt carrying that level of risk.

9.16   RESIDUAL VALUE

In practice it is not feasible to forecast free cash flows for more than perhaps six or eight years ahead. In calculating enterprise value, therefore, it is necessary to estimate the so-called **residual** or terminal value of the company at the end of the forecast period. This is its value as a going concern at that point in the future. Enterprise value is the present value of the forecast free cash flows for n years (where n is the number of years free cash flows are forecast) plus the present value of the residual value of the firm at year n. There are a number of methods used in the securities industry to estimate residual or terminal value. A common approach is to estimate residual value at year n as a multiple of the year n forecast EBITDA or free cash flow. The multiple builds in an assumption about the future growth in earnings and cash flows. Alternatives include estimating terminal value as:

- a multiple of the forecast book value of the firm's assets at year n;
- the replacement value of the assets at year n;
- the resale value of the firm's assets at year n.

The last approach (resale value) simply ignores any value the firm might have as a continuing entity. It ignores factors such as goodwill and assumes that the business is worth no more than the physical break-up value of its assets.

Finally, terminal value can be estimated by forecasting the growth in free cash flow from year n onwards and then using the constant growth perpetuity formula. For example, if the forecast free cash flow for year n is £1 million and it is assumed that this will grow at 5% in perpetuity then the free cash flow for year $n+1$ will be £1,050,000. Assume that the required return (discount rate) is 12.8%. Then the terminal value of the firm at year n is calculated as follows:

$$\text{Terminal Value} = \frac{£1,050,000}{0.128 - 0.05} = £13,461,538$$

This terminal value has to be discounted back n years and then added to the present values of the free cash flows that were forecast for n years. In practice terminal value often tends to be a large component of the valuation produced by discounted cash flow models and critics of the methodology point out the sensitivity of the result to the assumptions that determine terminal value.

9.17   WACC AND GEARING/LEVERAGE

There is an obvious objection to the use of WACC in discounting free cash flows. Clearly the fact that interest payments are tax deductible is an advantage. However even if this effect is taken away it seems that if a firm increases its gearing or leverage (the proportion of debt used to fund the business) its WACC can be reduced at a stroke. In that case why do companies not simply replace expensive equity with cheaper debt? It appears that this would increase the net present value of free cash flows by lowering the discount rate.

There does seem to be something wrong with this result. Intuitively it seems that the value of a firm should depend on 'real-world' factors such as profitability and return on capital, not on how it happens to be funded. After all, in theory a single investor could buy up all the company's equity and debt. It seems strange that the value of the investment could be affected by the way in which the investor chooses to take returns out of free cash flows—via interest or via dividend payments.

9.17.1   Return on Assets

One response to this problem is to argue that a firm's resources consist of the stream of free cash flows generated by its assets. What WACC is trying to measure is the required return on the firm's total assets, a rate that in the absence of tax distortions is unaffected by the proportion of equity and of debt capital funding the business. The figure can be applied to the free cash flows to calculate firm value. In the absence of tax distortions, the argument runs, firm value is not affected by the level of borrowing or leverage. Leverage only affects how firm value, as calculated by present valuing the free cash flows, is apportioned between the debt and equity stakeholders.

9.18   CONSTANT RETURN ON ASSETS: CASE STUDY

Let us assume that this argument is correct and that return on assets is constant regardless of gearing. We will take a case this time in which interest payments cannot be offset against tax. We have the following data to establish a company's cost of capital:

Risk-free rate $= 7\%$
Market risk premium $= 5\%$
Market portfolio return $= 12\%$
Equity beta $= 1.2$
Debt beta $= 0.2$
Equity/(debt + equity) $= 70\%$
Debt/(debt + equity) $= 30\%$

The required return on the company's equity and on its debt are calculated by CAPM:

$$\text{Return on Equity} = 7\% + (1.2 \times 5\%) = 13\%$$

$$\text{Return on Debt} = 7\% + (0.2 \times 5\%) = 8\%$$

The weighted average cost of capital is the cost of equity weighted by the proportion of equity, plus the cost of debt weighted by the proportion of debt:

$$\text{WACC} = (13\% \times 0.7) + (8\% \times 0.3) = 11.5\%$$

9.18.1 Increasing the Proportion of Debt

We will assume that this calculation establishes the return on the company's assets, and that the 11.5% figure is not affected by gearing. What happens if the company increases its proportion of debt to (say) 40% without any changes to the nature of the underlying business? The riskiness of the debt will obviously increase. Let us suppose that the debt beta rises to (say) 0.3. Then the required return on debt has to be recalculated:

$$\text{Return on Debt} = 7\% + (0.3 \times 5\%) = 8.5\%$$

The return on assets is constant at 11.5%. So the required return on equity will no longer be 13%. In fact it must be 13.5%:

$$\text{Return on Assets} = 11.5\% = (13.5\% \times 0.6) + (8.5\% \times 0.4)$$

The required return on equity has increased because of the increased level of gearing or leverage.

9.19 ASSET BETA

An alternative to using WACC is to establish the required return on assets directly by calculating an **asset beta** and inserting the result into the CAPM formula. Asset beta measures the change in the value of the whole firm for a 1% change in the market portfolio. It is also the weighted average of the beta of the company's equity and the beta of its debt.

In the example from the previous section we used the following data:

Equity beta $= 1.2$
Debt beta $= 0.2$
Equity/(debt + equity) $= 70\%$
Debt/(debt + equity) $= 30\%$

Therefore:

$$\text{Asset Beta} = (1.2 \times 0.7) + (0.2 \times 0.3) = 0.9$$

CAPM tells us that:

$$\text{Return on Total Assets} = \text{Risk-free Rate} + (\text{Asset Beta} \times \text{Market Risk Premium})$$

Therefore:

$$\text{Return on Total Assets} = 7\% + (0.9 \times 5\%) = 11.5\%$$

9.19.1 Increasing the Proportion of Debt

What happens if the proportion of debt rises to 40%? If we accept the argument that return on assets is unaffected by gearing then it follows that the asset beta is also unaffected by the level of gearing. The asset beta should not change because the underlying assets of the company are not affected by how they are funded. However the debt will become more risky because of the higher level of gearing. Assume as before that the debt beta rises to 0.3:

$$\text{Asset Beta} = 0.9 = (\text{Equity Beta} \times 0.6) + (0.3 \times 0.4)$$

Therefore the equity beta is no longer 1.2:

$$\text{Equity Beta} = \frac{0.9 - (0.3 \times 0.4)}{0.6} = 1.3$$

Given the higher beta number CAPM tells us that the cost of equity has also risen:

$$\text{Required Return on Equity} = 7\% + (1.3 \times 5\%) = 13.5\%$$

This is the same value we calculated using the WACC method, when we assumed that the return on assets is a constant.

9.20   COMPANY VALUE AND GEARING/LEVERAGE

This is a complex subject, but in the real world there are reasons why a company's value and its required return on assets are not entirely independent of the level of debt in the business. For one thing, we ignored the effects of taxation in our last example. Companies do seem to replace equity with debt when the relative tax advantage for investors shifts in favour of holding debt securities. In these circumstances it appears that firms can increase their borrowing and at the same time reduce their overall cost of capital.

What determines a company's asset beta? High beta firms often operate in highly cyclical sectors such as information technology. They may also have high levels of fixed costs. In favourable business circumstances demand for their products rises sharply and they outperform the market. In difficult trading conditions they are hit hard by falling sales and by having to support their fixed cost base out of shrinking revenues.

9.21   CHAPTER SUMMARY

A share or common stock can be valued as the present value of the expected dividend stream. In practice it is not possible to forecast dividends for more than a few years ahead. Therefore the dividend discount method requires an assumption that dividends will continue to grow at a given rate or rates after a certain point in time, or an assumption about the resale value of the share after a certain point in time. The constant growth dividend discount model tells us that the prospective price/earnings ratio can be calculated from the dividend payout ratio, the required return on equity and the assumed dividend growth rate. Many equity analysts use an alternative to the dividend discount model which involves establishing firm or enterprise value by discounting free cash flows. Free cash flows are derived from EBITDA forecasts. The value of the equity is firm value less the value of the debt. All discounted cash flow models require a discount rate. The Capital Asset Pricing Model developed in the 1960s remains a standard model used in the securities industry to establish the required return on a security given its risk. Risk in this context is measured not by the total variation in the returns on the security but by the risk that the security would add to a diversified market portfolio. This is established by the beta of the security. Free cash flows are conventionally discounted at a discount rate that blends the required return on a company's shares with the required return on its debt, taking into account the ability of the firm to offset interest payments against its tax liabilities.

Interest Rate Forwards and Futures

Satisfaction with the present induces neglect of provision for the future.
Francis Bacon

10.1 CHAPTER OVERVIEW

Interest rate forwards and futures are derivative contracts based on underlying money market interest rates. In this chapter we begin by considering a key product in this category known as a **forward rate agreement** (FRA). An FRA is a bilateral over-the-counter derivative contract directly negotiated between two parties fixing the rate of interest on a notional loan or deposit for a period of time in the future. We review the FRA settlement procedure and how the forward interest rate can be established through cash market interest rates. We consider a typical hedging application for a corporate, using an FRA to lock into a future funding rate. Interest rate futures are the exchange-traded equivalent of forward rate agreements. Because they are freely tradable they have the advantage of liquidity. They are also guaranteed by a clearing house. We explore the structure of key interest rate contracts such as the three-month Eurodollar futures traded on the Chicago Mercantile Exchange and the three-month euribor futures contract traded on Eurex. We explore trading and margining procedures and the role of the clearing house. Finally we assess the trading and hedging applications of interest rate futures and how they can be used to lock into a known investment or borrowing rate for a future period of time.

10.2 FORWARD RATE AGREEMENTS

An FRA is a bilateral contract agreed between two parties fixing the rate of interest that will apply to a notional principal sum of money for an agreed term in the future, the contract period. The principal or contract amount written into the FRA contract never changes hands. It is used to calculate the settlement amount due on the transaction. One party to the agreement is said to be the 'buyer' and the other the 'seller', although in fact nothing is ever literally bought or sold.

- **Buyer**. The buyer of the FRA contract is compensated in cash by the seller if the benchmark interest rate for the contract period turns out to be above the rate agreed in the contract.
- **Seller**. The seller of the FRA contract is compensated by the buyer if the benchmark interest rate for the contract period turns out to be below the agreed rate.

Corporate borrowers who wish to hedge against rising interest rates are natural buyers of FRAs. Money market investors who wish to protect themselves against declining interest rates are natural sellers of FRAs. A forward rate agreement is a derivative instrument in that its value is derived from cash market interest rates. FRAs are very similar to the short interest rate futures contracts traded on futures exchanges, except that they are over-the-counter transactions. An over-the-counter derivative contract is a legal and binding agreement made directly between two parties. As such it cannot be freely traded and carries counterparty risk — the risk that the other party to the contract might fail to fulfil its obligations.

10.2.1 Dealing Limits and Terms

Forward rate agreements are dealt by banks in a wide range of currencies. To protect themselves against counterparty default risk, banks will only allow their dealers to enter into FRA contracts with known counterparties whose credentials have been checked by the bank's internal credit function. In addition, the bank will impose a limit on the value of contracts that can be entered into with a given counterparty at any one moment in time. This is in order to avoid **concentration risk** — the risk that if the bank has too many deals on its books with one counterparty it will incur serious losses if that counterparty suffers financial distress. In the London market FRAs are normally dealt on the terms and conditions laid out by the British Banking Association (FRABBA terms).

10.3 FRA APPLICATION: CASE STUDY

BIGCO is a corporate borrower with a loan from a bank. The company pays a rate of interest linked to current money market rates. The principal of the loan is $100 million and interest is paid every six months in arrears. The rate of interest is fixed twice a year at six-month dollar LIBOR plus a fixed spread of 50 basis points (0.50%). The borrowing rate for the next six-month period (183 days starting from spot) has just been set at 7%, but the chief finance officer (CFO) is concerned that rates for the following period might be appreciably higher. This would have a detrimental effect on the company's cash flows and its profitability.

The CFO buys an FRA from a bank (not necessarily the same bank the loan was taken out with). The terms of the contract are set out in Table 10.1.

The contract period of 6v12 ('six against 12 months') means that the FRA covers a six-month contract period starting six months after spot. The actual number of days in this six-month period will be used to calculate the payments due under the FRA contract. In this example it is 182 days:

Table 10.1 FRA contract details

Notional amount:	$100 million
Contract currency:	US dollars
Contract rate:	7.15% per annum
Contract period:	6v12 months (a 182-day period)
Settlement date:	6 months (183 days) after spot
Maturity:	12 months (365 days) after spot
Reference rate:	Six-month US dollar LIBOR
Day count:	Actual/360

- BIGCO will be compensated in cash if six-month dollar LIBOR for the contract period turns out to be above the FRA contract rate of 7.15% per annum;
- if six-month dollar LIBOR for the contract period turns out to be below 7.15% per annum BIGCO will have to compensate the bank which sold the FRA;
- the compensation payments will be based on a notional principal of $100 million.

10.3.1   Settlement Payment on the FRA

The settlement date on the sample contract is six months after spot. At that point the actual market interest rate for the period covered by the contract will be known to both parties. In our example it will be established by reference to the London Interbank Offered Rate. The FRA contract will specify where that rate can be found, typically on an electronic news service such as Bloomberg or Telerate.

Let us suppose that the dollar LIBOR rate for the contract period is fixed at 8.00% per annum. The bank that sold the FRA has to pay BIGCO a cash sum in compensation for rising interest rates, covering a period of 182 days. The payment will be calculated using the appropriate actual/360 day count for US dollars:

Settlement or Compensation Payment at Maturity

$$= \text{Notional Amount} \times (\text{LIBOR} - \text{Contract Rate}) \times \frac{\text{Days in Contract Period}}{360}$$

$$= \$100 \text{ million} \times (0.08 - 0.0715) \times \frac{182}{360}$$

$$= \$429{,}722.22$$

10.3.2   Payment on Settlement Date

If the FRA was settled at maturity the compensation payment would indeed be $429,722.22. However in the FRA market the payment is usually paid on the settlement date, at the beginning of the contract period. The practice is to discount the settlement amount at the LIBOR rate so it can be paid at the start of the contract period. In our example the settlement date is six months after spot; the relevant dates for the contract are shown in Figure 10.1.

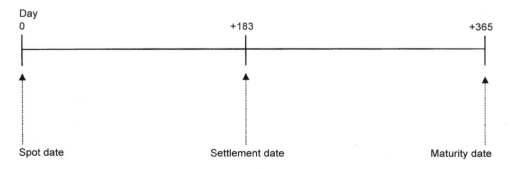

Figure 10.1   Relevant dates for the FRA

The settlement amount \$429,722.22 due at the maturity of the FRA would be discounted back for 182 days at the LIBOR rate for the contract period, which we assumed was 8.00% per annum:

$$\text{Settlement Amount} = \frac{\$429,722.22}{1 + (0.08 \times 182/360)} = \$413,017.94$$

10.3.3   Compensation Formula

The full compensation or settlement formula is as follows:

$$\frac{\text{Notional Amount} \times (\text{LIBOR} - \text{Contract Rate}) \times \text{Contract Days}/360}{1 + (\text{LIBOR} \times \text{Contract Days}/360)}$$

The interest rates in this formula are in decimal format. The contract days is the actual number of days in the FRA contract period. For dollars and currencies in the eurozone this is divided into a 360-day year. For sterling FRAs the base is 365 rather than 360. The advantage of making the settlement payment at the start of the period covered by the contract is that it reduces the risk that the other party to the contract might default on its obligations. Note that the dollar LIBOR rate for the contract period will actually be fixed by the British Banking Association two business days before the FRA settlement date.

10.4   ALL-IN BORROWING COST

Recall that BIGCO is paying LIBOR + 50 basis points per annum on its underlying borrowing. It buys an FRA at a rate of 7.15% per annum. If LIBOR turns out to be 8.00% then it is paid 0.85% per annum on the FRA contract by the bank. This means that its effective borrowing cost is:

$$8.00\% + 0.50\% - 0.85\% = 7.65\% \text{ p.a.}$$

This is simply the FRA contract rate of 7.15% per annum plus the 50 basis points fixed spread over LIBOR it pays on its underlying loan. In fact whatever LIBOR turns out to be for the contract period BIGCO's net cost of borrowing for that period will be fixed at 7.65% per annum. For example, if LIBOR is 6.50% then BIGCO will pay 7.00% per annum on its loan but will have to pay out annualized compensation of 7.15% − 6.50% = 0.65% to its counterparty on the FRA. The net funding cost for the period is:

$$7.00\% + 0.65\% = 7.65\% \text{ p.a.}$$

For BIGCO buying the FRA is simply a hedge against rising interest rates. The CFO of the firm can lock into a known interest rate for the forward period covered by the contract. The hedge shares a common feature with other hedges that are assembled using forward or futures contracts. It establishes a fixed borrowing cost for the contract period, which is helpful in terms of managing the finances of the business; the disadvantage is that the company cannot benefit from a fall in interest rates over the contract period. It is locked in at a fixed rate.

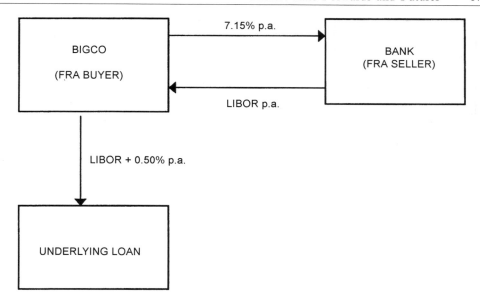

Figure 10.2 Loan plus FRA

10.5 FRA PAYMENT LEGS

Figure 10.2 illustrates the position of BIGCO after the FRA is dealt in a somewhat different way. It shows the payment due on the contract as two different legs, which in practice are netted out. Under the terms of the FRA BIGCO owes the bank 7.15% per annum on the $100 million notional. The bank owes BIGCO LIBOR% per annum on the $100 million notional. If (for example) LIBOR turns out to be 8.00% then the bank owes BIGCO 8.00% per annum for that six-month period. BIGCO owes the bank 7.15% per annum for that six-month period. In practice the payments on the contract are netted out and the bank pays BIGCO 0.85% × 182/360 × $100 million discounted back six months to the start of the contract period.

The diagram in Figure 10.2 illustrates the fact that BIGCO's net cost of borrowing for the period covered by the FRA is 7.65% per annum. The LIBOR leg received on the FRA contract simply cancels out the LIBOR element due on the underlying loan.

10.6 FRA MARKET QUOTATIONS

Dealers quote forward rate agreement prices on screens in much the same way as they do deposit rates. Price screens show the dealers' offer and bid rates for regular contract periods, although FRA traders will quote rates for irregular periods (sometimes called 'broken dates') on request.

Suppose that a dealer quotes the following rates for 6v12 dollar FRAs:

Offer 7.15% − Bid 7.12%

- The dealer is selling FRAs at a rate of 7.15%.
- The dealer is buying FRAs at a rate of 7.12%.

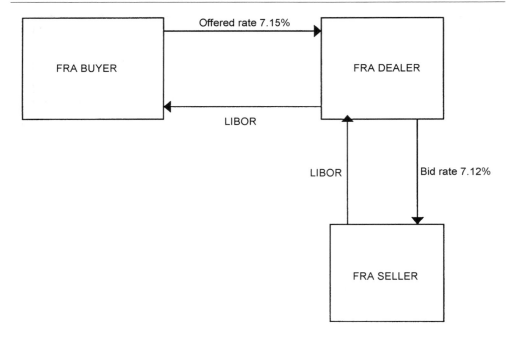

Figure 10.3   Matched FRA deals

Settlement is six months after spot. The maturity date is 12 months after spot. The contract period is a six-month period starting in six months. Imagine that as a result of making these quotations, the dealer sells a 6v12 FRA at 7.15% per annum to a counterparty. The dealer is then lucky enough to find a second counterparty who wishes to deal on exactly the same dates and the same notional principal, but this time the dealer buys an FRA at 7.12% from the second counterparty. The impact of making the two trades is illustrated in Figure 10.3.

10.6.1   Market Risk and Counterparty Risk

In Figure 10.3 the dealer makes a three basis point spread on the two deals combined, and the interest rate exposures are hedged. If interest rates rise the dealer will have to pay compensation to the FRA buyer, but will receive compensation from the FRA seller. However, since the deals are made directly with the two counterparties there is still counterparty risk to consider. In fact the counterparty risk is not on the notional principals on the trades, which are never exchanged. All that is ever exchanged on each deal is the difference between the fixed contract rate and the LIBOR rate for the contract period.

In practice, counterparty risk can be managed by setting position limits and also by taking collateral from counterparties. Increasingly, the position limits imposed on traders are determined by complex risk calculations rather than simple rules of thumb. For example, a dealer will be told to reduce the risk on a trading book when the potential losses (based on a statistical analysis) look as though they could exceed a predefined level. Counterparty risk could also be managed if a third party such as a clearing house agreed to guarantee the payments.

10.6.2 Shading FRA Rates

In reality the average FRA dealer will have many deals on the book and it is unlikely that all of the interest rate exposures will exactly match out. If this is the case a dealer may decide to 'shade' or adjust his or her quoted bid and offer rates to help offset the interest rate risks. For example, if a dealer has a net exposure to rising interest rates and wishes to reduce the exposure then he or she is a potential buyer of FRAs. The dealer may decide to quote rates into the market that will encourage sellers of FRAs to trade with the dealer rather than with other banks.

10.6.3 Shading Rates: Example

Suppose that the current market rate for 6v12 dollar FRAs is as follows:

Offer 7.15% − Bid 7.12%

A dealer who is exposed to rising interest rates for this contract period might decide to increase his or her offer rate to (say) 7.16% and at the same time increase the bid rate to (say) 7.13%.

- **Offer Rate**. The dealer is offering (selling) 6v12-month FRA contracts at 7.16%, which is a less attractive rate than the market rate of 7.15%. This will tend to discourage buyers.
- **Bid Rate**. The dealer is prepared to pay 7.13% to counterparties who wish to sell 6v12-month FRAs, a more attractive rate than 7.12%. This will tend to encourage sellers.

The dealer could also manage any residual interest rate risk on the trading book by using exchange-traded interest rate futures, which are the subject of a later section in this chapter. Interest rate futures in major currencies such as the US dollar have the advantage of being quick and cheap to transact and are highly liquid. In fact, the prices of interest rate futures are commonly used by dealers to establish FRA rates.

10.7   THE FORWARD INTEREST RATE

Forward rate agreements are derivatives of cash money market transactions and most deals cover short-term periods. Typical periods are:

3v9
6v9
6v12
9v12

The first of these periods 'three against nine' is a six-month period of time starting three months after spot and ending nine months after spot. The others are respectively 'six against nine', 'six against 12' and 'nine against 12'.

The contract rate on a forward rate agreement is an interest rate for a period of time starting in the future. It is, as the name of the instrument suggests, a forward interest rate rather than a cash market rate. As such its theoretical or 'fair' value can be calculated from cash market interest rates using the same approach we employed in Chapter 6 when deriving forward rates from the yield curve for par bonds. The difference this time is that most FRAs cover contract periods inside one year and the calculations are normally based on simple interest formulae, without compounding.

10.7.1   Arbitrage Relationships

We wish to calculate the theoretical 6v12-month US dollar forward interest rate. We will call this rate f_{6v12}. We have the following information on cash interest rates from the money markets (for simplicity we will ignore the effects of bid/offer spreads and transaction costs in this example). The rates are annualized and interest is calculated on a simple interest basis using an actual/360 day count:

$$6 \text{ months (183 days) rate} = 7.00\% \text{ p.a.}$$

$$12 \text{ months (365 days) rate} = 7.20\% \text{ p.a.}$$

These rates and the time periods they apply to are illustrated in Figure 10.4. This also shows the 6v12-month rate f_{6v12}.

It is clear that the cash market rates and the forward interest rate f_{6v12} cannot move too far out of alignment, otherwise profitable arbitrage opportunities will open up. Suppose, for example, that it is possible to borrow for 12 months (365 days) at 7.20% and deposit funds for six months (183 days) in the cash market at 7.00%. Suppose further that we can sell a 6v12-month FRA at a rate of (say) 7.50%. We can construct a simple arbitrage trade as follows:

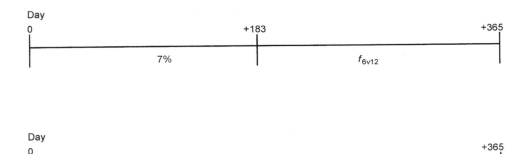

Figure 10.4   Cash market rates and the forward rate

- borrow \$1 for 12 months (365 days) at 7.20% per annum;
- invest \$1 for six months (183 days) at 7.00% per annum;
- lock into a reinvestment rate of 7.50% for the six-month (182-day) period starting in six months by selling a 6v12-month FRA.

The repayment amount due on the borrowing is:

$$\$1 \times \left\{ 1 + \left(0.072 \times \frac{365}{360} \right) \right\} = \$1.0730$$

The proceeds from the first six-month deposit are:

$$\$1 \times \left\{ 1 + \left(0.070 \times \frac{183}{360} \right) \right\} = \$1.0356$$

The proceeds from reinvesting this money for another six months (182 days) at a guaranteed rate of 7.50% p.a. are:

$$\$1.0356 \times \left\{ 1 + \left(0.075 \times \frac{182}{360} \right) \right\} = \$1.0748$$

The arbitrage profit is:

$$\$1.0748 - \$1.0730 = \$0.0018$$

10.8   FAIR FORWARD RATE

Clearly, the 'fair' 6v12-month forward interest rate in our example cannot be 7.50% per annum. It must be less than that, for the arbitrage opportunity to disappear. Let us assume that the cash market rates and the FRA rates are actually all in alignment and there is no arbitrage opportunity. Then it must be the case that:

$$\left\{ 1 + \left(0.072 \times \frac{365}{360} \right) \right\} = \left\{ 1 + \left(0.07 \times \frac{183}{360} \right) \right\} \times \left\{ 1 + \left(f_{6v12} \times \frac{182}{360} \right) \right\}$$

The left-hand side of this equation calculates the principal plus interest on the one-year loan at 7.20% per annum. For there to be no arbitrage this must equal the proceeds of \$1 invested for 183 days at 7.0% per annum, reinvested again at the 'fair' 6v12-month forward rate for a further 182 days. We can turn the equation round and then solve for f_{6v12}:

Fair Forward Rate $f_{6v12} =$

$$\left\{ \left(\frac{1 + (0.072 \times 365/360)}{1 + (0.07 \times 183/360)} \right) - 1 \right\} \times 360/182 = 0.0715 = 7.15\% \text{ p.a.}$$

If the 6v12-month FRA can only be sold at 7.15% per annum then the arbitrage profit disappears. The proceeds from investing a dollar for six months and locking into a reinvestment rate by selling a 6v12-month FRA will exactly equal the cost of borrowing for 12 months. The formula we used is as follows (the interest rates should be inserted as decimals):

Theoretical Forward Rate =

$$\left\{ \left(\frac{1 + \left(\text{Long Period Rate} \times \dfrac{\text{Days in Long Period}}{\text{Year Basis}} \right)}{1 + \left(\text{Short Period Rate} \times \dfrac{\text{Days in Short Period}}{\text{Year Basis}} \right)} \right) - 1 \right\}$$

$$\times \left(\frac{\text{Year Basis}}{\text{Days in the Forward Period}} \right)$$

where:

Long period rate = cash market interest rate to the second date in the forward period (in our example the 12-month rate of 7.2% p.a.)

Days in long period = actual number of days to the second date (in our example 365)

Short period rate = cash market interest rate to the first date in the forward period (in our example the six-month rate of 7% p.a.)

Days in short period = actual number of days to the first date (in our example 183)

Year basis = 360 or 365 depending on the currency

Days in forward period = actual number of days between the first and second dates in the forward time period (in our example 182)

10.8.1   Forward Rates in Practice

This of course is a simplified calculation, ignoring the effects of bid/offer spreads and other costs associated with borrowing and lending transactions, but it establishes a method for calculating the theoretical forward rate of interest from cash market interest rates. In fact a forward offer or lending rate should be calculated from the cost of borrowing funds in the cash market for the 'long period' (the market offer rate) and the rate for depositing funds for the 'short period' (the market bid rate). The forward bid rate should be calculated from the cash market bid rate for the 'long period' and the market offer rate for the 'short period'. Note also that the formula used above is only applicable to money market deals with time periods of one year or less, which use simple interest calculations. We showed in Chapter 6 how to calculate forward interest rates for time periods more than one year ahead using compound interest rates.

In practice FRA rates in major currencies such as the US dollar tend to be derived from the interest rate futures market (covered in the following sections). This is highly liquid and provides a relatively straightforward way in which an FRA dealer can manage the risks on his or her dealing book. As a result the bid/offer spreads on dollar FRAs may be narrower than the rates that would be derived from cash market deposits. On the other hand, it must still be the case that cash market interest rates, FRA rates and the rates derived from interest rate futures prices cannot move too far out of alignment, otherwise profitable arbitrage trades will open up.

10.9   FINANCIAL FUTURES

Commodity futures contracts have been traded on exchanges such as the Chicago Board of Trade (CBOT) and the Chicago Mercantile Exchange (CME) for many years.

They are a natural extension of trading in physical commodities such as wheat, coffee and orange juice. Farmers can sell futures as a means of locking into a price for selling their crops on future dates at an agreed price. Similarly, buyers of the commodities can buy futures contracts as a means of establishing a purchase price on future delivery dates. By contrast, financial futures are relatively recent in origin, first successfully introduced on the CME (otherwise known as the 'Merc') in 1972.

10.9.1 Definitions

The conventional textbook definition of a financial futures contract says that it is an agreement made on an organized exchange to buy or sell:

- a standard amount of a specified financial instrument;
- on a specified date or range of dates in the future;
- at an agreed price.

Some contracts such as the US Treasury bond futures traded on the CBOT follow this definition reasonably well, since there is indeed a physical delivery process (see Chapter 11 for more details of bond futures). A buyer of US Treasury bond futures who has not closed out the contracts before the delivery month will take delivery of bonds and will be invoiced against delivery as if it were a cash market transaction. A seller of US Treasury bond futures who has not closed out contracts before the delivery month will deliver bonds and be paid the invoiced amount. In practice, though, the great majority of contracts are closed out before delivery. However in the case of contracts such as interest rate futures the traditional definition is a little misleading, since there is no actual delivery process. The contracts are always **cash-settled**. In this respect interest rate futures are rather like their over-the-counter relatives, forward rate agreements.

10.9.2 Trading Methods

Futures contracts are either traded by open outcry in trading pits, or on electronic screen-based trading systems. The CME and the CBOT currently operate both systems in tandem. CME interest rate products can be traded virtually 24 hours a day. At the time of writing pit trading on the floor operates from 7:20 a.m. until 2:00 p.m. Chicago time Monday to Friday. After these hours trading resumes on GLOBEX, which is the CME's automated order-entry and matching system and is used by market participants around the world. The London International Financial Futures Exchange (LIFFE) and Eurex, the combined Swiss–German exchange, are wholly electronic markets. Trading on LIFFE is now effected through a computer system called LIFFE-Connect; the physical trading floor finally closed for business in 2000.

Standardization and Security

Unlike over-the-counter contracts, financial futures are standardized products. This is in order to encourage active and liquid trading. On the other hand, they are guaranteed by the clearing house associated with the exchange which eliminates (or greatly reduces) counterparty risk.

10.10   CME EURODOLLAR FUTURES

The three-month Eurodollar futures contract traded on the CME is one of the most liquid financial futures contracts in the world. It is widely used by banks and other financial institutions as a means of hedging short-term interest rate exposures, or as a means of taking a leveraged position in anticipation of a rise or fall in interest rates. As we have seen in Chapter 2, Eurodollars are simply US dollars held on deposit in international accounts. The CME contract is based on the LIBOR on a notional three-month $1 million Eurodollar deposit starting at a specific date in the future. The contract specification for regular trades is set out in Table 10.2.

Table 10.2   CME Eurodollar futures contract

Unit of trading:	Eurodollar term deposit with a principal value of US $1,000,000 and a three-month maturity
Delivery/expiry months:	March, June, September, December (standard months)
Last trading day:	11:00 a.m. London time (5:00 a.m. Chicago time) two business days before the third Wednesday of the contract month
Quotation:	100.00 minus the rate of interest
Tick size:	0.01 (representing in interest rate terms one basis point per annum)
Tick value:	$25
Final settlement:	Based on the three-month Eurodollar LIBOR rate established at 11:00 a.m. on the last trading day

Source: CME.

The contract is based on the rate of interest for a notional $1 million three-month Eurodollar deposit commencing on the third Wednesday of the contract month (March, June, September or December). The contract amount is purely notional — buyers and sellers simply receive or pay the difference between the rate at which they buy or sell the contracts and the rate at which they close the position. Open contracts are automatically closed on the last trading day, when settlement is made against the British Bankers Association LIBOR rate for three-month dollar deposits established at 11:00 a.m. on that day. The LIBOR rate is deducted from 100.00 to establish the final close-out price of the futures contracts.

10.11   EURODOLLAR FUTURES QUOTATIONS

The price of the Eurodollar futures contract is not quoted as an interest rate but in terms of 100.00 minus the interest rate for the contract period. For example, a futures price of 95.05 implies an interest rate for the three-month future period covered by the contract of 4.95% per annum. The convention was adopted to make life simpler for traders — they know that if interest rates are rising they should be selling interest rate futures, in the same way that they should be selling Treasury bill or bond futures.

Tick Size and Value

The minimum price movement on regular CME Eurodollar futures trading — the tick size — is one basis point or 0.01% per annum. The contract is based on a $1 million three-month (90-day) deposit. Each one basis point move represents a profit or loss on the contract of:

$$0.01\% \times \$1 \text{ million} \times 90/360 = \$25$$

10.11.1 Fair Futures Price

The 'fair' interest rate for the future period covered by the contract and hence the contract value can be established through the cash market interest rates in exactly the same way as we did for forward rate agreement contracts. For example if the three-month (90-day) cash market deposit rate is 4.50% p.a. and the six-month (180-day) cash market deposit rate is 4.75% p.a. then the theoretical forward rate f_{3v6} for three against six months (a 90-day period) can be calculated by assuming that the return from a six-month investment equals the return from a three-month investment rolled over at the three against six months forward rate f_{3v6}:

$$\left\{1 + \left(0.0475 \times \frac{180}{360}\right)\right\} = \left\{1 + \left(0.0450 \times \frac{90}{360}\right)\right\} \times \left\{1 + \left(f_{3v6} \times \frac{90}{360}\right)\right\}$$

Therefore:

$$f_{3v6} = 4.94\% \text{ p.a.}$$

If the futures contract is trading at fair value it should trade at around 95.06. In dealing rooms the interest rate implied by the Eurodollar futures price is taken to be the market's best estimate of what the three-month dollar cash market interest rate will be for the future period covered by the contract. It is taken as an indicator of the market's opinion about trends in short-term interest rates and as factoring in the consensus view on interest rate rises or cuts likely to be imposed by the central bank.

10.12 TRADING EURODOLLAR FUTURES: CASE STUDY

Suppose that the March Eurodollar futures contract is currently trading at 95.05. This implies a future rate of interest for the three-month period starting on the third Wednesday in March of 4.95% per annum. We are of the opinion that interest rates are set to fall more sharply than is anticipated by the market, as the Federal Reserve Bank seeks to stimulate the flagging US economy. We therefore buy 100 Eurodollar futures at 95.05.

The contracts reach their final trading date on the Monday before the third Wednesday in March. On that day the BBA dollar LIBOR rate for the three-month period covered by the contract is fixed at (say) 4.75% p.a. The futures will therefore settle at a price of $100.00 - 4.75 = 95.25$. Since we bought the futures at 95.05 we have made 20 ticks per contract, at $25 per tick. Ignoring funding and transaction costs, our net profit on the trade is calculated as follows:

$$\text{Profit} = 20 \text{ ticks} \times 100 \text{ contracts} \times \$25 = \$50,000$$

As we will see in the next section, futures contracts traded on exchanges operate on a **margined** basis. This means that if we wish to open the futures position we would have to lodge initial margin, which is a performance deposit against the risk that we might fail to meet our obligations.

10.13   FUTURES MARGINING

Only members are allowed to trade directly on a futures exchange. They may do so on their own account, or on behalf of clients or other non-members such as brokers who are acting for their clients. Once a deal is struck the clearing house associated with the exchange steps in to become the effective counterparty to both sides. Since the performance of the clearing house is guaranteed by the members of the exchange this greatly reduces concerns about credit risk. It also means that a trader who buys and sells the same number of contracts for the same contract month has a directly offsetting position and the trades simply cancel out.

Clearing House Security

The CME clearing house is financially backed by its members and by a special trust fund. The clearing house associated with the London International Financial Futures Exchange is the London Clearing House (LCH). LCH has also become the central counterparty for cash equity trades made on the London Stock Exchange. The clearing house of the combined Swiss–German derivatives exchange Eurex is Eurex Clearing AG which is a wholly-owned subsidiary of Eurex Frankfurt AG.

10.13.1   Initial and Variation Margins

A clearing house has to ensure that receipts from traders making a loss are available to make payments to the traders who are in profit. As a safety measure the clearing house requires all traders to put up collateral, which is known as **initial margin**, against their open positions. The initial margin exists simply to protect the clearing house, the members of the exchange, and their clients, against default. A client who is not a member of the exchange and who wishes to open a position must post initial margin with his or her broker who will handle all payments with the clearing house. Smaller members do this via a clearing member of the exchange, a large investment bank or securities house which deals directly with the clearing house.

10.13.2   Mark-to-Market

Open futures positions are regularly **marked-to-market**, normally at the end of every trading day. This means that the closing or settlement value of the contracts is compared with yesterday's settlement value and profits or losses are credited to or debited from the client's account with their broker. The client may be called upon to deposit additional margin as a result of losses, or can withdraw cash from the account as a result of profits. It may be possible, depending on the terms and conditions stipulated by a particular broker, to put up tradable securities such as Treasury bills and bonds against the initial margin requirement rather than cash.

10.14 MARGINING EXAMPLE: EURIBOR FUTURES

To illustrate the operation of the margin system in detail we will look this time at a relative of the CME Eurodollar futures contract. This is the three-month euribor futures contract traded on Eurex (there is a very similar euribor contract traded on LIFFE). The Eurex contract specification is set out in Table 10.3.

The tick value on the euribor contract is calculated as follows:

$$€1 \text{ million} \times 0.005\% \times \frac{90}{360} = €12.50$$

10.14.1 Trading Strategy

Consider a trading strategy in which we believe short-term interest rates in the euro are set to fall more sharply than is already factored into the price of euribor futures. The March contract is currently trading at 95.25. This implies a rate of interest for the three-month period starting on the third Wednesday of March of 4.75% per annum.

We buy 100 contracts at 95.25 and lodge initial margin with our broker. The settlement price at the end of the trading day is 95.20. As the contract description makes clear, this is calculated from the average of the last five trades in the March futures contract that day. The fall in the contract price is 0.05 which represents five basis points in interest rate terms, or a 10 tick fall in the value of the contract (each tick represents half a basis point). Since we have a long position in the futures and they have lost value

Table 10.3 Three-month euribor futures traded on Eurex

Unit of trading:	€1 million three-month time deposit based on the European Interbank Offered Rate (euribor)
Delivery/expiry months:	March, June, September, December
Last trading day:	Two trading days before the third Wednesday of the expiry month
Quotation:	100 minus the rate of interest to three decimal places
Tick size (minimum price movement in the contract):	0.005 (representing an interest rate change of 0.005%, or one half of one basis point)
Tick value:	€12.50
Daily settlement price (for the daily mark-to-market calculation):	The average of the last five trades of the day weighted by volume
Final settlement price (for the final close out on the last trading day):	Based on the euribor rate for three-month time deposits in the euro at 11:00 central European time on the last trading day of the contract

Source: Eurex.

we will have to pay variation margin via our broker to the clearing house to make good this loss. The amount due is calculated as follows:

$$100 \text{ contracts} \times 10 \text{ ticks} \times €12.50 = €12,500$$

We can see why this must be so if we look at the notional value of the position we have created. It is 100 contracts times the notional contract value of €1 million. This is €100 million. The implied interest rate for the forward three-month period covered by the contracts has changed by 0.05% per annum. Therefore the loss on our position must be:

$$€100 \text{ million} \times \frac{0.05}{100} \times \frac{90}{360} = €12,500$$

10.14.2   Outcome of the Strategy

Table 10.4 summarizes the variation margin payments and receipts on the assumption that we run the position for three trading days. The assumed settlement price for the mark-to-market at the end of day one is 95.20. At the end of day two it is 95.28. On day three we close the position by selling 100 March euribor futures at 95.31.

Table 10.4   Variation margin payments

Day 1
Bought at 95.25
Settlement price = 95.20
Variation margin payable = -10 ticks $\times 100 \times 12.5 = -€12,500$

Day 2
Settlement price = 95.28
Variation margin receivable = 16 ticks $\times 100 \times 12.5 = €20,000$

Day 3
Sale price = 95.31
Variation margin receivable = 6 ticks $\times 100 \times €12.5 = €7500$

The final variation margin payment is due to us because we sold the contracts at 95.31, which is three basis points or six ticks above the day two settlement price used in the mark-to-market calculation at the end of day two. When we sell the 100 March contracts we will also receive back our initial margin. The position is now closed and the clearing house no longer requires our collateral.

10.14.3   Net Profit and Loss

The net profit from our trading campaign (ignoring funding and transaction costs) can be calculated by totalling the variation margin payments and receipts:

$$\text{Net Profit} = -12,500 + 20,000 + 7500 = €15,000$$

This can also be calculated directly from the prices at which we bought and sold the 100 euribor futures contracts. We bought at 95.25 and sold at 95.31, a difference of 12 ticks. Therefore the net profit must be:

$$12 \text{ ticks} \times 100 \times 12.50 = \text{€}15,000$$

The notional value of the position we created by buying the contracts was €100 million. The implied interest rate for the three-month future period covered by the contract has changed in interest rate terms by six basis points in our favour (equivalent to 12 ticks on the contract price). Six basis points for a three-month period on €100 million gives us our profit of €15,000:

$$\text{€}100 \text{ million} \times \frac{0.06}{100} \times \frac{90}{360} = \text{€}15,000$$

10.14.4 Last Trading Day and Spread Trades

If we kept our position open until the last trading day of the contract the final settlement price would be based on the actual three-month euribor rate for the period covered by the contract. There would be a final variation margin calculation and the contracts would simply expire. If we wished to maintain the position we would have to 'roll' into another contract month by asking our broker to deal contracts in that month.

Many traders set up **spread trades** rather than simple long or short futures positions. At its simplest this involves buying one contract month (for example, March) and selling another contract month (for example, June). Since the risks offset each other to an extent this has the effect of reducing the initial margin that has to be deposited at the outset of the trade. The daily variation margins will also net out against each other. The objective of a simple spread trade is to profit when the prices of the futures contracts converge or diverge (reflecting changes in the shape of the yield curve) and/or to profit from misalignments in the pricing of the contracts.

10.15 INTEREST RATE FUTURES HEDGE: CASE STUDY

Like FRAs, interest rate futures can be used to hedge interest rate exposures. Consider, for example, the case of a money market investor who needs to reinvest the proceeds from a Eurodollar deposit in three months' time. Today is mid-March. In mid-June the investor will have exactly $10 million to reinvest in the money market for a further three-month (90-day) period.

The risk that the investor runs is that short-term dollar interest rates will fall sharply in the meantime. Suppose that the investor knows he or she will be able to deposit money with a bank for that future period at three-month LIBOR minus 1/16%. The problem is that the investor does not know in advance what the LIBOR component is going to be.

10.15.1 The Hedge Ratio

To hedge this risk the investor decides to buy three-month Eurodollar futures on the CME. If interest rates fall the contracts will gain in value because they are priced in terms of 100 minus the rate of interest. The investor will receive positive variation margin on the futures in compensation for the loss of interest when the $10 million sum is reinvested in the money markets. The notional size of the CME contract is $1 million so the investor has to buy 10 contracts to hedge the interest rate exposure. The tick size is 0.01 and the tick value is $25:

$$\text{Hedge Ratio} = \frac{\text{Position to Hedge}}{\text{Notional Contract Size}}$$

$$= \frac{\$10 \text{ million}}{\$1 \text{ million}} = 10 \text{ contracts}$$

Suppose the investor buys 10 June futures at 94.52. This implies an annualized rate of interest for the three-month period starting on the third Wednesday of June of 5.48%.

10.15.2 Hedge Performance

Next suppose that when the futures expire in mid-June the three-month dollar LIBOR is fixed at 5.35% per annum. In that case we can calculate the all-in reinvestment rate actually achieved by the investor.

● The investor can reinvest the $10 million at 5.2875% p.a. (the LIBOR rate of 5.35% minus 1/16%). At the end of the three-month reinvestment period this will generate interest of:

$$\$10 \text{ million} \times 0.052875 \times 90/360 = \$132{,}187.50$$

● The June Eurodollar futures will close at $100 - 5.35 = 94.65$.
● The profit from the 10 futures contracts is $(9465 - 9452) \times 10 \times \$25 = \$3250$.
● Add the profit from the futures position to the interest of $132,187.50 gained from reinvesting $10 million for three months and the total is $135,437.50. The annualized return on $10 million is:

$$\frac{\$135{,}437.50}{\$10{,}000{,}000} \times 100 \times 360/90 = 5.4175\% \text{ p.a.}$$

There is a simpler way to derive this figure. It is the 5.48% p.a. rate that the investor locked into through buying the futures contracts, less the 1/16% spread below LIBOR achieved on reinvesting funds in the cash market:

$$5.48\% - 0.0625\% = 5.4175\% \text{ p.a.}$$

10.16 FUTURES STRIPS

We will consider in Chapter 13 how to use interest rate futures to hedge interest rate swaps using a series or **strip** of interest rate futures with different expiry months. In this section we will briefly explore a similar kind of strip hedge, but this time for a bank that has to manage the risk on a fixed rate loan. We know from the previous example that

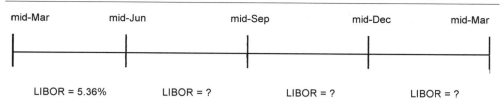

Figure 10.5 Bank's funding costs to finance a one-year loan

interest rate futures can be used to lock in a reinvestment rate for a future period. It follows that a strip of futures can be used to lock in a borrowing rate for a series of future dates.

10.16.1   Strip Hedge: Example

Suppose that a bank has to quote a rate of interest in mid-March for a one-year fixed rate Eurodollar loan to a corporate borrower. The loan principal is $10 million and interest payments will be made quarterly in arrears. The bank can fund itself at LIBOR flat. The LIBOR rate for the first period of the loan is 5.36% p.a. This can be locked in through borrowing in the money markets. The problem for the bank is that it does not know the rate of interest it will have to pay to refinance the loan on future dates. The situation is illustrated in Figure 10.5.

For simplicity we will assume that the annual period covers 360 days and that each three-month period has exactly 90 days. The bank can lock into funding rates for the periods from June to September, September to December and December to March by selling an appropriate number of interest rate futures contracts. Since the exposure to be covered on each refunding date is always $10 million, the bank will have to trade 10 June, 10 September and 10 December contracts. It has to sell contracts because if interest rates rise it will have to pay more in funding costs but it will receive compensating margin payments on the short futures position. As we have seen, interest rate futures prices move inversely with the interest rate for the future period.

10.16.2   Futures Prices

Table 10.5 shows the current Eurodollar futures prices for the contracts that cover these periods and the rates of interest implied in these prices.

In a simple case like this it is often possible to approximate quite closely the funding rate the bank can achieve through the futures hedge by calculating the simple

Table 10.5 Interest rate futures prices

Future period	Contract month	Contract price	Implied interest rate
Mid-Jun to mid-Sep	June	94.52	5.48% p.a.
Mid-Sep to mid-Dec	September	94.44	5.56% p.a.
Mid-Dec to mid-Mar	December	94.31	5.69% p.a.

arithmetical average of the cash rate and the forward rates implied in the futures prices. In this example:

$$\frac{5.36\% + 5.48\% + 5.56\% + 5.69\%}{4} = 5.52\% \text{ p.a.}$$

The bank can lock into a funding rate of approximately 5.52% per annum by borrowing for the first three months at LIBOR and dealing a strip of interest rate futures to guarantee the rate for the subsequent funding periods. In the next section we show how to calculate the result with more precision. It will be important to use the precise method when calculating a fixed interest rate from a longer strip of futures.

10.16.3   More Precise Calculation

The cost of funds for the bank is calculated as follows. Firstly we work out the cost of funding \$1 over one year at the cash market rate and at the forward rates guaranteed by the interest rate futures contracts:

$$\left\{1 + \left(\frac{0.0536}{4}\right)\right\} \times \left\{1 + \left(\frac{0.0548}{4}\right)\right\} \times \left\{1 + \left(\frac{0.0556}{4}\right)\right\}$$
$$\times \left\{1 + \left(\frac{0.0569}{4}\right)\right\} = 1.0564$$

We then subtract the \$1 principal to derive the implied interest rate:

$$\text{Interest Rate} = 1.0564 - 1 = 0.0564 = 5.64\% \text{ p.a.}$$

This is an annual equivalent rate. It was calculated based on the actual amount of interest that would be due at the end of the one-year time period. We know that a quoted rate of interest with quarterly compounding is always less than the annual equivalent rate (the rate with annual compounding). The quarterly compounded equivalent of 5.64% per annum with annual compounding is approximately 5.52% per annum:

$$\left(1 + \frac{0.0552}{4}\right)^4 - 1 = 5.64\%$$

10.16.4   The Bank's Spread

Having calculated a break-even funding rate of 5.52% p.a. (with quarterly payments) the bank will then add a spread on top to establish its lending rate. Note that in practice this calculation will only establish the *approximate* cost of funds to the bank. We assumed that the interest payment dates on the loan coincided with the expiry dates on the Eurodollar futures contracts, which in practice is unlikely to be the case.

10.17   FRAS AND FUTURES COMPARED

FRAs have certain advantages over interest rate futures when used for trading and to hedge interest rate exposures.

- **Flexibility.** The terms of an FRA are highly flexible because it is a contract between two parties. The contract period, the notional amount and the currency are all negotiable. Futures are standardized.
- **Margins.** A bank counterparty may ask for initial margin as collateral but daily variation margins (which are an inconvenience) are not normally required.

On the other hand interest rate futures have their own advantages.

- **Liquidity.** Futures are normally highly liquid contracts (at least the nearby expiry months) and positions can easily be closed out. FRAs are bilateral agreements that can only be closed out by negotiation between the two parties (although in the case of a standard contract the current value is very easy to establish).
- **Clearing House.** The performance of futures contracts is guaranteed by the clearing house. In the case of FRAs the two parties take on counterparty risk.

10.18   CHAPTER SUMMARY

A forward rate agreement is a cash-settled derivative contract based on the rate of interest for a period of time starting in the future. The buyer is compensated by the seller if the reference interest rate for the period (normally LIBOR) turns out to be above the contract rate. Otherwise the seller is compensated by the buyer. FRA dealers quote bid and offer FRA rates for regular dates on screens, although contracts can be tailored to meet the needs of individual customers. The theoretical rate for the forward period covered by an FRA contract can be calculated from cash market interest rates. In practice FRA rates in major currencies such as the dollar are closely related to the prices of interest rate futures. Key contracts include the three-month Eurodollar futures traded on the Chicago Mercantile Exchange and the three-month euribor futures contracts traded on Eurex and on LIFFE. These are guaranteed by the clearing house associated with the exchange. A trader or hedger who wishes to buy or sell futures contracts has to post initial margin and open positions are marked-to-market on a daily basis. Interest rate futures are used to take speculative positions on changes in short-term interest rates. They are also used by corporations, investors, banks and derivatives traders to hedge against interest rate risk. The prices of interest rate futures contracts are taken to establish the market's consensus expectations on the future direction of short-term interest rates.

APPENDIX: STATISTICS ON DERIVATIVES MARKETS

Table 10.6 shows the notional amounts outstanding in the global over-the-counter derivatives markets at the end of 1999 and 2000. The figures are in billions of US dollars.

Table 10.7 shows the notional amounts outstanding globally on organized derivatives exchanges by instrument at the end of 1999 and 2000 (in billions of US dollars).

Table 10.6 Size of OTC derivatives markets

	End-Dec 1999	End-Dec 2000
Grand total	88,201	95,199
Total FX contracts	14,344	15,666
Outright forwards and FX swaps	9593	10,134
Currency swaps	2444	3194
Currency options	2307	2338
FRAs	6775	6423
Swaps	43,936	48,768
Interest rate options	9380	9476
Total equity-linked contracts	1809	1891
Equity forwards and swaps	283	335
Equity options	1527	1555

Source: BIS. Reproduced by permission of the Bank for International Settlements.

Table 10.7 Size of exchange-traded derivatives markets

	Dec 1999	Dec 2000
Futures		
Total	8284.9	8308.2
Interest rate	7913.9	7892.2
Currency	36.7	74.4
Equity index	334.3	341.7
Options		
Total	5236.8	5817.1
Interest rate	3755.5	4734.2
Currency	22.4	21.4
Equity index	1458.9	1061.4

Source: BIS. Reproduced by permission of the Bank for International Settlements.

11
Bond Futures

But in the importance and noise of to-morrow
When the brokers are roaring like beasts on the
floor of the Bourse . . .

W.H. Auden

11.1 CHAPTER OVERVIEW

In the previous chapter we looked at futures contracts on short-term interest rates. Exchange-traded futures are also available on a range of major government bonds. In the present chapter we explore the structure and application of futures contracts on US Treasuries, UK gilts and German bunds. We explain the contract specifications and explore basic trading strategies. These contracts have a physical delivery mechanism although the contracts are written on notional bonds. We explain how the delivery and settlement procedures operate and how the exchanges calculate the conversion factors that are designed to adjust for the relative values of the actual bonds deliverable against the contracts. We then look at how bond forward and futures contracts are priced and explain concepts such as basis, basis risk, the implied repo rate and the cheapest to deliver bond. We consider the limitations of the conversion factors published by the exchanges and the behaviour of the cheapest to deliver bond. Finally, we explore some practical applications of bond futures in hedging positions in underlying bonds and in implementing asset allocation decisions. We develop methods for hedging exposures to the cheapest to deliver (CTD) bond and to non-CTD bonds.

11.2 DEFINITIONS

A financial futures contract is an agreement to buy or sell on an organized exchange:

- a standard amount of a specified financial instrument;
- at a specified date in the future (or within a range of dates);
- at an agreed price.

As we saw in Chapter 10 when exploring interest rate futures, the buyer or seller of futures contracts has to pledge collateral as a performance guarantee. This is known as **initial margin**. If a trader keeps a position open it is regularly marked-to-market against the futures settlement price and the trader is subject to margin calls (or will receive margin payments). In the current chapter we focus on bond futures contracts, their applications and how they are priced. The examples are based on: the US Treasury bond futures traded on the Chicago Board of Trade (CBOT); the bund futures traded on Eurex; and the UK gilts futures contracts traded on the London International Financial Futures Exchange (LIFFE).

11.3   THE CBOT US TREASURY BOND FUTURE

The contract specification of the 30-year US Treasury bond futures traded on the CBOT is described in Table 11.1.

11.3.1   Contract Size and Tick

Each contract is based on a $100,000 par value position in a notional US Treasury bond with a 6% coupon. The underlying bond is purely notional; there is no such instrument. The exchange publishes a list of actual Treasury bonds that are deliverable against the contract, and a range of so-called **conversion factors** which are designed to adjust for the different values of the bonds that are deliverable against the contract.

The futures price is quoted as a percentage of par with a tick size (minimum price move) of 1/32%. For example, a quotation of 105-16 means that the contract is trading at $105 and 16/32 per $100 nominal, which is $105.50 in decimal format. The value of a one tick move in the price of a contract is calculated as follows:

$$1/32\% \times \$100,000 = 0.0003125 \times \$100,000 = \$31.25$$

This tells us that for every contract we trade, every one tick movement in the value of the contract represents a $31.25 profit or loss on the position. Like the quoted prices of the underlying Treasury bonds, the bond futures price is a clean price. When a bond is delivered against a short futures position the seller will add the accrued interest on to the invoice.

11.4   INVOICED AMOUNT

Most buyers and sellers of bond futures close out their positions before the delivery month is reached. However during the delivery month a trader who is short US Treasury bond futures is entitled to go through the delivery process and deliver bonds to an assigned trader who is long bond futures. The seller has the option of which

Table 11.1   CBOT 30-year US Treasury bond futures

Unit of trading:	$100,000 par value of a notional US Treasury bond with a 6.00% coupon
Delivery months:	March, June, September, December
Quotation and tick size:	The futures price is quoted as a percentage of par with a tick size (minimum price move) of 1/32%
Tick value:	$31.25
Delivery:	The contract is written on a purely notional bond. A range of actual bonds can be delivered against the contract provided they have a maturity of at least 15 years from the first day of the delivery month. The CBOT publishes a set of conversion factors which adjust the invoice amount based on which bonds are actually delivered. Accrued interest is charged on the bonds that are delivered
Delivery date:	Any business day in the delivery month
Last trading day:	Seven business days before the last business day of the delivery month

Source: CBOT.

business day in the delivery month to deliver bonds and receive the invoiced amount from the buyer. The calculation of the invoiced amount is based on the price of the futures contract established by the clearing house. This is then adjusted by the **conversion factor** for the bonds that are actually to be delivered against the contract. The conversion factor is necessary because some bonds are more valuable than others, due (primarily) to differences in coupon rates. The calculation of the factor is discussed in detail in the next section.

The invoiced amount for the US Treasury bond futures is calculated as follows:

$$\text{Clean Price} = \text{Conversion Factor of Delivered Bond} \times \frac{\text{Futures Price}}{100} \times \$100,000$$

To this is added the accrued interest on the bond that is delivered up to the delivery date.

11.5   CONVERSION FACTORS

The conversion factor for the delivered bond is its clean price per \$1 par value at a yield to maturity of 6.00% (the coupon on the notional bond specified in the contract) on the first day of the delivery month. The time to maturity in the calculation is actually rounded down to the nearest quarter year. For example, 20 years and four months becomes 20.25 years.

Table 11.2 shows three bonds that were eligible for delivery against the December 2001 US Treasury bond futures contract, with their respective conversion factors.

- The clean price of the 5.25% coupon Treasury maturing on 15 November 2028 for settlement 1 December 2001 at a yield of 6.00% is \$0.9006 per \$1 nominal. The maturity date in this calculation is rounded back to the nearest quarter year from the assumed 1 December 2001 settlement date, which produces a date of 1 September 2028.
- The clean price of the 7.25% coupon Treasury for settlement 1 December 2001 at a yield of 6.00% is \$1.1463 per \$1 nominal. Again the maturity date is rounded back to the nearest quarter year from the assumed settlement date, in this case to 1 June 2022.

The conversion factor for a 6.00% coupon bond priced to yield 6.00% would be exactly one. The clean price per \$1 notional at a yield of 6% would be \$1.

11.5.1   Delivery and Settlement

Notice of delivery has to be given by the seller to the CBOT before delivery actually takes place and the seller has to state precisely which bond will be delivered. On the

Table 11.2   Deliverable bonds and conversion factors

Coupon	Issue date	Maturity	Factor
5.25%	16 Nov 1998	15 Nov 2028	0.9006
7.25%	17 Aug 1992	15 Aug 2022	1.1463
9.00%	22 Nov 1988	15 Nov 2018	1.3141

actual delivery day the bonds are transferred to the buyer and the invoiced amount to the seller.

Let us suppose that a futures seller decides to deliver bonds on 12 December 2001 against the December 2001 contract. The delivery price is set by the clearing house as 101-24. The seller notifies the exchange that the 5.25% coupon Treasury maturing on 15 November 2028 is to be delivered. The conversion factor is 0.9006. The last coupon on the bond was paid on 15 November 2001 and therefore 27 days have elapsed since the last coupon to delivery on 12 December. There are 181 days in the bond's current coupon period. The accrued interest on the bond on the delivery date is:

$$\frac{\$5.25}{2} \times \frac{27}{181} = \$0.3916 \text{ per } \$100 = \$0.003916 \text{ per } \$1$$

The invoiced amount per contract is:

$$\left(\text{Conversion Factor} \times \frac{\text{Futures Price}}{100} \times \$100,000 \right) + \text{Accrued}$$

$$= \left(0.9006 \times \frac{101.75}{100} \times \$100,000 \right) + \$0.003916 \times \$100,000$$

$$= \$92,028$$

11.5.2   Problems with Conversion Factors

The conversion factor is a simple means of adjusting the Treasury bond futures price to a price that is appropriate for the particular bond that is delivered:

* bonds with coupons lower than 6.00% will have factors below one;
* bonds with coupons higher than 6.00% will have factors above one and the invoiced amount is greater.

Unfortunately, as we will see later in this chapter, price factors do not fully adjust for the real value of the bonds that are deliverable against the futures contract. At any one time there tends to be one of the deliverable bonds that is the most attractive for a seller to hold and deliver against a short bond futures position.

11.6   LONG GILT AND EURO-BUND FUTURES

The long gilt futures contract traded on LIFFE in London is similar in structure to the CBOT US Treasury bond contract:

* the contract is based on £100,000 nominal notional gilts with a coupon of 7%;
* delivery can take place any business day in the delivery month at the seller's option;
* bonds that are eligible for delivery have maturities of between 8.75 and 13 years;
* the contract months are also March, June, September and December;
* the quote is in decimals per £100 nominal to two decimal places;
* the tick size is 0.01 and the tick value is £100,000×0.01%=£10.

LIFFE publishes a list of conversion factors (which it calls **price factors**) designed to adjust for the relative values of the gilts that are deliverable against a given contract month.

11.6.1   Euro-bund Futures

The bund futures traded on Eurex differs from both the US Treasury bond and the LIFFE gilt futures in that there is only one delivery date in the delivery month, the 10th calendar day of the month, or the next day if this is not a business day. The contract specification is set out in Table 11.3.

11.6.2   Bund Futures Settlement and Delivery

The settlement price for the daily mark-to-market in bund futures is normally based on the last five trades in the day. The final settlement price is determined at 12:30 p.m. on the last trading day, normally based on the average of the last 10 trades in the futures contracts. The conversion factor of a deliverable bond is based on the clean price of the bond at a yield of 6.00% for settlement on the 10th day of the delivery month. Unlike the US Treasury bond futures, the maturity date on the bond is not rounded in the calculation.

One of the bonds deliverable against the December 2001 bund futures was the 5.25% coupon German government bond maturing 4 July 2010:

- for settlement 10 December at a 6.00% yield the clean price of this bond is €0.950514 per €1 nominal
- therefore the conversion factor is 0.950514.

Table 11.3 Eurex bund futures contract

Unit of trading:	€100,000 par value of a notional German government bond with a 6.00% coupon
Delivery months:	March, June, September, December
Quotation and tick size:	The futures price is quoted as a percentage of par to two decimal places. For example, a quotation of 102.45 means €102.45 per €100 nominal. The tick size (minimum price move) is 0.01%
Tick value:	The value of a one tick move in the price of a contract is 0.01% × €100,000 = €10
Delivery:	The contract is written on a notional bond. Eurex lists a number of bonds that can be delivered against a short position in the futures. These are German government bonds with 8.5 to 10.5 years remaining to maturity on the delivery date. The exchange publishes a list of conversion factors which adjust the invoiced amount based on which bonds are actually delivered. Accrued interest is charged on the bonds that are delivered
Delivery date:	The 10th calendar day of the delivery month or the next trading day if this is a non-business day
Last trading day:	Two trading days before the delivery day in the delivery month. Trading ceases at 12:30 p.m. Central European Time

If this bond was delivered against a short futures position on 10 December 2001 the seller would invoice (per contract) the clean price of the futures adjusted by the conversion factor applied to a notional contract size of €100,000. To this would be added the accrued on the delivered bonds up to 10 December 2001.

11.7 FORWARD BOND PRICE

Calculating the fair value for delivering a bond on a forward date is based on an arbitrage argument, sometimes known as the **cash-and-carry** method. Suppose that for settlement tomorrow the 8.875% coupon US Treasury is trading at a clean price of $134.50. Accrued interest is $2.0594 so the dirty price is $136.5594. We wish to calculate a break-even clean price for delivering the bond to a client 30 days after tomorrow. This is a forward contract rather than a futures since it is agreed on an over-the-counter basis between ourselves and the client.

Our strategy is to buy the bond cash for a total settlement amount of $136.5594 so that we have the bond available to deliver to the client in 30 days. We will fund the position via repo. The repo rate is 4.50% per annum. In 30 days we will have to repay principal plus interest on the repo transaction:

$$\text{Interest Due} = \$136.5594 \times 0.045 \times \frac{30}{360} = \$0.5121$$

$$\text{Principal} + \text{Interest} = \$136.5594 \times \left\{ 1 + \left(0.045 \times \frac{30}{360} \right) \right\} = \$137.0715$$

In order to break even on the forward deal we must charge our client a total dirty price of $137.0715 on the forward delivery date to cover the principal and interest repayment on our loan. On that date the accrued interest on the bond is calculated to be $2.7949. Therefore the clean price we have to charge the client to break even on the forward contract is:

$$\$137.0715 - \$2.7949 = \$134.2766$$

This is the 'fair' forward clean price of the bond for delivery 30 days from tomorrow. It is calculated as follows:

Forward Clean Price =
    Cash Dirty Price + Funding Cost − Accrued Interest on the Forward Date

$$\$134.2766 = \$136.5594 + \$0.5121 - \$2.7949$$

11.8 CARRY COST

The relationship between the forward clean price and the cash price of the bond can be expressed in terms of the net cost of carrying a position in the underlying bond for forward delivery:

$$\text{Net Carry} = \text{Funding Cost} - \text{Coupon Income Earned}$$

$$\text{Forward Clean Price} = \text{Cash Clean Price} + \text{Net Carry}$$

In our example the coupon income earned over the 30-day period consists of net accrued interest of $2.7949 - $2.0594 = $0.7355. The **net carry** is the interest cost of funding the bond position via repo minus the coupon income earned over the holding period. In our example it is $0.5121 - $0.7355 = -$0.2234. Adding this to the cash clean price of $134.50 gives a break-even forward clean price of $134.2766.

11.8.1 Positive and Negative Carry

In the above example the forward clean bond price is actually lower than the cash clean price. This is because the accrued earned on the bond over the 30-day holding period is greater than the cost of funding the position via repo. The position is said to have **positive carry**. If the coupon income was *less* than the funding cost then holding the bond and funding the position via repo would result in negative carry. The break-even forward price would be above the cash bond price. Note that if a coupon is physically paid out on a bond during the 'carry' period this has to be factored into the calculation of net carry. In that case:

$$\text{Net Carry} = \text{Funding Cost} - \text{Coupon Received}$$

$$-\text{Income from Reinvesting the Coupon} - \text{Net Accrued Interest Earned}$$

$$\text{Net Accrued Interest Earned} =$$

$$\text{Accrued Interest on the Forward Date} - \text{Accrued Paid on Cash Purchase Date}$$

11.9 THE IMPLIED REPO RATE

A repo is a transaction in which a trader sells a bond at an agreed price and agrees to buy it back at a later date. In effect, the trader is borrowing money for the period of the repo using the bond as collateral. In a classic repo the title to the bond is transferred but any coupon payments are handed over to the original owner. The repo rate is the rate of interest charged by the lender of funds against the collateral. It is either stated explicitly in the agreement or (in some cases) implied in the difference between the sale and repurchase price. The interest on a dollar or a euro repo is based on the actual term of the repo divided into a 360-day year. (See Chapter 2 for more details on repo.)

In the previous section we worked out that the break-even or 'fair' forward price to deliver an 8.875% coupon US Treasury in 30 days was $134.2766 plus accrued. This was based on the assumption that a long position on the bond could be funded for 30 days at a repo rate of 4.50% per annum.

Suppose, however, that a counterparty is prepared to take delivery of the bond in 30 days at a clean price of $134-10 or $134.3125 plus accrued interest. Instead of using the actual repo rate for funding a 30-day position in the bond to calculate the fair forward price, we can work backwards from the actual forward price at which we could deal and calculate the repo rate that is implied in this price. This is known as the **implied repo rate**. We have the following equation:

Forward Clean Price =

Cash Dirty Price + Funding Cost − Accrued Interest on the Forward Date

We are able to sell the bond forward to the counterparty at a forward clean price of $134.3125. The cash dirty price as before is $136.5594, the bond will be delivered in 30 days and the accrued interest on the bond on that date is $2.7949. Let r be the implied repo rate expressed as a decimal. Inserting these values into the above equation we have:

$$\$134.3125 = \$136.5594 + \left(\$136.5594 \times r \times \frac{30}{360} \right) - 2.7949$$

Rearranging this equation:

$$r = \frac{\$134.3125 - \$136.5594 + \$2.7949}{\$136.5594} \times \frac{360}{30}$$

$$= 4.8155\% \text{ p.a.}$$

The implied repo rate — the repo rate implied in the actual price at which we can sell the bond forward — is 4.8155% per annum. This is a money market rate, quoted on a simple interest basis and using the actual/360 day count convention.

11.9.1 Interpreting the Implied Repo Rate

The rules for interpreting the implied repo rate are simple.

- If the implied repo rate is higher than the actual rate at which a cash bond position can be carried this is a sign that the forward contract is trading above its theoretical fair value. It may be possible to create a profitable cash-and-carry arbitrage by buying the cash bond and simultaneously selling the (overpriced) forward contract. The cost of funding the position at the actual repo rate will be more than offset by the settlement price received for delivering the bond.
- If the implied repo rate is below the actual funding rate via repo this means that the forward price is below the theoretical fair value. It may be possible to create an arbitrage by buying the underpriced forward contract and establishing a short position in the bond.

In practice, what looks like a profitable arbitrage opportunity can sometimes disappear when transaction costs and spreads are factored into the equation.

11.10 THE CHEAPEST TO DELIVER BOND

The conversion factors published by the exchanges are easy to work with but do not provide an exact method for making deliverable bonds comparable to each other. They make certain simplifying assumptions. The CBOT conversion factors are based on a settlement date which is taken to be the first day in the delivery month, although in fact delivery can be on any business day during the month. In addition, the maturity date of a bond is rounded down to the nearest quarter year.

These problems do not apply to the bund futures traded on Eurex, but one serious difficulty remains in the case of all bond futures contracts, the fact that conversion factors are based on pricing all deliverable bonds at the yield of the notional bond underlying the bond futures contract, regardless of maturity. In reality the yield curve tells us that the yields on bonds of different maturities are rarely identical; what is more the shape of the yield curve changes over time. The advantage of the conversion factor calculation is that it is simple. It allows the exchange to calculate and publish conversion factors for deliverable bonds when the contract begins to trade, and they remain constant throughout the life of the contract. This makes it easy to use bond futures for hedging purposes.

The disadvantage of the conversion factor system is that at any one time one of the deliverable bonds tends to provide the greatest profit (or smallest loss) if it is delivered against a short position in the futures contract, compared to the other deliverable bonds. This is known as the **cheapest to deliver** or CTD bond. In practice a bond futures contract tends to behave as if it is a contract on the CTD bond since that is the issue most likely to be delivered against it.

11.10.1 Determining the CTD

The CTD bond can be calculated as the deliverable bond that maximizes the profit or minimizes the loss obtained by:

* selling one futures contract;
* buying the bond in the cash market;
* funding the bond purchase via a repo transaction;
* delivering the bond against the futures contract.

In effect determining the CTD involves calculating theoretical futures prices based on each deliverable bond and then comparing these with the actual futures price. The bond that would maximize the profit or minimize the loss involved in selling the futures contract at its actual price and carrying the bond to deliver against the futures is the CTD.

11.11 CTD CALCULATION: EXAMPLE

In a previous section we worked out a 30-day forward price on the 8.875% coupon US Treasury trading at a clean price of $134.50 in the cash market. At an actual repo funding rate of 4.50% the fair forward price was given by the following calculation:

Forward Clean Price

= Cash Dirty Price + Funding Cost − Accrued Interest on the Forward Date

= $136.5594 + $0.5121 − $2.7949 = $134.2766

Let us suppose this time that we propose carrying the bond via repo and delivering it against a short Treasury bond futures contract. The delivery against the futures will take place in 30 days and the repo rate, as before, is 4.50%. The conversion factor for the bond as published by the exchange is 1.2931. If we are to break even on carrying the bond for delivery against the futures the following equation must hold:

Futures Price × Conversion Factor of Bond to be Delivered =

$$\text{Forward Clean Price of Delivered Bond}$$

Therefore:

$$\text{Futures Price} = \frac{\text{Forward Clean Price of Delivered Bond}}{\text{Bond's Conversion Factor}}$$

We have already calculated the forward clean price of the bond we propose to deliver. It is $134.2766. We know that it has a conversion factor of 1.2931. Therefore:

$$\text{Futures Price} = \frac{\$134.2766}{1.2931} = \$103.8408$$

Or put another way:

Futures Price

$$= \frac{\text{Cash Dirty Price of Bond} + \text{Funding Cost} - \text{Accrued on Delivery}}{\text{Conversion Factor}}$$

$$= \frac{\$136.5594 + \$0.5121 - \$2.7949}{1.2931}$$

$$= \$103.8408$$

11.11.1 Additional Steps

Of course the actual futures price at which we can deal may not be $103.8408. What we have done is simply to calculate what it would have to be for us to break even on carrying one particular bond to deliver against the futures. Suppose that the futures contract is actually trading on the exchange at 103-26, which is $103.8125 in decimal format. The clean price received for delivering our bonds would be:

$$\$103.8125 \times 1.2931 = \$134.2399$$

We know that the break-even clean price for delivering our bonds against the futures is actually $134.2766. Therefore we would lose $0.0367 per $100 through carrying a position in the bonds and arranging to sell them in 30 days through a short futures position. Using this methodology our bond will be the CTD if it is the bond among the list of deliverable securities that loses the least amount of money by carrying it via repo to deliver against a short futures position. It will be the bond with the highest implied repo rate. (Note though that the daily profits and losses on the cash bond and the futures will not necessarily cancel out *during* the 30 day 'carry' period.)

11.12 SELLERS' OPTIONS

In fact it is a fairly common result, to lose money through carrying and delivering cash bonds against bond futures. It can apply even to the CTD bond. This may seem strange, since the fair value of a bond futures is often derived from the cost of carrying a position in the CTD, as follows:

Theoretical Futures Price =

$$\frac{\text{CTD Cash Dirty Price} + \text{Funding Cost} - \text{Accrued on Delivery}}{\text{CTD Conversion Factor}}$$

From this equation it seems that the futures should trade at a price that produces zero profit and loss if we fund a position in the CTD and arrange to sell the bonds by shorting the futures. What the equation ignores is the fact that the seller of bond futures is granted a number of options, which always includes the choice of which eligible bonds to deliver. In the case of US Treasury bond futures and UK gilt futures it also includes the option of which day in the month to deliver bonds. These 'sellers' options' explain why the bond futures contract can trade below the theoretical fair value calculated simply from the cost of carrying the CTD bond. The seller of bond futures has valuable options, and in compensation the buyer demands a slightly lower futures price.

11.13   CTD BEHAVIOUR

As the futures contract approaches expiry, net carry diminishes to zero and the futures price adjusted by the CTD conversion factor should (in theory) converge on the price of the CTD. One problem with this, however, is that the CTD is not always the same bond. When the CTD changes the bond futures will suddenly start to track the new CTD, which makes its behaviour rather unpredictable. It is beyond the scope of this book to explore the CTD behaviour in detail, but one relationship is relatively straightforward, that between the CTD bond and market yields:

- when current market yields are above the coupon of the notional bond in a bond futures contract the CTD will tend to be a long-duration bond with a low coupon and a long maturity;
- when interest rates are low the CTD tends to be a high coupon, shorter-dated bond with lower duration.

To illustrate this effect, Figure 11.1 shows the price of two semi-annual 6.00% coupon bonds for a range of yields from 1% up to 15%. The bonds are identical except that one has 16 years and the other 28 years to maturity. At a yield of 6.00% both bonds trade at par. At yields below 6% the shorter-duration bond is the cheaper of the two, and at yields above 6% the longer-duration bond is the cheaper of the two.

11.14   HEDGING WITH BOND FUTURES

Bond futures are used by bond traders, interest rate derivatives traders, commercial banks, corporations, pension funds, mutual funds, insurance companies and money managers. Each user has specific trading and risk management goals. These might include:

- protecting the value of portfolio assets;
- limiting opportunity losses;
- enhancing the returns on portfolios.

The first two objectives can be achieved through a variety of hedging strategies. For example, a pension fund manager holding a portfolio of US Treasury bonds may be

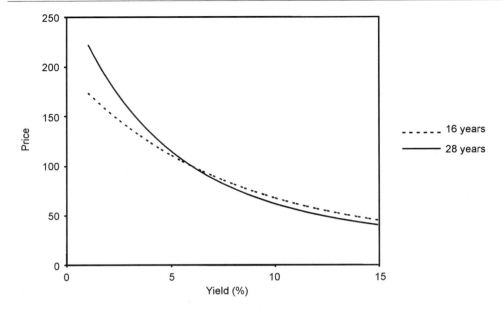

Figure 11.1 Price/yield curve for two bonds with different maturities

anticipating a rise in interest rates. If rates do rise the value of the portfolio will decline. To protect the value of the assets the manager sells US Treasury bond futures. If interest rates rise the profit on the futures position helps to offset losses on the cash bonds.

11.14.1 Hedging CTD Bonds: Example

Let us suppose that a portfolio manager holds $10 million of the current cheapest to deliver Treasury bond and is concerned about rising interest rates. The bond is in fact the 8.875% coupon Treasury we used to illustrate the forward and futures price calculations in the previous sections. It is trading at $134.50 clean. It is the current CTD with a conversion factor of 1.2931. The portfolio manager decides to short against this the near-dated Treasury bond future which is trading at $103-26 or $103.8125 per $100 nominal.

The manager might consider selling 100 CBOT Treasury bond futures contracts with a total nominal value of $10 million. In fact this is not quite correct since in theory every one tick move in the futures price will be associated with a 1.2931 tick move in the CTD bond price. This is because in the calculation of the theoretical fair value of the futures contract we use the CTD bond's conversion factor:

Theoretical Futures Price =

$$\frac{\text{CTD Cash Dirty Price} + \text{Funding Cost} - \text{Accrued on Delivery}}{\text{Conversion Factor of CTD}}$$

Therefore the change (Δ) in the futures price should match changes in the CTD price divided by the conversion factor of the CTD:

$$\Delta\text{Futures Price} = \frac{\Delta\text{CTD Price}}{\text{CTD Conversion Factor}}$$

In our example it requires a change of 1.2931 ticks in the CTD bond to produce a change in the theoretical fair value of the futures of one tick. The manager therefore has to sell a slightly increased number of contracts:

$$\frac{\$10\text{ million}}{\$100,000} \times 1.2931 = 129 \text{ contracts (rounded)}$$

11.14.2   Performance of the Hedge

Suppose that soon after the hedge is put in place the bond price falls from \$134.50 to \$133.50 in decimal terms (a loss of 32 ticks) in response to rising interest rates. On the \$10 million value of the portfolio this represents a loss of:

$$-0.01 \times \$10 \text{ million} = -\$100,000$$

In theory the futures price should change by less than the 32 tick move in the price of the CTD:

$$\frac{32}{1.2931} = 25 \text{ ticks}$$

The tick value on the bond futures contract is \$31.25. On a short position in 129 futures a 25 tick price change would generate a profit of:

$$25 \text{ ticks} \times 129 \times \$31.25 = \$100,781$$

11.15   BASIS RISK

In practice the hedge will normally tend to work fairly well in the type of case just considered, because the futures contract will closely track the CTD bond. Any inaccuracy in the hedge will primarily be due to the fact that the number of futures traded has to be rounded, and the fact that traded prices are rounded to the nearest tick. What dealers call the **basis risk** — the risk that the cash and the futures price may not move by the same amount — is relatively small. There remains of course the risk that the CTD bond may change over the period and the manager's cash and futures positions will cease to track each other closely. In addition, the efficiency of the hedge will be affected by timing decisions on when to sell the futures and when to close out the position.

The hedge ratio we used to determine the number of futures contracts that have to be sold to hedge the CTD bond was as follows:

$$\text{Hedge Ratio} = \frac{\text{Nominal Value of Portfolio}}{\text{Contract Nominal Value}} \times \text{Conversion Factor of CTD}$$

Conversion factors approximate the relative price sensitivities of cash bonds in relation to the futures contract. For example, a conversion factor of 1.2931 means that the price sensitivity of the CTD cash bond is roughly 129% that of the futures contract:

$$\Delta \text{CTD Bond Price} \cong \Delta \text{Futures Price} \times \text{CTD Conversion Factor}$$

Because this relationship holds we can use the conversion factor to determine the hedge ratio — how many futures contracts must be sold to offset the losses on a CTD cash bond position. If the conversion factor were two the cash bond would be twice as volatile as the futures contract in terms of its price sensitivity. Therefore two futures contracts would have to be sold for every $100,000 nominal of the cash bond.

The hedging methodology we have used has its limitations when the portfolio of bonds to be hedged consists of non-CTD bonds. Futures contracts track most closely the price changes in the CTD. The hedge ratio we used was based on the assumption that we are hedging the CTD; the calculation uses the conversion factor of the CTD and will fail to make the correct adjustment for the different price sensitivity of a non-CTD bond.

11.16 HEDGING NON-CTD BONDS

A way to describe the relationship between price changes in the CTD and price changes in non-CTD bonds is to bring in the concept of the price value of a basis point (PVBP). PVBP measures the change in the dollar value of a bond for a one basis point change in yield. The following relationship should hold:

$$\text{PVBP Futures} = \frac{\text{PVBP CTD}}{\text{CTD Conversion Factor}}$$

If we own a portfolio of non-CTD bonds the following relationship should hold between the price sensitivity of the bonds in the portfolio and the price sensitivity of the futures contracts:

$$\frac{\text{PVBP Portfolio}}{\text{PVBP Futures}} = \frac{\text{PVBP Portfolio}}{\text{PVBP CTD/CTD Conversion Factor}}$$

Or rearranged:

$$\frac{\text{PVBP Portfolio}}{\text{PVBP Futures}} = \frac{\text{PVBP Portfolio}}{\text{PVBP of CTD}} \times \text{Conversion Factor of CTD}$$

A commonly used hedge ratio calculation for hedging non-CTD bonds with bond futures is based on this reasoning:

$$\text{Hedge Ratio} =$$

$$\frac{\text{Nominal Value of Portfolio}}{\text{Contract Nominal Value}} \times \frac{\text{PVBP Portfolio}}{\text{PVBP of CTD}} \times \text{Conversion Factor of CTD}$$

11.16.1   Hedging non-CTD Bonds: Example

Suppose that the portfolio to be hedged consists of $10 million nominal value of the 6.125% Treasury maturing on 15 August 2029. We use a bond calculator to estimate PVBP for the bonds and the CTD bonds which the futures will track.

- The PVBP of the bonds to be hedged is estimated at $0.1429 per $100 nominal — for a one basis point change in yield the bond will change in value by approximately 14.29 cents per $100 nominal.
- The CTD is the 8.875% Treasury with a conversion factor of 1.2931. The PVBP of the CTD is estimated at $0.1299 — for a one basis point change in yield the bond will change in value by approximately 12.99 cents per $100 nominal.

The number of US Treasury bond futures that should be sold to hedge the portfolio is therefore:

$$\frac{\$10 \text{ million}}{\$100,000} \times \frac{\$0.1429}{\$0.1299} \times 1.2931 = 142$$

If we were hedging the CTD bond we would short 129 futures. However, in this case the bonds we are hedging are more sensitive to changes in yield than the CTD (and hence the bond futures) so we have to increase the number of futures contracts in our hedge.

11.17   OTHER USES OF BOND FUTURES

A trader or portfolio manager can buy futures to lock in a purchase price for a bond in anticipation of receiving cash in the future.

Suppose that a portfolio plans to invest $10 million in the current CTD in one month's time. This is the 8.875% Treasury with a conversion factor of 1.2931. The manager is concerned that falling yields will drive up the bond price over the next few weeks and wishes to lock in a purchase price today by buying CBOT Treasury bond futures. The hedge ratio we used for hedging CTD bonds will calculate the number of futures to buy:

$$\text{Hedge Ratio} = \frac{\text{Nominal Value of Portfolio}}{\text{Contract Size}} \times \text{Conversion Factor of CTD}$$

The manager should buy 129 contracts. If the bonds to be purchased are non-CTD bonds then the manager has to adjust for the specific price risk on the bonds to be purchased relative to the futures contracts.

11.17.1   Asset Allocation

Many portfolio managers look to asset allocation as a means of achieving returns above the market benchmark. Financial futures provide a quick and efficient means of adjusting the proportion of assets held in shares, bonds and cash. Compared to cash market transactions the brokerage fees on futures are low, transaction times are short and relatively large trades can be executed without major impact.

Suppose a UK fund manager runs a portfolio worth £100 million split 70% in UK shares and 30% in gilts. The FT-SE 100 index is currently at a level of 6000. The manager anticipates a fall in the stock market and wishes to increase the proportion of the fund held in bonds to around 40%. One alternative is to sell shares and use the proceeds to buy bonds. However this is expensive in terms of brokerage, and the portfolio manager would also like the flexibility of being able to move quickly back into the equity market if a recovery starts.

The current CTD is the 6.25% gilt maturing on 25 November 2010 with a conversion factor of 0.9505874 trading at par. Assuming that the manager wishes to establish a long position on £10 million nominal of the CTD he or she should buy:

$$\frac{£10 \text{ million}}{£100,000} \times 0.9505874 = 95 \text{ long gilt futures}$$

If the portfolio manager wishes to establish a position in another bond the number of futures contracts should be increased or reduced by the ratio of the PVBP of the bond over the PVBP of the CTD.

11.17.2   Shorting the Equity Market

The next step is to establish the equivalent of a short position on £10 million worth of shares that tracks the FT-SE index. This is implemented by selling FT-SE futures contracts. (See Chapter 14 for more details on equity futures.) The point value on the major FT-SE futures contract traded on LIFFE is £10 per full index point. So the nominal value of each FT-SE futures contract when the cash index is trading at 6000 is:

$$6000 \times £10 = \$60,000$$

Therefore the portfolio manager must sell approximately 167 FT-SE futures contracts:

$$\frac{£10 \text{ million}}{£60,000} = 167 \text{ contracts}$$

In the case of traditional 'buy side' portfolio managers the futures would normally be used only as a temporary asset allocation mechanism, allowing the manager time to physically sell the shares and buy the bonds in the cash market. Alternatively, the manager might use the futures to make the switch quickly and then decide later whether to make it permanent or restore the original asset allocation.

On the other hand 'long–short' hedge funds are prepared to take long or short positions in futures simply to implement their market view or their judgement on the relative values of two financial assets. A hedge fund manager, for example, could buy gilt futures and short US Treasury bond futures if he or she thought that UK interest rates had not yet reached their low point, whereas yields in the US were set to rise again from recent lows.

11.18   CHAPTER SUMMARY

A bond futures contract is an agreement made through an organized exchange to deliver or take delivery of a fixed nominal amount of a notional bond on a fixed date in the future, or between a range of future dates. The 30-year US Treasury bond future traded on the CBOT is one of the most actively traded contracts in the world. Each contract is based on $100,000 par value of a notional US Treasury with a 6% coupon. The seller decides which day in the delivery month to deliver bonds and receive the invoiced amount. The seller also decides which bonds to deliver. The exchange publishes a list of conversion factors designed to adjust for the different values of the deliverable bonds. The invoiced amount is the futures price adjusted by the bond's conversion factor plus accrued interest on the bond up to the delivery date. Long gilt futures traded on LIFFE are very similar to 30-year US Treasury bond futures. Bund futures traded on Eurex differ in that there is only one delivery day in the delivery month. Bond future positions are guaranteed by the clearing house and are subject to margin procedures. The theoretical or 'fair' price for delivering a bond on a future date can be established through a 'cash-and-carry' argument. This establishes a break-even price for delivering the bond from the cost of buying the bond in the cash market plus the net cost of carrying the position for future delivery, funded via repo. The cheapest to deliver bond is the bond that is cheapest to deliver against a short position in bond futures. It has the highest implied repo rate. The CTD is not always the same bond, and it changes in response to factors such as market yields. Bond futures can be used to hedge bond portfolios. If the bonds to be hedged are not the CTD bonds then the hedge ratio has to be adjusted using a price risk measure such as PVBP. Bond futures can also be used to change a fund's asset allocations by overlaying positions in bonds with positions in futures contracts.

Interest Rate Swaps

...where an open communication is preserved among nations, it is impossible but the domestic industry of every one must receive an encrease from the improvements of the other.

David Hume

12.1 CHAPTER OVERVIEW

In this chapter we consider one of the fundamental tools of the modern capital markets, the interest rate swap. A standard or 'plain vanilla' interest rate swap is an agreement to exchange regular cash flows on regular payment dates. The swap has two legs. One is based on a fixed rate of interest, and the return leg is based on a floating or variable rate of interest. We look at how the payments on the swap are calculated and netted out against each other. We consider the trading and hedging applications of interest rate swaps for corporate borrowers and institutional investors, and issues relating to the credit or default risk on swaps. Nowadays the market for swaps is extremely competitive and dealers working for major banks stand ready to quote two-way swap prices in a wide variety of currencies for a range of maturity dates (up to 30 years and beyond) and with different payment frequencies. We look at how dealers quote swap rates either as outright fixed rates or in terms of a spread over the yield on government bonds. The spread is determined by the credit risk on swap transactions and also by supply and demand factors. Many issuers of fixed coupon bonds use swaps to switch their liabilities to a floating rate basis. We consider why this should be the case and where the benefits lie. Finally we look at cross-currency swaps, in which the payments are made in two different currencies.

12.2 SWAP DEFINITIONS

A swap is a contract between two parties:

- agreeing to exchange cash flows;
- on regular future dates;
- where the two payment legs are calculated on a different basis.

A swap is a bilateral over-the-counter agreement directly negotiated between two parties, at least one of which is normally a bank or other financial institution. A swap agreement once made cannot be freely traded, but on the other hand the contract can be tailored to meet the specific needs of a particular counterparty. Traditionally swaps were dealt without a central counterparty acting as guarantor. This means that both sides have counterparty risk — the risk that the other party to the deal might default on its obligations. One side or both may ask for collateral or seek to change some of the terms of the contract in order to protect itself against default risk. The level of default risk varies greatly on swaps, however. In many swap agreements the notional principal is never exchanged and is not at risk. In addition, starting in September 1999 the London Clearing House (LCH) now offers a service called **SwapClear** under which it will act as central counterparty to bilaterally negotiated swap transactions.

A payment leg on a swap may be based on a rate of interest, an equity index or the price of a physical commodity such as oil. In an **interest rate swap** both payment legs are based on a rate of interest applied to a notional principal sum of money. Normally one rate is fixed and the other is a variable or floating rate of interest linked to a key money market reference rate such as the London Interbank Offered Rate (LIBOR).

Basis Swap

In some swap contracts both payment legs are linked to a floating rate of interest but each is calculated on a different basis. For example, one payment leg might be linked to dollar LIBOR and the other to the yield on US commercial paper. This type of transaction is known as a **basis swap**.

A **cross-currency swap** is a deal in which the payments between the two parties are made in two different currencies. The payments can either be linked to a fixed or a floating rate of interest. Note that a cross-currency swap is a different type of deal from the FX swap contract which we encountered in Chapter 3. A cross-currency swap is an agreement to exchange regular cash flows in two different currencies on regular dates. An FX or forward swap is an agreement to exchange two currencies for one value date (usually spot) and to re-exchange the two currencies on a later date.

12.3   BASIC INTEREST RATE SWAP

The most common type of interest rate swap (IRS) is a fixed/floating swap in which payments are made in arrears and netted out against each other. Let us suppose that party A and party B enter into an interest rate swap transaction. The swap will start on the spot date.

- **Fixed Rate Payer**. A agrees to pay B a fixed rate of 6.00% per annum on a notional £100 million at the end of each year for the next three years.
- **Fixed Rate Receiver**. B receives the fixed rate and in return agrees to pay A a floating rate of interest annually in arrears for three years. This is based on 12-month sterling LIBOR on the same notional principal.

The maturity or **tenor** of the swap is therefore three years. There are three payment dates: one year after spot; two years after spot; and three years after spot. The payment legs due on each payment date are illustrated in Figure 12.1.

12.3.1   First Payment Date

The notional principal is never exchanged in the deal, it exists simply to calculate the annual exchange of cash. The payment legs on the swap are netted out against each other and one party pays the difference between the two interest amounts to the other.

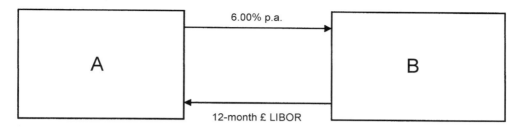

Figure 12.1   Payment diagram for interest rate swap

The first payment due on the swap will occur one year after the contract starts. In fact the LIBOR rate for this first period will be known on the date the swap contract is agreed and will be fixed in the contract. Let us suppose that it is fixed at 5.85% per annum. One year after the start date A will owe B 6.00% applied to the notional principal of £100 million. In return B will owe A 5.85% applied to the notional principal. The payments and receipts from A's perspective are as follows:

> Fixed Rate Payment = £100 million × 0.06 = −£6 million
>
> Floating Rate Receipt = £100 million × 0.0585 = +£5.85 million
>
> Net Payment = −£150,000

Therefore A pays over to B a net £150,000 one year after the swap start date.

12.3.2   Second and Third Payment Dates

There are two further payments due on the swap based on the difference between the fixed rate of 6.00% and the LIBOR rate for the payment period. When the year one payment is made the LIBOR rate for the second period will be re-fixed at whatever the British Bankers' Association's 12-month LIBOR rate happens to be at that point. Let us suppose that it is re-fixed at 6.10% per annum for the second year of the swap. This will determine the payments that are due at the end of year two. The payments and receipts from A's perspective are as follows:

> Fixed Rate Payment = £100 million × 0.06 = −£6 million
>
> Floating Rate Receipt = £100 million × 0.0610 = +£6,100,000
>
> Net Receipt = £100,000

The LIBOR rate for the third and final payment in the sequence will be re-fixed at the end of year two. This will determine the final payment or receipt due three years after the start of the swap. Since the swap had a maturity or tenor of exactly three years it will simply expire after the third payment is made. As we noted, the notional is not exchanged at the outset or at maturity. Figure 12.2 illustrates the sequence of payment dates on the swap deal.

Figure 12.2   Payments due on three-year annual swap

12.4   SWAP AS CASH PLUS FORWARD DEALS

Another way to look at the swap we have just described is as a package of spot and forward interest rate transactions. There are three components in the package: a cash market deal plus two forward deals. The swap consists of:

- an agreement to make a payment in one year based on the difference between 6.00% and the cash market one-year LIBOR rate;
- an agreement to make a payment in two years based on the difference between 6.00% and the forward LIBOR rate for the one-year period starting in one year;
- an agreement to make a payment in three years based on the difference between 6.00% and the forward LIBOR rate for the one-year period starting in two years.

12.4.1   Terminology and Documentation

Some market participants talk about the **fixed rate payer** and the **fixed rate receiver** on a swap deal. In our example A is the payer of the fixed leg and B is the receiver of fixed. Others would describe A as the **buyer** of the swap and B as the **seller**. Most swap contracts conform to standard documentation prepared by the International Swaps & Derivatives Association (ISDA). The two parties negotiate a master legal agreement using the ISDA terms and then any subsequent swap transactions are covered by this contract. This means that deals (at least standardized deals) can be transacted quickly by specifying the terms (fixed rate, maturity, payment frequency, etc.) and stipulating that they are covered by the master agreement.

12.4.2   Fixing Borrowing Costs

Why would either party enter into the swap deal we have just described? Banks and corporates use swaps to manage their interest rate exposures. Many banks also make markets in swaps and as such are prepared to quote two-way prices to potential counterparties.

In the example we described A is paying fixed on the swap and receiving LIBOR in return. This is a typical application for a corporate borrower. We will suppose that A has a three-year £100 million loan on which it pays a variable interest rate of 12-month LIBOR + 75 basis points. As Figure 12.3 illustrates, by overlaying this liability with the swap transaction the company effectively changes from a floating to a fixed rate obligation. The net cost of borrowing is fixed at 6.75% — the 6.00% swap rate plus the 0.75% spread over LIBOR on the loan.

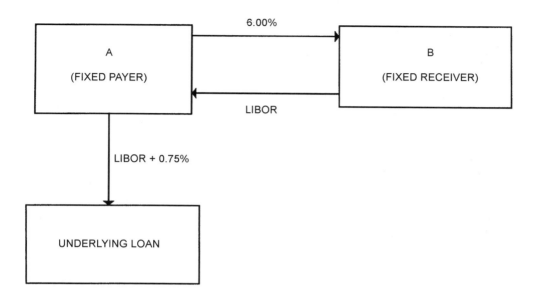

Figure 12.3   Using a swap to fix borrowing costs

12.5   TYPICAL SWAP APPLICATIONS

Interest rate swaps can be used to take directional views on interest rates. For example, a speculator who believes that rates will rise beyond market forecasts could pay fixed and receive floating on an interest rate swap. If interest rates do rise as predicted the speculator will benefit from cash payments representing the difference between the fixed rate and the (higher) floating rates of interest. However, many applications of swaps are concerned with hedging exposures to changes or fluctuations in interest rates. Since interest rate swaps are legal contracts directly negotiated between two parties, the terms can be extremely flexible. A dealer will adjust the swap payment dates and the notional principal amount to match the requirements of a hedger. We have set out four typical hedging applications below.

- **Case 1: Fixing a Borrowing Rate**. A company has borrowed funds on a floating rate basis but is concerned that interest rates will rise. Solution: the company enters into an interest rate swap with a bank paying fixed and receiving LIBOR. If interest rates do rise and LIBOR moves above the fixed rate on the swap the firm will receive net payments from the bank. This compensates the company for the increasing cost of borrowing. Alternatively the company can go back to the bank and agree to terminate the swap. If interest rates have risen sharply it will receive a substantial close-out payment.
- **Case 2: Asset Swap**. An investor would like to achieve a return linked to dollar money market interest rates. However money dealers will only pay LIBOR minus 1/16%. Solution: the investor enters into an asset swap transaction. This consists of buying a fixed coupon bond and entering into an interest rate swap to pay a fixed

rate and receive in return a floating rate of interest linked to LIBOR. Depending on the yield on the bond and on current swap fixed rates the investor may be able to achieve a net return above LIBOR on this package deal.

- **Case 3: Asset–Liability Management**. A bank is offering fixed rate mortgages to borrowers but funds itself primarily through short-term deposits. If interest rates rise it will pay more in funding than it is receiving in interest payments on the mortgage loans. This is a classic asset–liability management (ALM) problem for a lending bank. The bank's assets (its loan book) are misaligned with its liabilities (its funding). Solution: the bank enters into an interest rate swap in which it pays away the fixed receipts from the mortgage holders and receives in return a floating or variable rate of interest which it can use to service its borrowings.
- **Case 4: Switching to a Fixed Return**. A money market depositor is concerned that interest rates look set to remain at low levels for a number of years ahead and may in fact decline even further in a low inflation environment. Solution: the investor enters an interest rate swap to receive fixed and pay floating. The investor has locked into a fixed rate of interest and will not lose out as a result of declining money market rates.

12.6   INTEREST RATE SWAP: DETAILED CASE STUDY

The basic swap example we used previously to illustrate the nature of the swap transaction was somewhat simplified in that we did not take into account different interest rate conventions and day counting methodologies. It was also based on 12-monthly payments, which is relatively uncommon. In this section we explore a more detailed hedging application of interest rate swaps in which the appropriate conventions for calculating the payment legs on the swap are applied.

The case is that of a US company with debt of $300 million with five years remaining until maturity. The interest rate is set every six months on 6 June and 6 December at six-month US dollar LIBOR plus a 0.85% credit margin. The Chief Finance Officer (CFO) is concerned that interest rates may be set to increase from their recent historical lows. Any increase in borrowing costs would have to be passed on to customers, making the company's products less competitive in the marketplace. Alternatively, the company would have to absorb the rise in the cost of borrowing itself, which would erode its profit margins and affect the share price.

12.6.1   Swap Agreement

To protect the company from the expected rise in interest rates the CFO enters into a standard interest rate swap with a dealer. The terms of the contract are set out in Table 12.1.

The company has agreed to pay a fixed rate of 5.50% per annum on $300 million to the dealer for five years. This is payable in arrears in two semi-annual instalments. The accrued interest calculation is the same as that used with US Treasury bonds — that is, it uses the actual/actual day counting convention. (See Chapter 4 for more details on Treasury bonds.)

In exchange the swap dealer will pay the company six-month dollar LIBOR on $300 million in arrears every six months for five years, whatever the LIBOR setting for a

Table 12.1 Swap agreement: pay fixed, receive floating

Nominal amount:	$300 million
Trade date:	4 June 2001
Start or effective date:	6 June 2001
Maturity date:	6 June 2006
Fixed rate:	5.50% semi-annual actual/actual
Floating rate:	Six-month $ LIBOR actual/360
First floating fix:	5.32%

given period turns out to be. The accrued interest calculation is the one applied in the US money markets and with Eurodollar deposits — it uses an actual/360 convention. (See Chapter 2 for details on money market conventions.) Only the difference between the fixed and floating legs will be paid, either by the company or by the swap dealer. Swap cash flows are usually netted out wherever possible to reduce settlement risk — the risk that the other party might not make its return payment.

The trade date when the deal is agreed is Monday 4 June 2001. The LIBOR rate for the first six-month payment period starting 6 June 2001 is already known on the trade date since it is announced by the British Bankers' Association two business days before spot. In this case it has been fixed at 5.32% per annum. The swap starts on 6 June; that is the day on which interest begins to accrue on each payment leg.

12.6.2 First Payment Date

The first payment, for the first six-monthly (183-day) period 6 June–6 December 2001 will be paid in arrears on 6 December 2001.

The company's payment is:

$$\$300 \text{ million} \times \frac{0.055}{2} = \$8.25 \text{ million}$$

The swap dealer's payment is:

$$\$300 \text{ million} \times 0.0532 \times \frac{183}{360} = \$8.113 \text{ million}$$

The company pays the difference $8.25 million − $8.113 million = $137,000.

12.6.3 Second Payment Date

The next payment on the swap is for the 182-day period from 6 December 2001 to 6 June 2002. This is due in arrears on 6 June 2002.

The LIBOR rate for this second payment period will be set on 4 December 2001. Let us assume that the company's CFO was right about sharply rising interest rates and six-month LIBOR for this period is re-fixed at 5.70% per annum. Then the company's payment on the swap is still fixed at $8.25 million. The swap dealer's payment will be:

$$\$300 \text{ million} \times 0.057 \times \frac{182}{360} = \$8.645 \text{ million}$$

So the dealer pays the difference $395,000 on 6 June 2002.

12.6.4 Swap Payments and the Yield Curve

Since the swap is semi-annual and has an original maturity of five years there will be 10 payment dates. The first as we have seen is due on 6 December 2001. The final payment is due on 6 June 2006. Companies entering into swap transactions to change the nature of underlying liabilities will normally seek to arrange the swap payment dates to coincide with the dates on which interest is due on their borrowings.

In this example the first payment is from the company to the swap dealer. This is typical in a positive yield curve environment, which builds in expectations of future increases in interest rates. The positive first cash flow gives the swap dealer a small cushion against its exposure to rising interest rates. The overall 'winner' over the five-year maturity of the swap will depend on whether interest rate rises are greater than or less than the expectations built into the curve. (For details of how to derive forward interest rates from a yield curve see Chapter 6.) In practice though the swap dealer will tend to hedge out most if not all of the interest rate risk on the deal.

12.6.5 Net Result of the Swap

The company's net position including the swap deal is illustrated in Figure 12.4.

The net cost of borrowing for the company after the swap is approximately:

$$5.50\% + 0.85\% = 6.35\% \text{ p.a.}$$

This is very close to the true answer, although it ignores the different accrued interest calculations in the swap contract. The LIBOR payments in the case are calculated from

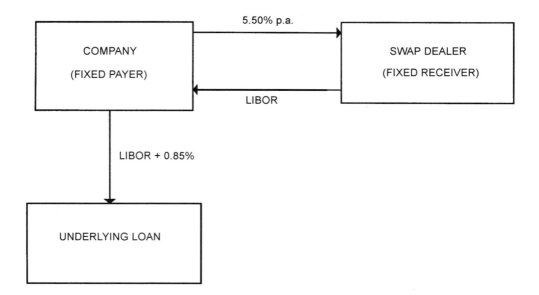

Figure 12.4 Company's net borrowing cost with the swap

six-month LIBOR using an actual/360 day count method. The fixed payments are also semi-annual but based on an actual/actual day count convention. The LIBORs in Figure 12.4 simply cancel out but the company also pays a spread of 85 basis points over LIBOR. We know that the actual/360 method understates the interest rate payment. To convert this to an actual/actual convention we have to multiply by 365 and divide by 360. The result can then be added directly to the 5.50% fixed rate to calculate the all-in cost of funding to the company:

$$\text{Spread in Actual/Actual Basis} = 0.85\% \times 365/360 = 0.86\%$$
$$\text{All-in Funding Cost} = 5.50\% + 0.86\% = 6.36\% \text{ p.a.}$$

The company has effectively changed the nature of its interest rate payments over the period of the swap from a floating rate of LIBOR + 0.85% to a fixed rate of 6.36% per annum.

12.7 STANDARD SWAP TERMS

The swap we have just considered is a standard, plain vanilla contract. It has the following characteristics:

- one party pays a fixed interest rate and the other a floating rate;
- the notional principal is not exchanged;
- the notional principal remains constant over the life of the swap;
- the fixed rate is constant over the life of the swap;
- the floating rate is LIBOR flat (i.e. exactly LIBOR) and is set in advance of each payment period;
- fixed and floating payments are due on exactly the same dates;
- payments are netted out and one payment is made in arrears at the end of each payment period.

The swap has a typical maturity at five years. Other common maturities are one, two, three, four, seven and 10 years. There has been a trend in recent times towards longer maturity deals, with 30 years and even more not uncommon. Payment periods can be annual, semi-annual or quarterly, though the bulk of US dollar swaps have semi-annual or quarterly payments. Other day counting conventions may be used in the calculation of accrued interest. For example, the fixed rate on a dollar swap may be based on the 30/360 convention used in some bond markets. In this convention each month has exactly 30 days and a year has 360 days (see Chapter 4). Alternatively both the fixed and the floating rate may be quoted in the actual/360 money market convention. In the case of sterling swaps the floating leg calculation is often based on the actual/365 convention used in the sterling money markets.

12.8 COMPARATIVE ADVANTAGE

If there is a difference between the relative costs of funding in the fixed bond market and the floating rate market this can be exploited through an interest rate swap. To see why this is so we will consider the case of Megacorp, a major multinational corporation with an AAA credit rating and a household name. The company needs to borrow $500 million over a five-year maturity. Its choices are to issue an annual coupon dollar Eurobond or raise the funds on a floating rate basis. It would prefer a floating rate commitment, to obtain a balance between the amount of fixed and variable rate debt it has outstanding on its balance sheet. Megacorp's likely borrowing costs are as follows — the company's strength allows it to issue low coupon bonds or borrow at LIBOR flat:

Megacorp borrowing costs	
Issue a fixed rate Eurobond:	Annual coupon rate 6.50%
Borrow on a floating basis:	Six-month LIBOR

Midicorp on the other hand is somewhat smaller but still a substantial and well-regarded business. It too needs to borrow $500 million over a five-year time horizon. However it would prefer a fixed interest rate commitment, given the concerns it has that increases in interest rates would affect the profitability of the business. It too has the choice of issuing fixed rate bonds or borrowing at a variable rate. Its likely borrowing costs are as follows — the higher costs compared to Megacorp reflect a lower credit rating:

Midicorp borrowing costs	
Issue a fixed rate Eurobond:	Annual coupon rate 7.50%
Borrow on a floating basis:	Six-month LIBOR + 0.60%

12.8.1   Funding Decision and Swap Agreement

Despite their funding preferences the two companies start by raising money in precisely the way they would prefer not to. Megacorp issues fixed coupon Eurobonds and Midicorp borrows on a floating rate basis linked to LIBOR. The two companies then contact a swap dealer who acts as an intermediary. The agreed terms for the swap transactions are as follows.

- The swap dealer will pay Megacorp 6.61% semi-annually in return for six-month LIBOR flat; the notional is $500 million and the maturity is five years.
- The dealer will receive 6.66% semi-annually from Midicorp and pay in return six-month dollar LIBOR flat; the notional is $500 million and the maturity is five years.

The swap fixed rates are quoted on a semi-annual bond basis (SABB) and the floating payments are quoted on a semi-annual money market basis (SAMMB) using the actual/360 convention. The net positions of both companies after the swap transactions are shown in Figure 12.5.

12.8.2   Result of the Swap Transactions

It seems that through this set of transactions 'everyone is a winner'. (We will ignore for the moment the fact that the interest rates in Figure 12.5 are quoted using a variety of different conventions.)

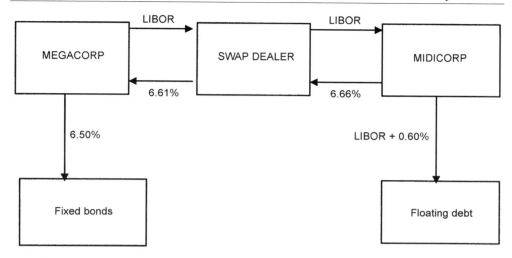

Figure 12.5 Swapping liabilities

- The net cost of borrowing to Megacorp is LIBOR + 6.50% − 6.61% which is LIBOR minus 11 basis points. This is 11 basis points better than the company could have achieved by borrowing in the floating rate market at LIBOR flat.
- The net cost of borrowing to Midicorp is LIBOR + 0.60% − LIBOR + 6.66% which is 7.26%. This is 24 basis points better than the company could have achieved by issuing a Eurobond with a coupon of 7.50%.
- The net benefit to the swap dealer for acting as an intermediary is five basis points per annum over the life of the swap transactions.

How can it be that everyone gains? The standard explanation for this is posed in terms of **comparative advantage**. Megacorp has an absolute advantage over Midicorp in its cost of funding in both the fixed rate and the floating rate market. It has a higher credit rating. However its relative advantage is greater in the fixed rate Eurobond market. The Eurobond market tends to be very 'name driven'—many buyers like issuers they are already familiar with—and some institutional investors can only invest in paper with a top credit rating. To tempt the bond investors Midicorp would have to pay a 7.50% coupon, a full 100 basis points more than Megacorp. On the other hand the floating rate market is prepared to lend to Midicorp at only 60 basis points more than the rate for Megacorp. The figures are set out in Table 12.2.

Table 12.2 Funding rates and credit spreads

Borrower	Fixed rate	Floating rate
Megacorp	6.50%	LIBOR
Midicorp	7.50%	LIBOR + 60
Spread	100 basis points	60 basis points

12.8.3 Exploiting the Different Credit Spreads

The discrepancy between the fixed and floating rate spreads in Table 12.2 is 40 basis points. This discrepancy in the relative perception of credit risk between the fixed and the floating debt market is exploited through the swap transactions. As a result of its swap deal Megacorp ends up borrowing at 11 basis points less than it would have done if it had borrowed in the floating market in the first place. Midicorp ends up borrowing fixed at 24 basis points less than it would have done had it issued a fixed rate bond in the first place. The swap dealer makes five basis points.

The sum of these various 'gains' adds up to the 40 basis point discrepancy between the credit spreads. It makes sense for Megacorp to borrow in the market in which it has the greater relative advantage (the fixed bond market). It then swaps its payments with Midicorp via the swap market and exploits the 40 basis points discrepancy.

12.8.4 Does Everyone Really Gain?

This is a complex argument and it is outwith the scope of this introductory volume to enter into the controversy in detail. One objection to the argument that 'everyone gains' from swapping liabilities is that while Megacorp and Midicorp have reduced their cost of funding this is achieved at the expense of acquiring counterparty risk on the swap transactions. Perhaps the two effects simply cancel out? In addition, there are costs associated with entering the swap deals. There are transaction costs and legal costs, but there may also be other hidden costs. For example it may be that the fixed coupon bond issued by Megacorp has an embedded call feature which allows the issuer to 'call' the bond back early and replace it with cheaper debt. But if Megacorp calls the bond early it may also have to unwind the offsetting swap transaction at some penalty.

12.9 CALCULATING ALL-IN GAINS

It may seem rather inequitable in the case that the smaller company Midicorp has gained more out of the deal than the multinational Megacorp. In fact to calculate the 'gains' more accurately we would have to make adjustments for the different interest rate conventions employed. In the case of Megacorp we will convert all the rates to semi-annual money market basis since it wishes to pay a rate of interest linked to six-month LIBOR. In the case of Midicorp we will convert all the rates to annual bond basis since its preferred funding method at the outset was via a fixed coupon Eurobond. To convert between annual and semi-annual rates we use the following equation:

$$1 + r_{\mathrm{a}} = \left(1 + \frac{r_{\mathrm{sa}}}{2}\right)^2$$

where:

r_{a} = rate of interest with annual compounding
r_{sa} = rate of interest with semi-annual compounding

To convert from a money market rate quoted using the actual/360 convention to a bond market rate we multiply by 365 and divide by 360. To convert from a bond rate to an actual/360 rate we divide by 365 and multiply by 360.

Megacorp's all-in funding cost is therefore calculated as follows.

- The firm pays a coupon rate of 6.50% on an annual bond basis. This equals 6.40% on a semi-annual bond basis. This is equivalent to 6.31% on a semi-annual money market basis.
- It receives a fixed swap rate of 6.61% on a semi-annual bond basis. This equals 6.52% on a semi-annual money market basis. In return it pays six-month LIBOR.
- Its net cost of borrowing is six-month LIBOR minus 21 basis points on a semi-annual money market basis. It has lowered its borrowing costs by 21 basis points.

Midicorp's all-in funding cost is calculated as follows.

- The company borrows at LIBOR plus 0.60% on a semi-annual money market basis. The company will receive six-month LIBOR on the swap. The remaining 0.60% spread equals roughly 0.61% on a semi-annual bond basis ($0.60 \times 365/360 = 0.61$).
- It pays 6.66% on the swap on a semi-annual bond basis. To this we add the 0.61% spread over LIBOR to obtain a total of 7.27% on a semi-annual bond basis.
- Its net cost of borrowing is 7.27% semi-annual which is 7.40% on an annual bond basis. It has lowered its borrowing costs by 10 basis points.

12.9.1   Profit for the Swap Dealer

Meantime, the swap dealer makes five basis points per annum on a semi-annual basis for five years. On a notional of $500 million this represents a net cash flow due every six months of $125,000. At a discount rate of 6.61% the present value is about $1,050,000. This is not of course a risk-free profit, since the swap transactions carry counterparty risk. The dealer may decide to take out protection against this risk, or the bank's internal credit specialists may take a slice of the dealer's profit to take over and manage the counterparty risk.

12.10   SWAP QUOTATIONS

In the early days of the swap market large corporates entered into swap agreements directly with each other. This exposed them to credit risk on their counterparty. It was also difficult to find a counterparty with matching requirements in terms of currency, principal amount and maturity.

Nowadays, most corporates, institutional investors and commercial banks enter swap contracts with swap dealers who work for the major investment and commercial banks. Swap dealers quote two-way rates on electronic information systems and over the telephone in a range of currencies and for standard maturities. These may be indication rates, in which case the actual rate for a deal will be a matter for negotiation with the counterparty. Dealers will also quote rates on demand for non-standard maturity dates and for structures that are non-standard in some way — for example, swap transactions in which the notional principal is not constant over the life of the contract.

Table 12.3   Two-way swap rates

Maturity	Swap rate
2 years	5.52–5.56
5 years	5.82–5.85
10 years	6.05–6.09

Fixed rate: semi-annual, actual/actual
Floating rate: six-month LIBOR, actual/360

12.10.1   Outright Swap Rates

Table 12.3 shows typical two-way swap rates for two, five, and 10-year maturity US dollar interest rate swaps.

In Table 12.3 the dealer's bid rate for 10-year dollar swaps is 6.05% with semi-annual payments. The dealer will pay 6.05% per annum on a semi-annual basis and receive in return six-month dollar LIBOR. The LIBOR rate is not shown in the quotation, it is assumed that the fixed rate is against LIBOR flat. Some market participants would say that the dealer is a **payer** of fixed at 6.05%, others that the dealer **buys** 10-year dollar swaps at that rate.

The dealer's offer rate for 10-year dollar swaps is 6.09%. The dealer asks for 6.09% fixed and will pay in return LIBOR flat. The dealer is a **receiver** of the fixed at 6.09%, a **seller** of 10-year swaps at that rate.

The fixed rates in Table 12.3 are quoted on a semi-annual bond basis and using the actual/actual day counting convention. The floating rate is quoted using the actual/360 money market convention. When a client asks for a firm rate dealers can quote rates using whatever is the most convenient convention for the client. For example, if a corporate borrower has raised funds through a dollar Eurobond the coupon payments will normally be made on an annual basis. If the corporate wants to receive fixed on a swap to switch into a floating rate liability the fixed rate can be expressed on an annual bond basis.

12.11   CREDIT SPREADS

Dealers may also quote swap rates in terms of a credit spread over the yield on the Treasury security with the nearest maturity. This is illustrated in Table 12.4.

In Table 12.4 the 5.23% figure is the yield on the reference US Treasury, based on the current mid-price of the bond (i.e. mid-way between the bid and the offer price). The reference Treasury will have a maturity of approximately 10 years and its yield establishes the risk-free rate for that maturity. The bid and offer swap rates are first quoted as spreads over the yield on the Treasury and then as outright fixed rates against dollar LIBOR. The dealer will pay 6.05% — a spread of 82 basis points over the

Table 12.4   Swap spreads: US dollar swaps

Maturity	Treasury yield	Swap spreads	Swap rates
10 years	5.23%	0.82–0.86	6.05–6.09

Treasury yield — on a 10-year dollar swap in return for LIBOR. On the offer or ask side the dealer will receive 6.09% and will pay LIBOR in return. This is a spread of 86 basis points over the risk-free rate.

Quoting the rates as spreads over the Treasury yield has a practical advantage in that the dealer's spread is less likely to change over the course of a day in comparison to the underlying risk-free rate. The dealer can quote a spread and if the counterparty accepts this number it can simply be added to the yield on the reference Treasury to establish the outright rate.

12.12   DETERMINANTS OF SWAP SPREADS

The spread over Treasuries on an interest rate swap in part reflects the market's current perceptions about the risk of default (assuming that no central counterparty is involved). This is similar to the situation with a straight bond issued by a bank or a corporate — it will trade at a spread over the Treasury yield and the spread will depend on the market's views on the risk that the issuer might default on its payments. However there is an important difference between the credit risk on a bond and on an interest rate swap.

- If an investor buys a bond the coupon payments and indeed the whole principal amount are at risk.
- If a party enters into an interest rate swap contract the worst that can happen is that it is due a future stream of positive cash flows (because interest rates have moved in its favour) and the swap counterparty is unable to meet its payment obligations. The risk is on the anticipated settlement of differences between the fixed and floating rates, not on the notional principal, which is never exchanged.

Since most swaps in major currencies such as the US dollar or the euro are contracted between financial institutions the typical level of credit risk is about the average for the banking sector, somewhere around the Standard and Poor's AA level. Swap spreads are also driven by straightforward supply and demand factors. For example, if fears that interest rates are set to rise sharply start to affect corporate borrowers there will be an excess of demand from those who wish to pay fixed and receive floating. Swap dealers will be able to demand higher fixed rates and a higher spread over the reference Treasury.

Hammersmith & Fulham

The London local authority of Hammersmith & Fulham transacted almost £3 billion notional in swap transactions in the late 1980s. When UK interest rates rose sharply the contracts became loss-making for the local authority. Unfortunately for the banks who were the counterparties, however, the UK courts subsequently decided that the swaps were *ultra vires*, that is, the local authority had no legal power to enter into the transactions in the first place. The deals were cancelled and the banks lost heavily. The case has entered the folklore of the swaps market and led to greater caution over the legal and credit implications of swap deals.

12.13 HEDGING SWAPS WITH TREASURIES

The link between the rate on Treasuries and the swap rate is also established by virtue of the fact that dealers can use Treasury bonds or bond futures to hedge their swap positions. For example, a dealer who agrees to pay fixed on a 10-year dollar swap in return for LIBOR can buy a 10-year US Treasury funded via a sale and repurchase agreement. This is illustrated in Figure 12.6.

Purchasing the Treasury bond protects the swap dealer against changes in the general level of interest rates. Assuming that funding the bond position via repo costs less than LIBOR (because it is a collateralized form of borrowing) the dealer can afford to pay a spread over the Treasury rate on the swap transaction.

12.13.1 Hedging in Practice

In practice of course a swap dealer will have many transactions on the book and much of the interest rate risk will cancel out — in some trades the dealer will be a payer of fixed (receiver of floating) and in others a receiver of fixed (payer of floating). The dealer has to make a decision on whether to hedge out any residual exposures to interest rate changes or whether this is a position he or she is happy to take.

Using Treasury bonds is not necessarily the best way to hedge interest rate exposures on swaps. If the government is shrinking the supply of government debt there may be constraints on buying a sufficient quantity of bonds at a reasonable price. Government buy-backs of debt tend to push up the prices of Treasury bonds and to lower the yields.

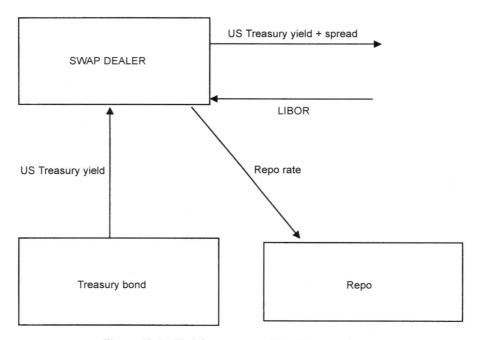

Figure 12.6   Hedging a swap with a Treasury bond

This was a major factor in the widening of US dollar swap spreads over the Treasury yield in the first year of the current century, particularly at the longer end of the yield curve. In fact as the yields on longer-dated US Treasury bonds became distorted in this way they became less useful as benchmark rates to price corporate bonds. Swap rates were sometimes used instead; a reflection of the deep liquidity in the US dollar swap market. We explore briefly in Chapter 13 another way to hedge swaps by using interest rate futures.

12.14   CROSS-CURRENCY SWAPS

In a cross-currency swap cash flows in one currency are exchanged on regular dates for cash flows in another currency. The principal is normally exchanged at the spot FX rate at the start of the swap and re-exchanged at the same rate on the final payment date. The interest payments can be calculated on a fixed or a floating basis. We will illustrate the mechanics using a simple example which also highlights the potential benefits of using cross-currency swaps to exploit a comparative funding advantage. In practice it is unlikely that the requirements of the two sides would exactly match, and the swap dealer would have to handle the mismatch.

In our case Americo Inc. is a highly-rated US company while Britco plc is a less highly-rated UK company. Both companies wish to borrow on a fixed-rate basis. Americo wishes to borrow £100 million and pay interest in sterling to finance its UK operations. Britco wishes to borrow $150 million and pay interest in dollars to fund activities in the United States. The spot FX rate is GBP:USD 1.5000. The borrowing rates for each company in dollars and in sterling are set out in Table 12.5.

Americo can borrow more cheaply in either currency, reflecting its higher credit rating. However its relative or comparative advantage is greater in dollars than in sterling due to its higher 'name recognition' in the US market. So Americo arranges dollar borrowings of $150 million at 7.00% per annum for five years. Britco arranges sterling borrowings of £100 million at 8.75% per annum for five years. The two firms then approach a swap dealer who agrees the following transactions.

- **Swap with Americo.** The swap dealer takes $150 million principal from Americo and gives the firm in return the £100 million it needs for its business operations. The principals will be re-exchanged at exactly the same FX rate in five years' time on the final swap payment date. The dealer agrees to pay Americo 7.00% per annum on $150 million for the next five years and will receive in return 7.75% per annum on £100 million.
- **Swap with Britco.** The swap dealer takes the £100 million from Britco raised through their funding and gives the firm $150 million. The principals will be re-exchanged at the same FX rate in five years' time on the final swap payment date. The dealer

Table 12.5   Borrowing rates for the two companies

Borrower	USD fixed rate	GBP fixed rate
Americo Inc.	7.00%	8.00%
Britco plc	8.50%	8.75%

agrees to pay Britco 8.75% per annum on £100 million for the next five years. In return Britco will pay 8.35% on $150 million.

12.14.1 Interest Payments

Figure 12.7 shows the annual interest payments on the two swaps and on the underlying loans.

The net borrowing cost for Americo is 7.75% per annum on £100 million. This is a 'gain' of 25 basis points compared to what their funding cost would have been if they had borrowed sterling directly. The net borrowing cost for Britco is 8.35% per annum on $150 million. This is a 'gain' of 15 basis points compared to what their funding cost would have been if they had borrowed dollars directly. The position of the swap dealer is as follows:

$$\text{Dollar Payments and Receipts} = 8.35\% - 7.00\% = +1.35\%$$
$$\text{Sterling Payments and Receipts} = 7.75\% - 8.75\% = -1.00\%$$

Every year the swap dealer is due to receive a net 1.35% on $150 million which is $2.025 million. The dealer is due to pay a net 1.00% on £100 million which is £1 million. There is a residual currency risk on this position but it can be hedged using forward foreign exchange contracts. The deal could also be structured such that Americo or Britco take some or all of the foreign exchange risk.

12.4.2 Principal Exchange

It might seem odd that the dollar and sterling principal amounts are re-exchanged at the maturity of the swap at the same spot rate at which they were exchanged at the outset of the swap. Why is it not done at the five-year forward FX rate? We know from Chapter 3

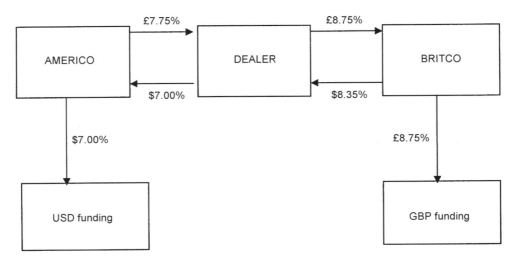

Figure 12.7   Swap and loan annual interest payments

that a forward FX rate is calculated from the spot rate and the interest rate differential between the two currencies. In the cross-currency swap deal the interest rate differential is already taken care of through the regular exchange of payments based on the interest rates in the two currencies. So we can use the initial spot rate of GBP:USD 1.5000 for the re-exchange of the two currencies. This is of course helpful to Americo and Britco since they will need $150 million and £100 million respectively to redeem their debt when it matures in five years. Note though that the principal re-exchange feature increases the potential credit exposure on the swap.

12.15   CHAPTER SUMMARY

A standard or 'plain vanilla' interest rate swap is a bilateral legal agreement made directly between two parties to exchange cash flows based on a fixed and a floating rate of interest on regular dates. The cash flows are netted out and payment is made to one party or the other. Normally payments are made in arrears and the reference floating rate is based on LIBOR. The first payment is known when the contract is agreed. Thereafter the payments will depend on whether LIBOR decreases or increases in the future. A 'vanilla' IRS is a package that combines a cash market transaction with a series of forward interest rate contracts. Because they are over-the-counter deals swaps carry default risk. However this is reduced if the notional principal is not exchanged and can be eliminated if a clearing house acts as central counterparty. IRS rates are quoted by dealers working for major banks in terms of the fixed rate versus LIBOR. This rate can also be shown as a spread over the yield on risk-free government bonds. Swaps are widely used by corporates, banks and investors to hedge interest rate exposures. In major currencies such as the US dollar swap rates are becoming key reference rates, given the deep liquidity of the market. A non-vanilla IRS is one in which the standard terms are adjusted. For example, the notional principal may vary over the life of the deal, or both legs may be based on a floating interest rate. A cross-currency swap is one in which the payment legs are in two different currencies; normally the principal is exchanged at the start and re-exchanged at the same FX rate at maturity.

APPENDIX: SWAP VARIANTS

There are many variants on the basic 'plain vanilla' interest rate swap structure. The following are some of the more common.

- **Amortizing Swap**. The notional principal reduces during the life of the swap. This is useful for a corporate hedging an amortizing loan or bond issue, in which the principal is paid off in instalments and decreases over time.
- **Accreting Swap**. The notional principal increases during the life of the swap.
- **Rollercoaster Swap**. The notional principal first increases and then reduces over the life of the swap.
- **Basis Swap**. A floating-for-floating swap in which the two legs use a different reference rate. For example, one party to the swap pays a cash flow linked to LIBOR and receives in return a cash flow linked to the commercial paper rate.

- **Callable/Putable Swap**. With a callable swap the fixed payer can terminate the contract early. With a putable swap the fixed receiver can terminate early.
- **Extendable Swap**. One party has the option to extend the life of the swap.
- **Forward Start or Deferred Swap**. The fixed rate is set when the swap is transacted but the swap starts on a date later than spot and accrues interest from that date.
- **LIBOR In-Arrears Swap**. The LIBOR for the floating leg is fixed (normally) two business days before the payment date rather than at the beginning of the payment period.
- **Rate-Capped Swap**. The floating rate payment is capped at a maximum level.
- **Swaption**. An option to enter into a swap contract either as the payer or the receiver of the fixed rate. See Chapter 19 for details.
- **Zero Coupon Swap**. A fixed against floating swap in which the fixed cash flow is calculated using a zero coupon rate. There are no interim payments on the fixed leg, only a lump sum payment normally at maturity.

13
Interest Rate Swap Valuation

Investment is an activity of forecasting the yield on assets over the life of the asset; ...
speculation is the activity of forecasting the psychology of the market.

John Maynard Keynes

13.1 CHAPTER OVERVIEW

In this chapter we investigate the value of an interest rate swap contract when the deal is first agreed, and methods for revaluing a swap given subsequent changes in market interest rates. We compare two well-established valuation methods: the zero coupon and the forward rate methods. These two approaches are shown to produce the same valuation when applied to a standard fixed–floating interest rate swap. The chapter introduces the concept of a **par swap** in which the present value of the fixed leg of the swap equals the present value of the floating leg. We show how spot or zero coupon rates can be extracted from the fixed rates on par swaps using the bootstrapping method. The zero coupon and forward rate revaluation methods are then compared with two simpler and still widely used methods of valuing single swaps: the bond and the replacement swap methods. The former treats a swap as a combination of a fixed coupon bond and a floating rate note and reprices the hypothetical fixed rate bond at the latest market swap rate. The latter method calculates the profit and loss that would result from entering into a new swap that offsets the original swap transaction. In a more detailed final section we explore how swaps can be priced and hedged using interest rate futures contracts and forward rate agreements.

13.2 VALUING A SWAP AT INCEPTION

We start by exploring the value of a swap when the deal is first entered into. To do this we will consider the case of a swap dealer who has just entered into an interest rate swap on a notional $100 million with exactly three years from the start date of the swap until maturity. The payment legs on the swap are as follows:

- the dealer pays a fixed rate of 8% per annum annually in arrears;
- the dealer receives in return 12-month dollar LIBOR annually in arrears.

For simplicity we will assume that interest payments on both the fixed and floating legs are calculated using an actual/actual day count method. The dealer's payments and receipts on the swap are illustrated in Figure 13.1.

The dealer's cash flows are illustrated in Figure 13.2, with amounts shown in $ millions. At the end of each year the dealer pays $8 million and receives the LIBOR rate for that year applied to a notional principal of $100 million.

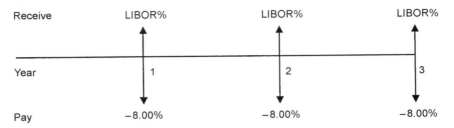

Figure 13.1   Dealer's payments and receipts on a three-year annual swap

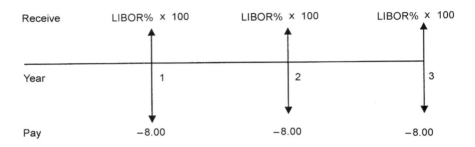

Figure 13.2   Swap cash flows

13.2.1   Swap as an FRN Plus a Fixed Coupon Bond

The dealer's cash flows can be looked at in another way. They look as if:

- the dealer has sold (is short) a three-year annual $100 million par bond paying a fixed 8.00% coupon;
- the dealer has bought (is long) a three-year $100 million par floating rate note paying 12-month dollar LIBOR.

The cash flows from the hypothetical bond and FRN combination are illustrated in Figure 13.3. In years one, two and three the dealer pays coupons of $8 million and receives LIBOR% times $100 million, whatever LIBOR happens to be for each particular 12-month payment period.

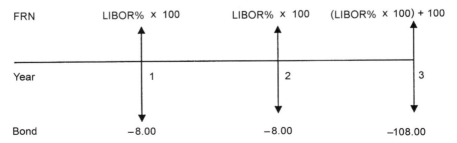

Figure 13.3   Three-year swap as an FRN plus a fixed bond

At first blush there does seem to be an important difference between the actual swap and the hypothetical FRN plus fixed coupon bond combination illustrated in Figure 13.3. In the actual swap deal the notional $100 million principal is never exchanged. If the dealer was actually long an FRN he or she would be due a principal payment of $100 million at the end of year three. But in fact this turns out not to matter at all. The $100 million principal due to the dealer on the imaginary FRN is balanced by the $100 million principal repayment the dealer would have to make on the hypothetical 8% coupon straight bond he or she is short. These cancel out, so the actual cash flow at the end of year three on the combination of an FRN plus a straight 8% coupon bond would be:

$$(\text{LIBOR}\% \times 100) + 100 - 108 = (\text{LIBOR}\% \times 100) - 8$$

This is exactly the same as the year three cash flow on the swap.

13.3 VALUING THE SWAP COMPONENTS

We now know that the swap can be replicated by a combination of a straight bond and an FRN — the cash flows and the timings of the cash flows are identical. If we can price the package of straight bond plus FRN, then it follows that the swap must have the same value as that combination. If two structures, however differently assembled, generate identical cash flows then they should have the same value. Otherwise arbitrage deals can be constructed. From the dealer's perspective it must be the case that:

$$\text{Value of Swap} = \text{Value of FRN} - \text{Value of Fixed Bond}$$

To present value the two components of the swap we should use one, two and three-year zero coupon or spot rates and apply these to the cash flows. These rates can be generated from the fixed rates on one, two and three-year annual swaps using the bootstrapping methodology we employed in Chapter 6. Let us suppose that the swap rates for standard 'plain vanilla' one, two and three-year annual dollar swaps are as set out in Table 13.1.

We will assume that 6.00% is the spot rate for one year. We will also assume that the first LIBOR rate for the year one floating cash flow on the swap is fixed at 6.00%. The two-year spot rate z_2 can be established through a bootstrapping argument, as follows. Suppose we buy $1 principal of a hypothetical two-year bond paying an annual 7% coupon that is trading at par. Then the $1 cost of buying the bond must equal the receipts from selling the first $0.07 coupon at the one-year spot rate 6%, plus the receipts from selling the final $0.07 coupon plus $1 principal at the two-year spot rate z_2:

Table 13.1 Swap rates

Year	Swap rate
1	6.00% p.a.
2	7.00% p.a.
3	8.00% p.a.

Table 13.2 Swap rates, spot rates and discount factors

Year	Swap rate	Spot rate	Discount factor
1	6.00%	6.00%	0.94339623
2	7.00%	7.0353%	0.87286193
3	8.00%	8.1111%	0.79138828

$$1 = \frac{0.07}{1.06} + \frac{1.07}{(1 + z_2)^2}$$

Rearranging, we find that $z_2 = 7.0353\%$. Recall from Chapter 6 that a discount factor is simply the present value of $1 at the spot rate for the period. So the two-year discount factor DF_2 is calculated as follows:

$$DF_2 = \frac{1}{(1 + z_2)^2} = 0.87286193$$

Using the same logic we can establish from the swap rates in Table 13.1 the three-year spot rate z_3 and the three-year discount factor DF_3. These are shown in Table 13.2.

13.3.1 Valuing the Fixed Leg

The next step is to value the fixed leg of the swap by present valuing the three cash flows on the equivalent short bond position. We use the discount factors derived from the spot rates:

Value of Fixed Leg = Value of Fixed Bond =

$$(-8.00 \times 0.94339623) + (-8.00 \times 0.87286193) + (-108.00 \times 0.79138828) = -\$100$$

13.3.2 Valuing the Floating Leg

Valuing the floating leg of the swap requires a moment's thought. The position is equivalent to a long position in an FRN with a known first coupon due in one year which we have assumed is set at 6%, the current market one-year rate. So the one-year coupon payment from the FRN is $6 million. The problem seems to be that we do not know what the LIBOR rates for subsequent years will be. However this turns out not to be an issue at all. At the beginning of any year, after a coupon is paid, the FRN's price would reset to par. This is because the future value a year later would be par plus interest at LIBOR. If we discount this back at LIBOR for one year the present value must be par.

The future value of the FRN in one year is therefore par plus the coupon payment of $6 million. The one-year spot rate is 6%. Therefore the present value of the FRN is $106 million discounted at 6%:

$$\text{Value of Floating Leg} = \text{Value of FRN} = \frac{\$106}{1.06} = \$100$$

13.3.3   Value of the Swap

The fixed leg of the swap is worth −$100 million to the dealer and the floating leg is worth +$100 million. The net present value of the swap today is therefore zero. What we have been considering is a **par swap**—the fixed and floating legs add to zero. In practice because of spreads and commissions a swap dealer will normally enter into an interest rate swap transaction at the outset at a positive net present value—this is sometimes called the **initial net present value** (INPV) of the swap.

13.4   SWAP REVALUATION

The result in the last section is not surprising. When a swap agreement is made at par the present value to each counterparty is zero. The fixed rate on the swap—in the example 8.00% per annum—is set to be the coupon on a straight fixed rate bond trading at par. The floating leg is also worth par, because the LIBOR rate for the first floating payment has just been set and exactly the same rate is used to discount its cash flows back to today.

Since the swap is equivalent to a fixed coupon bond and an FRN we can use this fact to revalue the swap if market interest rates change. Suppose, for example, that on the same day the swap agreement we have been considering is made the three-year swap rate rises to 8.10%. Par rates for one and two-year swaps remain as before. The change in the three-year swap rate will affect the year three spot rate and discount factor. The spot rates and discount factors are recalculated in Table 13.3.

The value of the fixed leg of the swap will now change as follows:

Value of Fixed Leg = Value of Fixed Bond =

$$(-8.00 \times 0.94339623) + (-8.00 \times 0.87286193) + (-108.00 \times 0.78897603) = -\$99.7395$$

The value of the floating side is unchanged at:

$$\frac{\$106}{1.06} = \$100$$

The net present value of the swap to the bank is now:

$$\$100 - \$99.7395 = \$0.2605 \text{ per } \$100$$

On the $100 million notional principal of the swap this is a profit of approximately $260,500. This is a **revaluation** or mark-to-market profit for the dealer who is paying fixed on the swap. If the dealer entered into an offsetting swap with the same payment dates and notional principal he or she would receive a fixed rate of 8.10% on this second transaction as opposed to the 8.00% fixed rate paid on the original swap. The

Table 13.3   Recalculated spot rates and discount factors

Year	Swap rate	Spot rate	Discount factor
1	6.00%	6.00%	0.94339623
2	7.00%	7.0353%	0.87286193
3	8.10%	8.2211%	0.78897603

gain of 10 basis points per annum for three years is worth about $260,500 in present value terms.

13.5   REVALUATION BETWEEN PAYMENT DATES

We assumed in the last section that the swap was revalued at the new swap rate of 8.10% on the start date. If the swap is revalued after its start date and between payment dates then the floating leg may no longer be valued at par as it was in our example. Firstly, interest on the floating leg will have accrued at LIBOR; secondly, current discount rates may be above or below the LIBOR rate fixed for the first payment period. This parallels the situation with an FRN valued between coupon dates.

For example, suppose that the (annually paid) coupon on an FRN has been set at 6.00% for a given year, but now there are only six months left in the coupon period. At the end of the year when the coupon is paid and the LIBOR rate is reset for the next period, the FRN will be worth $106. Now suppose that the six-month interest rate is 7.00% per annum. The value of the FRN today is:

$$\frac{\$106}{(1 + 0.07/2)} = \$102.4155$$

This is a dirty price, including accrued interest. The FRN has accrued $3 in interest to date during the current coupon period, so its clean value net of accrued interest is $99.4155. The clean price is below the par value of $100 because the 6% coupon rate for the period is lower than the discount rate used to price the FRN. It should be noted that in practice the interest payments on dollar FRNs will normally be calculated using the actual/360 day count convention.

13.6   THE FORWARD RATE METHOD

Using spot rates to present value the cash flows on swaps is an extremely powerful tool that can also be applied to less standard swaps and indeed to entire portfolios of swaps. It derives its rigour from the fact that each future cash flow is discounted at the unique and correct rate for the period. However the approach we used to value the floating leg can seem a little strange at first—particularly the notion that the hypothetical FRN will reset to par on a payment date. This section looks at an alternative approach to valuing the floating leg of an interest rate swap, known as the **forward rate** method. The steps taken to apply this method are as follows:

- calculate the forward rates implied in the fixed rates on par swaps and in the spot rates derived from these (forward rates could also be derived from the rates on FRAs or interest rate futures; see Chapter 10 for details);
- make the assumption that floating rates for forward periods on the swap will be the same as the implied forward rates;
- use the forward rates to calculate the floating leg cash flows;
- discount these cash flows at the appropriate spot rates.

Table 13.4   Spot and forward rates derived from swap rates

Year	Swap rate	Spot rate	Discount factor	Forward rates
1	6.00%	6.00%	0.94339623	
2	7.00%	7.0353%	0.87286193	8.0808%
3	8.00%	8.1111%	0.79138828	10.2950%

13.6.1   Forward Rate Method: Case Study

The example we use here is the same swap agreement we valued previously. The notional is $100 million and the term is three years with annual payments. The dealer has agreed to pay 8.00% per annum in arrears and in return will receive LIBOR. The dealer can be considered as being short a fixed coupon bond and long an FRN with annual LIBOR resets. The first LIBOR is fixed at 6.00%. The par and spot rates are shown again in Table 13.4, but this time also with the implied forward rates.

The implied rate of interest f_{1v2} for reinvesting cash between year one and year two is 8.0808%. This is calculated using the method we employed in Chapter 6. For no arbitrage to occur the return on a one-year investment at the one-year spot rate 6.00% reinvested at f_{1v2} should equal the return on a two-year investment at the two-year spot rate 7.0353%:

$$\$1.06 \times (1 + f_{1v2}) = 1.070353^2$$

Therefore $f_{1v2} = 8.0808\%$.

The implied forward rate f_{2v3} between year two and year three calculated in the same way is 10.2950%. The fixed side of the swap is valued by present valuing the fixed cash flows on a straight 8% coupon bond. The answer as we saw previously is $-\$100$. The floating leg is valued like an FRN except this time we assume that the implied forward rates tell us what the cash flows will be for years two and three. (We assumed that the first payment is already fixed at the one-year rate of 6.00% at the start of the swap.) The hypothetical FRN would have the cash flows set out in Table 13.5.

The next step is to discount these cash flows at the one, two and three-year discount factors:

Value of Floating Leg = Value of FRN =

$$(\$6.00 \times 0.94339623) + (\$8.0808 \times 0.87286193) + (\$110.2950 \times 0.79138828) = \$100$$

The fixed leg of the swap is worth $-\$100$ and the floating leg $+\$100$ to the bank, a net present value of zero. This has to be the case, because the implied forward rates are derived from the par and spot rates. If nothing else it shows that the methods we are

Table 13.5   Cash flows on the floating leg

Year	Cash flow
1	$6.0000
2	$8.0808
3	$110.2950

Table 13.6   Recalculated forward rates

Year	Swap rate	Spot rate	Discount factor	Forward rate
1	6.00%	6.00%	0.94339623	
2	7.00%	7.0353%	0.87286193	8.0808%
3	8.10%	8.2211%	0.78897603	10.6322%

using are internally consistent—it also provides us with a useful cross-check on our answers.

13.7   SWAP REVALUATION USING FORWARD RATES

We calculated previously that if the swap rate changed on the start date to 8.10% then the value of the fixed leg to the dealer changes to −$99.7395. The value of the floating leg is unchanged at $100. To recreate this result for the floating leg using the forward rate method we must recalculate the forward rates. As Table 13.6 shows, the change in the three-year swap rate to 8.10% increases the implied forward rate between years two and three.

How does this affect the value of the floating leg in the swap?

Value of Floating Leg = Value of FRN =
$$(\$6.00 \times 0.94339623) + (\$8.0808 \times 0.87286193) + (\$110.6322 \times 0.78897603) = \$100$$

Using the forward rate method we have the same revaluation profit and loss as calculated previously. The fixed leg is worth −$99.7395 per $100 notional to the bank. The floating leg is unchanged at $100 per $100 notional. On the $100 notional million swap the revaluation profit and loss is approximately $260,500.

13.8   VARIANT ON THE FORWARD RATE METHOD

The following is a variant on the forward rate method which is easy to set up on a spreadsheet and which can be used to value a wide range of swaps. We will assume as before that we wish to revalue the three-year annual swap on $100 million notional. The fixed leg on the swap is 8.00% and the new three-year swap rate used to revalue the deal is 8.10%. We are revaluing the swap on the start date.

- **Step 1**. Calculate spot and forward rates from the fixed rates on par swaps. The rates are shown again in Table 13.7.

- **Step 2**. Calculate the fixed and floating cash flows on the swap, using the forward rates for LIBOR. The resulting cash flows are given in Table 13.8.

Table 13.7   Swap rates

Year	Swap rate	Spot rate	Discount factor	Forward rate
1	6.00%	6.00%	0.94339623	
2	7.00%	7.0353%	0.87286193	8.0808%
3	8.10%	8.2211%	0.78897603	10.6322%

Table 13.8   Fixed and floating cash flows on the swap

Cash flow	Dealer pays	Dealer receives
Year 1	−8,000,000	6,000,000
Year 2	−8,000,000	8,080,808
Year 3	−8,000,000	10,632,249

Table 13.9   Present value of fixed and floating cash flows

Cash flow	Discount factor	PV fixed	PV floating
Year 1	0.94339623	−7,547,170	5,660,377
Year 2	0.87286193	−6,982,895	7,053,430
Year 3	0.78897603	−6,311,808	8,388,590
Totals		−20,841,873	21,102,397

- **Step 3**. Discount the cash flows at the appropriate discount factor for each period and calculate the net present value. The results are illustrated in Table 13.9.

The net present value is −$20,841,873 plus $21,102,397 which sums to approximately $260,500.

The fixed rate on a par swap (with zero net present value) in fact is simply the single rate which, when the fixed cash flows are calculated at that rate, produces a present value equal to the present value of the floating cash flows, where the forward LIBOR rates are established by the forward rates of interest. In the example we have worked through the dealer entered into the three-year swap paying a fixed rate of 8.00%. At inception the present value of the fixed equals the present value of the floating leg.

13.9   SWAP RATE AND LIBOR RATES

The following relationship holds for a par swap: the fixed rate is the weighted average of the cash LIBOR rate for the first payment period and the forward interest rates for the subsequent periods, where each rate is weighted by the appropriate discount factor.

For example, in the swap we have been considering the cash market one-year rate is 6%. This should be weighted by the one-year discount factor. The forward rate for one year starting in one year, f_{1v2} (in our example 8.0808%), should be weighted by the two-year discount factor. And so on. When the swap was entered into the weighted average is exactly 8.00%:

$$\frac{(0.06\times0.94339623)+(0.080808\times0.87286193)+(0.102950\times0.79138828)}{0.94339623 + 0.87286193 + 0.79138828}=0.08 \text{ or } 8.00\%$$

13.9.1   Observing Forward Rates

In our example we actually derived the forward interest rates from the spot rates and ultimately from the fixed rates on par swaps. In fact in a developed capital market such as the US, forward interest rates can be observed directly because of the existence of products such as forward rate agreements (FRAs) and interest rate futures. FRAs are quoted in terms of a forward interest rate, and interest rate futures are quoted in terms of 100 minus an implied future interest rate. What is more they can be used to lock into borrowing or lending rates for periods in the future. The swap rate for a period can be calculated from the forward rates derived from FRAs and interest rate futures. And FRAs and futures can be used to hedge the risks on interest rate swaps, as we will illustrate later in this chapter.

13.10   APPROXIMATE SWAP REVALUATION METHODS

The zero coupon and forward rate valuation methods provide robust methods for valuing standard 'plain vanilla' swaps and a range of more exotic products. However they can take some time to set up. It is possible to approximate the profit and loss revaluation on a single swap using a simpler method, sometimes called the **bond method**. In this approach the swap is again valued as a combination of fixed rate bond plus FRN. However, the straight bond is valued using a single discount rate rather than spot rates. The method values the fixed leg of the swap accurately at its inception:

$$\frac{-8.00}{1.08} + \frac{-8.00}{1.08^2} + \frac{-108.00}{1.08^3} = -\$100$$

Inaccuracies occur with this method when the fixed leg is revalued using a new swap rate or on a date other than the start date of the swap. For example, suppose as before that we revalue the fixed leg of our example swap on the start date at a new swap rate of 8.10%. The new present value of the fixed leg cash flows per $100 when discounted at a constant rate of 8.10% is given by the following calculation:

$$\frac{-8.00}{1.081} + \frac{-8.00}{1.081^2} + \frac{-108.00}{1.081^3} = -\$99.7428$$

Adding the floating leg value of $100 this values the swap at about $257,200 compared to $260,500 using the more accurate zero coupon and forward rate methods. The advantage of the bond method, however, is that it can easily be carried out on a simple bond calculator.

13.10.1   Replacement Swap Method

An alternative to the bond method, which produces the same results, is the **replacement swap** method. We assume again that the dealer has just entered into a three-year annual swap on a notional of $100 million paying fixed at 8.00% and receiving LIBOR. If the three-year swap rate changes to 8.10% later on the start date of the swap, the dealer could in theory enter into an offsetting three-year swap, paying LIBOR and receiving 8.10%. This is illustrated in Figure 13.4.

The LIBORs cancel out. The dealer's net cash flows are plus $100,000 (i.e. $100 million×0.1%) each year for three years. Discounted at a constant 8.10% the present value is just over $257,200. The method yields the same answer as the bond method, it is even simpler, but it suffers from the same inherent problem. It produces inaccurate results when the cash flows on the original and offsetting swaps are different in size and/ or occur on different dates.

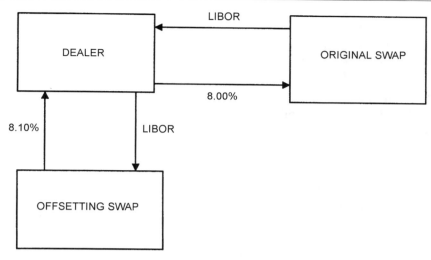

Figure 13.4   Cash flows with replacement swap

13.11   FRAS, FUTURES AND SWAP RATES

FRAs and interest rate futures contracts can be used to fix borrowing and lending rates for future time periods. To illustrate this fact suppose we carry out the following transactions.

- On 15 June we borrow $100 million at LIBOR for three months with the intention of rolling this loan over in three months' time at whatever the LIBOR rate happens to be at that time. The LIBOR rate for the initial three-month loan is 6.00% per annum.
- At the same time we sell 100 September Eurodollar futures contracts expiring 15 September. The yield curve in this case is assumed to be flat, so the futures will trade at a price of 94.00 (implying a rate for the forward period of 6.00% per annum).

On 15 September we will pay interest on the three-month loan at the quarterly rate of $6.00\%/4 = 1.5\%$. (For ease of explanation here we ignore the actual/360 day count convention that applies in the case of Eurodollar loans.) Suppose, however, that on the rollover of the loan on that date three-month LIBOR is now 10% per annum. The quarterly borrowing rate for September–December is therefore 2.50%. The September interest rate futures contracts will expire at 90.00 (100 − LIBOR) so we will receive settlement of 1% of the notional value of the contracts. Subtracting this from our borrowing cost for the quarter, our effective quarterly borrowing rate is fixed at 1.50% or 6.00% per annum.

13.11.1   Swap Alternative

As an alternative to this strategy, we could borrow $100 million on 15 June for six months on a floating rate basis with quarterly payments. The next step is to enter into a six-month swap as follows:

- notional principal $100 million;
- pay 6.00% per annum fixed with quarterly settlements;
- receive floating with quarterly settlements, with the first period rate set at three-month LIBOR which is 6.00% per annum.

The first payment on the swap is due on 15 September. The payment is zero — the rates for both the fixed and floating rates are 6.00%. On 15 September we suppose, again, that the LIBOR rate for September–December is reset at 10.00% per annum or 2.5% for the quarter. We will receive a net payment on the swap representing 1.00% of the notional value (a quarter of the difference between 10.00% and 6.00%). So once more our effective quarterly borrowing rate for September–December is 1.5% or 6.00% per annum.

In this simple example the futures and swap hedges have achieved the same result. It is not surprising then that swap dealers use futures prices to price swaps, and futures contracts to hedge exposures on swaps. In fact we saw in the previous section that the fixed rate on an interest rate swap is based on a series of forward interest rates. Since these rates can be established though the rates on FRAs and the prices of interest rate futures it follows that a series (known as a 'strip') of FRAs or futures can be used to establish the rate of interest on the fixed leg of an interest rate swap. This is illustrated in the final section of this chapter.

13.12   PRICING A SWAP FROM FUTURES: CASE STUDY

Consider the following swap in which a swap dealer pays fixed and receives floating on a quarterly basis with payments made in arrears.

Trade date:	8 February 2001
Start date:	12 February 2001
First payment:	21 March 2001
Final payment:	19 March 2003
Notional amount:	$100 million
Fixed year basis:	Actual/360 basis
Floating year basis:	Actual/360 basis
First floating fix:	4.175%

Payments are made two business days after the last trading date of the relevant Eurodollar futures contract. The first payment is due on Wednesday 21 March 2001, two days after the last trading date of the March contract. The first period is a so-called 'stub' period because there are only 37 days from the swap start date rather than a full quarter of a year. The 4.175% floating rate fix for the stub period is the 37-day cash market interest rate.

Two business days before that first payment, on Monday 19 March 2001, the LIBOR rate for the next payment on the swap due on Wednesday 20 June 2001 will be fixed. Monday 19 March is also the last trading day of the March 2001 Eurodollar futures contract. Two business days before the second payment on the swap, on Monday 18 June 2001, the LIBOR rate for the September payment will be fixed. And so on.

The fair fixed rate for a par swap is the rate that will produce fixed cash flows whose present value equals the present value of the floating rate cash flows. To establish the swap rate in this example we take the following steps.

13.12.1   Step 1: Establish Future Interest Rates

The Eurodollar futures prices covering the relevant swap payment periods are set out in Table 13.10. The 20 June payment on the swap (made in arrears) is based on the three-month LIBOR rate from 21 March 2001 to 20 June 2001. This is the period covered by the March 2001 three-month Eurodollar futures contract, which according to the table is trading at 95.82, implying a rate of interest of 4.18% per annum for the period. The 19 September payment on the swap is based on the LIBOR rate from 20 June to 19 September 2001. This period is covered by the June 2001 interest rate futures contract which is trading at 95.66, implying a rate of interest for the period of 4.34% per annum. And so on.

13.12.2   Step 2: Calculate Discount Factors

The spot rate for the stub period to 21 March 2001 is 4.175% p.a. The spot rate for the next period to 20 June 2001 can be calculated as follows. For no arbitrage to occur the return on $1 placed at the spot rate for the period to 20 June must be the same as that achieved by:

- placing $1 at 4.175% p.a. on a cash deposit maturing on 21 March;
- locking into a future interest rate of 4.18% p.a. for the following three-month period to 20 June by buying March 2001 futures at 95.82.

If z is the spot rate to 20 June 2001 it must be true that:

$$\left\{1 + \left(0.04175 \times \frac{37}{360}\right)\right\} \times \left\{1 + \left(0.0418 \times \frac{91}{360}\right)\right\} = \left\{1 + \left(z \times \frac{128}{360}\right)\right\}$$

Solving this equation:

$$z = 4.1913\% \text{ p.a.}$$

Table 13.10 Eurodollar futures prices and implied rates

Swap payment	Days in period	Futures contract	Futures price	Implied future rate p.a.
20/06/01	91	Mar 01	95.82	4.18%
19/09/01	91	Jun 01	95.66	4.34%
19/12/01	91	Sep 01	95.35	4.65%
20/03/02	91	Dec 01	95.17	4.83%
19/06/02	91	Mar 02	95.08	4.92%
18/09/02	91	Jun 02	94.98	5.02%
18/12/02	91	Sep 02	94.88	5.12%
19/03/03	91	Dec 02	94.79	5.21%

It is easier to work with discount factors based on spot rates than with the spot rates themselves. As we have seen, a discount factor is simply the present value of $1 discounted at the spot rate for the period. The factor for the 37-day stub period is:

$$\frac{1}{1 + (0.04175 \times 37/360)} = 0.9957274$$

The factor for the next period to 20 June 2001 is the present value of $1 due on that date:

$$\frac{1}{[1 + (0.04175 \times 37/360)] \times [1 + (0.0418 \times 91/360)]} = 0.9853164$$

The following formula is a more direct method for working out discount factors:

$$\text{Discount Factor for a Period} = \frac{\text{Discount Factor in the Previous Period}}{1 + (\text{Future Rate Between Periods} \times \text{Days in Period}/360)}$$

For example, the discount factor for the period to 20 June 2001 is given by:

$$\frac{0.9957274}{1 + (0.0418 \times 91/360)} = 0.9853164$$

The discount factor for the period to 19 September is given by:

$$\frac{0.9853164}{1 + (0.0434 \times 91/360)} = 0.9746242$$

Table 13.11 sets out the period discount factors for the payment dates of the swap. These are derived from the stub rate and then from the future interest rates implied in the futures prices.

13.12.3   Step 3: Present Value the Floating Leg Cash Flows

The floating leg cash flow on a given date is found by multiplying the notional amount by the cash rate for the stub period and by the future rate for a subsequent period, adjusted for the number of days in the period. Then each cash flow is present valued using the appropriate discount factor.

Table 13.11   Period discount factors

Payment date	Days	Cash/future rate p.a.	Discount factor
21/03/01	37	4.175%	0.9957274
20/06/01	91	4.18%	0.9853164
19/09/01	91	4.34%	0.9746242
19/12/01	91	4.65%	0.9633014
20/03/02	91	4.83%	0.9516822
19/06/02	91	4.92%	0.9399918
18/09/02	91	5.02%	0.9282133
18/12/02	91	5.12%	0.9163536
19/03/03	91	5.21%	0.9044424

Table 13.12   Floating leg cash flows and present values

Date	Floating cash flow	Present value
21/03/01	429,097	427,264
20/06/01	1,056,611	1,041,096
19/09/01	1,097,056	1,069,217
19/12/01	1,175,417	1,132,281
20/03/02	1,220,917	1,161,925
19/06/02	1,243,667	1,169,036
18/09/02	1,268,944	1,177,851
18/12/02	1,294,222	1,185,965
19/03/03	1,316,972	1,191,126
	Total	9,555,761

For example, the floating cash flow due on 21 March 2001 is:

$$\$100 \text{ million} \times 0.04175 \times 37/360 = \$429{,}097$$

$$PV = \$429{,}097 \times 0.9957274 = \$427{,}264$$

Table 13.12 shows the whole sequence of floating leg cash flows, their present values and the sum of the present values.

13.12.4   Step 4: Find the Swap Rate

The swap rate is the single rate such that the present value of the fixed leg cash flows when calculated at that rate is also $9,555,761. It can be found by trial and error, by first making a guess at the answer. Each fixed cash flow is then calculated as:

$$\text{Notional Principal} \times \text{Assumed Swap Rate} \times \text{Days in Period}/360$$

For example, assuming a swap rate of 5% p.a. the fixed cash flow due on 21 March 2001 is:

$$\$100 \text{ million} \times 0.05 \times 37/360 = \$513{,}889$$

The fixed cash flows are then present valued using the appropriate discount factors. At a fixed rate of 5% p.a. the sum of the present values is in fact more than $9,555,761 so the correct swap rate must be lower than 5%. By trial and error the correct rate is seen to be approximately 4.7439% p.a. The fixed cash flows at that rate are given in Table 13.13.

Mathematically the 4.7439% p.a. swap rate we have just calculated is the weighted average of the stub period interest rate and the future interest rates, where the weights are the period discount factors. In our example we also have to adjust for the fact that the periods are of unequal length. This is achieved, as the fourth column of Table 13.14 shows, by multiplying each discount factor and interest rate by the number of days in the period over a 360-day year. The weighted interest rates are summed and divided by the sum of the discount factors adjusted for the number of days in each time period.

Table 13.13 Fixed cash flows and present values

Date	Fixed cash flow	Present value
21/03/01	487,566	485,483
20/06/01	1,199,150	1,181,542
19/09/01	1,199,150	1,168,720
19/12/01	1,199,150	1,155,142
20/03/02	1,199,150	1,141,209
19/06/02	1,199,150	1,127,191
18/09/02	1,199,150	1,113,067
18/12/02	1,199,150	1,098,845
19/03/03	1,199,150	1,084,562
	Total	9,555,761

Table 13.14 Weighting the cash and future interest rates

Date	Rate p.a.	Days in period	Rate × discount factor × days/360	Discount factor × days/360
21/03/01	4.175%	37	0.004272638	0.102338645
20/06/01	4.18%	91	0.010410963	0.24906609
19/09/01	4.34%	91	0.010692169	0.246363347
19/12/01	4.65%	91	0.011322805	0.243501193
20/03/02	4.83%	91	0.011619246	0.240564106
19/06/02	4.92%	91	0.011690365	0.237609042
18/09/02	5.02%	91	0.011778511	0.234631696
18/12/02	5.12%	91	0.011859653	0.231633839
19/03/03	5.21%	91	0.011911255	0.228622939
		Totals	0.095557606	2.014330897

The weighted average is:

$$\frac{0.095557606}{2.014330897} = 4.7439\% \text{ p.a.}$$

13.13   SWAP HEDGING

In the example in the last section, if the dealer enters the swap at par he or she will pay the calculated swap rate of 4.7439% and receive in return a floating rate of interest. The notional amount is $100 million and the day count for both legs is actual/360. If the dealer does not have an offsetting swap he or she can hedge by trading interest rate futures. A standard procedure commonly used to calculate the hedge requirement is to recalculate the value of the swap given a one basis point change in future interest rates.

Assume, for example, that the March 2001 futures price rises by one tick from 95.82 to 95.83, implying a one basis point fall in the future interest rate from March to June 2001. We can then revalue the fixed and floating legs of the swap we priced in the previous section, which we assume was entered into at a fixed rate of 4.7439%. The results are as follows:

$$PV \text{ floating} = \$9,553,498$$

$$PV \text{ fixed} = -\$9,555,988$$

$$NPV = -\$2490$$

The price value of one basis point (PVBP) on the Eurodollar futures contract is $25. That is, each one basis point change in the interest rate is worth $25 profit or loss per contract. So to hedge this risk the dealer should buy:

$$\frac{\$2490}{\$25} = 100 \text{ March 2001 futures}$$

To complete the hedge the dealer repeats this procedure for each of the payment periods of the swap and buys a 'strip' of interest rate futures. In theory the dealer should also hedge against changes in the rate for the stub period, although in practice this is often ignored for lack of a suitable hedging vehicle.

13.13.1   Convexity Effects

In the above example the dealer pays fixed, receives floating and can hedge the risk of falling interest rates by buying interest rate futures. The hedge will work well for small changes in interest rates. However for larger changes the dealer's loss on the swap resulting from the revaluation of the fixed leg will exceed the profits from the long futures position. The dealer is effectively short a fixed rate bond through the swap and will suffer the effects of negative convexity (or concavity). The losses on the fixed leg will increase in a more than linear fashion as interest rates fall, while the profits will increase less sharply as rates rise. On the other hand the profit or loss on the futures contracts used to hedge the swap arising from each successive one basis point change in interest rates is always $25 per contract.

Precisely the opposite situation applies if the dealer receives fixed, pays floating and hedges by selling Eurodollar futures. The dealer is effectively long a straight bond. The effect of positive convexity means that the profit on the fixed leg will rise in a more than linear fashion as interest rates fall, and fall less sharply as rates rise. But profits and losses on the futures always change in a strictly linear manner; the imbalance this time is in the dealer's favour. The dealer should charge for concavity by paying a lower fixed rate than that implied in the futures prices. The dealer should also pay for the benefits of convexity by receiving a lower fixed rate on the swap than that implied in the futures prices.

13.14   CHAPTER SUMMARY

A standard 'plain vanilla' interest rate swap can be considered as a combination of a fixed coupon bond and a floating rate note. The swap can be valued by working out the present values of the fixed and floating legs. To do this accurately the cash flows should be discounted using the appropriate spot rates or discount factors. An approximate answer can be obtained by present valuing the cash flows on the fixed leg at a single discount rate. This is easy to perform on a bond calculator. An alternative valuation method is to calculate forward interest rates (or derive forward rates from forward rate agreements or interest rate futures) and use these to establish the payments on the floating leg of the swap. A par swap is one in which the present value of the fixed leg equals the present value of the floating leg. Spot rates and forward rates can be derived from the fixed rates on par swaps using the bootstrapping methodology. An interest rate swap can be priced from a series of FRAs or interest rate futures. The fixed rate on a standard or 'vanilla' swap is a weighted average of the cash market rate that establishes the first payment, plus the forward interest rates that establish subsequent payments. A swap can also be hedged using FRAs or futures. One common approach is to work out the change in the value of the swap for a one basis point change in interest rates and calculate the number of interest rate futures contracts required to match that profit or loss. A futures hedge will be somewhat inaccurate for large changes in interest rates because the price value of a basis point on futures is constant whereas the profits and losses on the swap are non-linear.

14
Equity Index Futures and Swaps

14.1 CHAPTER OVERVIEW

Index futures contracts are widely used to take trading positions and to hedge the exposures on baskets of shares. In this chapter we explore how they are quoted, traded and settled as well as the operation of the margin system. We consider a number of applications of index futures in hedging, trading and asset allocation. We consider how index futures are priced and the effect of the cost of carrying positions in the underlying shares on the pricing. This leads to a discussion of the cash–futures relationship, known in the market as 'the basis'. We demonstrate how a classic index arbitrage trade is assembled and how the potential profit can be calculated. Index and stock futures contracts are traded through exchanges and are standardized. Their equivalent in the over-the-counter market is the equity swap contract. We look at a standard or 'vanilla' equity swap deal, the terms of the contract and how the payments on the swap are calculated. We also consider how equity swap traders can manage their risks using portfolios of shares or futures contracts. We explore applications of equity swaps and some important variations on the basic structure including a floating principal swap. Throughout the chapter there is a focus on the practical applications of futures and equity swaps and the advantages and potential drawbacks of using them in different market conditions.

14.2 INDEX FUTURES

An equity index futures contract is an agreement:

- made between two parties;
- on an organized futures exchange;
- to exchange cash compensation payments;
- based on the movement in the value of an equity index.

There is no physical delivery of the underlying portfolio of shares that comprise the index. This contrasts with commodity or bond futures where there is a physical delivery process.

One of the most actively traded contracts in the world is the S&P stock index futures contract traded on the Chicago Mercantile Exchange (CME). The contract was first introduced in 1982 and accounts for most US equity index futures trading. Trades can be transacted on the CME by 'locals' dealing on their own account or by traders belonging to member firms who are acting on behalf of their firm or its clients. The underlying index is calculated by Standard and Poor's and is based on the value of 500 leading US shares weighted by market capitalization. It would be too cumbersome to deliver all the 500 shares in the correct proportions against the futures contract. Instead, each full S&P index point is assigned an arbitrary $250 monetary value and profits and losses on the futures are settled in cash.

Cash Settlement

A trader who buys 10 S&P 500 index futures contracts at a level of 1000 points and who later sells at 1050 points will receive a net cash payment of $10 \times 50 \times \$250 = \$125,000$ less brokerage.

The CME has also introduced a 'mini' S&P futures contract which is aimed at the retail market and which can be traded electronically. In this contract each full index point is worth $50. Other major index futures contracts include the FT-SE 100 futures, based on the index of the top 100 blue-chip UK shares, which is traded on LIFFE. Each full index point is worth £10. LIFFE has also introduced a 'mini' FT-SE 100 contract aimed at the retail market worth £2 per point. Index futures on the leading German index, the DAX 30, are traded on Eurex, the joint Swiss–German exchange. Each full index point is worth €25.

14.2.1 Role of the Clearing House

The role of the exchange and the associated clearing house is to facilitate trading in the contracts. The clearing house acts as central counterparty and guarantees the performance of all contracts. It ensures that for every bought or 'long' contract there is a 'short' or sold contract so that cash is available from one set of market participants to pay out to those who are in profit. Opening an index futures position (whether buying or selling) involves depositing collateral called **initial margin** with a broker, who handles payments made to and received from the clearing house. Open positions are marked-to-market and are subject to margin calls from the clearing house.

14.3   INITIAL AND VARIATION MARGIN

To illustrate the margining procedures we will consider a short trading campaign based on FT-SE 100 index futures contracts. Trading in this contract is now conducted electronically through the LIFFE-Connect computer system (the London trading floor was finally closed in 2000). The contracts are cleared and guaranteed by the London Clearing House (LCH). The contract specification is set out in Table 14.1.

14.3.1 Trading Campaign: Day One

The June FT-SE futures is currently trading at around 6000 index points and a trader decides to buy 10 contracts. To transact the order the trader contacts a broker. The broker asks for initial margin, effectively a performance deposit. The LCH sets minimum

Table 14.1 FT-SE 100 futures contract

Underlying:	FT-SE 100 index
Quotation:	FT-SE index points
Point value:	£10 per full index point
Tick size (value):	0.5 index points (£5)
Delivery months:	March, June, September, December

Source: LIFFE.

initial margin which is based on the volatility of the futures contract and is therefore liable to change over time. However, a broker will normally ask for more than the minimum initial margin, depending on the relationship with the client. We will suppose that the broker in this case asks for £4000 initial margin per contract and therefore £40,000 on the whole trade. The trader lodges the money with the broker, who in turn pays margin over to the clearing house (via a clearing member, if the broker is not itself a clearing member).

The broker transacts the order electronically. We will assume that 10 June contracts are bought at exactly 6000 index points. The other side of the trade is taken by the seller of the June futures. However trading is anonymous and the buyer and seller are not known to each other. As soon as the deal is transacted the LCH interposes itself as central counterparty. It becomes the seller to the buyer, and the buyer to the seller. The clearing house does not itself initiate trades. It simply clears and guarantees transactions, and to protect itself against default it operates the margin system.

Our trader could close the long futures position out later the same trading day by selling June futures. Instead, we will suppose that the trader decides to retain the position overnight. In this case it will be marked-to-market based on the closing or settlement price of the June futures contract. Suppose that the settlement price is 5970 index points, 30 points below the purchase price. The trader will receive a margin call to pay £3000:

$$\text{Variation Margin Due} = -30 \text{ points} \times 10 \text{ contracts} \times £10 = -£3000$$

The cash goes via the trader's broker to the clearing house. The clearing house needs this money because if the futures falls in value the money collected from the longs is credited to the accounts of the shorts — the market participants who are short FT-SE index futures contracts. If the trader does not meet the margin call the broker will close out the position, sell the 10 contracts and return the initial margin minus losses and costs.

14.3.2 Trading Campaign: Day Two

The trader has had to pay £3000 variation margin, but the position is still open. Suppose that at the close of the next trading day the June futures settlement price is fixed at 6020. This is a rise of 50 points from the previous day's settlement price. This time the trader receives variation margin:

$$\text{Variation Margin Received} = 50 \text{ points} \times £10 \times 10 \text{ contracts} = £5000$$

The futures price has risen, driven upwards by the cash FT-SE index, ultimately by the prices of the constituent shares. Variation margin payments are paid into the clearing house by the shorts (via their brokers) and are credited to the dealing accounts of the longs (via their brokers).

14.3.3 Trading Campaign: Day Three

Finally, on the third day the trader decides to close the position by putting in an order to sell 10 June futures either 'at best' (at the best available market price) or on a limit order basis (at a price that is not less than a stipulated level). We will suppose that the broker transacts the sell order at 6030. The trader is entitled to a final variation margin payment because the contracts were sold 10 points above the last settlement price:

$$\text{Variation Margin Received} = 10 \text{ points} \times £10 \times 10 \text{ contracts} = £1000$$

The position is now closed. This is the effect of having one central counterparty. Effectively, the trader has bought 10 June futures with the clearing house acting as counterparty. The trader is also short 10 June futures with the clearing house as counterparty. As far as the clearing house is concerned these trades simply cancel out and the trader has zero net position. The trader can take back the £40,000 initial margin (with interest, if this has been negotiated in the brokerage agreement).

14.3.4 Net Profit and Loss

The net profit on the whole trading campaign (ignoring funding and transaction costs) is the sum of the variation margin payments:

$$\text{Net Profit} = -£3000 + £5000 + £1000 = £3000$$

Alternatively, it is the price at which the futures were sold less the price at which they were bought times the index point value times the number of contracts traded:

$$\text{Net Profit} = (6030 - 6000) \times £10 \times 10 = £3000$$

14.4 EXCHANGE DELIVERY SETTLEMENT PRICE

The mark-to-market procedure is repeated every day until the FT-SE futures position is closed out. The futures contracts expire on the third Friday of the delivery month and trading ceases at 10:30 a.m. London time on that date. At the expiry of the contract all remaining open positions are marked-to-market and closed at the exchange delivery settlement price (EDSP).

- The EDSP is based on the average level of the cash FT-SE 100 index between 10:10 a.m. and 10:30 a.m. on the last trading day.
- In the absence of a physical delivery mechanism this ensures that the futures contract value will converge on the cash index level at expiry.

If a position is retained until the last day there is a final variation margin payment based on the EDSP and then the contracts simply expire — there is no physical delivery of shares.

14.5   MARGIN AND BROKERAGE ARRANGEMENTS

On LIFFE there is a daily variation margin payment due if the settlement price has changed from yesterday's settlement even by a small amount. Some exchanges run a system of **maintenance margins**. The difference is that the settlement price of the contract has to move beyond a threshold level before there is a margin call.

Some brokers are prepared to accept securities such as government bonds as collateral against the initial margin requirement rather than cash. The securities cannot then be lent out elsewhere. The collateral may be subject to a 'haircut'. This means that if the margin due is (for example) £40,000 then securities worth more than £40,000 will have to be pledged. This is to protect the broker against falls in the market value of the collateral.

14.5.1   Spread Trades

If a trader buys one contract month, say the June FT-SE futures, and sells another month, say the September contracts, then this is a **spread trade**. There is an offset in the profits and losses on the two positions but the total position is still open and will be marked-to-market on a daily basis. The two contract months are based on the same underlying but have different expiry dates and will normally trade at different prices. The long position does not completely match out with the short position, although the risk on the combined trade is less than if a trader has a simple long or short position in one delivery month. The initial margin requirement will be adjusted to reflect the offset.

Spread trades are used to take advantage of anomalies between the pricing of different contract months, or to take a view on whether the spread between the prices is likely to narrow or widen. An **intermarket spread** trade involves buying futures based on one equity index (such as the S&P 500) and selling futures based on a different index (such as an index based on smaller capitalization companies). The objective is to profit from changes in the relative values of each market.

14.6   HEDGING WITH INDEX FUTURES: CASE STUDY

Index futures can be used to hedge against potential losses in a cash portfolio of shares due to short-term falls in the market. In the following case a UK portfolio manager owns a portfolio of UK shares and wishes to use futures to hedge the equity risk. The details of the portfolio are as follows:

Current market value = £10 million
Beta = 1.2

Suppose that the FT-SE is currently trading at 6000 but the market is under short-term pressure. If it falls sharply the portfolio manager runs the risk of failing to meet quarterly performance targets on the fund. Of course the manager could simply liquidate the portfolio — sell the shares and put the money into cash. However this would incur hefty transaction costs, and if the market rallied the manager would either have to start buying back shares, or run the risk of underperforming competitors who have stayed invested in the market.

The portfolio manager instead decides to sell FT-SE index futures as a temporary hedge or protection device. If the market falls the fund will lose money on the cash portfolio, but will earn variation margin payments on the short futures contracts in compensation. One problem to bear in mind though is that the portfolio is not a market portfolio — it does not exactly replicate the behaviour of the FT-SE. The beta of 1.2 tells us that it is slightly more risky than the FT-SE 100 index. (Chapter 9 has details on the calculation and the applications of beta.)

Beta

A beta of 1.2 means that for a 1% movement in the market the portfolio should change in value (in the same direction) by approximately 1.2%. The beta of a portfolio is normally calculated as the weighted average of the betas of the constituent stocks (weighted by market value). The individual stock betas are based on historical price movements.

14.6.1   Calculating the Hedge Ratio

The first issue to resolve is how many FT-SE futures contracts the manager should sell to hedge against the risk of losses on the portfolio. This is the **hedge ratio**. One way to tackle the question is to take some arbitrary fall in the FT-SE and calculate the loss on the portfolio. Then we can calculate how many futures contracts the portfolio manager would have to short to exactly recover that loss.

For example, we could assume that the index drops 150 points from its current level of 6000. We work out the percentage drop in the market:

$$\text{Percentage Change in FT-SE} = \frac{150}{6000} \times 100 = 2.5\%$$

The beta of the portfolio suggests that if the FT-SE drops by 2.5% then the portfolio will fall by a greater amount:

$$\text{Percentage Change in Portfolio} = 2.5\% \times 1.2 = 3\%$$

On a £10 million portfolio this translates into a loss in cash terms of £300,000.

The final question to answer is how many futures contracts the manager would have to short to recover a loss of £300,000 on the cash portfolio. We will assume that the futures move in line with the cash market, and fall by exactly 150 points. Each full index point on the FT-SE futures is worth £10. Therefore:

$$\text{Futures Contracts} \times 150 \times £10 = £300,000$$
$$\text{Futures Contracts} = 200 \text{ (sell)}$$

14.6.2 Hedge Ratio Formula

A simpler way to calculate the hedge ratio (the number of futures to sell) is to work out the value of the futures contracts in **cash equivalent terms**. If the FT-SE cash market is trading at 6000 then each futures contract represents a position in a portfolio of shares worth £60,000 (some fund managers call this the 'associated economic exposure'):

$$6000 \times £10 = £60,000$$

Buying one index futures is therefore equivalent to buying a portfolio of shares tracking the FT-SE worth £60,000. Selling one index futures is equivalent to running a short position in the market portfolio to the value of £60,000. The portfolio manager in our case has to cover a long position in shares worth £10 million, so clearly selling one index futures is not sufficient. As a first step we can divide the market value of the portfolio by the nominal value of a futures contract:

$$\frac{£10 \text{ million}}{£60,000} = 167 \text{ futures}$$

However, we know from the beta measure that the portfolio is more sensitive to market events than the FT-SE itself, so the portfolio manager has to increase the number of contracts in the futures hedge:

$$\text{Number of Futures} = 167 \times 1.2 = 200 \text{ futures (sell)}$$

The complete hedge ratio formula is as follows:

$$\frac{\text{Value of Portfolio} \times \text{Portfolio Beta}}{\text{Cash Index Level} \times \text{Point Value}} = \frac{£10 \text{ million} \times 1.2}{6000 \times £10} = 200 \text{ futures (sell)}$$

14.7 HEDGE EFFICIENCY

There are a number of reasons why an index futures hedge such as the one we have just considered is liable to be less than perfect in practice.

- **Basis Risk.** We assumed that the cash FT-SE and the FT-SE futures simply move in line with each other. In practice, futures contracts do not exactly track the day-to-day changes in the underlying index. The relationship between the cash index level and the futures price is known as the **basis**. The basis can change over time and so there is **basis risk** on the hedge — the underlying index and the futures may not move exactly in line with each other.
- **Tracking Error.** We assumed when we constructed the hedge ratio that beta is a reliable indicator of the tracking relationship between the portfolio and the FT-SE 100 index (and also that it remains constant). Beta is based on historical evidence and the future relationship between the portfolio and the index may not reflect past behaviour.
- **Liquidity Risk.** The daily profits and losses on the portfolio are unrealized (paper) profits and losses until the shares are actually sold. The futures position is marked-to-market and variation margin is paid or received on a daily basis. This can be an

inconvenience for the portfolio manager (money has to be set aside to meet potential margin calls); at worst it could present a serious cash flow problem.

- **Rollover Risk.** When we constructed the hedge we did not consider which expiry month the portfolio manager should trade. In practice most market participants tend to trade the 'near month' futures, the contracts with the nearest expiry month. These are normally the most liquid and so it is easier to trade in size without moving the price. However when the contracts expire the portfolio manager will no longer have a hedge in place. If the portfolio manager wishes to extend the hedge further this will involve 'rolling' the futures — that is, selling the next expiry month. This gives rise to **rollover risk** — the risk that the new contracts may not be trading at their fair valuation and the manager may have to sell them too cheaply.

Portfolio managers who sell index futures to protect against market losses normally use the contracts as a temporary hedge and buy contracts back if the market shows signs of recovery. The danger they face is that if they are short futures in a rising market any gains on their portfolio will be wiped out by losses on the futures, and they will underperform the competition. They face the risk of making an opportunity loss.

14.8   OTHER USES OF INDEX FUTURES

Portfolio managers also use index futures to assist with their investment timing. For example, a mutual fund might decide to buy futures contracts to establish a position in a market before the cash is actually received from investors. The fund manager may not wish to delay the investment, in case the market rises in the meantime. Later on the futures contracts can be closed out and replaced with physical shareholdings.

Portfolio traders working for banks can employ the same type of strategy. If they need to buy a portfolio of shares they can buy futures in the first instance to establish a position in the market at a given level, and then purchase the actual shares over a longer period of time. See Chapter 7 for details of the portfolio trading business.

14.8.1   Asset Allocation

Fund managers also use index futures as a means of adjusting their asset allocations by 'overlaying' a position in shares with futures contracts. This can be a lot quicker and cheaper in terms of transaction costs compared to physically buying one portfolio of shares and selling another.

As an example, let us suppose that an American portfolio manager wishes to shift funds from the US to the UK. The S&P is trading at 1200 and the FT-SE at 6000, the sum to be reallocated is $30 million and the GBP:USD exchange rate is 1.5000. The current US portfolio has a beta close to one and the fund manager wishes to establish an exposure to the UK market that tracks the FT-SE. The fund manager should short S&P futures and buy FT-SE futures, as follows:

$$\frac{\$30 \text{ million}}{\$250 \times 1200} = 100 \text{ S\&P futures (sell)}$$

$$\frac{£20 \text{ million}}{£10 \times 6000} = 333 \text{ FT-SE futures (buy)}$$

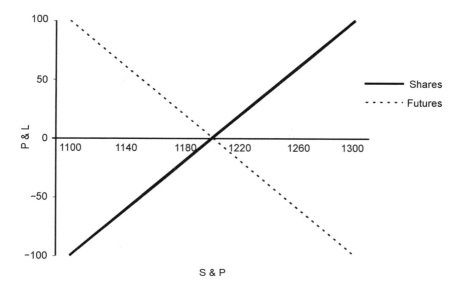

Figure 14.1   Selling S&P futures against a portfolio of US stocks

The £20 million in the numerator of this calculation is the sterling equivalent of $30 million at the spot FX rate:

$$\frac{\$30 \text{ million}}{1.5000} = £20 \text{ million}$$

This strategy 'overlays' a cash portfolio of US shares with futures contracts in order to switch to an exposure to the UK market. The effects are illustrated in Figures 14.1 and 14.2 (for simplicity this analysis ignores funding and transaction costs and assumes that the cash and futures values move in line). Assuming the short S&P futures position exactly offsets the profits and losses on the US share portfolio the fund manager has no exposure to the US market. The exposure is switched to the UK.

14.9   PRICING AN EQUITY FORWARD CONTRACT

The theoretical or **fair value** of an index futures contract is established using an arbitrage argument sometimes known as a cash-and-carry calculation. Fair value is also known as **equilibrium value**—the futures price should not stray far from that level, otherwise there are opportunities for profitable arbitrage. The cash-and-carry method derives from pricing forward contracts and is extended to exchange-traded futures. The theoretical forward price of a commodity or financial asset is derived from the cost of buying the commodity or asset in the cash or spot market, plus the cost of 'carrying' the position for forward delivery.

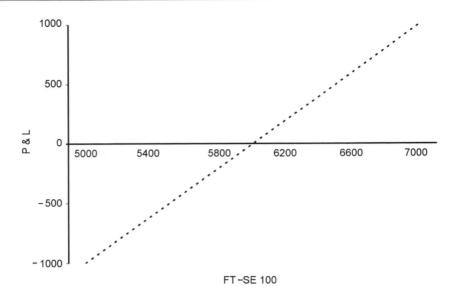

Figure 14.2   Long position in FT-SE futures

Suppose that we are asked to quote a price to a counterparty to deliver a share in one year at a fixed price. This is a **forward contract** because delivery takes place in one year and the delivery price is fixed in the contract. At the moment the share is trading at £10 in the cash market.

We could try to establish the forward price by taking a view on the direction of the share price. For example, if we believed that the price is set to fall sharply because of market or stock-specific events then we would be prepared to enter into the forward contract to deliver the share in one year at £10, in the confident expectation that we will be able to buy it later on for less than £10 to deliver to our counterparty.

Derivatives Pricing

This strategy is speculation, not valuation. The general rule when pricing a derivative product is to start with what it would cost to hedge the risks on the product and then to add on a reasonable profit margin. In normal market conditions most of the risks in the derivatives business are due to the fact that the hedging mechanisms used are not always as efficient as they might be.

14.9.1   The Cash-and-Carry Method

Our problem is that we are required to quote a fixed delivery price to our counterparty, but we do not know what it will cost us in the future to buy the share to

Spot   + 1 year

Borrow £10   Principal repayment = –£10
Buy one share cost = –£10   Interest = – £0.60
                                                   Dividend income = £0.20
                                                   Net cash flow = –£10.40

Figure 14.3 Cash flows resulting from carrying the share position

complete the delivery process. However we do know that one share would cost us £10 in the cash market. Our strategy is to buy the share in the cash market, borrow the money to do this, carry the share and then deliver it to the counterparty through the forward contract.

We have the following additional information available:

$$\text{One year funding rate} = 6.00\%$$

$$\text{Expected dividend income on the share during the next year} = £0.20$$

The principal repayment on the loan in one year is £10. The interest payment is:

$$£10 \times 0.06 = £0.60$$

Figure 14.3 illustrates the cash flows that result from carrying the position in the share to deliver against the forward contract.

Our break-even price for delivering the share in one year (assuming we have covered all our costs) is £10.40.

14.9.2 Components of the Forward Price

The forward price has two components: the cost of buying the share in the cash market, and the net cost of carrying the position to deliver the share in one year. The carry cost in turn has two components: the funding charge (interest payable) minus the dividends received on the share:

$$\text{Break-even Forward Price} = \text{Cash} + \text{Net Cost of Carry}$$
$$£10.40 = £10 + (£0.60 - £0.20)$$

$$\text{Net Cost of Carry} = \text{Funding Cost} - \text{Dividend Income}$$
$$£0.40 = £0.60 - £0.20$$

Properly speaking the net carry cost is likely to be slightly less than this because dividend payments received during the course of the year can be reinvested.

14.10   INDEX FUTURES FAIR VALUE

The fair value of a futures contract is established through a very similar calculation. It is calculated as the cost of buying a basket of shares in the cash market ready to have available to deliver on a future date, plus the cost of funding the position, less any dividends that will be received in the meantime. Although in fact there is no physical delivery on a futures contract, it is closed out at expiry against the index and therefore mirrors the behaviour of a market portfolio of shares that tracks the index.

Suppose that we wish to establish the fair value of a three-month FT-SE futures contract. We have the following data available:

Cash index level $= 6000$
Three-month sterling interest rate $= 6.00\%$ p.a.
Dividend yield on the FT-SE $= 2.00\%$ p.a.

Firstly, we establish the carry cost. The quoted interest rate and dividend yield are divided by four because they are annual rates and the futures expires in three months:

$$\text{Net Cost of Carry} = 6000 \times \frac{(0.06 - 0.02)}{4} = 60$$

Then we calculate the fair futures price:

$$\text{Fair Futures} = \text{Cash Index Level} + \text{Net Cost of Carry} = 6000 + 60 = 6060$$

$$\text{Fair Futures} = 6000 \times \left\{ 1 + \left(\frac{(0.06 - 0.02)}{4} \right) \right\} = 6060$$

Positive and Negative Carry

The fair value in this example is above the cash index level because the funding rate is higher than the dividend yield on the FT-SE. There is a negative net cost of carrying the shares which is passed on to the buyer of the futures by the seller. Not all trades have negative carry. For example, the coupon income on a bond is often higher than the cost of borrowing money to buy the bond. The seller of the futures can buy a bond to deliver against the futures and earn positive carry. This is passed over to the buyer of the futures contract in the form of a clean futures price at a discount to the cash clean price. See Chapter 11 for details on bond futures.

14.11   THE BASIS

The relationship between the cash and the futures price is known by traders as the **basis**. It is calculated in a number of different ways in the market:

$$\text{Basis} = \text{Cash} - \text{Futures}$$

or:

$$\text{Basis} = \text{Futures} - \text{Cash}$$

Here we will use the first definition. The basis on the FT-SE futures we have just priced is therefore calculated as follows:

$$\text{Basis} = 6000 - 6060 = -60 \text{ index points}$$

The negative number tells us that there is negative carry. The buyer of the futures (if it is trading at fair value) will have to pay 60 points in carry cost to the seller. This is fair, because the buyer always has the alternative of buying the underlying shares themselves rather than the futures. However the buyer would then suffer negative carry — the cost of funding the position (or the interest foregone from not being able to deposit the cash) is greater than the dividend income earned on the shares.

14.11.1   Theoretical and Actual Basis

In fact -60 points is the **theoretical basis**. It is derived from the theoretical fair value of the futures. In reality futures contracts do not always trade exactly at fair value. This can be the result of sheer supply and demand factors in the equity market:

- when the cash market starts to fall or look dangerous hedgers and speculators sell index futures aggressively;
- if subsequently the market starts to recover the shorts will look to close out their short positions by quickly buying back contracts.

Index futures tend to exaggerate movements in the underlying index. However when the futures contracts trade away from their theoretical value then valuable arbitrage opportunities open up. We illustrate how to exploit this situation in the next section.

14.12   INDEX ARBITRAGE TRADE

Let us suppose that there has been aggressive buying of the FT-SE futures that expires in three months. The three-month funding rate is 6% per annum. The dividend yield on the FT-SE 100 is 2% per annum. The fair value of the futures is therefore 6060. However we notice that the actual price of the contracts on the market is 6085. This provides us with an arbitrage trading opportunity. The strategy is as follows.

- **Long the Cash.** We borrow (say) £30 million for three months at 6.00% per annum and buy a basket of shares in the cash market worth £30 million that tracks the index (beta $= 1$).
- **Short the Futures.** We sell an offsetting number of the overpriced futures contracts at 6085. The cash index is trading at 6000 and each point is worth £10:

$$\text{Number of Contracts} = \frac{\text{£30 million}}{6000 \times \text{£10}} = 500 \text{ (sell)}$$

Selling 500 futures neutralizes the market risk on a £30 million portfolio of shares that tracks the index. We do not wish to take an outright position in the market. We want to exploit the mispricing of the futures contract.

14.12.1   Profit and Loss on the Arbitrage Trade

Finally, we will explore the net profit and loss on the strategy on the assumption that it is kept in place until the futures contracts expire. We will take two possible scenarios for the level of the FT-SE at the expiry of the futures: it is trading at 5700 (a fall of 5%); or it is trading at 6300 (a rise of 5%). The results are set out in Tables 14.2 and 14.3. Recall that if the FT-SE closes at 5700 the futures will be closed out at that level. Since they were sold at 6085 this is a profit. If the FT-SE closes at 6300 the futures are closed out at a loss.

14.12.2   Using the Basis Numbers

The net profit on the strategy is always £125,000. A quicker way to establish this figure is to look again at the theoretical basis of the futures, and also at their actual basis (calculated from the actual price of the futures contracts):

Table 14.2   Profit and loss if the index closes at 5700

FT-SE closes at 5700	Payments and receipts
Short 500 futures at 6085. Futures close at expiry at 5700	Variation margin received = $500 \times (6085-5700) \times £10 = £1.925$ million
Repay loan interest at 6% per annum (three-month loan)	Interest paid = £30 million $\times 0.06 \times 1/4 = -£0.45$ million
Dividends on shares at 2% per annum for three months	Dividends received = £30 million $\times 0.02 \times 1/4 = £0.15$ million
Buy £30 million shares with cash index at 6000. Index closes at 5700, a fall of 5%	Loss on shares = £30 million $\times -0.05 = -£1.5$ million
Net P&L	£125,000

Table 14.3   Profit and loss if the index closes at 6300

FT-SE closes at 6300	Payments and receipts
Short 500 futures at 6085. Futures close at expiry at 6300	Variation margin paid = $500 \times (6085-6300) \times £10 = -£1.075$ million
Repay loan interest at 6% per annum (three-month loan)	Interest paid = £30 million $\times 0.06 \times 1/4 = -£0.45$ million
Dividends on shares at 2% per annum for three months	Dividends received = £30 million $\times 0.02 \times 1/4 = £0.15$ million
Buy £30 million shares with cash index at 6000. Index closes at 6300, a rise of 5%	Profit on shares = £30 million $\times 0.05 = £1.5$ million
Net P&L	£125,000

Theoretical basis $= 6000 - 6060 = -60$
Actual basis $= 6000 - 6085 = -85$

There is a discrepancy between the theoretical and actual basis of 25 points. This discrepancy (sometimes called the **value basis**) is exploited through the index arbitrage trade:

$$\text{Arbitrage Profit} = 25 \text{ points} \times 500 \text{ futures} \times £10 = £125,000$$

The fact that the actual basis is a bigger negative number than the theoretical basis tells us that the carry cost built into the actual futures price is too high. We should sell the futures and buy the cash.

14.13   RUNNING THE ARBITRAGE DESK

In practice there are a number of constraints on index arbitrage trading that have to be factored into the equation.

- **Arbitrage Window.** Arbitrage opportunities of this kind do not persist for long. The effect of traders selling the overpriced futures and buying the cash will be to push down the futures price (and perhaps pull up the cash index). The arbitrage opportunity will quickly disappear.
- **Transaction Costs.** Even for a large trading operation there are transaction costs involved in buying shares and selling futures. Against this, electronic trading is reducing the costs and making it easier to assemble baskets of shares to offset against futures positions.
- **Tracking Error.** The arbitrage trader may decide to save on transaction costs by assembling a basket of shares that is likely to track the index rather than buying all the shares in the index. This leaves open the risk that the basket may not accurately track the index (while the futures at expiry will close at the cash index level).
- **Dividend Assumptions.** In the arbitrage trade we made an assumption about the dividends we would receive on the basket of shares. It may be that these are less than expected.
- **Borrowing Constraints.** The index arbitrage trade needs capital to generate a small (albeit a risk-free or low risk) profit.
- **Funding Costs.** As with many transactions involving derivatives, the ability to fund the strategy at keen interest rates is very important. High funding costs will eliminate the arbitrage profit.
- **Stock Borrowing Fees.** If the futures is trading 'cheap' relative to its fair or theoretical value the appropriate trade is to buy the futures and short the underlying stock. This incurs stock borrowing fees, and there is the risk that it may prove difficult (or expensive) to find the stock to borrow in the market.

Index arbitrage desks usually set a threshold level for the trade. If the futures deviates by more than this level from fair value the arbitrage trade is likely to be profitable, net of transaction costs. The threshold will differ between different banks, because it depends on such factors as funding and trading costs.

14.14   FEATURES OF INDEX FUTURES

Equity index futures have a number of features which can offer advantages to investors and traders compared to buying and selling shares and portfolios of shares in the cash market.

- **Leverage.** A relatively small deposit of initial margin provides access to a substantial equity exposure. If the cash FT-SE 100 index is trading at 6000 then each futures contract is equivalent to a market portfolio of shares worth £60,000. If an investor had £60,000 to invest a percentage could be used to make the margin deposit on futures and the rest kept in a safe money market deposit account.
- **Transaction Costs.** These are normally much lower when compared to buying and selling underlying shares. Brokerage charges on futures are low, there is no need for custodians and (in the UK) there is no stamp duty to pay to the government. It is relatively cheap and easy to switch exposures quickly.
- **Diversification.** Index futures provide easy access to a diversified portfolio of shares.
- **Liquidity.** The major contracts such as the S&P 500 futures are very actively traded and there are many market participants. Market access is easy and prices are determined in an open and transparent manner. It is also just as easy to take a short position as it is to take a long position.
- **The Clearing House.** Futures contracts are guaranteed by the clearing house.

There are some other features that can pose problems (although they can also provide trading opportunities).

- **Basis Risk.** The fact that futures do not exactly move in line with the cash market (the basis is not constant) means that hedging with futures is not an exact science. It also poses problems for fund managers who are using futures to track an index.
- **Rollover Risk.** Index futures do not last for ever. When a contract expires a trader who wishes to retain the position will have to 'roll' into the next delivery month. This may be trading cheap or dear relative to fair value.
- **Margin Calls.** The margin system helps to protect the stability of the exchange and to ensure that the clearing house can always meet its obligations. However it does mean that a trader is subject to margin calls, and may be forced to sell securities quickly to meet a margin call.
- **Standardized Contracts.** In order to make index futures contracts as actively traded as possible they have to be standardized. This may not suit an investor who, for example, would like to take an exposure to a subset of shares in the FT-SE rather than the whole index.

14.15   SINGLE STOCK FUTURES

The issue of standardization is now being addressed by the exchanges. Contracts have been introduced on a much wider range of indices, including the NASDAQ, the Russell 2000® index of smaller capitalization US companies, and the DJ STOXX index based on 50 leading European shares. In January 2001 LIFFE introduced futures contracts on individual shares. Contracts are available on leading international shares quoted in

Table 14.4   Universal stock futures contract

Currency:	GBP
Quotation:	Pence per share
Tick size:	0.5 pence
Contract size:	Normally 1000 shares
Delivery months:	March, June, September, December
Delivery:	Cash-settled
Last trading day:	Third Wednesday in delivery month

Source: LIFFE.

US dollars, euros and sterling. Table 14.4 sets out the contract specification for the stock futures on UK companies.

The contracts are cash-settled. Suppose for example an investor decides to take a long position in BT. The current share price is 450 pence and the investor would like to take an exposure of £72,000:

$$\text{Contract Value} = £4.50 \times 1000 \text{ shares} = £4500$$

$$\text{Contracts Purchased} = \frac{£72,000}{£4500} = 16 \text{ contracts}$$

The investor deposits initial margin with the broker. If the futures price later rises by (say) 30 pence per share the trader can close out by selling 16 contracts in the appropriate month:

$$\text{Profit} = £0.3 \times 1000 \times 16 = £4800$$

From this is deducted transaction costs (although the investor should earn some interest on the initial margin).

Smaller Investors

Some smaller investors seem to be put off from using futures contracts because of the margin system. They may find it inconvenient. It may also be because the daily mark-to-market makes it only too obvious when a futures position is unprofitable. In many ways this is a good thing, but for people accustomed to buying and holding shares it is a novel experience. Losses on bad share positions are unrealized until the shares are actually sold; it is always possible to convince oneself that the shares will recover. Daily margin calls concentrate the mind wonderfully.

14.16   EQUITY SWAPS

An equity swap is the over-the-counter answer to index and stock futures. In general terms, a swap contract is an agreement between two parties:

- to exchange cash flows;
- at regular intervals;
- over an agreed period of time.

Since swaps are dealt over-the-counter and not on exchanges they carry counterparty default risk (although we saw in Chapter 12 that the London Clearing House now has a facility under which it will act as central counterparty for certain classes of interest rate swaps).

In a standard or 'vanilla' **equity swap** there are two payment legs.

- **An equity payment**, based on the change in the value of a share or a basket of shares or an index.
- **An interest payment**, calculated on a fixed or a floating basis.

If the swap is a **total return swap** then the equity payment will be accompanied by a payment representing dividends on the share or basket or index.

14.17   EQUITY INDEX SWAP: CASE STUDY

A portfolio manager wishes to make a tactical asset allocation switch over the next year and to increase the fund's exposure to the UK equity market. The desired exposure is £100 million. Rather than sell off existing stocks or liquidate holdings in cash and bonds, the manager can enter into an index swap in which he or she:

- pays the swap dealer sterling LIBOR + 0.3% p.a. every three months for one year on a fixed notional £100 million principal;
- receives (or pays) a cash sum every three months that represents the change in the value of a notional £100 million portfolio tracking the FT-SE 100, plus the dividend yield on the index.

The index level at the start of the swap is 6000. The notional principal is fixed over the life of the swap. The swap payments are represented in Figure 14.4.

The LIBOR rate for the first payment date in three months is fixed at the start of the contract, as is the dividend yield. Let us suppose that the figures are as follows:

First three-month LIBOR fix = 5.70% p.a.
LIBOR + 0.30% = 6.00% p.a.
FT-SE dividend yield = 2.00% p.a.

The first payment takes place three months after the commencement of the swap. Suppose on that date the FT-SE 100 stands at 6150. This is a rise of 150 points or 2.5%

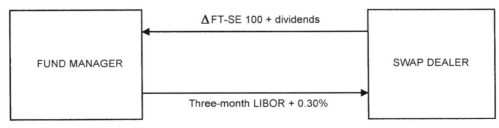

Figure 14.4   Payment legs on the equity swap

from the starting level of 6000. The payments and receipts on the swap are calculated as follows.

- **Index Change.** The dealer has to make a payment that represents the 2.5% rise in the FT-SE 100 index. On £100 million notional principal this is £2.5 million.
- **Dividend Yield.** The dealer has to make a payment representing the dividend yield on the notional principal for a three-month period. This is £100 million×0.02/4=£0.5 million.
- **Interest Payment.** The dealer is owed £100 million×0.06/4=£1.5 million.

The individual payments are netted out and cash is transferred from one counterparty to the other. In this case the fund manager is owed money by the swap dealer:

$$\text{Net Receipt} = £2.5 + £0.5 - £1.5 = £1.5 \text{ million}$$

14.17.1   Second Swap Payment

We have calculated the payment due three months after the start of the swap. At that point the three variables in the swap contract are re-fixed (in this swap the £100 million notional is a constant):

- the FT-SE start level is reset at 6150;
- the interest payment is re-fixed at the three-month sterling LIBOR plus 30 basis points;
- the FT-SE dividend yield is reset at the prevailing rate.

These variables are used to calculate the payment due in another three months' time. If, for example, the FT-SE fell back from 6150 to 5842.5 (a drop of 5%) then this time the fund manager would owe the swap dealer a sum of money representing the fall in the market. The payment is:

$$£100 \text{ million} \times 0.05 = £5 \text{ million}$$

To this is added the payment due to the dealer for the funding leg of the swap, less the dividend payment due to the fund manager.

14.17.2   Dividend and Interest Payments

In the above case we assumed that the dividend payment is calculated using a blanket dividend yield for the index as a whole. In practice the swap dealer may agree to pass over the actual dividends on the stocks that compose the index. We also assumed that the interest payments are made on a floating rate basis. An alternative is to fix the rate. In fact it is easy to convert between these alternatives using a fixed–floating interest rate swap. (See Chapter 12 for details of interest rate swaps.)

14.18   MANAGING THE RISK ON EQUITY SWAPS

The swap dealer in the above example clearly has a significant exposure to changes in the FT-SE 100 index. Perhaps the ideal hedge would be to find another counterparty willing to pay over the return on the market over the same period and prepared to

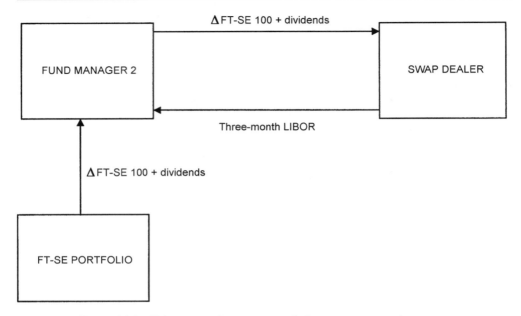

Figure 14.5   Using an equity swap to switch to a money market return

accept a rate of interest less than LIBOR + 0.30%. The counterparty might be a fund manager holding a large portfolio of UK stocks who believes that the market will perform poorly for a period of time but who is unwilling to physically liquidate holdings, perhaps because of transaction costs or because a sell-off may affect the prices.

Imagine that the dealer enters into an offsetting index swap with such a counterparty, Fund Manager 2. The dealer pays three-month LIBOR flat and receives the total return on the FT-SE 100. All payments are quarterly and the period of the swap is one year. The notional is fixed at £100 million. The position of Fund Manager 2 after the swap is shown in Figure 14.5.

Effectively, for the period of the swap, this second fund manager is converting from a volatile stock market return to a money market return. This is achieved without the significant transaction costs that would be incurred by selling off the portfolio and perhaps later having to build it back up again when the market shows signs of recovery. Depending on swap rates, it might also be possible to achieve a return above LIBOR.

14.18.1   Matched Swap Transactions

Next Figure 14.6 shows the position of the swap dealer on the assumption that both swaps are dealt — the original swap paying the index return, and the second swap receiving the index return.

Here the dealer collects the 30 basis points spread between the two funding rates. Of course it is unlikely that the swap dealer would be able to match two swaps as quickly and effectively as this suggests. In practice any offsetting tends to be partial and exposures do not exactly match. For example, Fund Manager 2 may be willing to pay

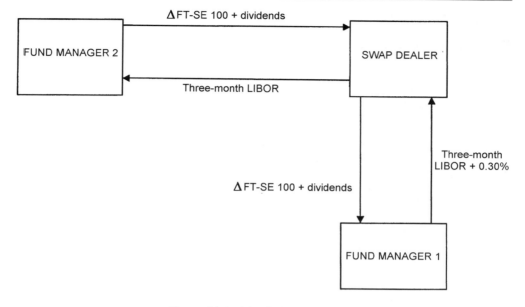

Figure 14.6   Matched equity swaps

the market return on the FT-SE over the desired period in return for LIBOR, but only
on a notional principal of £50 million.

14.19   HEDGING SWAPS IN THE CASH MARKET

If an offsetting swap is not available, another way for the dealer to hedge the equity
exposure is to trade in the underlying market. Figure 14.7 shows the original swap
transaction with the first fund manager. The dealer is paying the equity return and
receives LIBOR + 30 basis points. To hedge the risk this time the dealer buys a cash
portfolio of shares and funds the position at LIBOR.

The swap dealer captures 30 basis points on this set of transactions. However in
practice there are still some risks outstanding.

- **Counterparty Risk.** The counterparty might default on the swap and the hedge would
  have to be unwound or a replacement swap found (although the £100 notional is not
  at risk since it is never exchanged). The dealer may ask for margin to contain this
  risk.
- **Funding Risk.** The dealer may decide to fund the hedge on a weekly or even daily
  basis if rates are cheaper, and roll over the funding. This produces a mismatch since
  the rate received from the counterparty is based on three-month LIBOR.
- **Dividend Risk.** If the dealer agrees to pay over the actual dividends on the shares in
  the FT-SE this is covered by the hedge portfolio. If the dealer agrees to pay over a
  sum of money representing the forecast dividend yield on the index this may be more
  than the actual cash dividends received.

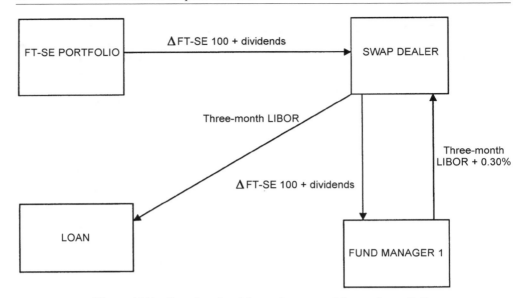

Figure 14.7   Covering the risk on the swap with a cash portfolio

- **Tracking Error.** The swap dealer may decide to buy a basket of shares designed to track the index rather than all 100 shares, to save on transaction costs. Then there is a risk that the basket may not track the index accurately.

Alternatively, the dealer could hedge the swap by buying index futures to cover the next swap payment date, and then 'rolling' the futures hedge into later month contracts to cover subsequent payment dates. This is likely to be cheaper in terms of transaction costs compared to buying a cash portfolio, but there is a basis risk — the risk that the futures position may not exactly match the profits and losses on the swap.

14.20   STRUCTURING EQUITY SWAPS

Equity swaps are over-the-counter structures and can be tailored to meet the needs of specific counterparties. One common variant is to allow the notional principal to fluctuate.
   The terms of our original FT-SE index swap were as follows.

Maturity: One year
Payments: Quarterly
Notional principal: £100 million (fixed)
Start index level: 6000

The client pays LIBOR + 0.30% p.a.
In return the swap dealer pays the total return on the FT-SE 100 (capital gain/loss plus dividend yield)

We assumed that on the first payment date the FT-SE 100 had risen 2.5% to 6150. The payment due to the counterparty for the rise in the index is therefore £2.5 million. If the index then fell back to 6000 on the next swap payment date this is a fall of 2.439%. The payment due to the swap dealer for the fall in the index is therefore:

$$£100 \times 0.02439 = £2.439 \text{ million}$$

In a typical **floating principal** swap the principal is also reset after a payment. In our example on the first payment date the notional principal would be reset to £100 million plus the payment of 2.5% of £100 million, that is to £102.5 million. Then if the index fell back to 6000 on the second payment date (a fall of 2.439%) the second payment is calculated as:

$$£102.5 \times 0.02439 = £2.5 \text{ million}$$

The floating principal approach replicates the changing value of a portfolio of stocks tracking the index, taking into account the cost of funding the position as well as capital gains/losses and dividends received. The internal rate of return on the cash flows will match the return on the equivalent index tracking portfolio, which is not the case for a fixed principal swap.

14.20.1   Single Stock Swaps and Baskets

Equity swaps need not be based on a well-known index such as the FT-SE 100. A counterparty may wish to receive the return on a basket of shares drawn from a particular sector such as pharmaceuticals or oil, or even the return on an individual share. In a so-called **quanto** swap the returns on a basket of shares are paid in another currency. This allows investors to take positions in foreign equity markets without settlement and custodian complications and without having to transact in the foreign exchange market.

   A swap may have two equity legs rather than just one. For example, a fund manager may decide to make a tactical asset allocation switch by paying away the returns on the S&P 500 index and receiving from the swap dealer a return based on the FT-SE 100. Typically the fund manager will own an underlying portfolio of US stocks and will simply pass over the returns in that market to the swap dealer.

   A further variant occurs when the equity leg of a swap is based on the higher of the returns on two market indices. Given the obvious attractions of such a structure the rate paid on the interest rate leg will be higher than on a standard or 'vanilla' equity index swap. Finally, a **blended** swap is one in which the equity payment is based on the weighted average of the returns on two or more indices.

14.21   BENEFITS OF EQUITY SWAPS FOR AN INVESTOR

Equity swaps have a number of advantages for an investor compared with buying and selling index futures or holding actual share portfolios.

- **No Basis Risk.** The equity leg payments in a swap are based purely on the change in the value of the underlying basket of shares. The return on futures positions depends not only on changes in the underlying market portfolio but also on unpredictable changes in the cash–futures relationship (the basis).

- **Transaction Costs.** There may be an upfront commission fee on an equity swap, or the swap dealer may simply make a return on the bid–offer spread. However, transaction costs can be appreciably lower than the cost of buying and holding the underlying shares (although there will be initial legal costs involved in setting up a master swap agreement).
- **Margins.** Index futures positions are inexpensive to transact but the daily margining system can be inconvenient for some users. Equity swaps avoid this problem by having a limited number of payment dates (although the dealer may reserve the right to call for margin on a monthly or even a weekly basis to manage the credit risk on the contract).
- **Perfect Tracking.** Equity swaps are highly convenient for index funds. As well as potentially lower transaction costs, they have the advantage over holding a portfolio of shares designed to match the index that there is no risk of tracking error. In addition, a tracking portfolio has to be restructured whenever there is a change in the composition of the index. This has proved expensive in the UK in recent years when companies such as Halifax plc joined the FT-SE 100 and the trackers were obliged to buy the stock in a rapidly rising market.
- **Customized.** Equity swaps are highly flexible and a dealer will be able to tailor a contract to meet the precise needs of the client. For example, the equity leg need not be linked to the return on a well-known market index but can be based on a specific basket of shares. By contrast futures contracts are standardized to encourage liquid trading.
- **Tax Benefits.** Some countries impose a special withholding tax on dividends paid to foreign investors. Such an investor could enter into a swap with a domestic bank (which is not subject to the withholding tax) and receive the return on a basket of shares including gross (or nearly gross) dividends.
- **Market Access.** In some countries shares can be highly illiquid, or there may be restrictions on ownership. Equity swaps allow foreign investors to gain exposure to such markets. If the swap is structured as a 'quanto' the returns can be paid in the investor's home currency. In addition, there is no need for the investor to become involved with the different settlement, accounting or regulatory systems of the foreign country.

One potential disadvantage of swaps is that, unlike index futures, they are over-the-counter contracts and therefore inherently illiquid. In addition, there is a credit risk, though not on the notional principal, only on the settlement of differences. However the sums involved can be quite considerable, more than is typical for traditional fixed–floating interest rate swaps. Partly for this reason many equity swaps employ quarterly or monthly rather than semi-annual payments, and maturities tend to be shorter than is the case with interest rate swaps. Credit risk may be managed by asking for initial margin and reserving the right to ask for additional collateral in defined circumstances, or by involving a third-party guarantor. A related problem is that of legal risk. If it is proved that a counterparty is acting **ultra vires** (that is, beyond their legal authority) in entering into the swap agreement in the first place then the contract may be cancelled by the courts.

14.22 CHAPTER SUMMARY

An index futures contract is an agreement made on an organized exchange to exchange cash payments based on the movement in a stock index. Contracts are cash-settled and there is no physical delivery of shares. When a futures position is set up initial margin has to be deposited and the contracts are regularly marked-to-market. On the last trading day they are closed out against the underlying cash index. The fair value of an index futures is the cash index plus the net cost of carrying a position in the shares that comprise the index. The relationship between the cash and the futures price is called the basis. If the futures price deviates from fair value it may be possible to construct an index arbitrage trade, buying the cash market and selling the futures, or vice versa. In practice it is necessary to take into account the effects of transaction costs on the likely profits. Index futures are used to hedge positions in shares and to implement asset allocation decisions as well as for trading purposes. Exchanges are currently introducing futures contracts on individual shares. An equity swap is an agreement between two parties to exchange payments on regular future dates. One payment leg is based on the change in the value of a share or a basket of shares (sometimes plus dividends) and the return leg is based on a fixed or floating rate of interest. Investors can use equity swaps to transform the nature of their assets and to gain exposures to changes in share prices without having to buy the actual shares. Equity swap dealers can use offsetting swaps or positions in shares or futures contracts to manage their risks. Because swaps are dealt over-the-counter they can be tailored to meet the needs of clients. However they are illiquid and carry credit risk.

15
Fundamentals of Options

Probability is expectation founded upon partial knowledge.
George Boole

15.1 CHAPTER OVERVIEW

This chapter introduces fundamental option concepts. It takes a 'building block' approach and describes the basic option strategies which we will apply in different combinations in later chapters. We describe the basic contract types — calls and puts; American and European-style options. We introduce and explain the key 'jargon' expressions used in the options market — strike or exercise price; expiry date; premium; intrinsic and time value; in-, at- and out-of-the-money; break-even point; and so on. These concepts are illustrated with practical examples. We introduce the idea of the expiry payoff profile of an option strategy and consider the profiles for four basic strategies — buying or selling a call option; buying or selling a put option. These are compared with the profit and loss profiles achieved by buying or selling the underlying shares. To relate the theory of options to the 'real world' of the financial markets we consider index option and stock option contracts traded on some key derivatives exchanges. We explain the specification of the contracts, how the option premiums are quoted and how to calculate the potential profits and losses on trades. Finally we review the fundamental concepts of intrinsic and time value and investigate how they relate to the quoted prices of options listed on exchanges. In the Appendix some common varieties of exotic options are described.

15.2 DEFINITIONS

Options contracts on commodities such as oil and grain have been in existence for many years. Options on financial instruments are relatively recent in origin but trading activity has expanded rapidly since the introduction of traded options contracts on exchanges such as the Chicago Board Options Exchange (CBOE) and the London International Financial Futures Exchange (LIFFE).

The buyer of a financial option contract has the right but not the obligation to buy or sell:

- an agreed amount of a specified financial asset, called the **underlying**;
- at a specified price, called the **exercise** or strike price;
- on or before a specified future date, called the **expiry date**.

For this right the buyer pays an upfront fee called the **premium** to the seller or writer of the option. Essentially the buyer of an option contract pays for the flexibility of not being obliged to exercise or take up the option. The buyer can exercise the option if the exercise or strike price is better than the market price of the underlying asset. Otherwise, the option can be left to expire worthless. This flexibility has a price, which is the option premium.

Exchange-traded options are standardized, but their performance is guaranteed by the clearing house associated with the exchange. Over-the-counter (OTC) option contracts are agreed directly between two counterparties, normally one of which is a bank or securities trading house. As a result the contracts can be customized to meet the needs of specific counterparties. However they cannot be freely traded and they do not carry the guarantee of a clearing house. For this reason there is default or counterparty risk on OTC options — the risk that the counterparty may fail to fulfil its obligations. To protect themselves against default risk option dealers may ask for collateral from their counterparties and will also limit the amount of deals they have outstanding with a particular counterparty at a given moment in time.

15.3   TYPES OF OPTIONS

There are two main varieties of option contract.

- **Call Option.** An option to buy the underlying at a given strike or exercise price is a call option. The buyer of a call has the right but not the obligation to buy the underlying asset at the strike price.
- **Put Option.** An option to sell the underlying at a given strike or exercise price is a put option. The buyer of a put has the right but not the obligation to sell the underlying asset at the strike price.

A so-called **American-style** option can be exercised on or before expiry. A **European-style** option can only be exercised on the expiry date of the contract. In fact these labels are purely historical and have nothing to do with where options are actually dealt. Most option contracts traded on exchanges are American options, including those traded on Eurex and LIFFE. OTC option contracts, regardless of where they are created, are often European. Because American options confer additional rights in terms of early exercise, in most circumstances they are more expensive than European contracts.

Bermudan Options

For those who like the flexibility of early exercise but who do not wish to pay the full cost of an American option, the market has created alternative contracts known as Bermudan options. These can be exercised on specific dates up to expiry, for example, one business day a week.

In practice relatively few options are ever exercised. A trader who has bought an exchange-traded option can simply sell it back through the exchange if it becomes more valuable, rather than actually exercising the contract. Options are bought and sold as assets in their own right and many traders simply make profits on the difference between the purchase and the sale price. And in any event the majority of options expire worthless.

15.4 BASIC OPTION TRADING STRATEGIES

In the following sections we will consider the return and risk characteristics of the four basic option trading strategies:

- buy a call;
- sell a call;
- buy a put;
- sell a put.

We will start with a call option contract. The details of the contract are specified in Table 15.1.

Table 15.1 Call option contract

Type of option:	American-style call
Underlying:	One XYZ share
Exercise price:	£100 per share
Expiry date:	One year from today
Current share price:	£100
Premium:	£10 per share

The buyer of the option has the right but not the obligation to buy one share at a fixed strike price of £100 on or before the expiry date in one year. For this right the buyer has to pay an upfront premium to the option seller of £10 per share. In this example the exercise price and the current share price are exactly the same. This is known as an **at-the-money** (ATM) option.

Intrinsic Value

An American option that is at-the-money has zero intrinsic value. Intrinsic value is the value (if any) that can be realized through immediately exercising an option contract. Intrinsic value is either zero or positive because the buyer of an option is never obliged to exercise the option and make a loss through exercise.

If the underlying were currently trading at £120 then the £100 strike call option would be **in-the-money** (ITM) and would have £20 intrinsic value per share. The holder could exercise the right to buy the share at the strike price of £100 and then immediately re-sell the share on the cash market at £120. Ignoring funding and transaction costs, the value realized by exercising the option would be £20 per share. If on the other hand the underlying security was currently trading at (say) £80 then the £100 strike call option would be **out-of-the-money** (OTM). The share price would have to increase by more than £20 before it would be worth exercising the option. If an option is out-of-the-money it has zero intrinsic value.

15.4.1   Intrinsic versus Time Value

The option contract in Table 15.1 is at-the-money in relation to the spot price of the underlying share. It has no intrinsic value. The £10 premium charged by the seller is paid for the chance or probability that the share price *might* increase over the one-year time period remaining until expiry. The buyer of the option could make a substantial profit from this eventuality, while the maximum profit to the seller is the relatively small amount of premium collected upfront. The chance or probability element in an option premium is known as its **time value** (so-called because it is in part determined by the amount of time remaining to the expiry of the option).

- **Intrinsic Value.** Any money that could be released by exercising an option. In the case of a European option this can only be done at expiry. An American contract can be exercised on or before expiry.
- **Time Value.** The chance or probability element in an option premium. Even an option that is out-of-the-money (with zero intrinsic value) will have time value if it has any time remaining until expiry and assuming the share price can fluctuate. There is a chance that the option might move into the money before it expires.

The premium payable on an in-the-money option is comprised of its intrinsic value plus time value. For example, if the underlying was trading at £120 then a £100 strike call would have £20 intrinsic value, and a seller would charge a minimum of £20 for the option plus some time value. The premium payable on an at-the-money or out-of-the-money option is purely time value. It is paid simply for the chance or possibility that the option might subsequently move into the money and return a profit.

15.5   BUYING A CALL: EXPIRY PAYOFF PROFILE

One useful way to look at an option strategy is in terms of its profit or loss at the expiry of the option, net of the initial premium paid. At the expiry of an option there is a simple decision for the holder to make — either the contract is exercised or it is discarded as worthless. Put another way, an option at expiry has positive intrinsic value if it expires in-the-money; it has zero intrinsic value if it expires out-of-the-money or at-the-money.

Let us suppose that a trader buys the one-year at-the-money call in Table 15.1 with a strike of £100 and pays a premium of £10 per share to the seller. To keep the illustration simple we will ignore transaction and funding costs in this example — in particular we will ignore the fact that the premium has to be paid upfront whereas the decision on whether or not to exercise the option will be taken at expiration. Figure 15.1 illustrates the payoff on this strategy at the expiry of the call for a range of different levels of the underlying share price.

At expiry the owner of the call option will only exercise the contract when the underlying price is above the strike or exercise price — in this case, £100. For example, if the share was trading at £90 at expiry then the holder of the call would not take up the right to buy the share at a fixed price of £100 when it could be purchased more cheaply in the cash market. If the option is not exercised the loss is the £10 premium. However if the underlying share is worth more than £100 in the cash market then it makes sense to exercise the call. It has intrinsic value.

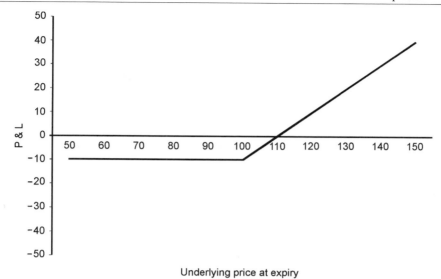

Underlying price at expiry

Figure 15.1   Expiry payoff profile for a long call position

Break-even Point

The break-even point is reached when the share is trading at £110. At that level the £10 initial premium is exactly offset (ignoring funding and transaction costs) by the £10 intrinsic value of the call. The call confers the right to buy a share at £100 that is worth £110 in the cash market and £10 could be realized by exercising the option.

15.5.1   Downside and Upside

In the jargon of the markets the buyer of an option has **limited downside risk** but **unlimited upside**. In other words, the maximum loss is restricted to the initial premium paid, simply because the buyer is not obliged to exercise an option that expires at- or out-of-the-money. On the other hand there is no limit to the profit that the buyer of a call option can make. The underlying share price could (in theory) rise to any level and the holder of the call has the option to buy the share at the fixed strike or exercise price.

15.6   COMPARISON WITH CASH POSITION

So far buying a call probably seems like a very attractive proposition (limited risk, unlimited return). However the initial premium is something of a dead weight on the profitability of the position. For example, rather than buying the £100 strike call the trader in our example could simply have bought the underlying share in the cash market at £100. Then if the share price rose to £110 the trader would have made a £10 profit, while because of the initial premium paid the option position would simply break even (although the initial outlay on the option position is far lower). For comparison

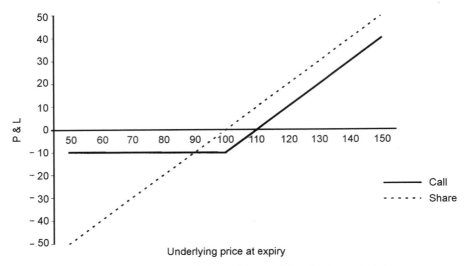

Figure 15.2   Long call versus long position in the underlying

purposes Figure 15.2 shows the profit and loss profile of the bought (long) call position against a position in the underlying share purchased in the cash market at £100.

15.7   SELLING A CALL: EXPIRY PAYOFF PROFILE

Next we look at the £100 strike call in Table 15.1 from the perspective of the seller or writer of the options. The initial premium collected by the seller is £10. In fact this is the most money the seller can ever make out of the option. If the option expires out-of-the-money the buyer will not exercise the contract and the premium is a profit. On the other hand, if the option expires in-the-money the buyer will exercise the call and has the right to buy a share at a fixed price of £100 that may be far more valuable in the cash market. Figure 15.3 illustrates the profit and loss profile of the seller of the call option at the expiry of the contract.

Figure 15.3 illustrates the payoff profile of a so-called 'naked' sold call option. The seller has an unhedged position. If the buyer exercises the option the seller has to deliver the share at a fixed price of £100 and buy it in the cash market at the current spot price, which could potentially be well above £100. As we will see later, sellers of call options normally hedge their risks, sometimes through offsetting options positions, sometimes through purchasing the underlying asset.

15.8   BUYING A PUT: EXPIRY PAYOFF PROFILE

In the next example we will explore the position of the buyer of a put option. The contract we will use is specified in Table 15.2.

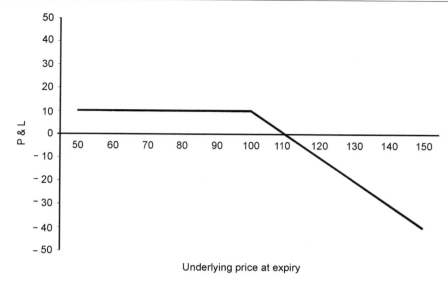

Underlying price at expiry

Figure 15.3   Expiry payoff profile of the short call

Table 15.2   Put option contract specification

Type of option:	American-style put
Underlying:	One XYZ share
Exercise price:	£100 per share
Expiry date:	One year from today
Current share price:	£100
Premium:	£10 per share

For the buyer of the put the contract is a 'bear' position, but the losses are limited to the initial premium.

- The buyer has the right but not the obligation to sell one share at £100 on or before the expiry date in one year.
- For this right the buyer has to pay an initial premium of £10 per share to the seller of the put option.

The contract in Table 15.2 is an at-the-money put option since the spot price is the same as the strike or exercise price. The contract has zero intrinsic value—that is, there is no profit to be made through immediate exercise. If the underlying share price was, for example, £90 rather than £100 then a put with a strike of £100 would have £10 intrinsic value since the holder of the put could immediately exercise the option and sell for £100 a share that is only worth £90 in the cash market. The holder of the put could buy the share for £90, exercise the option and 'put' the stock on the seller of the option for £100, and make a £10 profit. Of course if an option is in-the-money this would be reflected in a higher premium cost.

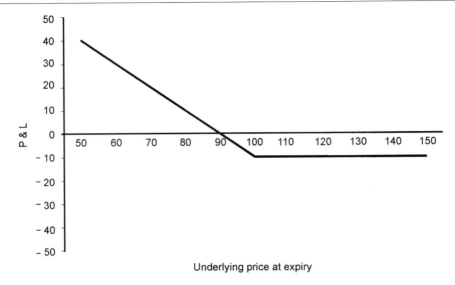

Figure 15.4   Expiry payoff profile of a long put option

Once again we can represent the profit and loss payoff profile of the buyer of the put option at the expiry of the contract for a range of different possible prices of the underlying share. The strike is £100 and the premium is £10. The profile is illustrated in Figure 15.4.

It would make sense for the holder of the put to exercise and sell the share at the fixed £100 strike when it is trading below £100 in the cash market at the expiry of the put option. We will take two examples: (i) the share price is £95; (ii) the share price is £90.

- **Share Price £95.** In this case the holder of the put option could buy the share in the cash market at £95 and sell it through the option contract at the fixed strike price of £100, making £5 on exercise (the £5 here is the intrinsic value of the option). From this must be subtracted the initial £10 premium paid so the net profit and loss to the holder of the call would be −£5 per share.
- **Share Price £90.** The holder of the call could make £10 from exercising the option, which just offsets the £10 premium paid upfront and the net profit and loss is zero.

If the share price is trading below £90 at the expiry of the put then the holder of the put will make a net profit (again ignoring funding and transaction costs). In this example the maximum loss to the holder of the put is the £10 premium and the maximum profit is £90. Unlike a bought call there is a maximum profit on a bought put because share prices can (in theory) keep rising indefinitely but they do not fall below zero.

15.9   COMPARISON WITH SHORTING THE STOCK

Owning a put option is a 'bear' position. The holder makes money when the underlying share falls in value. However it is far less risky than running a short position in

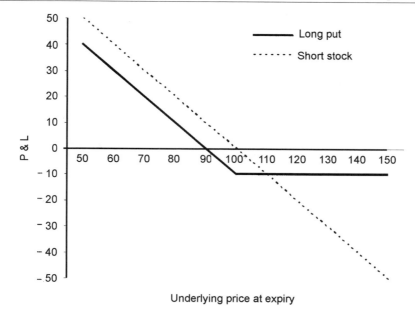

Figure 15.5   Long put versus short position in the underlying

the underlying share by borrowing the share and selling it in the cash market. The potential losses of a short seller are theoretically unlimited since the 'short' has to buy the share back in the cash market to return it to its original owner at the prevailing market price—which might be far above the sale price. Figure 15.5 shows the profit and loss payoff profile of the bought £100 strike put and at the same time (dotted line) the profile of a position in which the underlying is sold short at £100.

15.10   SELLING A PUT: EXPIRY PAYOFF PROFILE

Figure 15.6 shows the payoff profile at expiry of the put option in Table 15.2, this time from the seller's perspective. The strike of the put is £100 and the initial premium collected was £10 per share.

The maximum profit for the writer of the put option is the premium of £10 and the maximum loss is £90. If the share price closes at or above the strike at the expiry of the option the holder of the option will not exercise the contract and the seller has made a £10 profit. On the other hand if the share price is below £100 the holder of the put will exercise the contract. The break-even point occurs when the share is trading at £90. At that level the seller of the put will be sold a share for £100 which is only worth £90 in the cash market, making a £10 loss which is offset by the initial premium. Below £90 the position shows a net loss.

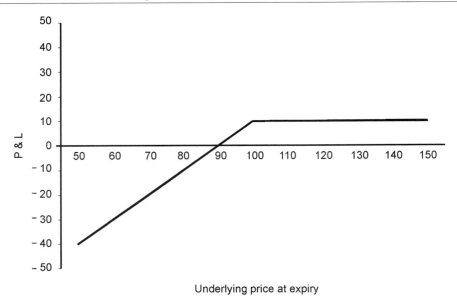

Underlying price at expiry

Figure 15.6   Expiry payoff profile of a short put option

In fact Figure 15.6 shows the payoff profile of a 'naked' short put option, that is, without a hedge in place. Normally speaking the seller of a put option will hedge the risks by trading other option contracts or by shorting the underlying — which will show a profit if the share price falls — to offset the losses on the put.

15.11   SUMMARY: INTRINSIC AND TIME VALUE

- The intrinsic value of an American call option is the amount by which the price of the underlying security exceeds the exercise or strike price of the option.
- The intrinsic value of an American put option is the amount by which the exercise price of the option exceeds the price of the underlying security.
- Strictly speaking when comparing the strike of a European option and the spot price of the underlying we should present value the strike since the option can only be exercised (and the strike price paid) at expiry. In practice many people ignore this factor and compute intrinsic value on a European option in the same way as for an American option.
- An option either has positive or zero intrinsic value. Intrinsic value by definition is never negative — the buyer of an option cannot be forced to exercise the option and make a loss on exercise. The maximum loss is the premium paid.
- Intrinsic value can only be realized before expiry through exercising an option in the case of an American contract. However the current value of an option will reflect any intrinsic value it may have.
- Even if an option has no intrinsic value, if there is any time remaining until expiration and the share price can fluctuate, the option will have time value.

- In the case of an at- or out-of-the-money call option, time value represents the probability or chance that the share might rise above the exercise price before expiry.
- In the case of an at- or out-of-the-money put option, time value represents the probability or chance that the share price might fall below the exercise price before expiry.
- From the perspective of the option seller, time value represents the risk involved in having to deliver a share (short call) or take delivery of a share (short put) at a fixed price.
- The term 'time value' derives from the fact that, all other things being equal, the longer the time to the expiry of an option the higher its time value. A long-dated option provides more profit opportunities for the holder than a short-dated option.

15.12 STOCK OPTIONS ON LIFFE

Call and put options on the shares of individual companies can be freely bought and sold on exchanges such as LIFFE and the CBOE. Table 15.3 shows closing prices for two share options traded on LIFFE on 4 June 2001.

The first column shows the underlying share and its current cash market mid-price. The second column shows a couple of the exercise or strike prices currently available for calls and puts on the share. The interval between exercise prices is set according to a scale determined by the exchange. It introduces new exercise prices when the underlying share price exceeds the second highest or has fallen below the second lowest exercise price currently available.

The remaining columns show the current prices of calls and puts for each strike price and for three future expiry dates. Quotations are in pence per share, to the nearest 0.5 pence. The contract size is either 100 or 1000 shares depending on the underlying share. The contracts are American style and are physically exercised — if the buyer of a call exercises the option he or she will receive shares and pay the strike price; if the buyer of a put exercises the option he or she will have to deliver shares and is paid the strike price.

15.12.1 Interpreting the Quotations

We will take some examples from the list.

Table 15.3 Share options traded on LIFFE

Option	Strike	Calls			Puts		
		Jun	Sep	Dec	Jun	Sep	Dec
Shell (629)	600	42	56	71.5	9	23	30
	650	15	31	46	32.5	48	54.5
Reuters (999)	950	93.5	140	176.5	38.5	77.5	103
	1000	67	116.5	154	62	103.5	129

Source: LIFFE.

- The Shell 600 strike June calls are trading at 42 pence per share. The underlying share is trading at 629 so the options are in-the-money by 29 pence in relation to the cash price. They have 29 pence intrinsic value and 13 pence time value.
- The Shell 650 strike June calls are trading at only 15 pence per share. They are out-of-the-money and the premium cost is all time value.
- The Shell 650 September calls are trading at 31 pence per share. They too are out-of-the-money but have a longer expiry date than the June 650 call and more time value.
- The Shell 600 puts (the right to sell at 600 pence) are out-of-the-money, with the underlying price currently at 629. They have zero intrinsic value. The 650 puts are in-the-money.

15.12.2 Additional Contract Details

Most stock option contracts on LIFFE have a contract size of 1000 shares and a tick value of £5 (1000 shares × the tick size of 0.5 pence per share). The premium is payable in full by the buyer of an option. The seller's position is subject to initial margin and a daily mark-to-market. Selling options is a risky business and the clearing house has to protect the system against default. It may be possible to pledge securities against the margin requirement with a broker, depending on the actual terms of the agreement.

LIFFE uses three separate cycles of expiry months for different stock options so they do not all expire at the same time.

- **The January Cycle (J)**. The nearest three expiry months from January, April, July and October.
- **The February Cycle (F)**. The nearest three expiry months from February, May, August and November.
- **The March Cycle (M)**. The nearest three expiry months from March, June, September and December.

All the options are American style and may be exercised on any business day up to and including expiry. Exercise must be by 17:20 on any business day or by 18:00 on the last trading day which is the third Wednesday of the expiry month. Trading is on the LIFFE-Connect computer system between (at the time of writing) 08:00 and 16:30 London time. When options are exercised the exchange assigns the exercise randomly to one or more sellers who are required to settle the transaction by delivering or taking delivery of the underlying shares.

Early Exercise

In general, there is more risk of early exercise in the case of shorter-dated in-the-money stock options than with other types of options. Holders of calls sometimes decide to exercise and acquire the stock when it appears that receiving the forthcoming dividend will more than offset the loss of time value.

15.13   CBOE STOCK OPTIONS

Table 15.4 shows IBM stock option prices in early trading on 7 June 2001. The prices are from the CBOE.

Table 15.4 IBM stock option prices on the CBOE

Option	Strike	Expiry	Calls premium	Puts premium
IBM (117.5)	110	June	8.90	0.45
	125	June	0.40	6.30
	110	July	11.20	2.60
	125	July	2.60	9.00

Source: CBOE.

The underlying IBM share price was $117.50. Premiums are quoted in dollars per share. We will take again a few examples from the table.

- The June $110 strike call is in-the-money but approaching expiry. Most of the $8.90 value of the option is intrinsic value.
- By contrast the June $125 strike call is out-of-the-money and the option premium of $0.40 is entirely time value.
- The $110 strike puts are out-of-the-money but the July series is more expensive than the June series because the options have more time value — there is more chance that the share price will fall below the strike by July compared to June.

The normal lot size in US stock option contracts is 100 shares.

15.13.1   Corporate Actions

The terms of stock options are not adjusted for regular cash dividends. Call options will tend to lose value when the underlying share goes ex-dividend, reflecting the fact that the holder of the call who exercises the option is not entitled to receive the forthcoming dividend. The effect is most marked with short-dated options. By contrast adjustments are made to the exercise prices of listed options when the company declares a stock split or when it is the subject of a takeover or merger.

15.14   FT-SE 100 INDEX OPTIONS

We explored in Chapter 14 the pricing and applications of index futures. Traders and hedgers can also use index options contracts to create positions in the market. The contract specification for the LIFFE FT-SE 100 index option (American-style exercise) is set out in Table 15.5.

Call and put option prices are quoted in index points, with a tick size (minimum price movement) of 0.5 index points. The value of a full index point is set by the exchange at £10, the same value as for the FT-SE 100 index future contract. The value of a tick is therefore half of £10 or £5.

15.14.1   Break-even Analysis

Quoting premiums in index points makes it easy to carry out break-even calculations. For example, a call trading at an exercise price of 6000 costing 50 index points would

Table 15.5   FT-SE 100 index options traded on LIFFE

Unit of trading:	Each full index point is worth £10. If the underlying index is trading at 6000 its value is £60,000
Quotation:	In index points
Tick size (value):	0.5 index points (£5.00)
Expiry months:	June and December plus such additional months that the nearest four calendar months are always available for trading
Exercise:	Exercise by 17:05 on any business day or by 18:00 on the last trading day of an expiring option
Last trading:	10:30 a.m. on the third Friday of the expiry month

Source: LIFFE.

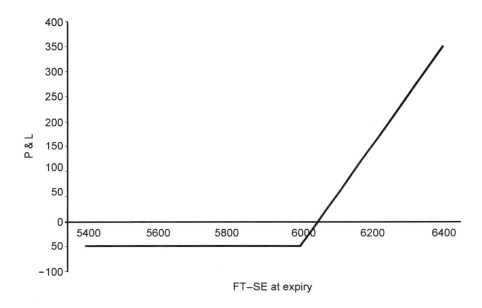

Figure 15.7   Expiry payoff profile of FT-SE index call option

break even at expiry (ignoring funding and transaction costs) when the index is trading above 6050. The cash value of the premium per contract is:

$$50 \times £10 = £500$$

Figure 15.7 shows the expiry payoff profile of the option per contract.

The contract described is the American-style version, which allows for early exercise. Exercise can be any business day for settlement on the next business day. The contract is cash-settled against the level of the cash FT-SE 100 index at 16:30. If the option is retained until expiry then cash settlement is based on the Exchange Delivery Settlement

Price (EDSP) which is based on the average level of the FT-SE between 10:10 and 10:30 on the last trading day.

The exchange introduces additional exercise prices if the FT-SE rises or falls below the second highest or lowest exercise prices currently available. There is also a European-style contract on the FT-SE traded on LIFFE which can only be exercised at expiry.

15.15 EARLY EXERCISE

In practice it rarely makes sense to early exercise an American-style option. Take the following case:

Option contract:	American FT-SE Index Option
Option type:	Calls
Exercise price:	5900
Expiry:	In one month
Premium value:	196 index points
Cash FT-SE index:	6000

Suppose we own 100 of these calls. If we early exercise the contracts against a cash index level of 6000 the cash settlement amount is calculated as follows:

$$\text{Cash Settlement} = 100 \times £10 \times (6000 - 5900) = £100,000$$

But if the contracts are trading on the market at 196 points per contract we can sell them and receive the total premium value:

$$\text{Premium Received} = 100 \times 196 \times £10 = £196,000$$

Early exercising the options simply destroys time value, because the options are killed off. If the options are sold they can be sold at the current market premium which includes their intrinsic value, plus time value.

15.16 S&P INDEX OPTIONS

The specification for the CME option on the S&P 500 is set out in Table 15.6. The underlying here is an S&P futures contract.

As always, the clearing house acts as an intermediary between buyers and sellers. The S&P contracts are American style and can be exercised on any business day. If the

Table 15.6 CME options on S&P 500 index futures

Contract:	S&P Option
Underlying:	One S&P 500 stock index futures
Index point value:	$250 per full index point
Expiry months:	Contracts are listed for all 12 calendar months
Tick size (value):	0.1 index points ($25)
Exercise prices:	At five or 10-point intervals

Source: CME.

Table 15.7   Closing prices of CME options on S&P futures

	Calls		Puts	
Strike	Jun	Sep	Jun	Sep
1225	50.90	89.30	2.10	30.80
1275	13.00	57.80	14.10	48.70
1325	0.90	33.60	51.90	73.90

Source: CME.

owner of an option exercises a contract, a seller of options is randomly assigned for exercise.

- **Calls.** If it is a call option the seller will acquire a short position in the futures at the strike price of the option.
- **Puts.** If it is a put option the seller will acquire a long position in the futures at the strike price of the option.

15.16.1   Premium

Premiums on the S&P options are quoted in index points. The dollar value of a premium is the quoted price times $250. Table 15.7 shows closing prices for S&P 500 index options traded on the CME for 6 June 2001.

On 6 June 2001 the June S&P futures closed at 1273.90. The September futures closed at 1284.20. We can use these values to interpret the option premiums in Table 15.7.

- **June 1225 Calls**. These are in-the-money relative to the June futures price by 48.90 points. The rest of the premium which is $50.90 - 48.90 = 2$ points is time value. This amounts to $500 per contract.
- **June 1325 Calls**. These are heavily out-of-the-money and the 0.90 points premium is all time value.
- **September 1225 Calls**. These are in-the-money relative to the September futures price by 59.20 points. The rest of the premium $89.30 - 59.20 = 30.10$ points is time value. The total premium of 89.3 points is worth $22,325 per contract.
- **September 1325 Puts**. These are in-the-money relative to the September futures by 40.80 points. The rest of the premium $73.90 - 40.80 = 33.10$ points is time value.

As we have seen, the option prices are quoted in S&P index points, with a point value of $250. The September 1325 put closed at 73.90 points which is:

$$73.90 \times \$250 = \$18,475$$

The September 1225 put closed at 30.8 or $7700. If we bought a September 1225 put at 30.8 points and kept the contract until the expiry of the options and of the futures in September then the index would have to trade below the strike minus the premium for us to make a profit (ignoring funding and transaction costs):

$$\text{Break-even Point} = 1225 - 30.80 = 1194.20$$

The expiry payoff profit for the contract is illustrated in Figure 15.8.

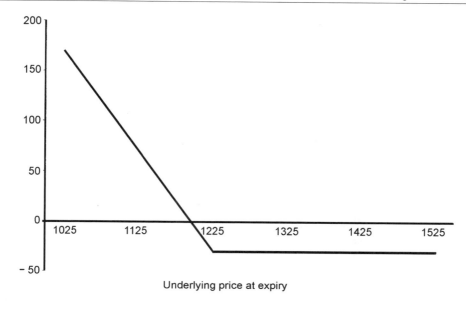

Underlying price at expiry

Figure 15.8 Expiry payoff profile of S&P put options

15.17 CHAPTER SUMMARY

An option is the right but not the obligation to buy or sell an underlying asset at a fixed price (the strike price) on or before a fixed date (the expiry date). A call option is the right to buy the underlying and a put is the right to sell the underlying. A European option can only be exercised at expiry. An American option can be exercised on or before expiry. The buyer of an option is not forced to exercise the contract and will have to pay an initial premium for this flexibility. The maximum loss for a buyer of an option is the premium, but the maximum profit can be far greater. The seller of an option is also known as the option writer. Selling options is risky because the maximum profit is the initial premium received whereas the maximum loss can be unlimited. Professional traders who sell options can manage this risk by buying and selling the underlying securities. An option premium has two components: time value and intrinsic value. Intrinsic value is either zero or measured as the difference between the price of the underlying and the strike price. An option that has intrinsic value is said to be in-the-money — if it can be immediately exercised it can be exercised at a profit.

Intrinsic value cannot be negative because the holder of an option is not forced to exercise. If the option strike is the same as the underlying the option is at-the-money. If the option could only be exercised at a loss it is said to be out-of-the-money (although it will not be exercised in this circumstance). Options on stock market indices such as the S&P 500 and the FT-SE 100 can be traded on exchanges, as well as options on individual shares. The buyer of an exchange-traded option has to pay the premium via their broker. Sold options are margined (because they are risky positions). The buyer of a call breaks even at expiry when the underlying trades at the exercise price plus the premium (plus transaction costs). The buyer of a put breaks even at expiry when the underlying trades at the exercise price less the premium (less transaction costs).

APPENDIX: EXOTIC OPTIONS

The term 'exotic option' is a rather loose one, but it is conventionally used to describe 'second generation' options whose terms differ in some way from the standard terms of a vanilla call or put option. This Appendix describes briefly some of the key structures used in the markets.

Asian or Average Price Options

The payoff from an average price call is the maximum of zero and the average price of the underlying during the life of the option minus the strike. The payoff from an average price put is the maximum of zero and the strike minus the average price of the underlying. Asian options are less expensive than conventional options since averaging prices over a period of time has the effect of lowering volatility. The more frequently the averaging is carried out the greater this effect, so that daily averaging reduces volatility more than weekly or monthly averaging. For the same reason geometric averaging reduces volatility more than arithmetic averaging.

A variant on the structure is the **average strike** option. Here the price of the underlying over some period of time is averaged out and the strike price is set to that average. The payout of an average strike call is the maximum of zero and the difference between the strike price and the price of the underlying on exercise.

Barrier Options

The payoff from a barrier option depends on whether the price of the underlying reaches a certain level during a specified period of time or during the whole life of the option. Barriers are either **knock-in** or **knock-out** options. A knock-in comes into existence only when the underlying price hits a barrier (sometimes called the **instrike**). A knock-out ceases to exist when the underlying price reaches a barrier (sometimes called the **outstrike**). Sometimes the buyer receives a pre-set rebate if the option is knocked out or fails to be knocked in.

With call options there are four possibilities.

- Down-and-in call: comes into existence if the stock price falls to the barrier.
- Up-and-in call: comes into existence if the stock price rises to hit the barrier.
- Down-and-out call: ceases to exist if the stock price falls to the barrier.
- Up-and-out call: ceases to exist if the stock price rises to hit the barrier.

The same possibilities exist with put options. For example, an up-and-out put ceases to exist if the stock price rises and hits a barrier above the current spot price. It will be less expensive than a standard put option and when used to protect against falls in the value of a share will provide cheaper protection than a vanilla option. However the 'insurance' will cease to exist if the stock price rises to hit the barrier or outstrike.

Bermudan Options

In an American option the holder can exercise at any time during the life of the option. With a Bermudan option the holder may only exercise at agreed times during the life of the option. Bermudan options provide more flexibility than European options because of the possibility of early exercise but are normally cheaper than standard American-style options.

Binary (Digital) Options

Binary options pay out a fixed amount or nothing at all. For example, a **cash-or-nothing** call pays out a fixed amount of cash if the underlying is above the strike at expiry, otherwise it expires worthless. Another variant is the **asset-or-nothing** call. This pays out a fixed amount of stock if the underlying price ends up above the strike, otherwise it pays nothing.

Chooser (Preference) Options

With a chooser or 'U-choose' option the holder can choose whether the option is a call or a put at a specified point in time. Normally the call or put will have the same time to expiry and strike price although more complex structures have been assembled where this is not the case. A trader or investor might buy chooser options when he or she believes that the underlying asset will be subject to price volatility but is uncertain whether the price will go up or down.

Compound Options

These are options on options. There are four main types:

● a call on a call;
● a put on a call;
● a call on a put;
● a put on a put.

In the case of a call on a call the buyer has to pay a premium upfront for the option to buy a call option. If the holder exercises that option he or she receives the underlying call and pays in return a further premium. The underlying call will normally have standard terms—it will be an American or European-style option with a fixed expiry date and a fixed exercise price.

Exchange Options

Exchange options are options to exchange two assets—for example, one stock for another, or one foreign currency for another. Effectively a convertible bond is an exchange option since the holder has the right but not the obligation to exchange a bond for equity or for another type of debt.

Forward Start Options

Forward start options are paid for now but start at some future date. Normally it is agreed that the strike will be set at-the-money on the start date.

Cliquet

A cliquet or ratchet option consists of a standard at-the-money option followed by a strip of forward start options whose strike will be set at-the-money on the forward start date.

For example, a cliquet option might consist of a one-year at-the-money spot start call option followed by strip of two forward start at-the-money call options each with one year to expiry. Suppose the underlying spot price at the outset is $100. If at the end of year one the underlying is trading at $110 the holder makes $10 on the one-year spot start option. The strike for the next option in the strip is set at-the-money at $110. If at the end of year two the underlying is trading at $115 the holder makes a further $5 profit. The strike for the final option in the strip is set at $115. If at the end of year three the underlying is back trading at $100 the final option expires worthless. However the holder has locked in the interim $15 gains.

Lookback Options

The payoff from a lookback option depends on the maximum or minimum price of the underlying asset during the life of the option. In a **floating strike** lookback call the strike is the minimum price achieved by the underlying during the life of the option. Its payoff is the extent to which the asset price at expiry exceeds that strike. It is a way of buying the underlying at the lowest price it trades at during the life of the option. In a floating strike lookback put the strike price is the maximum price of the underlying during the life of the option. Its payoff is the extent to which that strike price exceeds the asset price at expiry. A lookback put is effectively a way of selling the underlying at the highest price it achieves during the life of the option.

The payoff from a **fixed strike** lookback call option at expiry is the extent to which the highest price achieved by the underlying over the life of the option exceeds the strike. Lookback options are normally more expensive than conventional call and put options.

Ladder Options

Ladder options are similar to cliquets in that the holder can lock in profits made during the life of the contract. In a **fixed strike** call the payoff at expiry is the difference between the strike and the highest of a series of threshold prices or 'rungs' achieved by the underlying during the life of the option, or the spot price at expiry, whichever is greater.

In a **floating strike** ladder option the initial strike is reset whenever the underlying price hits a prescribed 'rung' in the ladder rather than (as is the case with a cliquet) on specific dates. For example, consider a ladder call with the initial strike set at $100 and rungs set at $10 intervals above that level. If the underlying hits $110 at any point the strike is reset to $110 and the $10 profit is locked in. If the underlying subsequently reaches $120 a further gain of $10 is achieved and the strike is again reset, this time to $120.

The more rungs there are in the ladder the more a ladder option resembles a lookback option (see above) whose payoff is based on the best level of the underlying during the life of the option. Ladder options, like cliquets, are more expensive than standard options.

Quanto Options

A quanto is an option based on a variable quantity of an underlying asset. An example is a call option based on the performance of a basket of UK shares that is payable in US dollars. The payoff from the option depends on the sterling value of the basket, which is a variable, and also on the GBP:USD exchange rate which introduces a further variable. The writer of the option is faced with a problem in managing a hedge for the FX exposure because the sterling value of the basket is a variable quantity.

Multi-asset Options

The payoff from a multi-asset option depends on the values of two or more underlying assets. A simple example is a **basket option** whose payoff is typically determined by the weighted average value of a portfolio of underlying assets. Another example is a 'best of' call whose payoff depends on the highest price achieved by two or more underlying assets. By contrast the payoff on a **spread** or outperformance option depends on the difference between the prices of two assets.

Shout Option

These are similar to cliquets and ladder options except that the strike is reset by the holder rather than at predetermined times or price levels. For example, if the initial strike is $100 and the asset price reaches $120 the holder can 'shout' and lock in a gain of $20. The strike will be reset at $120. The total gain at expiration will be $20 plus any intrinsic value on a call with a strike set at $120.

16
Option Valuation Models

By a model is meant a mathematical construct which, with the addition of certain verbal interpretations, describes observed phenomena. The justification of such a mathematical construct is solely and precisely that it is expected to work.

John von Neumann

16.1 CHAPTER OVERVIEW

In subsequent chapters we will use the standard option pricing model originally developed by Black, Scholes and Merton. We will explore the practical applications of the model in pricing options and option strategies, and the sensitivities of the model as measured by the so-called option 'Greeks': delta, gamma, theta, vega and rho. The current chapter is designed to provide a more detailed insight into how options are priced, and as such may be skipped over by readers who are more concerned with applications rather than theory. At the same time this chapter is not intended to cover the more complex mathematics of option pricing. The reading list at the end of the book lists titles that develop the subject in a rigorously mathematical fashion. We start here by showing that an option pricing model has to meet certain constraints, and move on to demonstrate one of the key results in the world of options, the **put–call parity** relationship. A simple option valuation model is developed using a one-step and then a three-step binomial tree, and we show how the volatility of the underlying can be incorporated into the model. As more and more steps are added to the tree the option value that is calculated will converge on the value calculated by the famous Black–Scholes option pricing model. We present the Black–Scholes equation in a manner that can easily be set up in an Excel spreadsheet and conclude by showing how the model can be adapted to cover securities that pay dividends. Finally, we look at some of the simplifying assumptions made by the model, the circumstances in which they tend to break down, and how option traders try to compensate for these problems in practice. In an Appendix we show how to calculate the volatility of an asset based on its historical returns. Volatility is a key input in option pricing.

16.2 FUNDAMENTAL PRINCIPLES

Until 30 or so years ago there was no generally agreed method in existence to price options. Valuations were sometimes based on little more than sentiment. In this situation a trader who was bullish about a share might tend to value calls more highly than someone who was bearish about its prospects. Conversely, the bull would tend to regard puts on the share as virtually worthless, while the bear would be an avid buyer. Some practitioners used a set of rough 'rules of thumb'—for example, pricing at-the-money options as a set percentage of the current cash price of the underlying. Other dealers used their 'feel' for the market and traded on prices that were in fact remarkably close to Black–Scholes values.

A useful first step in understanding how option models operate is to consider the fundamental relationship that must hold between the value of an option and the price of the underlying. In the following sections we explore this relationship by testing and proving a series of propositions relating to options on shares (stock options, in US parlance).

Statement 1

The minimum value of an American call on a share is either zero or the difference between the spot price of the share and the exercise price of the call.

This proposition simply says that the intrinsic value of an American call is either zero or the profit (if any) that can be made by immediately exercising the option. The statement also holds true of a European call when the exercise price is discounted back to a present value so that it is directly comparable with the spot price of the underlying.

Statement 2

An American call on a share can never be worth more than the underlying share.

If this statement were not true arbitrage profits could be generated. For example suppose that a trader could buy a share at £100 and sell a call on the share at a higher premium, say £101. The trader owns the share so is fully protected if the call is ever exercised. The first two statements can be combined to show that for any given price level of the underlying there is a minimum and a maximum value for an American call. It must lie between the two dotted lines in the graph in Figure 16.1.

16.3 EUROPEAN OPTIONS

The analysis so far can be extended to European-style options.

Statement 3

The minimum value of a European call option is either zero or the difference between the spot value of the share and the present value of the exercise price.

To see why statement three must be true consider the European call option described in Table 16.1. For simplicity we will assume that the share pays no dividends and use simple interest in the discounting calculation.

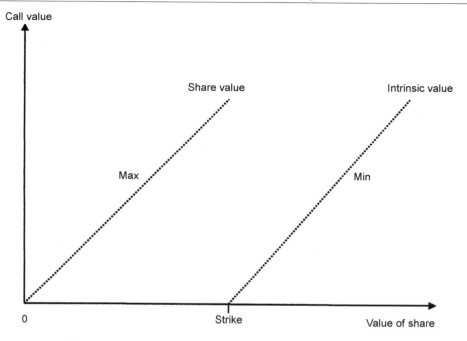

Figure 16.1   Minimum and maximum value of an American call

Statement three says that the minimum value of this option is given by the following calculation:

$$£95 - \frac{£100}{1.1} = £4.09$$

To test this proposition let us suppose that the option can be purchased at a lower premium, say £2. We can then construct an arbitrage as follows:

- buy the call for £2;
- borrow £2 to pay the premium at 10% interest;
- sell the share one year forward at its forward fair value of £95 × 1.1 = £104.50.

The net cash flow today is zero. We can easily show that the strategy has a positive payoff at the expiration of the option for any given price level of the share. Table 16.2 takes a range of price levels between £80 and £100 for illustration.

Table 16.1   Details of a European call

Spot price of share (*S*)	£95.00
Exercise price (*E*)	£100.00
Maturity (*t*)	One year
Interest rate (*r*)	10.00% p.a. simple interest

Table 16.2 Payoff of the arbitrage strategy at expiry

Share price	80	90	100	110	120
Call value	0	0	0	10	20
Loan repayment	−2.2	−2.2	−2.2	−2.2	−2.2
Value of forward position	24.5	14.5	4.5	−5.5	−15.5
Net	22.3	12.3	2.3	2.3	2.3

This is an arbitrage strategy which always has a positive payout, so something has gone wrong. The problem lies with the assumed £2 premium of the call. If the call is bought at a premium of £4.09 the loan repayment amount would be £4.50 which achieves zero payoffs in some circumstances. If the premium is higher than £4.09 the combined strategy has negative payouts in circumstances when the share price is trading above £100 at expiry. So the minimum option premium must be £4.09.

16.4 EARLY EXERCISE

Since they confer additional rights in terms of early exercise it may appear that American options must be more valuable than European options. However this is not always the case.

Statement 4

It never pays to exercise an American call on a non-dividend-paying share early.

Consider an American call with an exercise price of £100 when the underlying share is trading at £110. There is one year until expiry and interest rates are 10.00% per annum. The share pays no dividends.

The holder of the option could make £10 through immediate exercise. However it would be more profitable to short the underlying share at £110 and invest the proceeds for one year to earn interest. The short is covered by the call option in the event that the share price rises. Another way to view this situation is to say that the trader could simply sell the £100 strike call in the market. With one year remaining until expiry it will have time value over and above the £10 intrinsic value that would be realized through early exercise. Since an American call on a share that does not pay dividends should not be exercised early, it follows that an American call on such a share should be worth exactly the same as a European call.

On the other hand it can be profitable to exercise an in-the-money American put option early when the share does not pay dividends. To take an extreme case, suppose the share is trading at close to zero with low volatility and the put has an exercise price of £100 with one year to expiry. Since the share price cannot be negative there is very little scope for further profit from the put option and the cash received from early exercise could be invested immediately rather than at expiration. The interest earned is likely to exceed any additional profit the put could generate. Since there are sometimes advantages to early exercise it follows that American puts are always more valuable than European puts when the share pays no dividends and when interest rates are positive.

16.5   PUT–CALL PARITY

One of the most fundamental results in option pricing is known as **put–call parity**. This demonstrates that there is a fixed relationship between the value of European call and put options with the same strike and expiry. For European options the formula states that:

$$P + S = C + PV(E)$$

where:

P = value of the put
S = value of the underlying share
C = value of the call (same expiry date as the put)
E = exercise price of the put and the call

To test the formula we will consider a call option with the details set out in Table 16.3.
 We will compare this call with the value of a one-year put also struck at £100. We can construct two portfolios A and B consisting of the following assets:

Portfolio A	Portfolio B
1 share	1 call struck at £100
1 put struck at £100	1-year deposit of PV(E) paying $r\%$

The two portfolios have the same value at the expiry of the options for any given price level of the underlying. For example, if the share price is £90 at expiry then A is worth £90 plus £10 intrinsic value on the put option. The option in B is worthless but the principal and interest on the deposit amounts to £100. Conversely, if the share is trading at £110 at expiry the put option in A will have no value and the total value of the portfolio is £110. In B the deposit will amount to £100 to which must be added £10 intrinsic value from the call. Since the two portfolios have exactly the same payoffs in all circumstances it follows that they should have exactly the same value today. The current value of portfolio B today can be calculated as follows:

$$£5 + \frac{£100}{1.1} = £95.91$$

This implies that portfolio A is also currently worth £95.91. Since the share is trading at £95 today this means that the value of the put option is £0.91. This is the result predicted by the put–call parity formula:

Table 16.3   Details of call option for put–call parity

Spot price (S)	£95.00
Exercise price (E)	£100.00
Expiry (t)	One year
Interest rate (r)	10.00% p.a. simple interest
Call value	£5.00

$$P + S = C + \text{PV}(E)$$

So:

$$P = C + \text{PV}(E) - S$$

$$P = £5 + \frac{£100}{1.1} - £95$$

$$= £0.91$$

16.6 SYNTHETIC FORWARD AND FUTURES POSITIONS

The put–call parity formula for a non-dividend-paying stock can be rearranged as follows:

$$C - P = S - \text{PV}(E)$$

If the strike of the call and the put are both set at the forward price of the underlying for the expiry date of the options it follows that $\text{PV}(E)$, the present value of that strike, will equal the spot price S. To take our previous example, suppose the spot price of the underlying share is £95, the expiry date is one year and the one-year interest rate is 10% simple interest. This time the strike of the call and the put are both set at the forward price. In that case:

$$\text{Forward Price} = £95 \times 1.1 = £104.50$$

$$\text{Exercise Price} = £104.50$$

$$\text{PV}(E) = \frac{£104.50}{1.1} = £95 = \text{Spot Price}$$

From the put–call parity formula we have:

$$C - P = S - \text{PV}(E)$$

But in this instance $\text{PV}(E) = S$. It follows that:

$$C - P = 0 \quad \text{and} \quad C = P$$

In words, the call and the put should have exactly the same value. If we buy a European call and sell a European put struck at the forward price for the expiry date of the two options the combination has zero net premium. In fact it is a synthetic long forward position. If the underlying is trading above the strike at expiry we will exercise the long call; if the underlying is below the strike the short put will be exercised against us. Either way the combination will produce a long position in the underlying on the expiry date established at the strike of the two options. Traders often use this relationship to construct arbitrage trades or to build forwards and futures out of pairs of options.

When the share pays dividends the put–call parity formula can be modified as follows:

$$P + S - \text{PV}(D) = C + \text{PV}(E)$$

where D is the dividend expected to be paid during the life of the option.

16.7   PUT–CALL PARITY AND AMERICAN OPTIONS

Put–call parity applies only to European options. For American-style options with the same strike and expiry it is possible to state only certain inequalities. For instance:

$$C - P \leqslant S - \text{PV}(E)$$

We know that the value of an American put can be greater than that of a European-style put. Therefore $C - P$ may be reduced in value, so it can be less than $S - \text{PV}(E)$. If the shares pay dividends the put value P will be further increased (and the call value C reduced).

16.8   BINOMIAL TREES

We have developed some constraints on how an option model has to work and discussed the fundamental put–call parity relationship. A useful next step in understanding how the Black–Scholes option pricing model operates is to construct what is known as a **binomial tree**. We will start with a one-step tree and price a call option on an underlying share using the tree.

The assumption we will make is that the underlying share can only move up by a factor of 1.25 and down by a factor of 0.75 over one time period. This is illustrated in Figure 16.2.

Now we consider the payoff of a call option on this share with a strike of £100. At time one the call is either worth £25 or zero — either it has £25 intrinsic value or it expires worthless. This is illustrated in Figure 16.3.

Let us suppose that we sell the option and want to establish its fair value at time zero. We will label this value C. We start by covering the risk on the short option position by constructing the following hedged portfolio at time zero:

- sell one call with a value C;
- buy Δ (delta) shares worth $\Delta \times$ £100;
- borrow £B at (say) 10.00% simple interest.

The following equations are to be satisfied at time one:

$$(\Delta \times £125) - (£B \times 1.1) = £25 \tag{1}$$
$$(\Delta \times £75) - (£B \times 1.1) = £0 \tag{2}$$

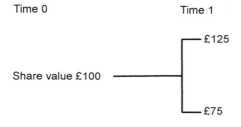

Time 0   Time 1

                                    ┌─ £125
Share value £100 ─────────────────┤
                                    └─ £75

Figure 16.2   One-step binomial tree for a share

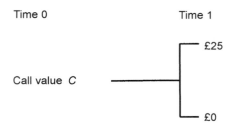

Figure 16.3   Value of the call option at expiry

Equation (1) says that if the share price closes at £125 the £25 intrinsic value we will have to pay out on the short call must be covered by the value of the Δ shares we bought in our hedge portfolio, less the principal plus interest repayment on the $£B$ we borrowed.

Equation (2) says that if the share price closes at £75 the calls will have zero intrinsic value. This should equal the value of the Δ shares we bought less the principal plus interest on the borrowing.

16.8.1   Solving the Equations

Equation (2) can be rearranged to say:

$$(£B \times 1.1) = (\Delta \times £75)$$

Inserting this into equation (1) we have:

$$(\Delta \times £125) - (\Delta \times £75) = £25$$

Therefore:

$$\Delta = 0.5$$

Delta (Greek letter Δ) is otherwise known as the **hedge ratio**. A delta of 0.5 tells us that for every call we write we have to buy 0.5 shares to neutralize our exposure to movements in the share price. If we sell calls on 100 shares we have to buy 50 shares. This is called a delta hedge and the resulting hedged position is called in the market a **delta-neutral** position. The option delta can be calculated directly as follows:

$$\Delta = \frac{C_u - C_d}{S_u - S_d}$$

where:

C_u = value of the call if the share price goes up
C_d = value of the call if the share price goes down
S_u = value of the share when it moves up
S_d = value of the share when it moves down

$$\Delta = \frac{25 - 0}{125 - 75} = 0.5$$

Since we have a value for delta we can insert this into equation (1) and calculate the amount borrowed at time 0:

$$(0.5 \times £125) - (£B \times 1.1) = £25$$

Therefore:

$$B = £34.09$$

At time zero we know that we have to buy 0.5 shares at £100 per share to construct the hedge portfolio. Therefore for all the cash flows to match at time zero the following equation must hold:

$$C + B = \Delta \times £100$$

This equation says that the cost of buying delta shares at time zero is met by borrowing £B plus the premium amount £C received for selling the call. Using the values for delta and B previously calculated it must be the case that $C = £15.91$.

16.8.2   Call Value Formula

It is possible to simplify the calculation of C by using a little bit of algebra that simply encapsulates the steps we worked through previously. Let:

$$p = \frac{(1 + r) - d}{u - d}$$

where:

$r = $ interest rate for the period as a decimal
$d = $ the factor that moves the share price down from its spot price in the binomial tree
$u = $ the factor that moves the share price up from its spot price in the binomial tree

Here:

$r = 0.1$
$d = 0.75$
$u = 1.25$

Therefore:

$p = 0.7$

The call value C is given by the following equation:

$$C = \frac{(p \times C_u) + [(1 - p) \times C_d]}{1 + r}$$

where:

$C_u = $ value of the call at time one if the share price rises
$C_d = $ value of the call at time one if the share price falls

Here:

$$C_u = £25$$
$$C_d = £0$$

Therefore:

$$C = £15.91$$

This is a type of weighted average payout calculation but one that is based on the assumption that we can fully hedge the risk on the option. Under this special assumption the 'probability' of the share price rising to £125 and the intrinsic value of the call equalling £25 is 70%. The 'probability' of the share price falling to £75 is 30%. The average of the two payouts weighted by the 'probability' of achieving each payout is discounted back one period at a 10% simple interest rate. These pseudo-probabilities apply in a so-called 'risk-neutral' world in which we can exactly match the exposure on the option by creating a delta hedge portfolio. Note that the 'expected' share price at time one is the weighted average of the two possible share prices at time one weighted by the 'probability' of attaining each value:

$$\text{Expected Value} = (125 \times 0.7) + (75 \times 0.3) = 110$$

16.9   EXPANDING THE TREE

Of course the binomial tree we have developed is highly simplistic. Firstly, we assumed that the share price could only move up to £125 and down to £75 over one time period. In reality the share price will tend to move up or down by much smaller steps, and then take a series of further steps. Secondly, the factors u and d that moved the share price from its current level were simply invented for the purposes of illustrating the concept of a binomial tree. It would be helpful if we could apply factors that derive from the **volatility** of the underlying share. Intuitively, the more volatile the share, all other things being equal, the more the share price is likely to fluctuate from its current level, and the more expensive the option should be. (We show in detail how to estimate volatility in an Appendix to this chapter, based on the standard deviation σ of the historical returns on an asset.)

To illustrate how we can cope with these issues we will construct a three-step binomial and price a European call on a share that pays no dividends. The details of the share and the option are as follows:

Underlying cash price $S = 300$
Exercise price $E = 250$
Annual risk-free rate $r = 10\%$ continuously compounded
Time to maturity $t = 0.25$ years
Volatility $\sigma = 40\%$

16.9.1   Incorporating Volatility

To construct a tree that matches the volatility of the underlying we will calculate the factors u and d using values proposed by Cox, Ross and Rubenstein:

$$u = e^{\sigma\sqrt{t/n}}$$

$$d = 1/u$$

where:

e = 2.71828, the base of natural logarithms
σ = volatility, the annualized standard deviation of returns on the share (here 0.4)
t = time to option expiry in years (here 0.25)
n = number of steps in the binomial tree (here 3)

In this example:

u = 1.1224
d = 0.8909

Using these values for u and d we construct a three-step binomial tree for the shares. This is illustrated in Figure 16.4. The first 'up-move' value 337 is simply the starting spot price of 300 times the up-move factor $u = 1.1224$. From 337 the share can either move up one step further to 378 at the up-move factor 1.1224, or down to 300 at the down-move factor $d = 0.8909$ and so on.

16.9.2   Constructing the Call Value Tree

Next, we construct a second tree that represents the values of the 250 strike call in response to changes in the value of the underlying. We can easily fill in the numbers at the end nodes — at expiry the option is worth zero or the price of the underlying less the strike price. This is illustrated in Figure 16.5. For example, at the top right of the share

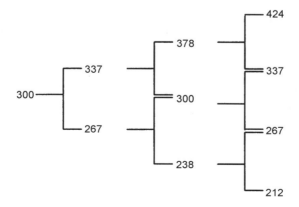

Figure 16.4   Three-step share binomial tree

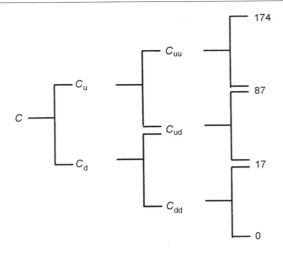

Figure 16.5   Call option binomial tree

tree in Figure 16.4 the share is trading at 424. In that case the 250 strike call will be worth 174.

In Figure 16.5 C is the value of the call at the outset. C_u is the value if the share takes one step up; C_{uu} if the share takes two steps up. C_d is the value if the share takes one step down; C_{dd} if the share takes two steps down. C_{ud} is the value if the share takes one step up and then a step down (it is the same as the value if the share takes a step down and then back up).

At each step we can now evaluate the call option exactly as if it were a one-step binomial. Let us take the value C_{uu}. To establish this value we start by calculating the 'probability' number p in the same way that we did for a simple one-step binomial. The formula (this time using a continuously compounded interest rate) is as follows:

$$p = \frac{e^{r(t/n)} - d}{u - d}$$

where:

u = the up-move factor
d = the down-move factor
r = the annual interest rate as a decimal
t = the time to maturity in years
n = the number of binomial steps in the tree

The values in this example are:

u = 1.1224
d = 0.8909
r = 0.1
t = 0.25
n = 3

Therefore:

$p = 0.5074$
$1 - p = 0.4926$

The value of the call C_{uu} is the present value of:

- the call value if it takes a further step up (174) times the 'probability' that this will occur (50.74%)

plus

- the call value if it takes a step down (87) times the 'probability' that this will occur (49.26%)

$$C_{uu} = [(174 \times 0.5074) + (87 \times 0.4926)] \times e^{-0.1(0.25/3)} = 130$$

16.9.3 The Complete Call Value Tree

The complete tree is set out in Figure 16.6. The value of the call today with 0.25 years to expiry is roughly 61. Note that the option we have priced is a European call option without dividends. If it was an American put it would be essential to check at any node in the tree that the option is not worth less than its intrinsic value. This is because an American-style put may be exercised early in some circumstances and should therefore never trade at less than its intrinsic value.

16.10 BLACK–SCHOLES MODEL

As we increase the number of steps the call value calculated in the three-step tree will converge on the result produced by the famous **Black–Scholes** option pricing model.

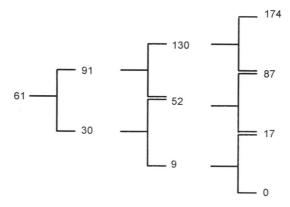

Figure 16.6 Three-step call value tree

The model was developed by Fischer Black, Myron Scholes and Robert Merton in the 1970s and is a vital tool in modern finance. Myron Scholes and Robert Merton were awarded the Nobel prize for their work on the model in 1997, Fischer Black sadly having died just two years before.

For a European option with no dividends Black–Scholes gives the following value:

$$C = [S \times N(d_1)] - [E \times e^{-rt} \times N(d_2)]$$

where:

$$d_1 = \frac{\ln(S/E) + (r \times t) + (\sigma^2 \times t/2)}{\sigma\sqrt{t}}$$

$$d_2 = \frac{\ln(S/E) + (r \times t) - (\sigma^2 \times t/2)}{\sigma\sqrt{t}}$$

$N(d)$ = cumulative normal density function, i.e. the area to the left of d under a normal distribution curve with mean 0 and variance 1. The Excel function to use is NORMSDIST( )

$\ln( )$ = natural logarithm of a number to base e = 2.71828. If $\ln(x) = y$ then $\exp(y)$ = x. In other words, $e^y = x$. The Excel function to use is LN( )

σ = volatility (as a decimal)

t = time to expiry (in years)

r = continuously compounded interest rate (as a decimal)

e = 2.71828, the base of natural logarithms. The Excel function for e to the power of the value in brackets is EXP( )

The formula says, in effect, that the value of a call is the spot price (S) minus the present value of the exercise price (E), where S and E are weighted by the probability factors $N(d_1)$ and $N(d_2)$. The first factor $N(d_1)$ is delta (Δ), the hedge ratio. The model uses continuous compounding in the present value calculation.

16.10.1 Example

In a previous example we constructed a three-step binomial to evaluate a call option with the following data. The call value was calculated to be approximately 61:

Underlying cash price $S = 300$
Exercise price $E = 250$
Annual risk-free rate $r = 10\%$ (0.1 as a decimal)
Time to maturity $t = 0.25$ years
Volatility $\sigma = 40\%$ (0.4 as a decimal)

The Black–Scholes formula will give the following value:

$$C = [S \times N(d_1)] - [E \times e^{-rt} \times N(d_2)]$$

where:

$$d_1 = \frac{\ln(S/E) + (r \times t) + (\sigma^2 \times t/2)}{\sigma\sqrt{t}}$$

$$d_2 = \frac{\ln(S/E) + (r \times t) - (\sigma^2 \times t/2)}{\sigma\sqrt{t}}$$

In this example the complete values (using Excel) are as follows:

$\ln(S/E) = \text{LN}(S/E) = 0.1823$
$d_1 = 1.1366$
$d_2 = 0.9366$
$N(d_1) = \text{NORMSDIST}(d_1) = 0.8721$
$N(d_2) = \text{NORMSDIST}(d_2) = 0.8255$
$S \times N(d_1) = 261.64$
$E \times N(d_2) = 206.38$
$e^{-rt} = \text{EXP}(-rt) = 0.9753$
$E \times e^{-rt} \times N(d_2) = 201.28$
$C = [S \times N(d_1)] - [E \times e^{-rt} \times N(d_2)] = \mathbf{60.36}$

The three-step binomial answer of 61 was in fact fairly close. The value P of a European put can be established by put–call parity. Otherwise:

$$P = [E \times e^{-rt} \times N(-d_2)] - [S \times N(-d_1)]$$

16.11 BLACK–SCHOLES WITH DIVIDENDS

Black–Scholes can be adjusted to price European options on shares paying dividends. The following version of the formula assumes that dividends are paid out in a continuous stream and is commonly used to price index options:

$$C = [S \times e^{-qt} \times N(d_1)] - [E \times e^{-rt} \times N(d_2)]$$

where:

q = continuous dividend yield as a decimal

$$d_1 = \frac{\ln(S/E) + [(r - q) \times t] + (\sigma^2 \times t/2)}{\sigma\sqrt{t}}$$

$$d_2 = \frac{\ln(S/E) + [(r - q) \times t] - (\sigma^2 \times t/2)}{\sigma\sqrt{t}}$$

In the case of an individual share it is not quite realistic to assume that dividends are paid in a constant stream. If a share is predicted to pay a future cash dividend D then one common approach is to present value D back from the ex-dividend date at the risk-free rate and subtract this from the spot price of the underlying. Replace S with S−PV(D) throughout and then:

$$C = [\{S - PV(D)\} \times N(d_1)] - [E \times e^{-rt} \times N(d_2)]$$

16.12   BLACK–SCHOLES ASSUMPTIONS

The Black–Scholes model makes some simplifying assumptions about the world which have a tendency to break down in extreme market conditions. The model makes the following assumptions.

- That the returns on the underlying follow a normal distribution, the famous bell curve. Many analysts believe there is a skew in the actual returns on assets, particularly equities, which means that in reality there is a bigger chance of significant price falls than is built into the shape of the bell curve. This is sometimes known as the 'fat tail' problem — the actual distribution of returns on shares is skewed.
- That the returns on the underlying follow a continuous random walk in which the last price movement bears no relationship to the next price movement and in which prices are not subject to sudden 'jumps'. This may be a realistic assumption in a normal market but not in a market crash.
- That it is possible to delta hedge option positions by buying and selling the underlying without transaction costs and without liquidity constraints. In the real world option traders do face transaction costs and liquidity problems and will not readjust their delta hedges on a continuous basis.
- That the volatility of the underlying is known and remains constant throughout the life of the option. In a market crash, however, experience suggests that panic sets in and volatility can increase sharply.

In practice option traders can compensate for the limitations of the model by adjusting the volatility at which they sell options. For example, if the underlying is not particularly liquid and hard to trade it will be difficult to manage the risks on a short option position. To compensate, the trader will increase the price of the options such that the implied volatility is greater than the actual historical volatility of the underlying (where **implied volatility** is the volatility assumption built into an actual option premium).

16.13   CHAPTER SUMMARY

An option pricing model has to meet certain constraints. A European call on a share is worth a minimum of zero or the difference between the spot value of the underlying and the present value of the strike price. An American call on a share that does not pay dividends should never be exercised early and therefore is worth the same as a European call. There are circumstances in which it does make sense to early exercise an American put option so it can be worth more than a European put. One of the most fundamental results in options is the put–call parity relationship for European contracts. This says that the combination of a long call and a short put both struck at the futures price can be used to replicate a long futures position in the underlying. A long put and a short call can replicate a short futures position. Put–call parity does not hold for American options. A simple option pricing model can be constructed using the binomial tree methodology. The first step is to generate a tree that represents the movements in the underlying share. The intrinsic value of the option at expiry is then calculated. By 'working backwards' along the tree the value of the option today can be calculated. As more steps are added to the tree the result converges on the option value calculated by the Black–Scholes model. Black–Scholes can easily be set up on an Excel spreadsheet and adapted for assets that pay out dividends. In practice the assumptions made by the model may not work very effectively in extreme markets. Traders tend to compensate for this by adjusting the implied volatility they use to price and trade options. Implied volatility is the volatility assumption built into an actual option premium. The implied volatility is based on the actual historic volatility of the underlying but also on forecasts of future events.

APPENDIX: MEASURING HISTORIC VOLATILITY

In the options market historic volatility is measured as the standard deviation of the returns on the underlying over some historical period of time. It is normally annualized. The percentage returns are calculated by taking the natural logarithms of the price relatives rather than simple percentage price changes. The Excel function that calculates the natural log of a number is LN( ). It is the inverse of the EXP( ) function.

Using natural logs has very useful consequences. For example, suppose that a share is trading at 500 and the price rises to 510. The **price relative** is the new share price divided by the old price:

$$\frac{510}{500} = 1.02$$

The simple percentage price change is calculated as:

$$\frac{510}{500} - 1 = +2\%$$

But suppose then that the share price falls back again to 500. The simple percentage fall in price is:

$$\frac{500}{510} - 1 = -1.96\%$$

The problem is that simple percentage changes calculated in this way cannot be added together. If the share price starts at 500 and ends at 500 then the total change in the share price is actually zero. If we add 2% and −1.96% we get +0.04%. Using natural logarithms cures this problem:

$$\ln\left(\frac{510}{500}\right) = +1.98\%$$

Table 16.4 Calculation of historic volatility

(1) Day	(2) Price	(3) % Price change	(4) Deviation (%)	(5) Deviation^2 (%)
0	500			
1	508	1.59	1.37	0.02
2	492	−3.20	−3.42	0.12
3	498	1.21	0.99	0.01
4	489	−1.82	−2.04	0.04
5	502	2.62	2.41	0.06
6	507	0.99	0.77	0.01
7	500	−1.39	−1.61	0.03
8	502	0.40	0.18	0.00
9	499	−0.60	−0.82	0.01
10	511	2.38	2.16	0.05
		Average = 0.22		Sum = 0.33

$$\ln\left(\frac{500}{510}\right) = -1.98\%$$

Table 16.4 illustrates the calculation of historic volatility using natural logarithms. The price of the underlying security starts at 500 on day zero. In column (2) we show the closing price of the stock over the next 10 trading days (covering two calendar weeks). Column (3) calculates the natural logarithm of the price relatives. For example, the percentage change in the share price between day 0 and day 1 is calculated as:

$$\ln\left(\frac{508}{500}\right) = +1.59\%$$

The average daily percentage change in the share price is +0.22%. Column (4) calculates the extent to which each daily percentage price change deviates from the average. For instance, +1.59% is +1.37% away from the average. The next number in the sequence, −3.2%, is −3.42% away from the average. Column (5) squares the deviations. The sum of the squared deviations shown at the bottom of the column is 0.33%.

Sample variance is a statistical measure of the extent to which a set of observations in a sample diverges from the average or mean value. In Table 16.4 we used 10 observations based on the change in the share price over two calendar weeks. The sample variance is calculated as follows:

$$\text{Variance } \sigma^2 = \frac{\text{Sum of Deviations}^2}{\text{Number of Observations} - 1}$$

$$= \frac{0.33\%}{10 - 1} = \frac{0.0033}{9} = 0.000367 = 0.0367\%$$

The reason we divide by one less than the number of observations is simply to adjust for the fact that we are using a sample of price changes (and a relatively small sample at that). Volatility is defined as the standard deviation of the returns on the share. It is the square root of the variance:

Standard Deviation $\sigma = \sqrt{\text{Variance}} = \sqrt{0.000367} = 0.0192 = 1.92\%$

What we have calculated is the **daily volatility** of the returns on the share. It was based on the average daily percentage price change over a series of trading days. Volatility is normally expressed on an annualized basis in the options market. If we assume that there are 252 trading days in the year then the annualized volatility is calculated as the daily volatility times the square root of 252:

$$\text{Annual Volatility} = \text{Daily Volatility} \times \sqrt{\text{Trading Days per Annum}}$$
$$= 1.92\% \times \sqrt{252} = 30.4\%$$

17
Option Pricing and Risks

A random element is rather useful when we are searching for the solution of some problem . . .

Alan Turing

17.1 CHAPTER OVERVIEW

In this chapter we review the main inputs to pricing an option using the Black–Scholes model and consider how changes in the inputs affect the value that is calculated. The model is described in Chapter 16. Here we focus on the sensitivity of the option value to changes in the key input assumptions — the price of the underlying security; the time remaining until expiry; the assumed volatility of the underlying share; and the cost of carrying a hedge position in the underlying. We explore the sensitivities of the model and the so-called option 'Greeks': delta, gamma, theta, vega and rho. Specifically, we look at how traders can use these measures in practice to manage the risks on option positions by trading in the underlying security, and the circumstances in which such hedges are likely to be more or less efficient. In the body of the chapter we look at how traders manage so-called 'delta exposures' — potential losses on option positions that arise from changes in the value of the underlying security. This is explored in more detail in an Appendix, with a description of how the gamma exposure on an option position can be hedged.

17.2 INTRINSIC AND TIME VALUE

The value of an option is composed of **intrinsic value**, which is either zero or positive, plus **time value**. Time value reflects the chance that the option may move into the money (or further into the money) before expiration. This chance is greater:

- the longer the time remaining until expiry;
- the greater the volatility of the underlying security.

The more time there is to expiry, the greater the opportunity for the option to be exercised profitably. Equally, the more volatile the underlying share, the greater the chance or probability of a substantial change in the price of the underlying. In the case of a call option, volatility increases the probability that the price of the underlying will be above the strike price. It also increases the risk of a fall in the share price, but the holder of a call is not forced to exercise the option if it is out-of-the-money. This represents an opportunity for the buyer of the option and a risk for the seller. Time value is the price of that opportunity and that risk.

Inputs to the Black–Scholes Model

According to the Black–Scholes option pricing model (adapted for a share that pays dividends) the value of an option is determined by five factors:

- the exercise or strike price of the option;
- the spot price of the underlying asset;
- the time to expiry of the option;
- the volatility of the underlying security;
- the net cost of carrying a position in the underlying security.

In the following sections we explore the value of a call option on a share and how the value is affected by changes in the inputs to the pricing model. The version of the Black–Scholes model used in this chapter assumes for simplicity that dividends paid on a share are spread evenly throughout the life of the option. The model itself is described in more detail in Chapter 16 in a way that will allow it to be set up on an Excel spreadsheet.

17.3   SPOT PRICE AND OPTION VALUE

The details of the option contract we will explore in this chapter are as follows:

Exercise type:	European-style call
Strike:	650 cents
Days to expiry:	30 days
Funding rate:	6.00% p.a.
Share dividend yield:	2.00% p.a.
Share volatility:	25.00% p.a.

Table 17.1 shows the fair value of the call for different price levels of the underlying share, keeping all the other inputs to the pricing model constant. It then shows how much of this value is intrinsic value and how much of it is time value. For example, if the underlying share is trading at 600 cents then the option (the right to buy the underlying at 650) is out-of-the-money and has zero intrinsic value. Therefore all the value calculated by the pricing model must be time value. On the other hand if the underlying share is trading at 700 cents then the option (which has a strike of 650) has 50 cents intrinsic value and therefore 5.49 cents of its total value must be time value. The results from Table 17.1 are then graphed in Figure 17.1.

17.4   TIME VALUE BEHAVIOUR

Table 17.1 and the graph in Figure 17.1 show that when the option is deeply out-of-the-money (for example, when the price of the underlying is at 600) then the option has zero intrinsic value, but also very little time value. In the graph the difference between the

Table 17.1   Share price, intrinsic value and time value

Share price	Option value	Intrinsic value	Time value
600	3.24	0	3.24
610	5.03	0	5.03
620	7.48	0	7.48
630	10.69	0	10.69
640	14.72	0	14.72
650	19.61	0	19.61
660	25.34	10	15.34
670	31.88	20	11.88
680	39.15	30	9.15
690	47.05	40	7.05
700	55.49	50	5.49

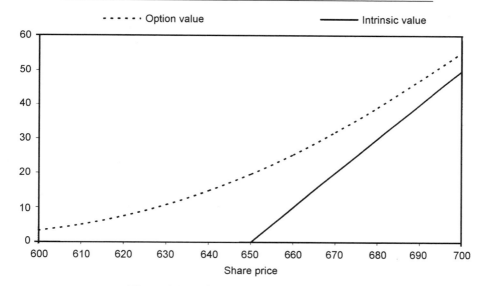

Figure 17.1   Share price and option premium

solid black line representing intrinsic value and the dotted line representing the total value of the option is time value. If the share is trading at only 600 cents it would have to rise by at least 50 cents before the 650 strike call will expire in-the-money. The probability of that happening over the next 30 days is relatively small, so the option has very little time value. On the other hand the probability is not zero, and has to be paid for through time value.

Table 17.1 and Figure 17.1 also show that as the share price increases to 650 (all other inputs to the model remaining constant) the time value of the option also rises. The probability of the option expiring in-the-money is increasing. Time value peaks when the call option is at-the-money when the price of the underlying and the strike are equal. Then as the option moves into the money, the total option value continues to increase as it acquires more and more intrinsic value, but the time value component of the option steadily declines.

Buying a deeply in-the-money call is rather like buying the actual share. Time value for an in-the-money option represents the additional amount the investor is prepared to pay, over and above the intrinsic value, for the privilege of holding an option with limited downside. Unlike holding the actual stock, the loss is limited to the premium. The more in-the-money the option is, however, the smaller the time value — there is less chance that the 'disaster insurance' which the option provides will actually be required.

17.4.1 A Simplification: Probability of Exercise

Although it is something of a simplification of the way in which the model actually works, capital market practitioners sometimes think of the value of a European-style option in terms of probability of exercise. In the case of an out-of-the-money call the probability of the option being exercised and becoming the underlying share is quite low. The probability of an at-the-money call being exercised and becoming the underlying is around 50%. If a call is very deeply in-the-money then the probability of it being exercised and becoming the underlying approaches 100%.

17.5   VOLATILITY

We have seen that according to the Black–Scholes model the value of an option is determined by five factors. The model and its inputs are illustrated in Figure 17.2.

The only really problematical input here is the volatility assumption. The spot price and the carry cost can be obtained from market information screens. The time to expiry and the strike are written into the option contract. How do we measure volatility and what data do we use to derive that measurement? A reasonable starting point is to look at the historical price behaviour of the underlying share over some period of time. The more variable the share price, the greater the risk to the seller of the option, the greater the opportunity to the buyer of the option, the higher the time value of the option.

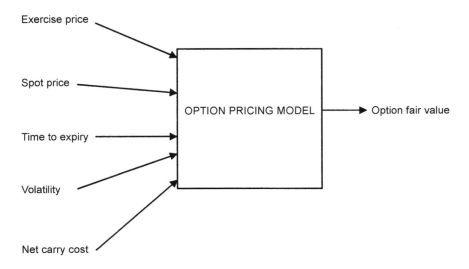

Figure 17.2   Inputs to the pricing model

Measuring Historic Volatility

Historical volatility is measured as the standard deviation of the percentage returns on the underlying security over an historical period, around the average return for that period. (The calculation is illustrated in the Appendix to Chapter 16.) It is sensible to base the calculation on the percentage returns on a share rather than the absolute changes in the share price because it makes it possible to compare volatility on shares that are trading at very different price levels. Standard deviation is the most common statistical measure of dispersion around a mean or average value.

When historic volatility is used to price options the assumption is that the past price behaviour of the underlying is a reliable guide to the future — the higher the historical volatility the greater the likelihood of substantial future fluctuations in the price of the underlying. It may not always be sensible to make this assumption. For example, there are weeks and months when stock prices experience periods of extreme turbulence, and historical volatility calculated on the basis of such data will be very high. Option traders may take the view that the market will settle back down again over the following months and that volatility will be lower than suggested by recent historical experience.

17.5.1 Implied Volatility

A major problem with measuring historic volatility is deciding which historical time period to choose. Should we look at the price behaviour of the stock over the last few months, or the last few years? Is the recent historical period atypical in some way? Are we heading for a period of relative calm or extreme turbulence? Should more recent price changes be given a greater weight in the calculation of historical volatility? To get round these difficulties option traders often take another approach. Rather than using a volatility assumption to calculate an option fair value, they take the actual price at which the option is trading in the market and calculate the volatility assumption implied in that price. This **implied volatility** can then be compared against historical experience and future volatility forecasts.

17.5.2 Annualizing Volatility

Although historic volatility may be calculated from daily or weekly movements in the share price, the practice in the market is to annualize the number (in the same way that interest rates are annualized). When annualizing volatility however the 'square root rule' comes into effect. Suppose for example that the volatility — the standard deviation of the percentage price changes — of a share per single trading day is 2%. This is daily volatility. If there are 252 trading days in a year then the annual volatility is given by:

$$2\% \times \sqrt{252} = 31.75\%$$

Intuitively, the square root rule is based on the idea that short-term fluctuations in the prices of securities tend to smooth out to some extent over a longer period of time. Annual volatility is therefore far less than daily volatility times the number of trading days in the year. Note that this may be a reasonable assumption to make in normal market conditions when shares are following something close to a 'random walk' and there is no statistical relationship between the previous movement in the share price and the next movement. In extreme circumstances such as stock market crashes these conditions may well not apply.

17.6   DELTA (Δ OR δ)

As well as calculating the fair value of an option, the Black–Scholes pricing model tells us about the sensitivity of the calculated option value to changes in the inputs to the model. This is what the option delta, gamma, theta, vega and rho measure. These so-called 'option Greeks' are essential to the management of risk in an options position. Delta is the most significant measure and in fact it is integral to the way in which the Black–Scholes model prices an option. Delta can be defined as follows.

Delta

Delta is the change in the option price for a small change in the price of the underlying security, assuming all other inputs to the model are held constant. Delta is often expressed as a ratio or a percentage. For example, if a bought call option has a delta of 0.50 or 50% this means that if the price of the underlying share increases (decreases) by one tick the option value will increase (decrease) by 0.5 ticks. A tick is the minimum allowed price movement in a financial asset, such as one cent or one pence.

17.6.1   Sign of Delta

Traders often give the delta of an option position a positive or a negative value. The sign tells us about the directional exposure of the position to changes in the price of the underlying.

- **Long Call.** The delta of a long (bought) call is positive. If a trader buys a call the option position increases (decreases) in value if the value of the underlying stock increases (decreases).
- **Short Call.** The delta of a sold call position is negative. If a trader sells a call the position loses value as the value of the underlying increases — the option becomes more expensive to buy back in order to close out the position. If the underlying falls in price the position gains in value because the option becomes cheaper to buy back. In this sense selling a call is like a short position in the underlying; hence the negative delta.
- **Long Put.** The delta of a long put option is negative. If a trader buys a put the option position increases (decreases) in value as the price of the underlying falls (rises).

- **Short Put.** The delta of a short put option is positive. If a trader sells a put the position increases in value as the value of the underlying rises (the option becomes cheaper to buy back to close out the position) and falls in value if the underlying falls. In this sense selling a put is like a long position in the underlying. Hence the positive delta.

Intuitively, the sign shows whether the position is a bull or a bear position. Positive delta means that the position makes a profit if the price of the underlying rises. Negative delta means the position is in profit if the underlying price falls. For example, let us suppose that a trader buys a put with a delta of -0.50 or -50%. This means that the value of the position increases by 0.50 ticks if the underlying share falls by one tick. As the underlying share declines in value the put becomes more valuable to the buyer. On the other hand if the underlying rises in value the put becomes less valuable to the buyer.

17.7   DELTA BEHAVIOUR

For standard or 'vanilla' options the absolute value of delta lies between zero and one (0% and 100%). A deeply out-of-the-money call has a delta approaching zero — it is highly insensitive to a small change in the underlying. As the option approaches the at-the-money point its delta increases until it reaches approximately 0.50 or 50%. Intuitively, when an option is at-the-money the probability of the option expiring in-the-money is around 50% and the option transmits around half of the price change in the underlying security. As the call moves increasingly in-the-money delta moves toward a limit of one or 100%. The option moves tick for tick with the underlying stock. As we saw before, a deeply in-the-money (ITM) option increasingly comes to resemble a position in the underlying security. A bought ITM call resembles a long position in the underlying. A bought ITM put represents a short position.

17.7.1   Delta as the Slope on the Option Curve

We illustrated previously the relationship between the price of the underlying and the value of a call option calculated by Black–Scholes. For ease of reference, this chart is reproduced again in Figure 17.3, this time showing just the curve of the option premium for different values of the underlying share.

Figure 17.3 also shows the slope or tangent on the option price curve when the option is at-the-money. This is delta. It is approximately 0.5 — for a one tick move in the share price the option moves in value by around 0.5 ticks. The slope of the curve approaches zero when the call is deeply out-of-the-money; the option is insensitive to small changes in the price of the underlying. The slope of the curve approaches one when the option is deeply in-the-money; the option value moves in line with the underlying for small changes in the price of the underlying — it is so far in-the-money that it simply behaves like a position in the actual share.

17.8   DELTA AS THE HEDGE RATIO

Delta is not only valuable as a sensitivity measure. It is used by option traders to hedge the risks on their trading books. For example, let us suppose that we have written calls

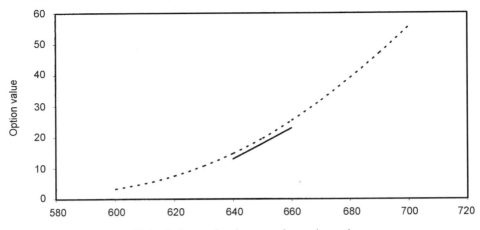

Figure 17.3   Delta as the slope on the option price curve

on 10,000 shares, each with a delta of 0.50. The position delta in this case is negative because we have sold calls. If the share price rises the options will become more valuable, which would be bad news for us. If the calls become more expensive it will cost us more to buy them back to close our short option position than we sold them for. Hence the loss on the position.

17.8.1   Position Delta

A useful way to look at the delta measure is to translate it into a **position delta**. We have sold calls on 10,000 shares and for a small movement in the underlying share price the calls will move by half as much as the shares:

$$\text{Position Delta} = -10,000 \times 0.50 = -5000 \text{ shares}$$

This means that (for small movements in the price of the underlying) we have the same market exposure as if we had a short position in 5000 shares. In simple terms, if the share price rises by (say) one cent we will lose the same amount of money on the options as we would if we were short 5000 shares. To hedge this position we could, quite simply, buy 5000 of the underlying shares. The delta of each purchased share is by definition plus one, so the net position delta is now zero. Any losses on our options position resulting from a small move in the underlying share price would be offset by profits on our share position. If the underlying share price rises by one cent we will lose $50 on the calls:

$$\text{Loss on Calls} = 1 \text{ cent} \times 0.50 \times -10,000 = -\$50$$

The calls will have increased in value by $50, and if we close our option position by buying them back they would cost $50 more than we sold them for. On the other hand the 5000 shares we bought to hedge our position have increased in value by $50 in total:

$$\text{Gain on Shares} = 5000 \times 1 \text{ cent} = \$50$$

Option portfolios hedged in this way so they are not exposed to small movements in the price of the underlying security are said to be **delta-neutral** or delta-hedged.

17.9   GAMMA (Γ OR γ)

Gamma is the change in delta for a small change in the price of the underlying security. The option curve in Figure 17.3 illustrates the fact that delta (the slope of the option price curve) is not a constant. It changes depending on which point on the option's price curve is taken. Delta is really only a reliable measure of the change in the value of an option for small changes in the underlying price. Delta assumes a linear relationship between the underlying share price and the value of the option. If the price of the underlying moves by a substantial amount then the actual option price change will be greater than predicted by delta. Delta is the analogue of the duration measure we explored in Chapter 5 when we considered the relationship between the price of a bond and current market interest rates. Like duration, delta itself is not a constant.

Gamma as Convexity

Gamma (convexity) measures the rate of change of delta. Gamma is a measure of the curvature in the relationship between the value of an option and the price of the underlying. The greater the amount of curvature, the more rapidly delta (the slope or tangent on the option price curve) will change.

17.9.1   Gamma Risk

Because option professionals use delta to manage the risk on their books they are exposed to changes in their position delta. In the previous delta hedge example it was assumed that we sold calls on 10,000 shares with a delta of 0.50. The position delta is therefore −5000 shares. In other words, for small movements in the share price the profit and loss on the options position will behave rather as if we were short 5000 shares — not 10,000, because the calls move half as much in price terms as the underlying shares.

To delta hedge this position we said that we should buy 5000 shares in the underlying. The hedge will work well for small movements in the underlying share price. We tested this. The problem is that it will not work at all well for large movements in the underlying share price. If the share price rises sharply the short call position will actually lose more money than predicted by the delta measure. This is the effect of gamma or convexity, the curvature in the option price graph. The 5000 shares we bought to hedge the risk will not match the losses on the options because the profit and loss profile on the shares in our delta hedge is always linear.

17.9.2   Sensitivity of the Delta Hedge

An option trader tends to think of the gamma problem in terms of the change in the delta, and the possibility that the trader might have to readjust their delta hedge. In our delta hedge example we sold calls on 10,000 shares with a delta of 0.50 as ratio, in share equivalent terms −5000 shares. We hedged the delta risk (the exposure to small movements in the underlying share price) by buying 5000 shares in the underlying.

Suppose that shortly after the calls are sold and delta-hedged the share price rises sharply, to the extent that the option delta is no longer 0.50, but in fact moves to 0.60.

In that case the position delta on the calls is now equivalent to being short 6000 shares. Now we have a problem. We can leave the hedge as it is, but we will be badly under-hedged if the share price keeps rising — the losses on the calls will greatly outweigh the offsetting profits on the 5000 shares in the delta hedge. Or we can readjust the delta hedge by buying another 1000 shares on top of the 5000 shares already held in the hedge portfolio. But then if the share price falls back sharply again the pricing model will tell us to sell some or all of those additional shares! This will crystallize a loss on the shares.

17.10   READJUSTING THE DELTA HEDGE

This last example illustrates the real problem with option trading. By and large sellers of options do not sell large quantities of 'naked' options. Such positions are extremely dangerous. The option seller can manage exposures to directional changes in the underlying share price by buying and selling the underlying. The risk is that if the underlying is more volatile than the option seller predicted when he or she priced and sold the options then the delta hedge will have to be readjusted at frequent intervals — realizing trading losses on the underlying shares used in the hedge. The trick is to assess the volatility of the underlying properly and price this into the premium charged for the option. In that case a trader should be able to readjust the delta hedge from time to time and still retain some of the option premium as a profit.

Of course in practice a trader will not rebalance the delta hedge every time the underlying price moves; transaction costs would quickly eat away at any profits that might be made. The skill in being an option trader lies in deciding what constitutes an exceptional movement in the price of the underlying that should be covered to guard against unacceptable losses. In practice, also, many of the delta risks in an option book will tend to cancel out — for example, a sold call is a short delta position but a sold put is a long delta position. If the underlying rises or falls by a small amount the profits and losses will offset each other to some extent. It is the residual delta risk in the trading book that is covered by trading in the underlying.

17.10.1   Measuring Gamma

Gamma, as we have seen, is the change in delta for a small change in the underlying price. It can be measured in a number of different ways. Perhaps the most useful way is to show gamma in share equivalent terms. In our example the trader sells calls on 10,000 shares with a delta of 0.50 or −5000 shares. If the gamma of the position is (say) 0.01 this means that for a one cent rise in the underlying price the delta will move to 0.51 or −5100 shares. In other words the profit and loss on the position will now behave as if the trader is short 5100 shares. So:

$$\text{Position Gamma} = -10,000 \times 0.01 = -100 \text{ shares}$$

Assuming the trader had bought 5000 shares at the outset to hedge the delta risk, the gamma measure tells the trader that he or she would have to buy a further 100 shares to rebalance the hedge if the underlying rose by one cent.

17.11   DELTA AND GAMMA BEHAVIOUR

The graph in Figure 17.3 also shows that gamma is at its highest when the option is at-the-money. The slope or tangent to the curve will change most sharply at that point for a given (small) change in the price of the underlying. It is the point of maximum curvature. By contrast the gamma for a deeply out-of-the-money or in-the-money option is low — the delta approaches zero and one in each case and becomes less and less sensitive to small changes in the stock price.

This phenomenon is illustrated in a different way in the graphs shown in Figures 17.4 and 17.5. The first graph shows the delta of the 650 strike call option with 30 days to expiry, where all the other inputs to the model are kept constant and only the price of the underlying share is changed. The second graph shows the same option but with only five days remaining until expiry.

The graphs show that when the call is deeply out-of-the-money its delta is close to zero and (for small changes in the underlying price) anchored at close to zero. The gamma is low, particularly when the option has only five days remaining until maturity. It would take a very substantial movement in the share price to have any appreciable

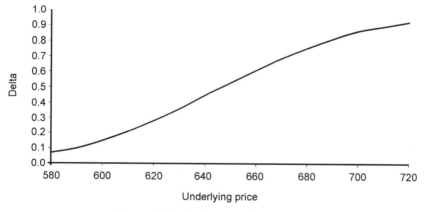

Figure 17.4   Delta curve for 30-day call

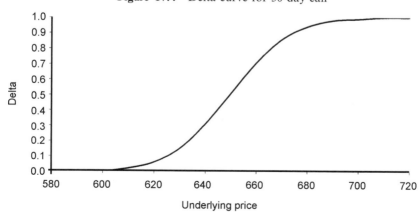

Figure 17.5   Delta curve for five-day call

impact on the delta. When an option is deeply out-of-the-money and approaching maturity it becomes increasingly certain that it will expire worthless; the delta is close to zero and insensitive to small changes in the share price.

Similarly, when the option is deeply in-the-money the delta approaches one and the gamma is also low. Intuitively, the probability of the call being exercised and becoming the underlying share is approaching 100% and a small change in the underlying share price is not going to have much of an influence on that level of certainty. The delta is one and anchored at one. This effect becomes more pronounced as the call approaches expiry and it becomes increasingly certain that it will be transformed into a position in the underlying share.

17.11.1   Gamma and Expiry

Figures 17.4 and 17.5 show that when the option is at-the-money and the delta is around a half there is maximum instability in delta (the gamma is at its highest). A small movement in the share price in either direction will sharply increase or decrease the delta. Figure 17.5 also shows that an at-the-money option approaching expiry has very high gamma. The delta will be around a half, but in response to small changes in the share price the delta will suddenly shift upwards towards one, or downwards towards zero.

This phenomenon matters particularly to option sellers because the higher the gamma on their position the more unstable their delta hedge is liable to be — and as we have seen, when a seller of an option keeps adjusting the delta hedge through buying and selling underlying shares, the seller can realize trading losses. If the share price rises the holder of a short call position will be told by the model to buy more shares in the delta hedge. If the share price then falls back the position will be less short delta and the trader will be told to sell shares at a lower price.

17.12   THETA (θ)

Delta measures the sensitivity of an option value to changes in the underlying share price, with all the other inputs to the model remaining constant. Gamma measures the sensitivity of delta. Mathematically, delta is the first derivative of the pricing model with respect to small changes in the underlying; gamma is the second derivative. Delta is also the hedge ratio used to manage exposures to changes in the share price acquired through trading options.

However there are other inputs to the Black–Scholes pricing model in addition to the cash price of the underlying share. It is possible to measure the sensitivity of the option value to changes in these inputs. Table 17.2 shows the changing value of a 30-day at-the-money (ATM) call with a strike of 650 as the option approaches expiry. All the other inputs to the pricing model have been kept constant — the strike, the price of the underlying, the volatility assumption and the carry cost. The relationship between the time to expiry and the value of the option is then graphed in Figure 17.6.

The table and the graph show, obviously, that the option loses time value as it approaches expiry. With less time remaining there is less chance that the option will expire in-the-money. The Greek letter that measures the sensitivity of the option value for a given change in time (typically one day) is theta. Theta measures the rate of decay

Table 17.2 Value of an ATM option as it approaches expiry

Time to expiry (days)	Option value
30	19.61
25	17.82
20	15.86
15	13.66
10	11.08
5	7.76
1	3.43
0	0.00

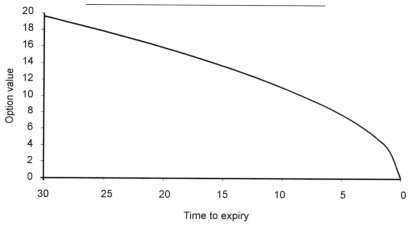

Figure 17.6 Time value decay curve

in the time value of an option. It is the slope or the tangent at any given point on the option value curve illustrated in Figure 17.6.

17.12.1 Acceleration of Time Decay

The graph in Figure 17.6 also illustrates the fact that the rate of time decay accelerates as the option approaches expiry — the slope or tangent on the curve is much more pronounced when the option has only five days remaining compared to when it has 30 days remaining to expiry. Theta is high for at-the-money options that are close to expiry. We have seen already that at-the-money options tend to exhibit the most extreme characteristics.

Sign of Theta

Theta is negative for bought calls and puts — the position loses value every day. For opposite reasons theta is positive for sold calls and puts. Every day (all other inputs to the model remaining constant) options lose value, which is good for the seller who could close his or her position out by buying the contracts back at a cheaper price.

17.13   VEGA

The value of an option is also sensitive to the assumption made about the volatility of the underlying. This sensitivity is measured by vega. Vega is the change in the option value for (typically) a 1% change in the assumed volatility of the underlying. Buying an option is sometimes known as a **long volatility** or long vega position. If the volatility assumption used to price the option increases the contract will become more valuable. This applies to both call and put options. Conversely, the seller of options hopes for declining volatility. (Vega is not in fact a Greek letter; some people use instead the Greek letter kappa.)

Table 17.3 shows the value of the 650 strike at-the-money 30-day call for different volatility assumptions. As volatility increases the value of the option increases in a more or less linear fashion. The data is then graphed in Figure 17.7.

The vega of this particular option is in fact about 0.74. This means that for a 1% change in volatility (all other inputs to the pricing model remaining constant) the option will increase or decrease in value by about 0.74 ticks (cents). Vega is the slope on the line in Figure 17.7 that shows the relationship between volatility and option value.

Table 17.3   Option value against volatility

Volatility	Option value
5%	4.87
10%	8.52
15%	12.21
20%	15.91
25%	19.61
30%	23.30
35%	27.00
40%	30.70

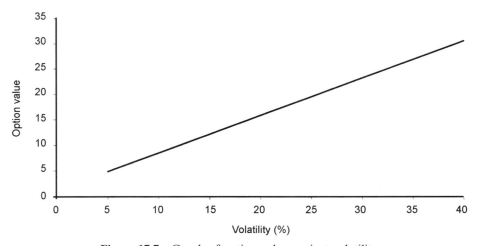

Figure 17.7   Graph of option value against volatility

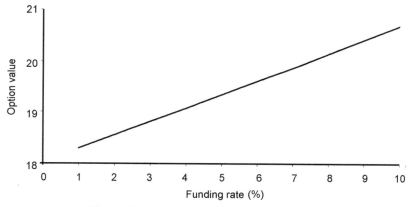

Figure 17.8 Option value against funding rate

17.14 RHO (ρ)

The final 'Greek' we will consider here is rho. Rho measures the change in an option's price (all other inputs to the model remaining constant) for a given change in the cost of funding, typically 1%. Figure 17.8 shows the value of the 650 strike at-the-money call as the funding rate is increased. It is a linear relationship and rho is the slope of the line in the graph.

Rho in this example is in fact 0.27. This means that for a 1% increase in the funding rate the call option value calculated by the model (all other inputs remaining constant) will increase by 0.27 ticks.

17.14.1 Rho on Call Options

The option pricing model operates by assuming that when an option is sold a riskless hedge can be put in place using the delta measure. In the case of a call option, delta tells the seller of the option how much of the underlying shares to buy to cover the exposure. The model assumes, in effect, that this is funded through borrowing, offset by any dividend income received on the shares bought to hedge the exposure. All other things being equal, when interest rates rise the value of call options also tends to rise. The sellers of calls pass on their higher funding costs to the buyers.

17.14.2 Rho on Put Options

On the other hand if interest rates rise the value of put options will fall. Sellers of put options are exposed to falls rather than rises in the price of the underlying share. To hedge this delta exposure they will run short positions in the underlying shares. As interest rates rise they will earn more money by investing the cash received from selling the shares short and can afford to pass the benefits on to the buyers of the puts.

17.14.3   Dividends

The version of the pricing model we have been using in this chapter has assumed that the underlying share pays dividends. It prices options using the net cost of carrying a hedge position in the underlying shares — funding minus dividends. If a dealer sells a call option he or she can hedge the delta risk (the directional exposure to rises in the share price) by buying the underlying shares. All other things being equal, the higher the rate of dividends earned on the shares carried in the delta hedge, the lower the price the dealer can charge for selling the options. Matters work in reverse for the seller of a put option. The seller of a put can delta hedge by borrowing and shorting the underlying shares. He or she will have to pass over dividends on the shares to the lender. The higher the dividends the more this will cost and (all other things being equal) the more the dealer will have to charge for selling the put options.

17.15   CHAPTER SUMMARY

According to the Black–Scholes model the value of a standard or 'vanilla' option is determined by the strike price, the price of the underlying, the time to expiry, the assumed volatility of the returns on the underlying asset and the cost of carrying a hedge position in the underlying. The first two factors determine whether the option has any intrinsic value. They also help to determine the time value of an option. An option that is out-of-the-money is a 'lower probability bet' than one that is at-the-money and will have less time value. The time value of an option is highest when it is at-the-money. The change in the value of an option for a small change in the price of the underlying is measured by delta. Delta is the slope or tangent on the option price curve. It is also the hedge ratio, the number the trader uses to decide how much of the underlying he or she should trade to manage the risk on an option position. Delta is not a constant and in fact is most unstable when an option is at-the-money and approaching expiry. The 'Greek' that measures the rate of change of delta is gamma. It is possible to gamma hedge a short option position by buying options, especially short-dated at-the-money options. The change in the value of an option as time elapses is measured by theta. It is negative for bought option contracts. Vega measures the change in the value of an option (all other inputs remaining constant) for a given change in volatility. It is positive for bought calls and puts. Rho measures the sensitivity of the option premium to a change in the funding rate. It is positive for bought calls and negative for bought put options.

APPENDIX: DELTA AND GAMMA HEDGING

In the main section of the present chapter we considered how traders can buy and sell the underlying security to hedge the delta risk on an option position. In this Appendix we look at a more detailed example of a delta hedge, and also explore how the gamma risk on an options position might be hedged. In the following example we are short (have sold) $6.51 strike calls on 500,000 shares. To value the options we have the following information:

Exercise price:	$6.51
Spot price:	$6.50
Time to expiry:	12 days
Funding rate:	5.75%
Dividend yield:	1.74%
Implied volatility:	25.00%

The implied volatility is derived from the price of option contracts traded openly in the market on the same underlying.

With the above values the Black–Scholes pricing model (adapted for a dividend-paying share) gives us a premium value for the option of 11.68 cents per share. On 500,000 shares this values our total option position at $58,400. The call delta derived from the model is 0.507. Therefore:

$$\text{Share Equivalent Delta} = 0.507 \times -500,000 = -253,500 \text{ shares}$$

Delta is negative here because we have sold calls; if the underlying share price rises the calls will become more expensive to buy back to close the position. A delta negative position is rather like being short the underlying. To delta hedge we should buy 253,500 shares. We have seen previously that for small movements in the share price the profits and losses on the options and the shares in the delta hedge will balance out.

Larger Movement in the Underlying Price

But what happens if the share price rise is greater than one cent? For a 10 cent rise in the share price the options, according to the Black–Scholes model, would cost 17.41 cents per share or $87,050 in total to buy back. Therefore:

$$\text{Loss on Calls} = \$58,400 - \$87,050 = -\$28,650$$
$$\text{Profit on Delta Hedge} = 253,500 \text{ shares} \times \$0.10 = \$25,350$$
$$\text{Net Loss} = -\$3300$$

The net loss in this instance is due to the effects of gamma. Delta only holds good for small changes in the price of the underlying. The short calls have actually lost more money for a 10 cent rise in the underlying share price than we would expect if we simply extrapolated from the option delta. The delta on the short option position was 0.507. For a 10 cent rise in the price of the underlying share this delta figure predicts a loss on the options position of:

$$-500,000 \times 0.507 \text{ cents} \times 10 = \$25,350$$

The actual loss, as we have seen, would be −$28,650. There is a discrepancy of $3300.

Delta–Gamma Adjustment

Traders sometimes make a simple adjustment to the delta prediction to get a better estimate of the actual movement in the value of the option position for a larger move in the price of the underlying. This is known as the **delta–gamma** adjustment. The gamma of the calls in this example is approximately 0.0135, or in share equivalent terms:

$$\text{Gamma} = 0.0135 \times -500{,}000 = -6750 \text{ shares}$$

For a 10 cent rise in the price of the underlying the gamma effect on the position profit and loss can be estimated as follows:

$$-\frac{10^2}{2} \times 0.0135 = -0.675 \text{ cents}$$

This means that the additional loss caused by gamma on top of the delta prediction for a 10 cent rise in the value of the underlying is estimated at approximately 0.675 cents per share. For calls on 500,000 shares this amounts to about −$3375. The delta–gamma adjustment can be a useful rule of thumb, but is liable to become increasingly inaccurate for larger movements in the price of the underlying. In effect it is a simple means of adjusting for the curvature in the relationship between the price of the underlying and the value of the options.

Gamma Hedging

We have seen that buying the underlying shares can manage the delta exposure on a short call option position. However, it does not cover the gamma exposure. The option position has a non-linear relationship with the price of the underlying, while the value of shares in the delta hedge moves in a linear fashion in response to changes in the share price. An alternative hedge might be to buy short-dated call options. These will have positive delta (they increase in value when the underlying price rises) and at the same time a substantial amount of positive gamma.

Suppose we consider buying the following short-dated at-the-money calls on the same underlying:

Exercise price:	$6.50
Implied volatility:	25.00%
Days to expiry:	Three days

With the spot price of the underlying at $6.50 the Black–Scholes model prices these options at 5.98 cents per share. The delta is 0.51 and the gamma is 0.0271. The gamma on the 12-day 651 strike calls we are short is 0.0135 so we have to buy fewer of the shorter-dated 650 strike calls to match the gamma risk. The ratio is calculated as follows:

$$\frac{0.0135}{0.0271} = 49.82\%$$

We are short calls on 500,000 shares. To match the risk we have to buy fewer of the short-dated 650 strike calls. The figure is calculated as follows:

$$500{,}000 \times 0.4982 = 249{,}100$$

Unfortunately this will not manage the delta exposure on our original position:

$$\text{Position Delta on Short 651 Calls} = 0.507 \times -500{,}000 = -253{,}500$$
$$\text{Position Delta on Long 650 Calls} = 249{,}100 \times 0.51 = 127{,}041$$

To hedge out the remaining delta risk we can buy approximately 126,500 shares in the underlying.

Remaining Risks on the Gamma Hedge

This combination of buying short-dated calls and buying the underlying will manage the delta and gamma risks on the short call position fairly effectively, unless the movement in the underlying share price is extreme. However it will not cover all of the risks. For example, there is a residual vega or volatility exposure. The vega on the short calls is 0.47. This means that for a 1% rise in volatility the loss on the options will be 0.47 cents per share, or $2350 for calls on 500,000 shares. However the vega on the long calls (extracted from the model) is only 0.24. For a 1% rise in volatility the profit on these options will be 0.24 cents per share, or $598 for calls on 249,100 shares. The net loss for a 1% rise in volatility would be about $1752.

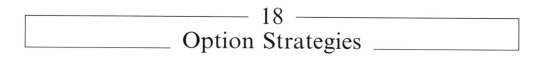

18
Option Strategies

So their combinations with themselves and with each other give rise to endless complexities, which anyone who is to give a likely account of reality must survey.

Plato

18.1 CHAPTER OVERVIEW

Options can be combined with other options and with positions in underlying securities in many different ways to construct a wide variety of trading strategies and risk management solutions. In this chapter we begin by exploring one of the most fundamental applications of options, hedging or protecting against potential losses on a position in an underlying security using put options. This can be combined with a sold call option on the underlying to construct a 'collar' strategy. If the strikes of the put and the call options are set at the right level the premiums of the two options cancel out and the strategy becomes a zero cost collar. The next set of strategies considered are spread trades, which are essentially trading rather than risk management applications of options. We explore trades that are designed to capitalize on directional movements in the underlying whilst at the same time limiting potential losses. We consider strategies designed to profit from changes in the volatility assumptions used to price options and to profit from the fact that options tend to lose value as time elapses. There is a focus in all the cases and examples in this chapter on the returns and potential risks of each strategy, how the risks can be managed in practice, and on the market circumstances in which a trader or investor is likely to employ that strategy.

18.2 HEDGING WITH PUT OPTIONS

A protective put strategy combines a long (bought) position in the underlying security with a long (bought) put option. The combination is designed to provide so-called 'downside risk' protection — that is, to hedge against short-term falls in the price of the underlying asset. If the put option is a physically exercised contract then it can be exercised when the price of the underlying falls below the strike; the underlying security is sold at the strike price, eliminating any further losses. If the put option is cash-settled then any losses that accrue on the underlying below the strike price of the option will be compensated for in the form of cash payments from the seller of the put option.

18.2.1 Options versus Futures Hedge

To illustrate the strategy we will take the example of an investor who owns a portfolio of shares in a UK company currently trading at 873 pence per share. The investor is concerned about the possibility of short-term falls in the value of the shares due to general turbulence in the equity markets. This could impact on the quarterly performance

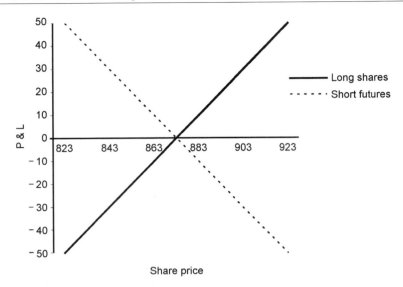

Figure 18.1   Futures hedge

figures of the fund. The manager could of course sell the stock and invest the proceeds in the money markets, or switch the proceeds into another financial asset. The problem is that doing this will incur transaction costs and might also trigger tax liabilities. In addition, the investor may have built up the shareholding over a period of time and would prefer not to switch out of the holding simply because of short-term turbulence in the market. And of course if the investor does make a switch there is the danger of incurring an **opportunity loss** — the loss of profits that would arise if the share price actually increased and the investor had sold out prematurely.

The investor could try to hedge the position in the shares by selling stock futures or cash-settled equity forward contracts (see Chapter 14 for details of equity futures and forwards). In this case if the share price falls then the investor will be compensated in cash through gains on the derivative contracts. The disadvantage is that the reverse would hold — any gains on the shares would be offset by cash payments the investor would have to make on the futures or forward contracts. Figure 18.1 illustrates the net position that would result from a futures or forward hedge. For simplicity we ignore carry cost here and assume that the futures price is exactly 873 pence.

18.3   PAYOFF FROM PROTECTIVE PUT

The advantage of covering the risks on a long (bought) position in shares with put options rather than with futures is that the investor can achieve 'downside' protection — insurance against losses arising from falls in the share price — whilst at the same time still being able to benefit from rises in the share price. In our example the investor owns shares trading at 873 pence per share. Let us suppose that the investor contacts a dealer and agrees to buy one-month European puts on the shares with a strike of 850 pence. The agreed premium is 19 pence per share.

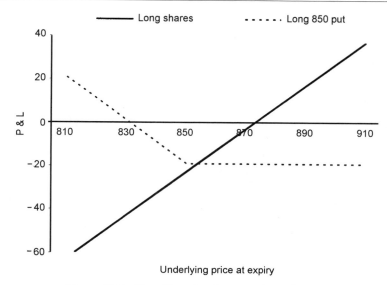

Figure 18.2   Payoff on the shares and on the put option

Figure 18.2 illustrates the profit and loss on the share and the profit and loss on the put at the expiry of the option contracts. The figures are in pence per share and for a range of different prices of the underlying. Note that in this and subsequent examples the analysis is simplified by ignoring the effects of the time value of money — in fact the premium would be paid upfront, whereas any payout from exercising the option would occur in one month's time.

Figure 18.2 shows the profit and loss on the shares as a diagonal line cutting through the current share price of 873 pence. If the share price rises the investor will make a profit; otherwise he or she will make a loss. It then shows the bought put option. The maximum loss on the put per share is the premium of 19 pence. The contract will only be exercised at expiry if the share price falls below the 850 pence strike. At share price levels below the strike the put is in-the-money. The point at which the put option (considered on its own) cuts through the zero profit and loss line is the strike minus the premium, that is 831 pence. Figure 18.3 now shows the combination payoff profile of the position in the shares and the 850 strike put. For comparison purposes it also shows what the profit and loss position in the unhedged share looks like.

18.3.1   Maximum Loss

The maximum loss per share on the hedged position at the expiry of the options is 42 pence. This is the combination of 19 pence premium (which is a sunk cost at expiry and never recovered) plus the difference between the share price at 873 pence and the 850 strike of the option. The put is an out-of-the-money option and the underlying can fall 23 pence before the protection afforded by the put comes into effect. If the put is physically settled then the investor will exercise the option and sell the underlying when it is trading below 850. In that case the investor will have lost 23 pence on the share (from the starting level of 873) plus the 19 pence premium. If the put is cash-settled then losses on the shares at price levels below 850 will be compensated in cash by payments received from the seller of the option.

18.3.2   Other Break-even Levels

There are a couple of other reference points that are of interest. What happens if the share price rises and the protection afforded by the put option is not required? The problem here is that the share price has to rise to 892 pence before the initial premium paid for the options is recovered. This contrasts with the unhedged position, where the position is in profit if the share price rises above 873 pence. Finally, the hedged and unhedged lines in Figure 18.3 meet when the share price is at 831. This is the point at which both strategies (hedged and unhedged) lose exactly 42 pence. In fact this would be a significant level for the investor. Provided the share price stays above 831 the investor is better off unhedged, i.e. without the put option.

Synthetic Call

Note that the hedged payoff profile in Figure 18.3 resembles a synthetic bought call option on the underlying. This is a common feature of options. They can be assembled in many different combinations, often replicating other option positions.

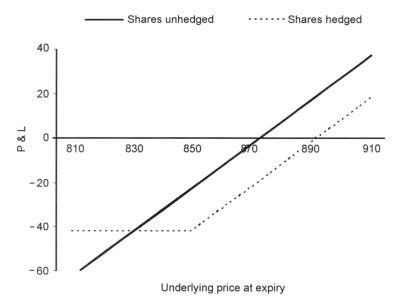

Figure 18.3   Hedged and unhedged position

18.3.3 Changing the Strike

Buying an out-of-the-money put option to hedge the risk on a share is rather like buying a cheap insurance policy — the options are relatively inexpensive, but the protection level is not particularly good. By way of contrast let us explore what would happen if the investor chose an at-the-money put option as insurance. The underlying as before is trading at 873 so the strike on an at-the-money put would also be 873 pence. Let us suppose that the investor has to pay 29 pence per share for these options. Figure 18.4 illustrates the payoff profile at expiry on the combined hedged position (long the shares, long the 873 strike put) at the expiry of the 873 strike put options.

The maximum loss this time is better at 29 pence per share. However if the share price rises rather than falls, it would now have to rise to 902 pence at the expiry of the options to recover the higher option premium. The figures for the 850 strike options were 42 and 892 pence respectively. By purchasing puts that are struck in-the-money the investor could further reduce the maximum loss on the combined position (to a level converging on zero) while further pushing out the price the share would have to rise to break even (to a level converging on infinity). Buying a deeply in-the-money put option is rather like establishing a short position in the underlying — there is a very high probability that the put will be exercised.

18.4   COVERED CALL WRITING

A further application of options is to generate additional income by selling call options against a holding of securities. This strategy is known as a **covered call**, or alternatively a buy–write strategy (because the underlying securities are bought and then calls are written or sold). To illustrate this strategy we will take the same basic circumstances from the previous sections — an investor who owns shares in a company that are

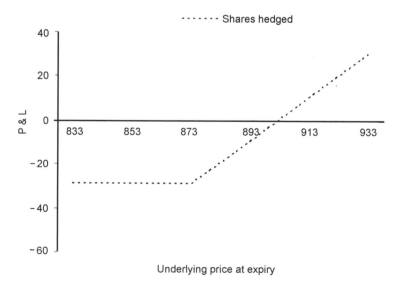

Figure 18.4   Hedged position with 873 strike put

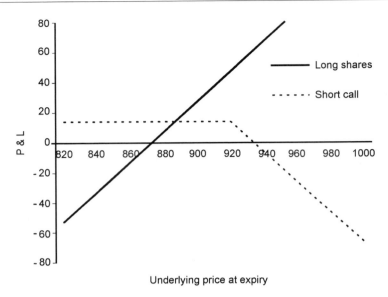

Figure 18.5   Payoff profile of the shares and the sold call

currently trading at 873 pence per share. The investor decides to explore selling one-month out-of-the-money calls against this holding at a strike of 920 pence per share. The premium earned is 14 pence per share. Figure 18.5 illustrates the profit and loss profile of the position in the underlying share and the short position in the 920 strike call at the expiry of the options.

Since the premium of the short call is 14 the call payoff profile (considered on its own) will cut through the zero profit and loss line at 934. At that level the investor will lose 14 pence on the exercise of the short call, which eliminates the premium initially collected on the option. Figure 18.6 now illustrates the payoff profile of the combined position — long the shares, short the 920 strike call sold at a premium of 14 pence per share. For comparison the original long position in the shares is also shown.

18.4.1   Maximum Profit

The maximum profit on the covered call strategy is 61 pence per share and this is achieved when the share is trading at 920. At 920 the calls will not be exercised and the investor retains the premium. In addition, the investor has made 47 on the long position in the underlying. At levels above 920 the profit on the covered call strategy flattens. If the calls that were sold are physically settled then above 920 they will be exercised and the investor will have to deliver the shares and receive in return the fixed strike of 920 pence per share. If the calls are cash-settled then any profit the investor earns on the shares above 920 will have to be paid out to the buyer of the 920 strike calls. Because the investor initially collected 14 pence in premium the share price can fall by 14 to 859 before the covered call strategy starts to lose money. Note that the covered call payoff profile resembles that of a synthetic short (sold) put option on the underlying security.

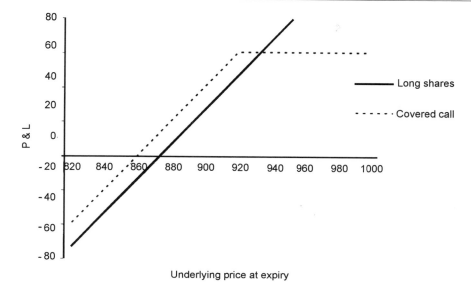

Underlying price at expiry

Figure 18.6   Covered call payoff profile at expiry

Use of Covered Call Strategies

Portfolio managers frequently sell call options against their holdings in shares to generate additional income for their fund. This can be particularly valuable in a dull or 'flat' market in which it is difficult to make acceptable returns without taking excessive risks. Covered call writing is far less dangerous than selling 'naked' call options. Normally the strike is set out-of-the-money so the risk of exercise is limited. If the risk of exercise increases then the fund manager may consider buying back the options and selling calls that are struck further out-of-the-money.

18.5   COLLARS

In the first protective put strategy we considered the investor bought an 850 strike put costing 19 pence per share to hedge against potential losses on a position in the underlying. The main drawback for the investor was the cost of the options. If the share price rises instead of falling it will have to rise by at least 19 before the investor starts to break even, net of the option premium paid. An alternative possibility is to buy the protective put and at the same time to sell a call option with the same expiry date. The advantage is that the investor will receive premium on the calls to offset the cost of the put options.

  Let us suppose that the investor buys the 850 strike put costing 19 pence and at the same time sells a 920 strike call with a premium of 14 pence. The combination is usually

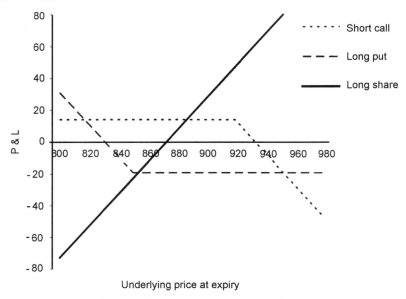

Figure 18.7 Components of the collar strategy

known as a **collar** strategy. Figure 18.7 shows the expiry payoff profile of the individual components of the collar: a long position in the share, a long position in the 850 put option and a short position in the 920 call.

18.5.1 Combined Payoff Profile

Next Figure 18.8 shows the combined payoff profile — the net profit and loss on the collar strategy for different levels of the underlying at the expiry of the options.

This time the combined payoff profile cuts through the zero profit and loss line at 878 pence. This is because the net premium on the two options is −5 so the share price would have to rise 5 pence from 873 at the expiry of the options to recover this sum and for the collar to break even. The maximum profit of 42 pence per share is achieved at the 920 strike of the calls; the maximum loss of 28 pence per share is achieved at the 850 strike of the puts.

18.6   ZERO COST COLLAR

A **zero cost collar** involves buying a put option and selling a call option with the strikes of the options set such that the two premiums exactly cancel out. Suppose as previously that the investor buys an 850 strike put against a holding in a share trading at 873 pence, but this time also sells a 905 strike call. The premium received for the call is 19 pence per share, which simply offsets the 19 pence cost of the puts, so there is zero net premium to pay. The payoff profile of the zero cost collar is illustrated in Figure 18.9.

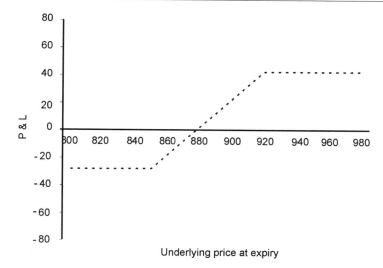

Figure 18.8 Expiry payoff profile of collar strategy

The net premium on the two options is zero so the combination strategy payoff profile cuts through the zero profit and loss line at 873. The investor can make 32 pence per share on the underlying before the call options are exercised. The investor can lose 23 pence per share before the protection afforded by the 850 strike puts comes into operation. Zero cost collars are popular with investors for the obvious reason that there is no net premium to pay. However there is a potential opportunity cost — if the share price rises above the strike of the sold call then the investor's returns are capped and he or she will underperform other investors who do not have the option position in place.

18.7   BULL SPREAD

In the previous examples we have used options to hedge the risk on a position in the underlying, or to generate additional returns against a holding in the underlying. In the remaining strategies explored in this chapter we consider ways in which call and put options can be assembled in combinations to establish trading positions. These strategies are used by traders (and potentially by hedge funds) rather than by traditional buy-side investors such as pension fund managers.

A **bull spread** is an appropriate strategy to put in place when a trader is moderately confident that the underlying will rise in price. There are in fact different ways to assemble the strategy. In the following example we will put it together in the first instance by buying calls and simultaneously selling calls with a higher strike price but the same time to expiry. The details of the options used are set out in Table 18.1. The data is for 30-day European options. The premiums were calculated using the Black–Scholes option model and assuming a 30.00% volatility on the underlying. The spot price of the underlying is 100. Premiums are quoted per share.

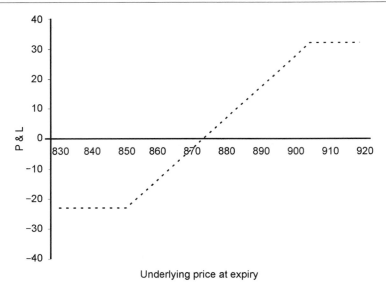

Figure 18.9   Zero cost collar payoff profile at expiry

Table 18.1   Options for the bull spread trade

Strike price of long call	95.00
Premium paid for long call	−6.57
Strike price of short call	105.00
Premium received for short call	1.63

The net premium due to be paid on the combined position is −4.94 per share. Figure 18.10 shows the payoff profile of the strategy at the expiration of the two options.

18.7.1   Maximum Profit and Loss

The maximum loss on the bull spread at expiry is the net premium of −4.94. The maximum profit is 5.06 per share. This profit is achieved when the share price is at 105 — it comprises a profit of 10 on the 95 strike long call, less the net premium paid. At price levels above 105 any gains on the 95 strike call will be exactly offset by losses on the 105 strike short call position. Again in this analysis we ignore the fact that the option premium is paid upfront while any profit from exercise is achieved at the expiry of the options; properly speaking we should adjust for the time value of money.

Uses of Bull Spread

The bull spread is an appropriate trade to put in place when a modest rise in the share price is expected, since the profits are capped above the strike of the short call. It has certain advantages when compared with buying a call on its own. The net cost and hence the maximum potential loss are lower, and the level the share will have to trade at the expiry of the options for the strategy to break even is lower. The position will normally be set up with positive delta and fairly neutral values for gamma, theta and vega.

18.7.2 Bull Spread with Puts

The bull spread we have just constructed can also be assembled by selling an in-the-money put with a strike of 105 and at the same time buying an out-of-the-money put with a strike of 95 to limit the losses in the event that the share price falls sharply. The advantage of setting up the trade in this way is that a positive net premium will be received at the outset. Taking into account the effects of the time value of money fully, however, the maximum profit and maximum loss figures will be identical.

18.8 BEAR SPREAD

A bear spread strategy is useful when a trader is moderately bearish about the under-lying. It generates a capped profit when the underlying falls in value, but a maximum loss if the underlying should happen to rise in value. We will assemble a bear spread using a long and a short put option using the data in Table 18.2. These are 30-day European options again priced at a 30% volatility with the underlying share trading at 100.

The net premium due to be paid on the combined position is −5.01. The maximum loss is achieved at expiry when the underlying is trading at 105, in which case the net premium is lost. The maximum profit (4.99) is attained when the underlying is trading at 95, below which level any profits on the long put option are offset by losses on the short

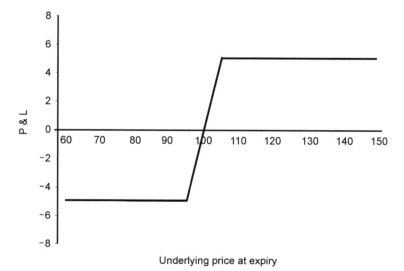

Figure 18.10 Bull spread expiry payoff profile

Table 18.2   Option details for the bear spread

Strike price of long put	105.00
Premium paid for long put	−6.36
Strike price of short put	95.00
Premium received for short put	1.35

95 strike put. Figure 18.11 shows the payoff profile of the strategy at the expiration of the two options (again ignoring the time value of money factor).

18.9   PUT RATIO SPREAD

In the previous spread trade examples it was assumed that the ratio of bought and sold options was one-for-one. In the following strategy a trader sells two options for every one option purchased. The options used are described in Table 18.3. The underlying share is again trading at 100, the options have 30 days until maturity and they are priced using a 30% volatility assumption.

18.9.1   Net Premium and Payoffs

Since two 96 strike puts are sold for every one 102 strike put that is bought, the trader pays a net premium of −1.09. At the expiry of the options, if the share price is above 102, none of the options will be exercised and the trader will have lost 1.09. If the share price is below 102 the trader will exercise the 102 strike put, and will recoup the net premium paid when the share is trading at 100.91. The maximum profit is realized when

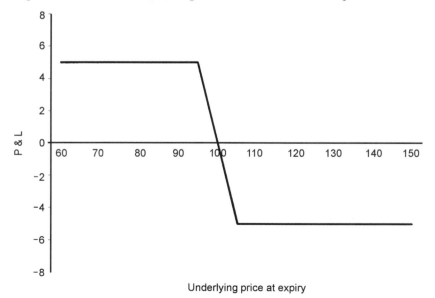

Underlying price at expiry

Figure 18.11   Bear spread expiry payoff profile

Table 18.3 Option details for put ratio spread

Strike price of short put	96.00
Premium received per share	1.65
Strike price of long put	102.00
Premium paid per share	−4.39

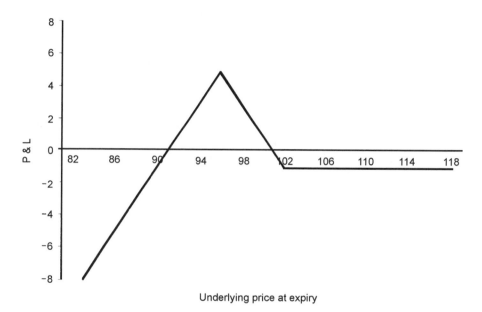

Underlying price at expiry

Figure 18.12 Put ratio spread expiry payoff profile

the underlying is trading at 96 because the puts the trader has sold will not be exercised until that point. The maximum profit is 102−96 less the 1.09 net premium paid, a total of 4.91. The expiry payoff profile of the strategy is shown in Figure 18.12.

Unlike a bear spread the profit is not capped when the 96 strike is hit. In fact it starts to fall because two puts were sold for every one bought. The profit and loss line then cuts through zero when the share price is at 91.09. The maximum loss on the strategy of 91.09 is realized when the underlying is trading at zero. At that level the loss on the two sold puts is 2 × −96 = −192. The profit on the bought put is 102 and the net cost of the options is −1.09. In this case the profit and loss line falls sharply below 96 because the trader has sold the 96 puts in a ratio of 2:1 to the bought 102 strike puts. The angle of the line can be adjusted by changing the ratio, although this of course will affect the net premium paid or received on the options.

Use of Put Ratio Spread

The put ratio strategy we explored might be appropriate for a trader who is moderately bearish about the underlying but who thinks it unlikely that it will fall below 96. Selling the two 96 strike puts helps to recoup almost all the premium paid for the long 102 strike put option.

18.10   CALENDAR OR TIME SPREAD

The final spread trade we will explore is known as a **calendar** or **time spread**. Essentially it is designed to exploit the fact that a shorter-dated option has a faster rate of time value decay—a higher absolute theta value—compared to a longer-dated option on the same underlying. To illustrate the concept we will assemble a strategy that involves buying and selling at-the-money calls on the same underlying. The options are specified in Table 18.4. The spot price of the underlying is 100. The sold calls have 30 days to expiry and the bought calls 60 days to expiry. Both options were priced at a 30% volatility.

The net premium paid on the options is −1.52. The net theta is positive 0.02. This means that if one day elapses (assuming other factors such as the price of the underlying remain constant) then the profit on the strategy will be 0.02 per share. The profit arises from the fact that the sold 30-day options have a higher rate of time decay compared to the 60-day options purchased.

Every day that elapses (all other things being equal) the short calls will tend to lose value and can be bought back more cheaply to close the position. The bought calls also lose value, but at a somewhat slower rate. The theta effect will actually generate slightly higher proportional returns for longer holding periods because the rate of time decay on the options is non-linear. For example, if 10 days elapse and all the other inputs to the option value remain constant then the sold 30-day calls would only cost 2.88 to repurchase while the 60-day calls will have dropped in value to 4.61. In that case:

$$\text{Net Profit per Share} = (3.54 - 2.88) + (4.61 - 5.06) = 0.21$$

18.10.1   Risks with Calendar Spread

The risk with the calendar spread trade, of course, is that all the other factors that determine the value of the options may not remain constant. In the example the two calls were struck at-the-money in relation to the spot price and the deltas would therefore net out—the delta of the sold call is negative and the delta of the bought call

Table 18.4   Option details for calendar spread

Premium received on 30-day sold call	3.54
Theta of 30-day sold call	0.06
Premium paid on 60-day bought call	−5.06
Theta of 60-day bought call	−0.04

is positive. For small directional movements in the underlying share price the net profit and loss on the position will be close to zero—any losses on one option will be compensated for by gains on the other. However the sold 30-day call will have higher gamma than the longer-dated bought 60-day call. In practice this means that the delta-neutrality will tend to break down for larger movements in the price of the underlying. If the share price rises sharply, for example, the losses on the sold call will exceed the profits on the bought call option.

18.11 VOLATILITY REVISITED

Perhaps the key input to the option pricing model is the assumed volatility of the underlying security. Certainly it is the variable that offers the most scope for disagreement. Historical volatility is calculated statistically as the standard deviation of the past returns on the security around the historical average return (see the Appendix to Chapter 16 for details of the calculation). But what time period should we use in the calculation? One approach is to go back many years in order to incorporate as much information about the behaviour of the asset as possible. But the underlying itself may have changed its characteristics over time. To take one extreme example, the Finnish mobile phone company Nokia used to be a conglomerate making a range of unexciting staple goods. Data from that historical period is unlikely to be very relevant to assessing the likely behaviour of the shares today. On the other hand, if we exclude too much historical data and base our volatility calculation only on recent experience we run the risk of failing to capture those extreme movements in the price of the underlying that occur very rarely. Some option traders try to resolve this problem by calculating a moving average of the historical volatility of the underlying, which weights its more recent behaviour more heavily than distant events. The logic is that the most recent experience is likely to provide a better indicator of the future.

18.11.1 Implied Volatility

Whatever the methodology, however, there is no getting round the fact that historical volatility is concerned with the past behaviour of the underlying. The outturn profits and losses on an option position will be determined by the actual behaviour of the underlying over the life of the option. One standard way around this problem is to operate the option pricing model 'in reverse'. Rather than calculating the value of an option from an estimated or assumed volatility, the method involves inserting the actual value at which the option is trading in the market and deriving the volatility assumption built into this price. This is called **implied volatility**.

Implied Volatility

Implied volatility is the volatility assumption built into an actual option price. It can be compared with the historical volatility of the underlying or with a forecast of future volatility to determine whether the option is trading 'cheap' or 'expensive'.

When implied volatility is calculated from publicly available data such as the prices of exchange-traded options the result at first sight is often a little surprising. It appears that traders tend to use different volatilities to price options on the same underlying that differ only in their strike price or in the time to expiry. For example, out-of-the-money puts on an equity index are often sold at higher implied volatilities compared to at-the-money and in-the-money put options on exactly the same index.

18.11.2 Volatility Smile

When the calculated implied volatilities are plotted against the strikes of the options the resulting graph is sometimes called a **volatility smile** (although in practice it can be something of a lopsided smile). This is a large subject and detailed treatment is outwith the scope of this book, but one commonly accepted explanation for this effect is that traders are compensating for some of the imperfections of the standard pricing model by adjusting the volatility assumptions they use to price options. The Black–Scholes model assumes that the returns on shares follow the bell-curve shape of the normal distribution. It appears empirically that there is a greater probability of major falls in equity markets than is captured by the normal distribution curve. It seems that traders cover this risk by increasing the prices (and hence the implied volatilities) of out-of-the-money put options.

A **volatility surface** is a three-dimensional graph which shows the implied volatilities of options on the same underlying for (on the x-axis) a range of different strike prices and (on the z-axis) a range of different expiry dates. Traders and risk managers use the data from volatility smiles and surfaces to pinpoint the correct volatility to use to value options on a given underlying, taking into account the actual strike and expiry date of the options.

18.11.3 Volatility Trades

Implied volatility is a useful concept since it helps traders decide whether the volatility assumptions currently being used by the rest of the market to price options are (in the judgement of the trader) realistic or otherwise. The trader can then 'buy volatility' if it is cheap or 'sell volatility' if it is overpriced. In simple terms, buying volatility means purchasing options (they increase in value as volatility assumptions increase). Selling volatility involves shorting or selling options (for opposite reasons).

18.12 VOLATILITY TRADING: CASE STUDY

In the following case study we will explore a typical volatility trade. The underlying in this example is the FT-SE 100 index, the index of the leading 100 UK shares. (See Chapter 15 for more details on index options.) Additional details are as follows:

Cash index level:	6000
Risk-free interest rate:	6.00%
FT-SE 100 index dividend yield:	2.25%
Value of a full index point:	£10.00

A trader looks at the price at which FT-SE options are being traded on the exchange. Two-month (62-day) European-style 6000 strike calls are trading at 264 index points or £2640 (each point is worth £10). The equivalent FT-SE puts are trading at 226 points. The trader then inserts the data into the Black–Scholes model adapted for an asset paying continuous dividends (see Chapter 16) and discovers that the market is selling the contracts at an implied volatility of 25.00% per annum. This is the volatility assumption that generates option prices of 264 and 226 points respectively.

The trader believes that 25.00% implied volatility is too high and that volatility is set to fall sharply as the market recovers from its recent concerns and uncertainties. The trader believes that volatility on the FT-SE will fall back to 20.00%, much closer to its long-run average. To capitalize on this the trader decides to sell (short) an at-the-money straddle on the FT-SE with 62 days to expiry. The total premium received on the straddle per call and put option contract sold is 490 index points, or £4900 at £10 per point.

Short Straddle

A short straddle strategy consists of selling a call and a put option on the same underlying with the same strike and the same time to expiry. If volatility declines then (assuming the other factors that determine the price of the options remain constant) both options will lose value and can be bought back cheaply at a profit.

18.12.1   Delta Risks

Rather than sell the straddle of course the trader could simply sell calls on the FT-SE 100 index outright. This is also a short volatility position in the sense that if volatility declines the options will decline in value and can be repurchased at a cheaper price. The problem is that selling a naked call is also a short delta position — the option will increase in value if the FT-SE rises and the trader would lose money. As an alternative the trader could consider selling put rather than call options on the FT-SE. This is a short volatility position, but at the same time it is also a long delta position — if the market rises the puts will move out of the money and will become cheaper to buy back; if the market falls the puts will move into the money and the position will become more expensive to close out.

By selling the straddle the trader starts out with a position that is roughly delta-neutral. The negative delta on the short calls is balanced by the positive delta on the sold put options. If the FT-SE rises (by a small amount) then the gains on the puts will offset the losses on the calls. If the FT-SE falls the reverse will occur.

18.12.2   Short Straddle Expiry Payoff

Figure 18.13 shows the payoff profile of the short straddle at the expiry of the two options for different levels of the FT-SE 100 index. The maximum profit is achieved when the index remains at 6000 — the trader earns the 490 points (£4900) total premium and both options expire worthless with zero intrinsic value. There are two break-even points. If the FT-SE closes at 6490 the premium initially earned on the options is exactly offset by the 490 point loss on the sold 6000 strike call (the put expires worthless). If the FT-SE closes

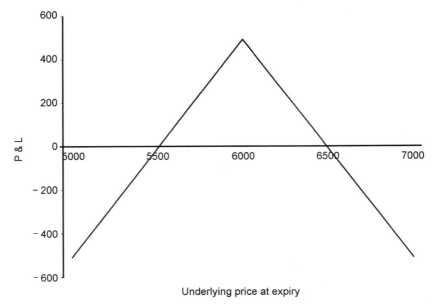

Figure 18.13   Expiry payoff profile of short straddle

at 5510 the premium is exactly offset by the 490 point loss on the sold 6000 strike put (the call expires worthless). Since this is a short volatility strategy it is no surprise to find that it generates its maximum profit when the index closes exactly where it started, at a level of 6000.

One fact that Figure 18.13 illustrates clearly is that selling a straddle is a very risky strategy. In theory there is no maximum loss. For this reason many traders would look to close the position by buying back the two options as quickly (and cheaply) as possible. What matters from this perspective therefore is not so much the payoff at expiry but the **current** value of the strategy.

18.13   CURRENT PAYOFF PROFILES

Figure 18.14 shows the **current** profit and loss profile of the sold 6000 strike call option. This shows the profit and loss on the position in response to immediate changes in the FT-SE. The assumption is that the call has been sold for 264 points with two months remaining to expiry and with the FT-SE at 6000. If the FT-SE rises above 6000 (and all the other factors that determine the price of the option remain constant) then the call will become more expensive to buy back and the trader would lose money closing the position. In theory the call can keep moving further and further into the money indefinitely, attracting more and more intrinsic value, so there is no limit to the potential losses. On the other hand if the FT-SE falls below 6000 the call will move out of the money and the trader could buy it back more cheaply at a profit. The maximum profit is the 264 point premium the call was initially sold for — the option can never be purchased for less than zero.

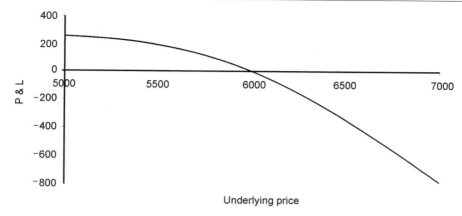

Figure 18.14 Current payoff profile on the sold 6000 call

Selling the call is a short delta position — it is rather like being short the underlying. The difference is that while the losses continue to mount when the index rises, the maximum profit if the index falls is 264 points or £2640.

18.13.1 Short Put Current Payoff

By selling a straddle the trader also sold a put option. Figure 18.15 shows the current profile and loss profile of the two-month 6000 strike put option in response to immediate changes in the underlying index. Selling a put is a positive delta position. It is rather like establishing a long position in the underlying, except the maximum profit that can be achieved is the premium initially earned (in this example 226 index points).

Figure 18.15 Current payoff profile of the sold 6000 put

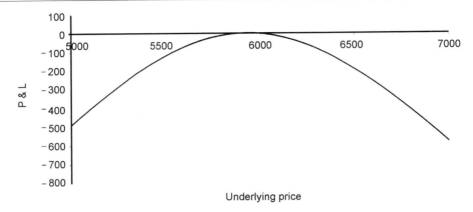

Figure 18.16   Current payoff profile of the short straddle

18.13.2   Short Straddle Current Payoff

The current payoff profile on the short straddle is illustrated in Figure 18.16. This combines the profiles for the call and the put option. The graph shows that for small movements in the underlying index the profits and losses on the two options cancel out. The call has negative delta and the put has positive delta so overall the short straddle is roughly delta-neutral. In simple terms, if the FT-SE rises the call will become more expensive to repurchase (it moves into the money) but the puts will become cheaper. The reverse process happens if the FT-SE falls by a small amount. However the graph also shows that the benefits of delta-neutrality will tend to break down for larger movements in the FT-SE 100 index. For example, if the index moves up sharply then the losses on the sold call will be considerable (the intrinsic value can increase indefinitely) whereas the maximum profit on the put is the 226 point premium at which the contract was sold.

18.13.3   Position Gamma

The problem is that while the straddle may be approximately delta-neutral (the deltas of the call and the put cancel out) it is gamma negative. Selling a call is a gamma negative position and so too is selling a put option. The practical consequence of this fact is that if the FT-SE rises or falls by more than a small number of points the straddle will no longer be delta-neutral (gamma is a measure of the instability of delta).

The consequences are rather unpleasant. If for example the FT-SE rises sharply then the short straddle position will become delta negative—effectively the trader is short the market in a rising market. The more the index rises, the more delta negative the position will become. The trader could attempt to restore delta-neutrality by buying FT-SE calls, futures or underlying shares. The danger then is that if the index should subsequently fall back sharply the trader will have to sell back some or all of those calls, futures or shares (which are no longer required) at a loss.

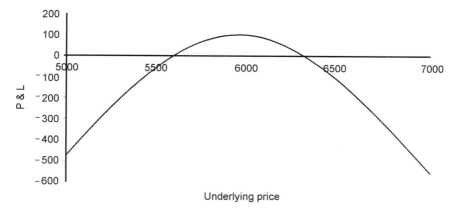

Figure 18.17   Current payoff profile at 20.00% volatility

18.14   PROFITS FROM THE SHORT STRADDLE

By now it may appear that the short straddle is rather a 'lose–lose' strategy. Certainly it loses money on a current profit and loss basis whether the index rises or falls. In fact there are only two events that can generate a trading profit on the short straddle position.

● **Declining Volatility.** A decline in the volatility assumption used by the market to price the options. If this happens the call and put options will lose value and the position can be closed out at a profit. The strategy has negative vega.
● **Time Decay.** Every day that elapses the options will tend to lose a certain amount of time value (all other things being equal). The strategy has positive theta.

Figure 18.17 shows what happens to the current value of the straddle (still with two months to expiry) for a range of different levels of the FT-SE on the assumption that volatility has dropped from 25.00% to 20.00% Provided the FT-SE has not moved appreciably from the starting level of 6000 the two options can be repurchased and the straddle position closed out at a profit.

Even if volatility does not decline there is still a chance of making money from the time value decay. Figure 18.18 shows the current value of the straddle for a range of different levels of the FT-SE, this time with one month remaining to expiry (both options still priced at 25.00% volatility). Provided the index has not moved directionally to any great extent and volatility has not increased materially, the straddle can be closed out after one month has elapsed at a (modest) profit.

18.15   OTHER VOLATILITY TRADES

One way to reduce the risk on a short volatility position is to sell calls and puts that are struck out-of-the-money. For example, the trader could sell a 6250 call and a 5750 put. This strategy is known as a **short strangle**. For a given change in the index the trade will lose less money than the short 6000 strike straddle (it is less short gamma). The problem

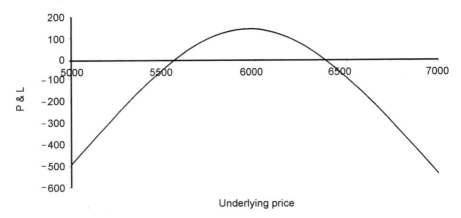

Figure 18.18   Current payoff profile, one month to expiry

is that for a given fall in volatility or a given period of time elapse it will generate less profit than the short straddle.

Selling volatility is typically a high-risk trade. The profit is limited to the premium charged for the options while the potential losses are unlimited. On the other hand, buying volatility carries limited risk and potentially unlimited profits. A long straddle consists of buying a call and a put on the underlying with the same strike and the same time to expiry. The loss is limited to the combined premium on the options. At expiry the call or the put options could generate unlimited (or at least very substantial) profits.

Long Straddle Application

A long straddle might be an appropriate trade to put in place when a trader feels that the underlying is due to break sharply out of a range but is not clear about the direction of the move. What the buyer of a straddle does not want is a dull or flat market with declining volatility.

Buying a straddle is a **long volatility** (long vega) trade because if volatility rises both options will increase in value. It will be roughly delta-neutral but gamma positive — meaning that the profits and losses on the call and put will cancel out for small movements in the market; for larger movements the profit on the option that is moving into the money will more than offset the losses on the option that is moving out of the money (the maximum loss on which is confined to the initial premium paid). A long straddle is short theta — both options are subject to the loss of time value.

18.16   CHAPTER SUMMARY

An investor who owns a security and is concerned about losses can buy put options as an insurance or protection device. This maximizes the potential losses on the securities but at the same time reduces the potential profits because of the cost of the option premium. The more in-the-money the put options are the better the level of protection they provide, but the more expensive they will be. Investors can generate additional income against their holdings in securities by selling call options. These are normally struck out-of-the-money to reduce the risk of exercise. A collar strategy consists of buying an out-of-the-money put and selling an out-of-the-money call to protect against losses on the underlying while reducing the net premium paid. In addition to their applications in hedging and risk management, options can also be used to implement trading strategies. A spread trade is assembled by buying or selling a combination of options. A bull spread is a strategy that pays a capped profit when the underlying rises, but which has a maximum loss if the underlying falls in price. A bear spread pays a capped profit when the underlying falls in price, with a maximum loss if the underlying increases in value. Traders can also use options to implement views about volatility. A short straddle is a short volatility position. It consists of selling two options on the same underlying with the same strike and the same expiry date. If volatility declines the straddle can be repurchased at a cheaper price. In addition to historic volatility, which is based on the historical returns on an asset, traders also use a measure called implied volatility. This is the volatility assumption implied in the actual premium quoted for an option. Implied volatility is used by traders as a measure of whether options represent good value or are overpriced (in which case they should be sold). A volatility smile is a graph which plots the implied volatility of options on the same underlying for a range of strike prices.

19
Currency and Interest Rate Options

News from a forrein country came,
As if my treasure and my wealth lay there.
Thomas Traherne

19.1 CHAPTER OVERVIEW

In previous chapters we have looked at option valuation models, fundamental option strategies and risk measures. In the current chapter we apply these concepts to currency (foreign exchange) and to interest rate options. We explore how currency options can be used to manage foreign exchange exposures, and how they compare against other instruments. We consider how exchange-traded contracts operate in practice and review the roles of the exchange and of the clearing house. Finally we outline the way in which the Black–Scholes option pricing model is commonly adapted to price currency options. Interest rate options can also be traded on an exchange or over-the-counter. We consider in this chapter how interest rate options are quoted and traded and how they are used to manage interest rate exposures. Specific products reviewed are caps and 'caplets'; floors and 'floorlets'; interest rate collars; options on short-term interest rate futures; and swaptions, which are options to buy or sell interest rate swaps. We consider trading and hedging applications of these various products and outline how interest rate options can be valued using a variant of the standard model. The chapter concludes with a summary of hedging or trading strategies (using cash or derivative products) that might be implemented for different interest rate forecasts.

19.2 CURRENCY OPTIONS

A currency or FX option is the right but not the obligation:

- to exchange two currencies;
- on the expiry date (on or before the expiry date in the case of an American option);
- at a fixed rate of exchange.

Currency options are traded over-the-counter by dealers or on exchanges such as LIFFE and the Philadelphia Stock Exchange (PHLX). The Philadelphia exchange is a major market for exchange-traded currency options and offers contracts in a range of major currencies against the US dollar, including the British pound, the Japanese yen, the euro and the Swiss franc. Contracts that are exercised are physically settled (the two currencies are exchanged at the exercise price). Table 19.1 shows the closing prices for a selection of PHLX £/$ options on Wednesday 30 May 2001.

Table 19.1   Sterling/dollar option premiums

Strike	June calls	July calls	June puts	July puts
1.410	1.95	2.42	0.30	0.88
1.420	1.26	1.81	0.55	1.27

Source: Philadelphia Stock Exchange.

19.2.1   Interpreting the Quotations

The contract size for sterling/dollar options is £31,250. The strike is quoted in Table 19.1 in dollars per pound and the option premiums are quoted in cents per pound. The quotations are interpreted as follows.

- A trader who buys one June 1.410 sterling call option acquires the right (but not the obligation) to buy £31,250 and to pay in return $31{,}250 \times \$1.410 = \$44{,}062.50$.
- The premium for this option is $31{,}250 \times \$0.0195 = \$609.375$ per contract.

Note that the 1.410 sterling call (the right to buy £31,250) is at the same time a dollar put (the right to pay $44,062.50 for the pounds).

- A trader who buys one July 1.420 put contract acquires the right but not the obligation to sell £31,250 and to receive in return $31{,}250 \times \$1.420 = \$44{,}375$.
- For this privilege the trader has to pay a premium of $31{,}250 \times \$0.0127 = \$396.875$. This is a sterling put and at the same time a call on the US dollar.

19.2.2   Trading Methods

Currency options on PHLX are traded by open outcry with orders coming in to the floor from brokers from around the world. The floor brokers can execute orders with other brokers or with a market maker. Contracts are guaranteed by the Options Clearing Corporation (OCC), which acts as an intermediary between buyers and sellers. This contrasts with over-the-counter currency option dealings in which market participants are exposed to the risk of counterparty default. Sellers (writers) of exchange-traded options have to post margin as collateral. Currency option contracts on PHLX are not automatically exercised at expiry. The buyer of a call or put option has to submit an exercise notification to his or her broker. The OCC assigns the exercise to a seller of the contracts and the two currencies are physically exchanged at the strike price.

19.3   HEDGING FX EXPOSURES: CASE STUDY

OTC and exchange-traded currency options can be used by corporates, traders and investors to hedge FX exposures. We will consider here a typical case.

In this example a US company exporting goods to the UK is paid in pounds sterling for the goods. It is the end of May and the firm is due to receive a payment of £10 million in July. The company could wait until July and sell the pounds at the prevailing spot rate. The problem is that if the pound weakens against the dollar the US firm will receive fewer dollars than expected and may lose money on the export transaction.

Alternatively, the company could contact a broker and buy sterling puts (dollar calls) on the Philadelphia exchange. The July 1.420 puts are trading at 1.27 cents per pound. The contract size is £31,250. The company should buy 320 contracts:

$$\frac{£10 \text{ million}}{£31,250} = 320 \text{ contracts}$$

The total premium cost of the contracts is:

$$\$0.0127 \times £31,250 \times 320 = \$127,000$$

19.3.1   Performance of the Hedge

Table 19.2 analyses the hedge and its potential benefits and drawbacks. The table shows the following values.

- Column (1) shows a range of possible spot GBP:USD rates in July.
- Column (2) shows the dollar amount the US company would receive from selling £10 million at that spot rate.
- Column (3) shows the dollar amount the company would receive if it hedged the FX exposure by buying the 1.420 strike sterling put, ignoring the initial premium.
- Column (4) shows the option premium.
- Column (5) shows the net of columns (3) and (4).
- Column (6) shows for each spot rate in column (1) the effective rate of exchange achieved if the company had hedged the FX exposure by buying the sterling put options.

For example, if the GBP:USD spot rate in July is £1 = \$1.36 then the corporate would receive \$13.6 million for the pounds at the spot rate.

On the other hand if the firm had bought the 1.420 strike sterling puts to hedge the exposure then the option would be exercised and the corporate would receive \$14.2

Table 19.2   Performance of the FX hedge strategy

(1)	(2)	(3) $ Hedged before premium	(4) Less premium	(5) Net $ hedged	(6)
Spot rate	$ Unhedged				Hedged rate
1.3600	13,600,000	14,200,000	127,000	14,073,000	1.4073
1.3800	13,800,000	14,200,000	127,000	14,073,000	1.4073
1.4000	14,000,000	14,200,000	127,000	14,073,000	1.4073
1.4200	14,200,000	14,200,000	127,000	14,073,000	1.4073
1.4400	14,400,000	14,400,000	127,000	14,273,000	1.4273
1.4600	14,600,000	14,600,000	127,000	14,473,000	1.4473
1.4800	14,800,000	14,800,000	127,000	14,673,000	1.4673
1.5000	15,000,000	15,000,000	127,000	14,873,000	1.4873
1.5200	15,200,000	15,200,000	127,000	15,073,000	1.5073
1.5400	15,400,000	15,400,000	127,000	15,273,000	1.5273
1.5600	15,600,000	15,600,000	127,000	15,473,000	1.5473

million for the pounds. Subtracting the $127,000 premium paid, the net dollar receipt is $14.073 million. The effective exchange rate achieved is:

$$\frac{\$14.073 \text{ million}}{£10 \text{ million}} = 1.4073$$

$$1.4200 - 0.0127 = 1.4073$$

To take one other example, if the GBP:USD spot rate in July is £1 = $1.560 then the dollars received from selling the pounds at that rate would amount to $15.6 million. If the corporate had bought the 1.420 strike sterling puts the options in this situation would expire worthless, and the firm would sell pounds for dollars at the more favourable spot rate. From the $15.6 million received must be subtracted the $127,000 premium, so the net dollar receipt on the hedged position would be $15.473 million. The effective exchange rate achieved is:

$$\frac{\$15.473 \text{ million}}{£10 \text{ million}} = 1.5473$$

$$1.5600 - 0.0127 = 1.5473$$

19.3.2 Graph of Hedged and Unhedged Positions

Figure 19.1 graphs the dollar receipts from selling the pounds for a range of GBP:USD spot prices. The solid line shows the dollars received at the spot rate, with no hedge in place. The dotted line shows the dollars received with the options hedge in place. The lines cross when the spot price is at $1.420 - 0.0127 = 1.4073$. At that exchange rate the

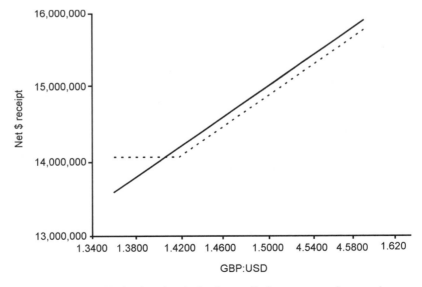

Figure 19.1 Hedged and unhedged payoffs for a range of spot prices

pounds could be sold for \$14.073 million on the spot market. The net amount of dollars received if the put was exercised would be $(10,000,000 \times 1.420) - \$127,000 = \$14.073$ million.

19.4   PRICING CURRENCY OPTIONS

The Black–Scholes option pricing model was originally written to price equity options, and then modified for dividend-paying shares. The inputs to the model are as follows:

- the current price of the underlying share;
- the option strike or exercise price;
- the expected volatility of the underlying;
- the cost of carrying a position in the underlying.

A modified version called the Garman–Kohlhagen model is widely used to value European currency options. A sterling call, for example, is simply the right to buy pounds (the underlying) and to pay in return a fixed price in US dollars. The pricing model is therefore modified as follows:

- the spot price of the underlying becomes the GBP:USD spot rate;
- the volatility is the volatility of the spot rate;
- the 'dividend yield' becomes the sterling interest rate, the yield on the currency that would be acquired by the buyer and sold by the seller if the call is exercised;
- the 'risk-free rate' is the dollar interest rate.

One way to view the carry cost is to realize that the seller of a sterling call can hedge the risk on this position by borrowing dollars and buying and investing pounds. Therefore the net cost of carrying this hedge has to be factored into the premium charged for a GBP:USD option.

19.4.1   Example

To illustrate the Garman–Kohlhagen approach we will price a sterling call (dollar put) with the following input data:

Spot GBP:USD rate (S) = 142 cents per £
Exercise style: European
USD rate ('risk-free rate') = 4.00% p.a.
GBP interest rate ('dividend yield') = 5.25% p.a.
GBP:USD volatility = 10.00% p.a.
Exercise price (E) = 142 cents per £
Time to expiry = 0.25 years

Interest rates are quoted on a continuously compounded basis. With these inputs the model calculates the following values:

$N(d_1) = 0.4850$
$N(d_2) = 0.4651$
$S \times N(d_1) \times e^{-0.0525 \times 0.25} = 67.98$
$E \times N(d_2) \times e^{-0.04 \times 0.25} = 65.39$
The value of the call $C = 67.98 - 65.39$
$\qquad\qquad\qquad\quad = 2.59$ cents per £

Although the option is at-the-money in relation to the spot rate, in fact it is actually slightly out-of-the-money in relation to the GBP:USD forward rate. Properly speaking the forward rate is the real reference point to determine the 'moneyness' of a European-style option since it can only be exercised at expiry. The three-month GBP:USD forward rate in this example will be lower than £1 = $1.42 (the pound will buy fewer dollars for forward delivery compared to spot delivery) because sterling is the higher yield currency. This means that in relation to the (lower) forward rate a call with an exercise price of 142 cents is struck slightly out-of-the-money. The delta of the call in this example is 0.48 or 48%.

19.5   INTEREST RATE OPTIONS

Interest rate options provide investors, traders and borrowers with a flexible means of managing interest rate risks and exposures. Since the time of the 1960s and 1970s central banks and governments around the world have gradually relaxed or abolished controls on currency exchange rates. As a result the short-term rate of interest (especially the repo rate) has become their main weapon against inflation, and from time to time also a means of strengthening or weakening the national currency. This has led, amongst other factors, to increased volatility in interest rates and the need for sophisticated tools to manage interest rate risks and exposures.

FRAs and Futures Hedges

A corporate borrower concerned about rising interest rates can buy a forward rate agreement (FRA) or sell interest rate futures on a derivatives exchange. However there is a potential drawback with this type of strategy. If interest rates should happen to fall rather than rise then the borrower would have to make a compensation payment to the seller of the FRA, or margin payments on the futures contracts to the clearing house. Of course these cash payments would be offset by lower interest costs on the borrower's underlying loans, but it would nevertheless suffer an 'opportunity loss'. Net of the payments made on the FRA or futures, its effective borrowing cost would be higher than if it did not have the interest rate hedge in place. (See Chapter 10 for details of FRAs and interest rate futures.)

19.5.1   Hedging with Interest Rate Options

An alternative strategy for a corporate borrower is to hedge interest rate exposures by buying over-the-counter (OTC) or exchange-traded interest rate options. An OTC interest rate call option is essentially an option to buy an FRA.

- If at the expiry of the option the LIBOR rate for the period covered by the contract is above the contractual rate (the strike price or rate) the corporate would exercise the call.
- It would then receive a cash compensation payment from the seller of the call. The payment is calculated in the same way as it would be for a standard FRA contract.
- If LIBOR is equal to or lower than the strike rate then the option contract expires worthless and no further payment is due to the seller.

Since the buyer of the option has the privilege of exercising the contract in favourable circumstances or otherwise allowing it to expire worthless, the buyer will have to pay an upfront premium to the seller of the option.

Interest Rate Puts

An investor who is concerned about falling interest rates might decide to buy an OTC interest rate put option. This is effectively the right but not the obligation to sell an FRA to the counterparty (normally a bank). The put option will be exercised at expiry if the cash LIBOR rate for the period covered by the contract is below the strike rate. The investor then holds a sold FRA contract which is cash-settled — that is, a cash compensation payment is received from the counterparty. If at expiration the LIBOR rate is equal to or above the strike rate the option is left to expire worthless and the investor has lost only the initial premium paid.

19.6 EXCHANGE-TRADED INTEREST RATE OPTIONS

Borrowers and investors can also use exchange-traded interest rate options to manage their interest rate risks and exposures.

- The buyer of an exchange-traded put option has the right but not the obligation to sell an interest rate futures contract.
- The buyer of an exchange-traded call option has the right but not the obligation to buy an interest rate futures contract.

Interest rate futures are quoted in terms of 100 minus the interest rate for the period of time covered by the contract. For this reason, as we have seen in Chapter 10, they work in the opposite way to FRAs which are quoted in interest rate terms.

- A borrower concerned about rising interest rates would consider selling interest rate futures or buying interest rate put options (the right but not the obligation to sell interest rate futures).
- An investor concerned about falling LIBOR rates would consider buying interest rate futures or buying interest rate call options (the right but not the obligation to buy interest rate futures).

19.7 EURODOLLAR OPTIONS

Table 19.3 shows settlement or closing prices for selected Eurodollar options traded on the Chicago Mercantile Exchange on 31 May 2001. The underlying is a three-month Eurodollar futures contract with a notional value of $1 million. As in the case of the

Table 19.3 Eurodollar option prices

Strike	Calls		Puts	
	Jul	Sep	Jul	Sep
9575	0.3900	0.4050	0.0100	0.0300
9600	0.1700	0.2150	0.0400	0.0850
9625	0.0500	0.0950	0.1700	0.2150

Source: CME.

underlying futures contract, one basis point represents $0.01\% \times \$1$ million $\times 90/360 = \$25$. The strikes are quoted in terms of 100 minus the interest rate for the period of time covered by the underlying futures contract.

To take one example from the table.

- The July 9600 call represents the right to buy the underlying Eurodollar futures contract at a strike price of 9600.
- This implies an interest rate for the three-month period starting in mid-July of 4.00% per annum.
- The premium cost in dollars per contract is 17 points $\times \$25 = \$425$.

Suppose we buy one July 9600 call and retain the position until the expiry of the contract. At that point the three-month Eurodollar interest rate is in fact fixed at 3.75% per annum. The underlying futures will close at 9625. We have the right to buy the futures at 9600. Our net profit per call option is calculated as follows:

$$\text{Profit on Exercise} = 25 \text{ points} \times \$25 = \$625$$

$$\text{Less Premium Paid} = \$425$$

$$\text{Net Profit} = \$200 \text{ per contract}$$

Looked at another way, the option contract represents an option to invest dollars at a fixed interest rate of 4.00% per annum for the three-month period starting in July with a notional principal amount of $1 million. The premium is 0.17%. If the interest rate for the period in fact turns out to be 3.75% per annum then the net profit on the option is:

$$\$1 \text{ million} \times (0.04 - 0.0375 - 0.0017) \times 90/360 = \$200$$

19.7.1 Eurodollar Put Options

We will take a second case from Table 19.3.

- The July 9600 put option represents the right but not the obligation to sell a July Eurodollar futures contract at a strike price of 9600.
- This implies an interest rate of 4.00% per annum for the future period.
- The premium in this case is $4 \times \$25 = \$100$.

If the Eurodollar interest rate for the period turns out to be higher than 4.00% per annum then the futures will close below 9600. The holder of the put will make a profit from exercising the option and selling the futures at 9600, from which must be deducted the initial premium paid. Ignoring funding and transaction costs, the break-even point will be when the Eurodollar interest rate is at 4.04% per annum. In that event the futures contract will close at 9596 and the buyer of the put option will recover the four points in premium paid at the outset.

Of course in practice Eurodollar option contracts need not be retained until expiry or even exercised in order to realize their intrinsic value. They are financial assets in their own right and can be freely traded on the exchange. The value of an option position will respond to changes in the input factors such as the current market price of the underlying interest rate futures contract, the remaining time to expiry and the volatility of the underlying future interest rate.

19.8   LIFFE EURIBOR OPTIONS

Interest rate option contracts are traded on other exchanges such as LIFFE and Eurex. The contract specification for the LIFFE contract on the three-month euribor interest rate futures is set out in Table 19.4. The notional is one million euros but the tick size in this case is half a basis point so the value of one tick is €1 million × 0.005 = €12.50.

The LIFFE euribor options are American-style contracts and can be exercised on any business day up to the last trading day. If the holder of a bought call or put option decides to exercise a contract they are assigned a long or short position in the futures contract for the delivery month at the strike price. The option premium is not paid in full at the time of purchase. Instead an initial margin is paid and the option position is marked-to-market on a daily basis, and as a result variation margin is either paid or received.

19.9   CAPS, FLOORS AND COLLARS

A cap is a series of European over-the-counter interest rate call options covering a different forward time period, each with the same strike price.

Cap as Strip of FRAs

In effect a cap is a series or 'strip' of call options on forward rate agreements. Borrowers can use the product to 'cap' or set a limit on their cost of borrowing over the whole period covered by the contract, while still being able to take advantage of falls in interest rates (since they are not obliged to exercise any of the options in the cap).

Table 19.4   LIFFE euribor options

Unit of trading:	One three-month euribor futures contract
Expiry months:	Quarterly months March, June, September, December plus 2 serial months
Exercise/expiry:	Exercise by 17:00 on any business day before the expiry day and up to 10:45 on the last trading day
Last trading day:	Two business days before the third Wednesday of the expiry month
Tick size/value:	0.005/€12.50

Source: LIFFE.

The cap premium is simply the sum of the premiums of the individual interest rate options that make up the structure. The individual options are sometimes known as 'caplets'. Prices on caps are often quoted as a simple percentage of the contract notional amount. This can be paid upfront or 'amortized' over the life of the contract — that is, paid in instalments.

19.9.1   Interest Rate Floors

A floor is a series of European over-the-counter interest rate put options each written at the same strike rate. In effect a floor is a series or strip of put options on forward rate agreements. They are bought by investors in order to establish a minimum rate of return on their investments over a period of time. If the interest rate for a given period turns out to be below the strike then the investor will exercise the put option which covers that period and receive a cash payment to compensate for the lower reinvestment rates on their underlying investments. In return, the investor has to pay a premium for the floor in a lump sum or in instalments.

19.9.2   Interest Rate Collars

A borrower can enter into an interest rate collar strategy by:

● buying an interest rate cap;
● selling an interest rate floor.

This strategy establishes both a maximum and a minimum rate of interest. If interest rates rise above the strike of the cap the borrower will exercise the interest rate calls in the cap and receive compensation payments. If interest rates fall below the strike of the floor, the interest rate puts will be exercised and it will have to make compensation payments to the buyer of the floor.

19.10   INTEREST RATE CAP: CASE STUDY

To illustrate how caps are used in practice we will take the case of a UK corporate which has to renew a £100 million loan in six months. The loan will be for three years with semi-annual payments and the rate is likely to be set by the lending bank at LIBOR + 75 basis points. The company's financial officer is concerned about the effects of possible interest rate rises on the profitability of the company, and decides to explore three possible strategies to cope with this problem.

1. Renew the loan in six months at LIBOR + 75 and do not hedge the interest rate risk.
2. Renew the loan as above, but also enter today into a three-year interest rate swap starting in six months paying fixed and receiving floating. The fixed rate on an appropriate forward start three-year sterling swap would be 7.25% semi-annual against six-month LIBOR.
3. Renew the loan as above, but also buy an interest rate cap covering the payment periods on the loan. A cap with a strike of 7.25% would cost 1.20% of the notional principal, payable upfront. Alternatively, the premium can be paid in six semi-annual

instalments to match the payment dates of the underlying loan, at a cost of 0.23% of the notional principal per period or 0.46% per annum.

The finance director decides to explore a number of scenarios for interest rates and to consider how each strategy would perform.

19.10.1   Scenario A: LIBOR is 6.50% Over the Life of the Loan

1. The cost of borrowing unhedged is LIBOR + 0.75% = 7.25% per annum.
2. The cost of borrowing with the swap in place is fixed at 6.50% + 0.75% + 7.25% −6.50% = 8.00% per annum.
3. The cost of borrowing with the cap in place is 6.50% + 0.75% + (2 × 0.23%) = 7.71% per annum. In this scenario LIBOR is below the strike of the cap so the options in the cap will not be exercised and therefore no payment is due. From the cost of borrowing must be subtracted the annual cost of the cap premium, which is twice the six-monthly payment of 0.23%.

19.10.2   Scenario B: LIBOR is 7.50% Over the Life of the Loan

1. The cost of borrowing unhedged is LIBOR + 0.75% = 8.25% per annum.
2. The cost of borrowing with the swap in place is fixed at 7.50% + 0.75% + 7.25% − 7.50% = 8.00% per annum.
3. The cost of borrowing with the cap in place is 7.50% + 0.75% − 0.25% + (2 × 0.23%) = 8.46% per annum. LIBOR is above the 7.25% strike of the cap so the options in the cap will be exercised. The corporate receives 0.25% per annum (the difference between LIBOR and the strike). The annual premium cost is 0.46%.

Table 19.5 shows how the three strategies perform under a wider range of different interest rate scenarios. Figure 19.2 translates these figures into a graph.

19.10.3   Interpreting the Results

Notice that with the benefit of hindsight the capped strategy is second best to one of the other two strategies:

• if interest rates fall then the best strategy is to be unhedged;
• if on the other hand LIBOR rises sharply then the best strategy is to have locked into a fixed borrowing cost via the swap.

Table 19.5   Interest rate hedge strategies

LIBOR	Unhedged LIBOR + spread	Swapped at 7.25%	Capped at 7.25%, premium 0.46% p.a.
5.50%	6.25%	8.00%	6.71%
6.50%	7.25%	8.00%	7.71%
7.50%	8.25%	8.00%	8.46%
8.50%	9.25%	8.00%	8.46%

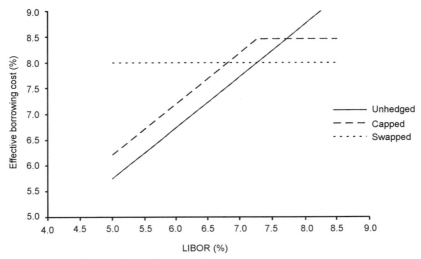

Figure 19.2   Graph of interest rate hedge strategies

The problem is that the finance officer does not know in advance the direction interest rates will take. The cap strategy offers 'something of both worlds'. If LIBOR falls then the options in the cap will simply not be exercised and the corporate is still able to take advantage of falling interest rates (which is not the case if the liability is swapped into a fixed rate). If LIBOR rises the corporate has established a maximum cost of funding (which is not the case if the interest rate exposure is left unhedged).

The main disadvantage of the cap strategy is the cost of the premium. This could be offset by selling a floor (a strip of interest rate puts) which will also establish a minimum cost of borrowing.

19.11   PRICING CAPS AND FLOORS

Interest rate options are often priced using a variant of the Black–Scholes model developed by Black in 1976 (see Chapter 16 for details of Black–Scholes). In the Black version of the model adapted for interest rate options the underlying is a **forward** interest rate and the volatility is the volatility of the forward interest rate.

The fair value of a European call is given by the equation:

$$C = [F \times N(d_1) - E \times N(d_2)] \times e^{-r_m t_m}$$

where:

F = forward interest rate
E = strike price
e = 2.71828, the base of natural logarithms
r_m = risk-free rate (continuously compounded) to the maturity of the caplet
t_m = time to maturity of the caplet (in years)
σ = annual volatility of the forward interest rate
$N(\ )$ = cumulative normal function

$$d_1 = \frac{\ln(F/E) + (\sigma^2 \times t_e/2)}{\sigma\sqrt{t_e}}$$

$$d_2 = d_1 - \sigma\sqrt{t_e}$$

t_e = time to expiry of the caplet (in years)

ln = natural logarithm of a number to base e

The value of the corresponding put option P is given by the equation:

$$P = [E \times N(-d_2) - F \times N(-d_1)] \times e^{-r_m t_m}$$

19.12 CAPLET VALUATION: EXAMPLE

To illustrate the application of the Black model we will take a cap written on six-month dollar LIBOR. The strike is 6.00% per annum and the nominal is $10 million. The first option or 'caplet' in the strip covers a six-month forward period of time (182 days) starting in six months (183 days). The forward rate for this period is 6.00% per annum. The expiry date of the first caplet is therefore in 183 days. The relevant dates for this caplet are illustrated in Figure 19.3.

The Black model assumes that the expected LIBOR rate for the forward period will have an average value of $F = 6.00\%$ and a standard deviation given by the volatility of that rate. The expected payout of the caplet (made in arrears, 182 days after the option expiry date) is F weighted by $N(d_1)$ minus E weighted by $N(d_2)$. This is then discounted back one year to establish the option premium. We use the following values to price the caplet:

Forward rate (F) = 6.00% p.a. (actual/360 basis)
Exercise price (E) = 6.00% p.a. (actual/360 basis)
1-year risk-free rate (r_m) = 5.43% p.a. (continuously compounded)
Time to caplet expiry (t_e) = 183 days = 0.5014 years
Volatility of F (σ) = 10% p.a.

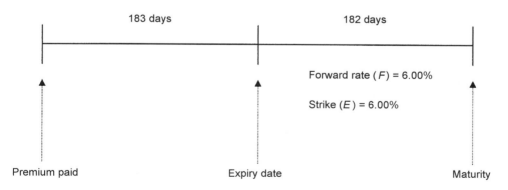

Figure 19.3 Caplet payment dates

With these inputs the Black model calculates the following values:

$d_1 = 0.0354$
$d_2 = -0.0354$
$N(d_1) = 0.5141$
$N(d_2) = 0.4859$

$$\text{Expected Payout at Caplet Maturity} = F \times N(d_1) - E \times N(d_2) = 0.1695\%$$

$$\text{Present Value} = 0.1695\% \times e^{-0.0543 \times 1} = 0.1605\% \text{ p.a. (actual/360 basis)}$$

This establishes a value C for the first caplet, which covers a six-month (182-day) period starting in six months. The rate is quoted on an actual/360 basis. In dollar terms on a notional of $10 million the caplet premium would cost:

$$\$10 \text{ million} \times 0.001605 \times 182/360 = \$8114$$

Valuing the whole cap is simply a matter of pricing the remaining interest rate caplets and summing the premiums.

19.13   VALUING FLOORS

Interest rate put options or 'floorlets' can be priced using the equation for P given above, or alternatively by put–call parity. This key result tells us that if C is the value of a European-style call then the value P of a European put with the same terms (strike, expiration-date and so on) is given by the following equation:

$$P = C - [(F - E) \times e^{-r_m t_m}]$$

This formula means that the value of the put equals the call value minus the present value of the difference between the forward rate and the strike price. If the strike E of the call and the put are both at the fair forward rate F then $PV(F-E) = 0$. So the call and put will have the same value. The value of a floor is simply the sum of the values of the constituent floorlets.

19.13.1   Issues with the Black Model

The Black model in its original form has some features that are open to criticism. It assumes that forward interest rates are variable with mean value F and standard deviation σ, whereas in practice short-term interest rates do not tend to move very far from their average values. This phenomenon is known as 'mean reversion'.

Traders either cope with this problem by adjusting the volatility assumption (often using different volatilities for each individual caplet in a cap) or by using more complex pricing models. The same sort of problem occurs when pricing bond options, particularly options on Treasury bonds, which do not deviate very significantly from their face value and in fact tend to 'pull' towards their face value with reducing volatility as they approach maturity.

19.14   SWAPTIONS

A swaption is an option on a swap. The buyer of a swaption has the right but not the obligation to enter into an interest rate swap with a given maturity and fixed rate of interest. The difference between a swaption and a cap or a floor is that the swaption can only be exercised once. A European cap or a floor is a strip of interest rate options each of which may or may not be exercised on its expiration date.

Swaption Types

In a **payer** swaption if the contract is exercised the buyer pays the fixed rate and receives in return the floating rate on an interest rate swap. In a **receiver** swaption if the contract is exercised the buyer pays floating and receives fixed on an interest rate swap.

A payer swaption might be purchased by a corporate or a bank which is concerned that interest rates will rise, but which does not want to lock into a rate of interest immediately by entering a standard interest rate swap contract. In that case it could not take advantage of any falls in interest rates until the swap matures. A receiver swaption might be purchased by an institutional investor or a bank which is concerned that investment rates will fall but which does not want to lock into a fixed return immediately by receiving fixed and paying floating on a swap. In each case the swaption provides flexibility. In return for the initial premium, the buyer has the right but not the obligation to enter into the underlying swap contract.

19.15   SWAPTION VALUATION

European swaptions can be valued using the Black model which we introduced earlier in this chapter. To illustrate this method we will consider the case of a European payer swaption with the following details:

Strike (E) = 6.00% p.a. (semi-annual, actual/actual)
Fair swap rate (F) = 6.00% p.a. (semi-annual, actual/actual)
Volatility of the swap rate = 15% p.a.
Expiry = 1 year
Notional principal = $100 million

The underlying swap starts in one year and has a tenor (maturity) of two years with semi-annual payments. The yield curve is flat at 6.00% per annum semi-annual. Figure 19.4 illustrates the relevant dates for the swaption and the underlying swap contract.

We want to price the swaption on its purchase date, with one year to expiration. Applying the Black model we have:

$$d_1 = \frac{\ln(F/E) + (\sigma^2 \times t_e/2)}{\sigma\sqrt{t_e}}$$

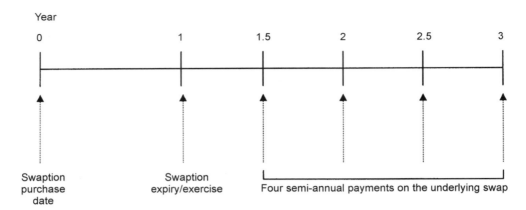

Figure 19.4   Swaption payment dates

$$d_2 = d_1 - \sigma\sqrt{t_e}$$

In our example:

$F = 0.06$ (semi-annual)
$E = 0.06$ (semi-annual)
$\sigma = 0.15$
$t_e = 1$ year
$d_1 = 0.0750$
$d_2 = -0.0750$
$N(d_1) = 0.5299$
$N(d_2) = 0.4701$
$F \times N(d_1) - E \times N(d_2) = 0.3587\%$ (the expected payout)

We apply the expected payout value 0.3587% to the notional principal $100 million (divided by two since the swap is semi-annual) on each of the four swap payment dates and present value the results:

Expected Payout $= 0.3587\%/2 \times \$100$ million $= \$179,350$

The expected payout is $179,350 on each of the four payment dates of the underlying swap. The full valuation of the swaption is set out in Table 19.6. The discount rate applied in each instance is 6.00% on a semi-annual basis. Note that the first payment due on the swap occurs in 1.5 years or three semi-annual periods from the purchase date of the swaption (0.5 years after its exercise date). The final payment is due three years or six semi-annual periods from the purchase date of the swaption. The premium value of the swaption on its purchase date is approximately $628,400 or about 0.6284% of the notional.

Table 19.6 Swaption expected payouts and valuation

Payment (years)	Expected payout	PV at 6.00%
1.5	$179,350	$164,131
2	$179,350	$159,350
2.5	$179,350	$154,709
3	$179,350	$150,203

Net Present Value = $628,393

19.16 INTEREST RATE STRATEGIES

To conclude this chapter, Table 19.7 sets out some possible strategies that a trader or hedger who expects interest rates to rise or fall might wish to consider. Of course these strategies do not all have the same risk/return characteristics. For example, buying a call or put option on an FRA is a strategy in which the maximum loss is limited to the initial premium paid. On the other hand the maximum profit to the seller of the option is the initial premium, whereas the maximum loss (unhedged) is much greater.

Table 19.7 Interest rate strategies

Market view	Possible strategy
Rising interest rates	• Short bonds or money market paper • Sell Treasury bill or bond futures • Buy forward rate agreements • Sell interest rate futures • Pay fixed, receive floating on a swap • Buy caplets (calls on FRAs) or caps • Buy exchange-traded interest rate puts • Sell floorlets (puts on FRAs) or floors • Sell exchange-traded interest rate calls • Buy payer swaptions • Sell receiver swaptions
Falling interest rates	• Buy bonds or money market paper • Buy Treasury bill or bond futures • Sell FRAs • Buy interest rate futures • Pay floating, receive fixed on a swap • Buy floorlets (puts on FRAs) or floors • Buy exchange-traded interest rate calls • Sell caplets (calls on FRAs) or caps • Sell exchange-traded interest rate puts • Buy receiver swaptions • Sell payer swaptions

19.17 CHAPTER SUMMARY

A currency or FX option is an option to exchange two currencies at a fixed exchange rate. The right to buy one currency is at the same time the right to sell the counter-currency. FX options are traded over-the-counter by dealers or on exchanges such as the Philadelphia Stock Exchange. Exchange-traded contracts carry the guarantee of the clearing house associated with the exchange. FX options can be used to hedge currency exposures. For example, a US company due to receive a fixed amount of pounds could buy a sterling put (dollar call) which is the right to exchange the pounds for dollars at a fixed rate. If the company can obtain a better rate in the spot market the option need not be exercised. Because the option provides flexibility the buyer of the contract has to pay premium to the seller. FX options are often priced by an adaptation of Black–Scholes called the Garman–Kohlhagen model. The key inputs are the spot exchange rate, the volatility of the exchange rate and the interest rates in the two currencies. An over-the-counter interest rate option is essentially an option to buy or sell a forward rate agreement. An exchange-traded interest rate option is an option to buy or sell an interest rate futures contract.

An interest rate cap is composed of a series or strip of individual interest rate options each of which may or may not be exercised. It can be used to establish a maximum borrowing cost, but at the expense of paying a premium. An interest rate floor is used to establish a minimum investment rate. A borrower who buys a cap and sells a floor has an interest rate collar. This establishes a maximum and a minimum cost of borrowing. If the strikes of the cap and floor are set appropriately the premium due from the floor will offset the premium payable on the cap and there is zero net premium to pay on the collar. A swaption is an option to enter into an underlying interest rate swap, either as the payer or the receiver of the fixed rate. It can be exercised only once. Interest rate options can be priced using the Black model. It is relatively simple to work with but tends to overstate the extent to which interest rates diverge from their average value. Traders cope with this by adjusting their volatility assumptions or by using more complex pricing models.

Glossary of Financial Terms

Accounts payable
Invoiced amounts owed by a business to its suppliers. In UK accounting known as creditors. Included amongst current liabilities in the company's balance sheet.

Accounts receivable
Invoiced amounts that are owed to a business. In UK accounting known as debtors. Included amongst current assets in the company's balance sheet.

Accreting swap
A swap in which the principal increases in each time period.

Accrued interest
Interest on a bond, loan, swap or other financial instrument that has accrued but has not yet been paid out.

Acquisition
The act of one company acquiring control of another. The takeover may be 'friendly' or 'hostile'. The buyer may offer cash for the shares of the target company or its own shares or a mixture of the two.

Actuary
A specialist in financial mathematics and statistics responsible for estimating the future claims on insurance companies and pension schemes. Nowadays firms of consulting actuaries are used by the trustees of pension funds to help evaluate the performance of asset managers and allocate investment management mandates.

Aftermarket
Dealings in a security after it has been launched in the primary market (the market for new issues).

Agency cross
When a broker acts as an agent for both the buyer and the seller in a share transaction.

Agent
Someone authorized to transact business on behalf of a client.

AGM
Annual general meeting.

Alpha
A share or portfolio with returns that exceed its required return adjusted for beta (i.e. its risk-adjusted return) is said to have positive alpha. In some investment management firms the fund managers who are responsible for picking shares they think likely to outperform the market (adjusted for risk) are known as 'alpha managers'. *See*: Beta; Capital asset pricing model.

American depository receipt (ADR)
A receipt issued by a US bank against shares in a foreign company held in custody for investors. A US investor wishing to invest in a foreign market may find it easier to buy ADRs than to buy the underlying shares directly. ADRs are priced in dollars and settlement procedures are the same as those for a US security. ADRs may trade over-the-counter or on an exchange.

American option
An option which can be exercised on or before expiry.

Amortization
The repayment of the principal on a loan in instalments over a period of time rather than all at the maturity of the loan. Alternatively, writing off an intangible asset such as goodwill from the balance sheet of a company through a series of charges to the profit and loss account.

Amortizing swap
A swap in which the principal is reduced in each time period.

Analyst
A specialist with expertise in a particular economy, market or class of securities who advises investors, traders and salespeople.

Arbitrage
Buying and selling in different marketplaces and making risk-free profits from the disparity between market prices. If an investor could buy a currency in one market and immediately sell it in another market at a better rate he or she would make an arbitrage profit. Sometimes used in a looser sense to include speculative deals such as buying shares in a new issue in the hope of selling the stock after the issue at a profit.

Asian or Asiatic option
Another name for an average price option.

Asset allocation
The process in portfolio management of deciding how to allocate money between broad classes of assets (shares, bonds, etc.) and different sectors and geographical locations (US, Asia Pacific, etc.).

Asset-backed commercial paper
Commercial paper secured on assets such as debtors (accounts receivable).

Asset-backed securities
Bonds backed by a pool of assets created or 'originated' by a bank or other financial institution, such as mortgages and credit card loans. The receipts from the loans are used to repay the bondholders.

Assets
A company's assets consist of tangible fixed assets such as plant and machinery, current assets such as stock and cash, and intangible assets such as goodwill. Financial assets held by investors include cash, shares and bonds.

Assignment
Formal notification from an exchange that the writer of a call (put) option must deliver (take delivery of) the underlying security at the exercise price. Alternatively, the process of transferring ownership of a contract such as a loan from one of the original parties to an acceptable replacement counterparty.

At-best order
An order to a broker to buy or sell a security or derivative contract at the best price available on the market.

At-the-money option
An option whose exercise price is equal to the current market price of the underlying. It has no intrinsic value.

Average price (or rate) option
In a fixed strike contract the payout is based on the difference between the strike and the average price of the underlying during the life of the option. In a floating strike contract the strike is based on the average price of the underlying during the life of the option and the payout is based on the difference between this value and the price of the underlying at expiry.

Back office
The part of a securities operation that settles the trades carried out by the dealers and brokers who work in the 'front office'.

Backwardation
When the forward or futures price of a commodity is less than the cash or spot price.

Balance sheet
The accounting statement that lists a company's assets and its liabilities and share capital. It is drawn up at a specific point in time, normally at the end of the company's financial year.

Balloon or balloon payment
A final payment instalment on a loan that is much greater than the previous payments.

Bancassurance
A business strategy in which a bank also provides products such as life assurance and pension plans.

Banker's Acceptance (BA)
A negotiable short-term debt security issued by a company typically to finance an international trade deal. Payment on the bill is guaranteed by a bank and the goods involved in the trade deal also serve as collateral. BAs trade at a discount to their face value.

Bank of England
The central bank for the UK. Since 1997 the Bank of England's Monetary Policy Committee has been responsible for setting UK interest rates independently of government. Its responsibilities for banking regulation have been transferred to the Financial Services Authority (FSA) and responsibility for issuing UK government Treasury bills and bonds has been transferred to the Debt Management Office (DMO), a separate agency of the UK government.

Bank for International Settlement (BIS)
The BIS is based in Basle and is often called the 'central banks' central bank' although most of its activities in this area have been taken over by the International Monetary Fund (IMF). The BIS acts to promote international cooperation in financial matters.

Barrier option
An option which either comes into existence or ceases to exist when the underlying asset reaches a threshold or barrier level. For example, an up-and-out put ceases to exist if the underlying rises to hit a knock-out or barrier level (also known as the out-strike) during the life of the option.

Basis
The relationship between the cash price of an asset and the forward or futures price. When the forward price is above the cash price the basis is negative. This represents the negative cost of carrying a position in the underlying to deliver on the future date. (The funding rate is higher than the income on the asset.) When the forward price is below the cash the basis is positive.

Basis point
In the money and bond markets one basis point equals 0.01%.

Basis risk
Specifically, the risk that arises because futures prices do not exactly track changes in the underlying asset, because of changes in the basis. More generally, used to mean the risk that results from potential changes in the relationship or 'basis' between two market factors. For example, a bank that funds itself via commercial paper and lends at a spread over LIBOR may be said to have a basis risk. The relationship between commercial paper rates and LIBOR is not a constant.

Basis swap

A swap in which both legs are based on floating interest rates but each is calculated on a different basis. For instance, one leg might be based on the rate on commercial paper and the other on LIBOR.

Basket option

An option whose payoff depends on the performance of a specific basket of assets. To price the option the dealer has to make an assumption about the correlation between the price movements of the constituent assets. Normally the assets will not be perfectly correlated and as a result of the offsetting movements in their prices the volatility of the basket will be less than the simple weighted average of the volatilities of the constituent assets in the basket.

BBA

British Bankers' Association. The BBA calculates LIBOR rates each business day for a range of currencies.

Bear

A bear is someone who thinks that a security, sector or market will fall in price. A bear market is one in which traders and investors are feeling negative and prices are falling or static.

Bear spread

A combination option strategy which pays a limited profit in the event that the underlying asset falls in value but which only suffers a limited loss if the underlying rises in value.

Bearer security

A security for which the owner of the physical certificate has full title. There is no register of ownership. Eurobonds are bearer securities.

Benchmark bond

A liquid government bond with a round maturity such as 10 years. Its price is actively followed in the market.

Bermudan option

An option that can be exercised on specific dates up to expiry, such as one day per week.

Beta

The percentage change in the price of a security for a 1% change in the market portfolio. Securities with betas higher than one are more volatile and hence more risky than the market, and their required returns are higher. Beta can be measured statistically based on historical price changes relative to a benchmark index.

Bid

The price a dealer is prepared to pay to buy a security. In the money markets, the interest rate a dealer will pay to borrow funds.

Bid/offer spread
The difference between the price a dealer will pay for buying and selling a security. In the money markets, the difference between the interest rate a dealer pays for borrowing and lending funds.

Big bang
The deregulation of the UK stock exchange in 1986.

Big figure
In the FX markets, the first decimal places of a currency rate quotation.

Binomial tree
A set of prices developed from the current price of the underlying asset such that at any 'node' in the tree the asset can either move up or down in price by a set amount and with a set probability. Used to price standard and exotic options and instruments such as convertible bonds.

Black model
A variant on the Black–Scholes model, used to price options on forwards and futures.

Black–Scholes
The European option pricing model developed by Fischer Black, Myron Scholes and Robert Merton in the 1970s. Refinements of the model still form the basis of many option trading systems used today.

Block trade
The sale or purchase of a large number of shares.

Blue chip
A top-name company whose shares may be considered to provide a consistent return.

Bond
A debt security issued by a company (corporate), a sovereign state and its agencies, or by a supranational body such as the World Bank. A straight or plain vanilla bond pays fixed amounts of interest—known as coupons—on regular dates. The principal or par value of the bond is repaid when the bond matures. Non-straight bonds have different features—for example, there may be no maturity date, or a variable coupon.

Bond option
An option on a bond.

Bond ratings
Ratings of the credit risk on bonds issued by agencies such as Moody's and Standard and Poor's. The highest S&P bond rating is AAA, called 'triple-A'. This means it is extremely unlikely that the issuer will default on its obligations. *See also*: Credit risk.

Book value
The net value of a fixed asset after depreciation. Alternatively, used to mean equity book value, i.e. the total assets of a company less its total liabilities.

Bookbuilding
The process used by the managers of a new issue to assess demand for the securities, set the issue price and sign up investors.

Bootstrapping
Deriving zero coupon or spot rates from the prices of liquid coupon bonds or from the par swap curve.

Bottom fishing
Buying shares when the price has fallen to low levels expecting the price to rise again.

Bottom-up
A style of portfolio management which is based on building a portfolio from the 'bottom up' based on individual stock selections. *See*: Top-down.

Boutique
A financial services firm that concentrates on a limited range of specialized activities.

Brady bonds
Bonds issued in the 1990s as part of a scheme to reschedule the debt of Latin American countries. The bonds were issued in US dollars and US Treasuries were used as collateral to guarantee some or all of the payments on the bonds. They are named after Nicholas Brady, the former US Treasury Secretary.

Break
A rapid and sharp decline in the price of a security or commodity.

Broken date
In the money markets, a non-standard term for a deal (e.g. 50 days).

Broker
A person or firm paid a fee or commission to act as an agent in arranging purchases or sales of securities or arranging contracts.

BTP
Treasury bond issued by the Italian government.

Buba
Bundesbank, the Federal German central bank.

Bulge bracket firm
An investment bank that is one of the small group of top firms with global capability. Who is and who is not a member is much disputed. At the time of writing (2001) most

observers would agree on three names: Merrill Lynch, Morgan Stanley, Goldman Sachs. The expression comes from the heavy type on 'tombstone' advertisements used for the lead managers of issues.

Bull
Someone who thinks that a particular security or the whole market will increase in price. A bull market is one in which traders and investors are feeling positive and prices are rising.

Bull spread
A combination option strategy which pays a limited profit in the event that the underlying asset rises in value but which only suffers a limited loss if the underlying falls in value.

Bund
Treasury bond issued by the Federal German government.

Buy side
An analyst or fund manager working for an investment management firm is said to operate on the buy side. An analyst or security salesperson working for a securities house and providing investment ideas to fund managers is said to operate on the sell side.

Cable
The sterling–dollar exchange rate. So-called because deals used to be transacted through a trans-Atlantic cable.

CAC 40
An index of the top 40 French shares. Also used as a basis for index futures contracts.

Calendar or time spread
A combination option strategy that involves buying and selling options with different expiry dates to exploit differences in the rate of time decay or changes in volatility.

Call feature
A feature of many bonds that gives the issuer (the borrower) the right to redeem the bonds before maturity. The call price may be at par or slightly above par, depending on the terms of the bond.

Call money
A deposit or loan that is repayable on demand.

Call option
The right but not the obligation to buy the underlying asset at a fixed strike price.

Capital
Wealth used to create further wealth. Capital is provided by governments, corporates and households (in the last case often through investment vehicles such as pension

funds) and used by governments, corporates and supranational agencies such as the World Bank. Banks intermediate between suppliers and users of capital. The same word is also used to mean the different sources of funds available to a business, such as shares (equity capital) and loans (debt capital).

Capital adequacy
A system under which banks are obliged to maintain a required ratio of capital in proportion to assets such as loans. Assets are weighted according to their risk. Capital includes ordinary shares and preference shares (sometimes extended to subordinated debt and loan loss reserves). The system is designed to help prevent banks from over-extending themselves.

Capital asset pricing model (CAPM)
A model used to establish the required return on a security or a portfolio of securities given the level of risk. The required return on a security according to CAPM is the risk-free rate (the return on Treasuries) plus the market risk premium (the additional return on a diversified market portfolio of securities over and above the risk-free rate) adjusted by the beta factor for the security. *See*: Beta; Equity risk premium.

Caplet
One component of an interest rate cap.

Capped floating rate note
A floating rate note in which the rate of interest cannot exceed a given level.

Cash-and-carry arbitrage
Arbitraging between the cash and the futures market.

Cash security
Used to mean the underlying asset rather than a derivative of that asset. An IBM share is a cash security whereas an option on an IBM share is a derivative. A cash market is one in which the underlying assets are traded rather than derivatives.

Cash settlement
Settling a contract in cash rather than through the physical delivery of an asset or commodity. For instance, if an option contract is exercised and cash-settled then the seller simply pays the buyer the intrinsic value of the contract. The underlying asset is not exchanged.

Certificate of deposit (CD)
A negotiable money market instrument issued by commercial banks. A CD promises to pay the principal plus a fixed rate of interest at maturity, normally one year or less from issue. Longer-dated CDs may pay interest in a number of instalments.

Chicago Board of Trade (CBOT)
Started as a commodity market in the nineteenth century and has now developed major financial futures contracts such as contracts on US Treasury bonds.

Chicago Board Options Exchange (CBOE)
The major options exchange founded in 1973.

Chicago Mercantile Exchange (CME)
The other Chicago futures and options exchange. Also known as the 'Merc'. Its financial futures and options division is known as the International Monetary Market (IMM).

Chooser option
The buyer can decide at a preset time whether it is a call option or a put option. Also known as U-choose, as-you-like, call-or-put options.

Circuit breaker
In response to the 1987 crash the NYSE instituted measures called circuit breakers to reduce market volatility and increase investor confidence. Trading stops when the market moves through a trigger level.

Clean price
The price of a bond excluding interest that has accrued since the last coupon date.

Clearing house
The organization that registers, matches, monitors and guarantees trades made on a futures and options exchange. In London the London Clearing House (LCH) clears trades on all the derivatives exchanges. It is owned by the clearing members who are major financial institutions. More generally, an organization that settles payments between banks and other financial institutions.

Clearing member
Not all members of a futures and options exchange are clearing members. All trades must eventually be settled through a clearing member which deals directly with the clearing house.

Clearstream (formerly called Cedel)
With Euroclear, one of the two settlement systems for Eurobond trades. Based in Luxembourg.

Cliquet (ratchet) option
An option in which the strike is reset at specific dates according to the spot price of the underlying on that date, locking in any interim gains.

Closed-ended fund
An investment company with a limited amount of share capital. In the UK known as an investment trust.

Collared floating rate note
A floating rate note with a minimum and a maximum coupon rate.

Collateral
Cash or securities pledged against the performance of some obligation. A trader wishing to buy or sell futures contracts on an exchange has to put up collateral known as initial margin. If the trader loses money on the trade but is unable to pay, the clearing house has the right to discharge the trader's obligations from the collateral.

Collateralized debt obligation (CDO)
Debt securities based on the cash flows from a portfolio of bonds or loans. CDOs differ from simple pass-through securities in that different classes or tranches of securities are issued which have different payment characteristics. If the underlying collateral consists of bonds the securities may be known as collateralized bond obligations (CBOs). The portfolio may be actively managed by a fund manager or it may be a 'static pool' of assets.

Collateralized mortgage obligation (CMO)
Debt securities based on the cash flows from a pool of mortgage loans. The securities are sold in tranches with different risk/return characteristics. The securitization process that creates CMOs converts illiquid mortgage loans into liquid market assets. *See*: Mortgage-backed securities.

Commercial bank
A bank that makes loans, e.g. to corporations and governments. The loans may be funded through the money markets rather than through a retail banking business.

Commercial paper (CP)
Short-term unsecured debt securities issued by companies and banks. USCP is commercial paper issued in the US domestic market by both US and foreign companies, at a discount to face value. Euro-CP is issued in the Euromarkets and trades on a yield basis.

Commission
The fee charged by a broker to a customer for completing a purchase or sale.

Commodity
A physical item such as oil, gold or grain. Commodities are traded for spot and also for future delivery. There also exist options to buy and sell commodities.

Common stock
US expression for an ordinary share.

Compound option
An option on an option. For example, a call on a put is the right but not the obligation to buy a put option at a fixed premium.

Contagion risk
The risk that problems in a bank or a region may spread to other parts of the local or international financial system.

Contango
When the forward or futures price of a commodity is higher than the spot price. *See*: Backwardation.

Contract size
A unit of trading on a futures and options exchange. For example, the 30-year Treasury bond futures contract traded on the CBOT is for $100,000 par value of US Treasury bonds.

Conversion (price) factor
A factor used when bonds are delivered against bond futures which adjusts the invoiced amount according to the coupon and maturity date of the bond that is actually delivered.

Conversion premium
A measure used in the convertible bond market. It measures how much more expensive it is to buy shares by buying and immediately converting a convertible bond compared to buying the shares in the cash market.

Conversion ratio
The number of shares a convertible bond can be converted into.

Convertible bond
A bond that is convertible (at the option of the holder) into a fixed number of (normally) ordinary shares of the issuing company.

Convexity
A measure of the curvature in the relationship between the price of a bond and market interest rates. Used to adjust the change in a bond price predicted by duration, which assumes a linear relationship between price and yield. *See*: Duration.

Cost of capital
The rate of return that a business has to pay to providers of capital. The rate will depend on the riskiness of the business.

Cost of carry
The difference between the cost of financing a position in a security and the income received on the security. A trader borrowing money to buy a security will earn positive carry if the income from the security (interest or dividends) exceeds the funding cost. Otherwise the carry is negative.

Counterparty
The other party to a trade or contract.

Counterparty risk
The risk that a trading counterparty might fail to fulfil its obligations, e.g. fail to deliver securities on the agreed trade settlement date.

Coupon
The interest amount payable on a bond.

Coupon rate
The rate of interest on a bond. Annual coupon bonds pay it in one annual instalment, semi-annual bonds in two.

Covenants
Legal restrictions placed on a borrower to protect the interests of lenders.

Covered warrants
Warrants on shares and baskets of shares in other companies issued by banks and securities houses. *See*: Warrant.

Credit default swap
A contract in which a protection buyer pays a periodic or upfront fee to a protection seller. If there is a default on the referenced security or loan specified in the contract the buyer of protection either receives a cash compensation payment from the protection seller, or can deliver the security or loan to the protection seller (normally) at par. Where physical delivery is provided for the protection buyer often has the right to substitute an asset that is similar to the referenced security or loan stipulated in the contract. According to the BBA the notional outstanding on credit swaps is projected to reach $1.5 trillion by the end of 2002.

Credit derivative
A derivative whose payoff depends on specified credit events. These can include bankruptcy, liquidation, financial restructuring, the default on a loan or bond, or a credit rating downgrade. *See*: Credit default swap.

Credit enhancement
Methods used to enhance credit quality. In a securitization a third party such as an insurance company may guarantee payment in order to improve the credit rating of the bonds issued against the collateral. *See*: Securitization.

Credit rating
An assessment of the probability that a borrower or issuer of securities will make timely payments on its financial obligations.

Credit risk
The risk of default or non-payment on a loan, bond or contractual agreement such as a swap.

Credit spread
The additional return on a bond or loan over some benchmark rate, that is dependent on the creditworthiness of the borrower. Often it is expressed as a number of basis points over LIBOR, or the yield on a government bond. Sometimes the term is used to mean a bond that carries credit risk as opposed to a risk-free government bond.

Creditors
See: Accounts payable.

Cross-currency swap
An interest rate swap in which the payment legs are made in two different currencies. The principals are normally exchanged at the outset and re-exchanged at maturity.

Cum-dividend (cd)
The buyer of a cd security is entitled to the next dividend payment.

Cum-warrant
A bond with a warrant still attached. *See*: Warrant.

Currency option
The right but not the obligation to exchange one currency for another at a fixed exchange rate — the strike or exercise rate. Also known as an FX option.

Currency overlay
A strategy used in investment management to divorce decisions made on buying foreign assets from decisions on currency exposures. The manager can hedge the currency risk or take additional currency exposure.

Currency risk
The risk of losses resulting from movements in currency exchange rates.

Currency translation risk
The risk that results from translating foreign currency earnings back into the home currency when the consolidated accounts of companies with international operations are prepared.

Current assets
Short-term assets in a company's balance sheet including cash, debtors and stock or raw materials.

Current liabilities
Short-term liabilities in a company's balance sheet including creditors and short-term bank loans.

Current ratio
A company's current assets as a ratio of its current liabilities. A measure of how easily a company can meet its most pressing short-term obligations from short-term assets such as cash, debtors and stock that can be turned into cash.

Current yield
The coupon on a fixed rate bond divided by the clean price. Also known as running, flat or interest yield.

Custodian
A bank or institution that holds securities for safekeeping and handles administrative arrangements such as collecting coupons and dividends.

DAX
An index of 30 top German shares traded on the Frankfurt exchange. It is a total return index—dividends on the shares are assumed to be reinvested. Most equity indices such as the FT-SE 100 index do not take into account income from dividend reinvestment in their calculation.

Day count
The calendar convention applied to a quoted interest rate or yield.

Dealing spread
The difference between a trader's bid and offer price.

Debentures
In the US, bonds that are not secured by specific assets but are a general claim on the assets of the issuer. In the UK, bonds that are secured by specific assets such as property (mortgage debentures) or by a general claim on assets.

Debt
Money owed to creditors, lenders or buyers of debt securities.

Debt security
A tradable security such as a bond, Treasury bill or commercial paper that represents a loan made to the issuer.

Debtors
See: Accounts receivable.

Delivery
The process of delivering assets. In derivatives markets some futures and options contracts involve the physical delivery of the underlying security or commodity. For example, a buyer of bond futures receives physical bonds if he or she has not sold the contracts before the delivery month. *See also*: Settlement of differences.

Delivery month
The month when a futures contract expires and delivery or final cash settlement takes place. The most common months are March, June, September and December.

Delta
The change in the value of an option for a small change in the value of the underlying asset. Option traders use delta to hedge their books—it tells them how much of the underlying they need to buy or sell to protect against (small) changes in the price of the underlying.

Delta-neutral
An option position which is delta-hedged and therefore protected against small changes in the price of the underlying asset.

Depository receipt
A title to shares in a foreign company held by a bank and issued in local currency. Dividends are normally paid in local currency. *See also*: American depository receipt.

Depreciation
The process of writing off the purchase price of a physical asset through a series of charges to the profit and loss account.

Derivative
An instrument whose market price depends on the value of an underlying security such as a share or bond. A derivatives market is a market in which derivative securities are traded.

Digital option
Also known as a binary option. The payoff from the option is a fixed sum.

Dilution
The reduction in earnings per share caused by the creation of new shares in a company.

Dirty price
The total present value of a bond. Clean price plus accrued interest.

Discount factor
The present value of $1 at the spot or zero coupon rate for a specific time period, used to discount cash flows due at that period.

Discount rate
Generally, the rate used to discount future cash flows to a present value. Also, in the US money markets, the rate charged to banks when they borrow from the Federal Reserve acting as lender of last resort.

Discount security
A security such as a Treasury bill that pays no interest but trades below its face or nominal value.

Disintermediation
The process of cutting out an intermediary. Disintermediation occurs for example when companies issue bonds to raise capital directly from the market rather than borrowing the money from a commercial bank.

Diversification
Buying a portfolio of assets to reduce risk and take advantage of a range of investment opportunities.

Dividend
The payment per share a company makes to its shareholders. On ordinary shares it varies with the profitability of the firm. On preferred shares it is normally fixed.

Dividend cover
Earnings per share divided by dividend per share. It measures the extent to which the dividend payment is 'covered' by earnings. *See*: Dividend payout ratio.

Dividend discount model
A model used to value a share by discounting expected future dividend payments.

Dividend payout ratio
Dividend per share divided by earnings per share. The proportion of a company's earnings paid out in dividends. The reciprocal of dividend cover.

Domestic corporate bond
A bond issued by a company in its home market and in its home currency. Normally subject to regulation by government authorities.

Dow Jones Industrial Average (DJIA)
US index based on 30 leading industrial shares traded on the New York Stock Exchange. It is a simple average of the share prices (not weighted by market capitalization) it is but adjusted for stock splits.

Downside risk
The risk of making a loss on a trading position or an investment.

Dual currency bond
A bond that pays interest in one currency but which is denominated in another currency.

Duration
A measure of the value-weighted average life of a bond and of its sensitivity to changes in interest rates. *See*: Macaulay's duration; Modified or adjusted duration.

Duration matching
Matching the duration of assets with those of liabilities.

Earnings
The part of a company's profits that is available for distribution to its ordinary shareholders. Often a company will pay out a proportion of earnings in the form of cash dividends but retain the rest for reinvestment.

Earnings per share (EPS)
A company's earnings for a given financial year divided by the number of shares.

Earnings yield
The reciprocal of the price/earnings ratio.

EBITDA
Earnings before interest, tax, depreciation and amortization.

Economic value added (EVA)
A measure of whether or not a company achieves returns on invested capital above its cost of capital.

Efficient market theory
The theory that share prices reflect currently available information and fully discount expected future cash flows.

Eligible bill or paper
A bill that can be used as collateral by a bank to raise funds from the central bank.

Embedded option
An option that is embedded in a security or a structured financial product. For example, there is an embedded call option in a convertible bond.

Emerging markets
Developing countries with fledgling capital markets. Banks make loans to emerging market nations and also assist them in issuing bonds and other debt securities.

Equity
Ordinary shares or common stock. An equity holder is a part-owner of the business, receives dividend payments if the company makes a profit, and/or participates in the growth in value of the company. In accounting terms equity equals balance sheet assets less liabilities.

Equity collar
A strategy that involves buying out-of-the-money put options and selling out-of-the-money calls to protect against losses on the underlying asset whilst at the same time reducing (or eliminating) the net premium due. The disadvantage is that profits on the underlying are capped.

Equity risk premium
The additional return required by investors to hold a diversified portfolio of shares above the risk-free rate (the return on Treasuries). *See*: Capital asset pricing model.

Equity swap
An agreement between two parties to make regular exchanges of payments where one payment leg is based on the value of a share or a basket of shares. The other payment leg is usually based on a fixed or floating interest rate.

ESOP
Employee share option plan.

Eurex
The merged German–Swiss derivatives exchange. Contracts are traded electronically rather than on a physical trading floor.

Euribor
Reference rate set in Brussels for interbank lending in euros, the new European common currency. Its rival is euro LIBOR, set in London by the British Banking Association.

Eurobond
A bond denominated in a currency other than the currency of the country in which it is issued, and marketed to international investors normally via a syndicate of under-writing banks.

Euroclear
The Brussels-based institution that acts as a central clearing house for trades in Eurobonds. *See also*: Clearstream.

Euro-commercial paper (ECP)
Commercial paper issued in the Euromarkets. Short-term unsecured bearer notes issued by major corporations. Most issues are zero coupon with maturities ranging from one week up to one year and with a high credit rating.

Eurocurrency
A currency held on account outside the domestic market and outside the control of its regulatory authorities.

Eurocurrency deposit
Eurocurrency placed on deposit with a bank. The largest market is for Eurodollar deposits.

Eurodollar
A dollar held on deposit outside the US or in an international account in the US market.

Eurodollar futures
A futures contract traded on the Chicago Mercantile Exchange based on the interest rate on a notional three-month Eurodollar deposit for a future time period. The price of the contract is taken as an indication of the market's consensus expectations on future interest rates.

Euromarket
The international market for dealings in Eurocurrencies.

European Investment Bank (EIB)
The body formed by member states of the European Union to provide capital for regional development projects.

European option
An option that can only be exercised at expiry.

Ex-dividend (xd)
The buyer of a security trading xd is not entitled to the next dividend. It goes to the seller.

Ex-rights (xr)
The buyer of a share trading xr is not entitled to any rights to subscribe to new shares. *See also*: Rights issue.

Exchange
A market in which securities are traded. Some exchanges use open outcry trading methods. In others dealers are connected by telephones and/or computer screens.

Exchange delivery settlement price (EDSP)
The price used to settle a futures contract on the delivery day.

Exchange-traded contract
A derivative contract traded on an exchange rather than over-the-counter.

Exchangeable bond
A bond that is exchangeable (at the option of the holder) for a fixed number of shares of a company other than the issuer of the bond.

Exercise
The action taken by the holder of a call (put) option when he or she takes up the option to buy (sell) the underlying.

Exercise or strike price
The price at which the holder of a call (put) option takes up his or her right to buy (sell) the underlying asset.

Exotic option
An option that is not a standard call or put, e.g. a barrier, average price or binary option.

Expiry or expiration date
The last day of a contract.

Face value
The principal or par value of a debt security such as a bond or a Treasury bill. Normally the face value is repaid at maturity.

Fair value
The theoretical value of a financial asset, often established using a pricing model.

Fannie Mae (FNMA)
Federal National Mortgage Association. A private corporation sponsored by the US government set up to facilitate home lending in the US. It raises funds through the bond markets and buys mortgages from banks and other financial institutions.

Federal funds (Fed funds)
US banks are required to place funds with the Federal Reserve, the central bank. The Fed funds market is a method of trading any excess funds for overnight use via the Fedwire system to other banks that are short of funds. The Federal Reserve sets a target rate for the Fed funds rate to implement its monetary policy.

Federal Open Market Committee (FOMC)
The committee of the US Federal Reserve that sets interest rates and issues instructions on open market operations. The open market operations are conducted by the Federal Reserve Bank of New York which influences the Fed funds rate and hence the general level of interest rates by buying and selling securities and conducting repo operations.

Federal Reserve
The US central bank. Actually a system consisting of 12 regional Federal Reserve Banks, the Federal Reserve Board and the Federal Open Market Committee.

Fedwire
An interbank payments system in the US.

Fill-or-kill (FOK)
A type of order on an exchange which is either executed at the stipulated price or cancelled.

Financial future
An exchange-traded contract in which a commitment is made to deliver or take delivery of a financial asset on a future date or between a range of dates at a fixed price. In some contracts no physical delivery actually takes place and the contracts are settled in cash.

Financial institution or intermediary
A generic name for banks, investment management institutions, securities houses, brokers, insurance companies, etc.

Financial Services Authority (FSA)
The combined regulatory body in the UK that regulates the banking system, the securities industry, investment management, personal financial services and insurance.

Fixed interest or income security
Literally, a security which pays a fixed income on a regular basis until maturity. Often though it is used as a generic term for bonds.

Fixed price offer
In a UK new share issue, when the new shares are offered to the public at a fixed price rather than in a tender (auction).

Fixed re-offer price
An expression used in bond issues. The syndicate of underwriters re-offers the bonds at the same price to the market until the securities are all sold, when the syndicate breaks.

Flat price
Clean price.

Flex options
Exchange-traded options that have some flexibility as to their terms, e.g. the strike price can be non-standard.

Floating rate
A rate of interest such as LIBOR that varies over time.

Floating rate certificate of deposit
A CD with a coupon that resets periodically according to a benchmark rate such as LIBOR.

Floating rate note (FRN)
A bond whose coupon is linked to current market interest rates. The coupon resets e.g. every three months according to a benchmark rate such as LIBOR.

Floor broker
On a US exchange, someone who buys and sells securities on the floor of an exchange on behalf of clients.

Foreign bond
A bond issued by a foreign borrower in another country's domestic market.

Foreign exchange risk
The risk of losses resulting from changes in foreign exchange rates.

Forex
Foreign exchange.

Forward contract
An agreement to buy or sell a security, commodity or currency at an agreed price for delivery at some date in the future. A forward contract is a legally binding agreement made directly between two parties and is not traded on an exchange.

Forward exchange rate
The rate to exchange two currencies on a date later than spot.

Forward interest rate (forward–forward rate)
The rate of interest that applies between two dates in the future. Also known as a forward–forward rate. The forward yield curve is constructed using such rates.

Forward rate agreement (FRA)
A contract between two parties to make compensation payments based on the difference between a contractual interest rate for a forward time period and the actual market rate for that period.

Forward start option
An option that starts on a future date.

Forward start swap
A swap that starts on a date later than spot.

Freddie Mac (FHLMC)
Federal Home Loan Mortgage Corporation. US body set up to facilitate mortgage lending. It issues bonds backed by pools of mortgage loans.

Front running
When a trader creates a position on the trading book in anticipation of a large deal which may move the market.

FT-SE 100 Index
An index of the top 100 UK shares weighted by market capitalization.

Fundamental analysis
An analysis of the fair value of a share based on an assessment of the prospects of the company, its balance sheet, forecast earnings growth, etc. The work of an investment analyst in a bank, broking operation or fund management business.

Funded pension scheme
A pension scheme in which the regular payments are used to buy assets such as shares and bonds.

Fungible
Two securities or contracts are said to be fungible when they can be considered as identical and directly interchangeable.

Futures contract
An agreement transacted through an organized exchange to buy or sell a security or commodity at an agreed price for delivery at some date in the future. Futures contracts can be freely traded on the exchange. Some contracts such as index futures are cash-settled and no actual physical delivery takes place.

Futures option
An option to buy or sell a futures contract.

Gamma
The change in an option's delta for a small change in the price of the underlying security. Gamma measures how quickly delta changes and therefore how unstable a trader's delta hedge is likely to be. *See*: Delta.

Gearing (UK) or leverage (US)
The proportion of debt to equity in a company's capital structure. In a trading or investment situation gearing or leverage refers to making higher returns through a strategy that requires a relatively small outlay of capital. For example, an at-the-money call option will cost a fraction of the underlying share price, and the potential returns are very high if the share price rises sharply.

Gilt or gilt-edged security
A bond issued by the UK government.

Glass–Steagall Act 1933
US law (now repealed) preventing commercial banks from underwriting new issues or dealing in securities.

Global bond
A bond issued simultaneously in major markets around the world.

Goodwill
The price paid for a business over and above the value of its physical assets. This is commonly amortized over a period of time. *See*: Amortization.

Government securities
Bills, notes and bonds issued by governments.

Greeks
The market's name for the option sensitivity measures: delta, gamma, theta, vega and rho.

Greenshoe
A over-allocation option granted to the manager of an issue of new securities. In an initial public offering (IPO) the manager often seeks to sell more shares than the announced size of the issue. If the offer is oversubscribed and the share price holds up in the aftermarket the manager has the right under the greenshoe option to receive additional shares from the issuer. If the share price falls the manager can buy shares back in the aftermarket to satisfy the oversubscription.

Grey market
Trading in securities before they are issued.

Growth investment
A style of equity investment that favours growth shares.

Growth share or stock

Shares in a company whose earnings are expected to grow rapidly. The shares often trade on a high price/earnings ratio.

Haircut

When securities are pledged as collateral against a loan the lender will normally apply a 'haircut' and lend less than their current market value. This is to protect against falls in the value of the collateral.

Hard currency

Currency of one of the major developed countries.

Hedge fund

Originally a name for a 'long–short' fund which takes both long and short positions in securities. In this sense the fund may be relatively low risk since much of the risk is hedged out. It is also sometimes used though to mean funds that take highly leveraged or speculative positions, e.g. on currencies, interest rates, equity markets or market volatility.

Hedge ratio

The calculation of how much of the hedge instrument has to be traded to cover the risk on the asset to be hedged. For example, the number of futures contracts that have to be bought or sold to hedge an exposure on a share or a bond.

Hedging

Protecting against potential losses. For example, a borrower can buy a forward rate agreement as a hedge and will receive compensation payments if interest rates rise.

Herstatt risk

The risk in an FX transaction that payment is made to a counterparty which then fails to make the return payment in the other currency. Named after a German bank that failed in the 1970s.

High-yield bonds

Bonds with a credit rating lower than the Standard and Poor's BBB− rating but which pay a higher yield. They are sometimes called speculative or 'junk bonds'.

Historic volatility

The standard deviation of the historical returns on a security measured over a period of time, such as three months.

Holding period return

The annualized return on an investment that is held over some specified time horizon.

Hypothekenbank

A German mortgage bank.

Implied repo rate
The repo or funding rate implied in an actual bond forward or futures price.

Implied volatility
The volatility assumption implied in an actual option price.

In-the-money option
An option that has positive intrinsic value. In the case of a call, when the strike is below the current price of the underlying. In the case of a put, when the strike is above the current price of the underlying.

Index
A figure representing the changing value of a basket of securities, such as a stockmarket index. The index is set at some arbitrary value such as 100 or 1000 on the base date. Indices such as the FT-SE 100 are weighted by the market capitalization of the constituent companies. This means that a given percentage change in the share price of a large company will have a bigger impact than the same change in the price of a smaller company. Others such as the Dow Jones Industrial Average are not value weighted.

Index arbitrage
Arbitrage trade assembled by simultaneously buying and selling shares and index futures.

Index fund or index tracker
A fund that seeks to track or match the performance of a market index.

Index futures
A financial futures contract based on a market index. The contracts are cash-settled.

Index option
An option on a market index such as the S&P 500.

Initial margin
A trader on a futures and options exchange has to deposit initial margin as a performance deposit. This can be cash or (by agreement with the broker) some other acceptable collateral such as Treasury bills.

Initial public offering (IPO)
An offer to the public to buy shares in a company for the first time. Originally a US expression but it has become universal.

Insider trading
Trading on price-sensitive information not yet in the public domain. It is illegal in the US and Europe and in most countries now.

Instinet
An electronic broking business owned by Reuters.

Institutional investor
A firm such as a pension fund investing money on behalf of other people.

Instrument
A share, bond or some other negotiable security.

Intangible asset
A non-physical asset on a company's balance sheet, such as goodwill.

Interbank market
Dealings in the capital markets between banks. The bulk of foreign exchange deals, for example, are interbank.

Interest cover
A measure of a company's ability to meet its interest bill. Usually measured as profit before interest and tax for a given year divided by gross interest payable.

Interest rate cap, floor, collar
A cap is an option product typically sold to borrowers, which places a limit or 'cap' on their cost of borrowing. If the interest rate for a given time period covered by the cap is above the strike then the cap buyer will receive a compensation payment from the seller. A floor establishes a minimum interest rate level and may be sold to investors. A collar establishes both a minimum and a maximum interest rate.

Interest rate future
An exchange-traded contract based on the interest rate for a period of time starting in the future. The listed equivalent of the forward rate agreement. *See*: Eurodollar futures.

Interest rate margin
The difference between a bank's funding rate and its lending rate.

Interest rate option
An option based on an interest rate.

Interest rate swap
An agreement between two parties to exchange regular cash flows on regular dates for a specified time period. One payment is based on a fixed interest rate and the return payment is based on a floating rate, usually LIBOR. The rates are applied to the notional principal to calculate the payments, which are normally netted out.

Interest yield
See: Current yield.

Interim dividend
A dividend paid part of the way through a company's financial year.

Internal rate of return
The annualized return on a set of cash flows assuming that interim cash flows are reinvested or borrowed at a constant rate. Used to calculate the yield to maturity of a bond.

International Securities Market Association (ISDA)
A trade association for dealers in Eurobonds and other international securities, headquartered in Zurich.

International Swaps and Derivatives Association (ISDA)
A trade association for dealers in over-the-counter derivatives such as swaps, caps, floors, collars and swaptions. The ISDA Master Agreement is widely used as the legal basis for swaps.

Intrinsic value
The value that could be released from an option by immediate exercise. In the case of an American call it is the maximum of zero or the spot price of the underlying minus the strike. In the case of an American put it is the maximum of zero or the strike less the spot price of the underlying. Intrinsic value is either zero or positive.

Investment bank
Originally, a bank that underwrites and deals in securities such as bonds and shares. Now mainly used to mean a bank that operates in the capital markets, issuing and trading securities and derivatives, and which also advises on mergers, acquisitions and privatizations.

Investment grade bonds
Bonds that are rated BBB− and above by Standard and Poor's. Some investing institutions are only allowed to buy investment grade paper.

Investment manager
An individual or institution managing funds on behalf of clients. Also known as a fund, asset or portfolio manager.

Investment trust
The UK name for a closed-ended investment fund structured as a limited company whose shares are listed and traded on an exchange.

Issue price
The price at which a new security is issued including fees paid to underwriters and selling agents.

Issuer warrants
Warrants (long-dated options) issued by a company on its own shares, which trade in the form of securities. *See*: Warrant.

Jobber
The old name for a trader or market maker on the London Stock Exchange.

Junk bond
Below investment grade bond trading at a high yield.

Knock-out or knock-in level
The level of the underlying at which a barrier option ceases to exist or comes into existence. Sometimes known as the out-strike and the in-strike. *See*: Barrier option.

Ladder option
An option which locks in intervening profits during its life. Whenever the underlying hits a 'rung' or threshold price level the gains to that point cannot then be lost.

Lead manager
The bank or group of banks which takes the lead in arranging a syndicated loan or an issue of new securities and which takes the largest share of the fees. Also known as the bookrunner.

Leasing
Where a bank or other financial institution buys equipment and leases it to the end-user for a period of time. Often there is a tax advantage to a leasing deal.

Lender of last resort
Traditionally the role of the central bank. If it fears systemic risk it may stand ready to lend to an ailing financial institution when no one else will.

Leveraged buy-out (LBO)
When a company or subsidiary is bought funded mainly by debt.

Liabilities
Money owed by a company to its creditors, bondholders and other providers of debt such as banks. A company's assets less its total liabilities — its total net assets — belongs to its shareholders.

LIBID
London Interbank Bid Rate. The rate top banks pay for taking in Eurocurrency deposits in the London market.

LIBOR
London Interbank Offered Rate. The rate at which top-name banks lend money to each other for a specified term (e.g. three months) in the London market. LIBOR is a key market reference rate. It is set at 11 a.m. London time every business day by the British Banking Association. Key rates include US dollar LIBOR and euro LIBOR.

LIFFE
The London International Financial Futures Exchange.

Limit order
An order from a client to buy or sell a security or a futures or options contract where the client specifies a maximum purchase price or minimum sale price.

Limit price move
Some exchanges only allow price moves within certain limits in the course of a day. Trading is stopped if the limit is broken. This is intended to give the market time for reflection.

Limited liability
If a limited liability company goes into liquidation the shareholders can only lose their initial stake; their personal assets are not at risk.

Liquidation
Winding up a company. It may be voluntary or imposed by creditors.

Liquidity
There is a liquid market in a security if it is easy to find a buyer or seller without having to increase or lower the price to a great extent.

Liquidity preference theory
The theory that other things being equal investors prefer short-dated investments and have to be offered a higher return to buy longer-dated investments.

Liquidity ratio
A balance sheet ratio that measures how easily a company could pay off its short-term liabilities. *See*: Current ratio.

Liquidity risk
The risk that trading in a security, currency or other asset dries up and either prices cannot be found or are subject to sharp fluctuations. Also used in banking to mean the risk that arises from funding on a short-term basis and lending on a longer-term basis.

Listing
A listed company is one whose shares are quoted and traded on a recognized major market such as the NYSE. Listed companies have to provide a substantial amount of information on a regular basis about their trading and financial position. Normally a company selling shares in an IPO will also seek a listing on an exchange or exchanges.

London Metal Exchange (LME)
The market for trading metals and futures and options on metals.

London Stock Exchange (LSE)
The stock exchange for UK shares and gilts and also shares in foreign countries. Traditionally a quote-driven market based on market makers, it has also introduced an electronic order-matching system. *See*: SETS.

Long position or long
The position of a trader who has bought securities or futures or options contracts.

Lookback option
An option whose payoff is based on the maximum or minimum price of the underlying during the life of the option.

Macaulay's duration
The value-weighted average life of a bond.

Management buy-out (MBO)
When the existing management team buys a company or a subsidiary usually with the financial assistance of banks and/or private equity funds.

Mandatorily convertible or exchangeable bond
A bond that must be converted into or exchanged for shares on or before a certain date. *See*: Convertible bond; Exchangeable bond.

Margin call
A trader who has bought or sold contracts on a futures and options exchange receives a call to make an additional margin payment (on top of the initial margin deposited) if there is an adverse movement in the value of the contract.

Margin trading
In some markets such as the US it is possible to buy shares 'on margin' — that is by putting up a proportion of the purchase price and borrowing the rest from the broker.

Mark-to-market
Revaluing investments based on the current market price. For example, if an investor bought bonds for $1 million yesterday and they are now worth $1.1 million today the mark-to-market profit is $100,000. This is a paper or unrealized profit — the profit is only realized if the bonds are actually sold.

Market capitalization or market cap
The value of a company on the stockmarket. It is the current market price of a share times the number of shares issued. The book value of the equity in the company's balance sheet is often a much lower figure. The stockmarket attempts to value a firm as a going concern. Equity book value equals assets at historical cost less depreciation less liabilities.

Market expectations theory
The theory that holds that the yield curve builds in the market's consensus expectations about future interest rates and bond prices.

Market maker
A trader who makes a market in particular securities by quoting bid and offer prices.

Unlike a broker, who acts purely as an agent matching buyers and sellers, a market maker buys or sells securities on his or her firm's own account and runs a trading book.

Market risk
Also known as price or rate risk. The risk that results from the effects of changes in the market prices of securities or interest or exchange rates.

MATIF
The Paris-based futures and options exchange.

Maturity date
The date on which a bond matures and the face or par value is repaid. Also known as the redemption date.

Medium-term note (MTN)
MTNs were originally debt securities with maturities of two or so years and designed to fill the gap between commercial paper and bonds. These days the maturity can sometimes be 10 years and more. The main feature of MTNs is the issuance procedure. Borrowers set up an MTN programme and sell notes on a continuing basis rather than on a specific issue date. The notes are often sold via dealers acting as selling agents rather than underwritten.

Merchant bank
The old UK name for investment bank.

Mezzanine capital
A hybrid source of capital that lies somewhere between debt and equity. The term is often used to mean subordinated debt which ranks behind senior or secured debt for payment, but in front of ordinary shares. It could also include instruments such as preferred or convertible preferred shares. There are specialist funds dedicated to making mezzanine finance investments.

Middle office
The part of a trading operation that stands between the traders in the front office and the back-office staff who settle deals and manage cash payments. In practice their responsibilities can vary greatly. They range from helping dealers input trades into an electronic deal capture system, to working out the end-day profits and losses. Many banks feel that it is important for profits and losses to be checked by middle-office staff rather than by the dealers who created the positions.

Modern portfolio theory
A theory that measures the risk on a security or a portfolio based on the statistical variance of returns. An optimal portfolio is one that maximizes return for a given level of risk.

Modified or adjusted duration
The percentage change in the dirty price of a bond for a 1% change in yield.

Momentum investment
A style of investment which involves riding the market trend in a share or sector until it changes direction.

Monetary Policy Committee (MPC)
The committee of the Bank of England that sets short-term UK interest rates.

Money market
The market for short-term wholesale deposits and loans (up to one year) and for trading short-term negotiable securities such as Treasury bills and commercial paper.

Monte Carlo simulation
A method of establishing the value of a complex financial asset or portfolio of assets by setting up a simulation based on random changes to the variables that determine the value of the asset or portfolio. The average or 'expected' outcome is then calculated.

Morgan Stanley Capital International World Index (MSCI)
A closely followed benchmark index of share prices from around the world.

Mortgage-backed securities (MBS)
Bonds and notes backed by a pool of mortgages. The mortgage payments are earmarked to pay interest and principal on the bonds. In a simple pass-through structure all the investors receive the same pro-rata payments from the mortgage pool. In a collateralized mortgage obligation (CMO) different classes of securities are issued with different payment characteristics. For example, one class of bonds may receive all the principal payments from the mortgage pool until they are paid off. Then a second class of bonds receives the principal payments, and so on, until all the bonds have been paid off. *See*: Collateralized mortgage obligation.

Mutual fund
The US term for an investment vehicle managed by professional asset managers in which savers can pool their savings to invest in a diversified portfolio of securities. A mutual fund can be closed-ended (with limited capital) or open-ended (like a UK unit trust).

Naked option
An option position that is not hedged.

NASDAQ
National Association of Securities Dealers Automated Quotations. A computer system showing competing market maker quotations in US and foreign shares, and which also allows trade execution.

Nearby month
A futures or options contract with the nearest delivery or expiry date from the date of trading.

Negative convexity

Bonds with embedded call features can exhibit negative convexity. This means that the rise in the bond price for a given fall in yield is less than the fall in the bond price for the same rise in yield.

Negotiable security or instrument

A security that can be freely traded after it is issued. For example, CDs are negotiable securities whereas term Eurocurrency deposits with a bank are not.

Net asset value (NAV)

Equivalent to shareholders' equity. It is balance sheet assets minus liabilities.

Net present value (NPV)

The sum of a set of present values.

New issue

A new issue of shares, bonds or other debt securities.

New York Stock Exchange (NYSE)

The largest stock exchange in the world by market capitalization. Floor brokers match buy and sell orders on behalf of clients. Otherwise orders come in electronically from member firms and are processed by the specialists. The role of specialists is to manage the order-matching process. They can also act as a market maker if a broker is unable to match a trade.

Nikkei 225

An index based on the unweighted average of 225 shares traded on the Tokyo Stock Exchange. The Nikkei 300 is weighted by market capitalization.

Nil paid

An expression used in the UK in connection with rights issues. The holder of rights can sell them to another investor 'nil paid' and the buyer will then have to pay the rights price to the issuer to receive the shares.

Nominal interest rate

The stated or quoted rate of interest or yield on a loan or debt security.

Normal distribution

The classic bell curve whose properties were proved by Gauss. In the Black–Scholes model it is assumed that the returns on shares follow a normal distribution.

Nostro account

From the Latin for 'our'. A bank's payment account held at another bank. *See*: Vostro account.

Notional principal

The face value of a derivative contract such as a swap.

OAT
French government bond.

Off-balance-sheet
An item that does not appear in the assets or liabilities columns on a company's balance sheet. The item can still give rise to contingent claims.

Off-market swap
A non-par swap in which the present values of the fixed and floating legs are not identical. Normally one party will make an initial payment to the other in compensation.

Offer price (US: ask price)
The price at which a trader is prepared to sell a security. In the money markets, the interest rate a dealer asks for lending funds.

On-the-run bond
The most recently issued and actively traded US Treasury for a given maturity. The coupon on the bond is close to the current level of interest rates and many investors like to hold the bond.

Open-ended fund
A mutual fund or investment company that can continuously take in additional capital from investors and create new units in the fund. *See*: Closed-ended fund.

Open-ended investment company (OEIC)
A listed open-ended fund that can create new shares when it wishes. The shares trade on an exchange.

Open interest
The number of futures or options contracts for a given delivery month that are still open. It is usually shown as the number of open long contracts or equivalently the number of open short contracts (not both combined). Many traders start to close out contracts before the last trading day, reducing the open interest.

Open market operations
The activities of a central bank in the money market designed to influence short-term interest rates and implement monetary policy.

Open outcry market
A physical market in which trades are conducted by dealers calling out prices.

Open position
A long or short position in securities or other assets which is not yet closed out and which therefore gives rise to market or price risk until it is closed or hedged.

Operating profit or loss
A company's profits and losses arising from its day-to-day business operations.

Option
The right but not the obligation to buy or sell a given security or commodity at a fixed price (the exercise or strike price) on or before a specified date (the expiry or expiration date).

Order-driven market
A market in which client buy and sell orders are directly matched.

Ordinary share
A stake in the equity of a company, carrying an entitlement to participate in the growth of the business and (normally) voting rights. US: common stock.

Out-of-the-money option
In the case of a call, when the strike is above the price of the underlying. In the case of a put, when the strike is below the price of the underlying.

Outright forward FX
A forward foreign exchange deal in which two currencies are exchanged for a value date later than spot.

Outright purchase or sale
A sale or purchase of securities by a central bank without time limit, as opposed to temporary sales and purchases via repo.

Over-the-counter (OTC) transactions
Trades and deals that are agreed directly between two parties rather than through an exchange.

Paid-up capital
The part of a company's issued shares that has been paid for by shareholders.

Par
The face or nominal value of a bond or bill, normally repaid at maturity. Bonds are quoted as a percentage of par.

Par bond
A bond that is trading at par.

Par swap
An interest rate swap in which the present value of the fixed and the floating legs are equal.

Parallel curve shift
When the yield curve shifts up or down in parallel, i.e. the yield change is the same at all maturities. A 'twist' in the curve happens when there are non-parallel movements.

Parity
An expression used in the convertible bond market. It measures the equity value of a convertible bond. It is the bond's conversion ratio (the number of shares it converts into) times the current market share price.

Participating preference share
A preference share which pays an additional amount on top of the fixed dividend depending on the level of profits.

Pass-through security
A security backed by underlying loans such as mortgages. The cash flows from the loans are passed through on a pro-rata basis to make the principal and interest payments to the bondholders. *See*: Collateralized debt obligation.

Payback period
How long it takes to recover the initial negative cash flows on an investment. The traditional payback measure does not discount cash flows and hence ignores the effects of the time value of money.

Perpetual bond
A bond with no fixed maturity date. Coupons are paid in perpetuity. Sometimes called an undated bond.

Perpetual floating rate note
A floating rate note with no maturity date.

Perpetual preferred share
A preference share with no fixed maturity date.

Pfandbriefe
A bond issued by one of the German mortgage banks and backed by mortgage loans and loans to local government authorities.

Physical delivery
The process of delivering the underlying commodity or financial asset specified in a contract. Some derivative contracts involve physical delivery of the underlying at a pre-agreed price. In other cases the contracts are 'cash-settled' and one party pays the difference between the contract price and the price of the underlying in the spot market on the date the contract is settled.

Plain vanilla
The most standard form of a financial instrument, such as a straight coupon-paying bond with a fixed maturity.

Political risk
The risk of losses in financial markets that result from exceptional activities by governments, e.g. halting foreign exchange trading in the national currency, or imposing special taxes.

Portfolio insurance
A hedging technique much maligned (probably unjustly) in the aftermath of the 1987 stock market crash. It involves dynamically adjusting a hedge against losses on the market as the market moves by e.g. trading index futures.

Portfolio management
Also known as fund, asset or investment management. Managing money for individual and institutional investors such as pension funds by holding a diversified portfolio of assets. The assets might include shares, bonds, cash, money market securities, property, etc.

Portfolio trading
Buying and selling whole portfolios of shares.

Position
A trader or investor who has bought securities has a long position. Someone who has sold short has a short position. A trader with an open position is exposed to market risk unless it is hedged or closed out.

Preference shares (US: preference stock)
Preference shares pay (normally) a fixed dividend and do not carry voting rights. However the dividend must be paid before the ordinary shareholders receive a dividend.

Premium
In the options market the premium is the price of an option — the sum which the buyer pays to the seller for the rights granted by the contract. On other occasions the word is used when an asset is trading above some reference level — for example, a bond trading above par is said to be trading 'at a premium to' its face value.

Present value
The discounted value of a future cash flow or cash flows.

Price/book ratio
The market capitalization of a company as a ratio of the book value of the equity (i.e. its total net assets).

Price/earnings ratio
The most commonly used measure of relative value in the equity market. It is the current market price of a share divided by the historic or prospective earnings per share.

Primary dealer
A dealer in government securities. For example, the gilt-edged market makers in the London market.

Primary market
When a security is first issued it is said to be launched in the primary market. *See also*: Secondary market.

Prime rate (US)
The base rate of interest on dollar loans to companies posted by the largest banks in the US.

Private equity
A business or fund that takes equity stakes in unlisted companies or companies listed on smaller exchanges, often participating in management buy-outs and spin-offs from corporate restructurings. Normally this is with a view to selling the stake at a later date through a trade sale or an initial public offering.

Private placement
When new securities are placed directly with large institutional investors rather than through a public offer.

Privatization
When an operation in public ownership is turned into a company in the private sector through a share offer or trade sale.

Profit
Profit before interest and tax is sales and other revenues minus direct and indirect cost of sales. Profit after interest, tax, preference share dividends and adjustments for minority interests is earnings. It is profit attributable to the ordinary shareholders which is paid in dividends and/or reinvested in the business and added to the equity (shareholders' funds) in the balance sheet.

Project finance
Complex financing deals involving construction and engineering projects, often employing a mixture of sources of finance and sometimes with government involvement. The cash flows from the project service the payments due to the providers of capital.

Protective put
Buying a put option to protect against losses on an asset.

Proxy hedge
A hedge that involves using a related financial instrument that is to some extent correlated with changes in the value of the underlying asset to be hedged. For example, a trader who has sold options on a basket of shares might trade liquid futures contracts on a market index in the expectation that profits and losses on the shares and the

futures will offset. There is a risk that the correlation between the two may turn out to be lower than anticipated.

Pull-to-par
The movement in a bond price towards its par or face value as it approaches maturity.

Put–call parity
A fixed relationship between the fair value of European call and put options. It shows that a long or short forward position can be assembled from a combination of call and put options on the underlying with the same expiry date (when the strikes are set at the forward price).

Put feature
A feature of some bonds that allows the investor to sell the bonds back to the issuer before the maturity date.

Put option
The right but not the obligation to sell the underlying at a fixed strike or exercise price.

Quanto option
An option in which the payoff depends on an underlying denominated in one currency (such as the FT-SE 100 index) but is paid in another currency (such as the US dollar).

Quick ratio
A company's current assets minus stock as a ratio of its current liabilities. A measure of how easily it can pay off its most pressing debts with cash and other assets that can quickly be turned into cash. Also known as the acid test or acid ratio.

Quote-driven market
A market in which market makers (traders) quote bid and offer prices for securities.

Rainbow option
An option whose payoff depends on two or more underlyings. For example, an option based on the best performing of two equity indices over the time to expiry.

Ranking (subordination)
Some securities rank ahead of others in terms of entitlement to payments. Holders of senior debt must be paid before other bondholders are paid. Preference shareholders rank ahead of ordinary shareholders.

Ratings agency
Agencies such as Moody's, Standard and Poor's and Fitch which rate the default risk on corporate and sovereign debt.

Real interest rate or yield
An interest rate or rate of return on an investment excluding inflation.

Recovery rate
A measure of what can be recovered on a loan or bond that defaults, e.g. 50 cents in the dollar.

Recovery share
An unloved share trading at a low price that is deemed to be ripe for recovery.

Red herring
The initial prospectus in a new share issue, published before the issue price has been set. In the UK sometimes called a pathfinder prospectus.

Redemption
When the redemption value of a security is repaid to the investors.

Registrar
A bank or other institution employed by a company to maintain the share register and make dividend payments.

Reinvestment risk
The risk that arises with coupon bonds that coupons cannot in practice be reinvested at a constant rate. Hence the actual return on a coupon bond may be higher or lower than the yield to maturity at which it was originally bought.

Repo
Short for sale and repurchase agreement. In a repo a security is sold for cash with an agreement that it will be repurchased on a specified forward date. The original holder of the security is effectively borrowing money using the security as collateral, and will therefore pay a reduced borrowing rate. The other party is effectively borrowing the security for the term of the repo, perhaps to maintain a short position. Nowadays central banks lend money to commercial banks using the repo structure and the rate at which a central bank will lend against collateral has become the key money market rate.

Repo rate
The rate of interest charged by the lender of funds in a repo. Also used to mean the rate of interest for repo transactions between a central bank and commercial banks.

Reserve assets
Funds that commercial banks must have in cash or on deposit with the central bank in proportion to the deposits they take in.

Reset or refix date
The date when a floating rate on a swap is re-fixed for the next payment period.

Retained earnings
Company earnings not paid out in dividends and added to the equity in the balance sheet.

Return on capital
Profit before interest and tax as a proportion of the capital employed in the business (normally measured as long-term debt plus equity).

Return on equity
Profit attributable to the ordinary shareholders as a proportion of the equity capital in the business.

Return on total assets
Profit before interest and tax as a proportion of the total capital employed in the business (which equals total assets).

Reverse FRN
A special kind of floating rate note. The coupon rate moves inversely with current market interest rates. They are extremely sensitive to changes in interest rates.

Rho
The sensitivity of an option value to a change in interest rates, usually a one basis point change.

Rights issue
'Rights' is short for pre-emption rights. An offer to existing shareholders to buy new shares at a discount to the current market price. A shareholder can take up the rights or sell them on. *See also*: Ex-rights.

Risk management
Monitoring, evaluating and hedging against potential losses caused by changes in asset prices, interest rates, currency exchange rates, etc. Investment banks and securities houses have a risk management function which provides an independent assessment of the risk on trading positions.

Rollover
In listed derivatives, rolling a position over from one expiry or delivery month to a later month.

Running yield
See: Current yield.

S&P 500
Standard and Poor's 500. An index of 500 shares traded on the NYSE.

Samurai bond
A bond denominated in yen issued in the Japanese domestic market by a foreign issuer.

Savings and Loan Association (SLA)
US financial institution that takes in deposits and makes housing loans. Similar to the UK building societies.

Scrip dividend (US: stock dividend)
When an investor takes a dividend in the form of new shares rather than cash.

SEAQ
Stock Exchange Automated Quotations. The system in the UK for collecting and distributing competing market maker quotations for securities traded on the London Stock Exchange.

Secondary market
A market to buy and sell securities already launched through the primary market. *See*: Primary market.

Securities & Exchange Commission (SEC)
Federal agency responsible for regulating the securities industry in the US.

Securitization
The process of creating asset-backed securities by packaging up future cash flows such as the interest and principal repayments due on loans. Bonds are sold to investors which are backed by the underlying cash flows.

Security
The generic name for a negotiable (tradable) instrument such as a share, bond or bill.

Sell-side
Analysts, salespeople and traders working for investment banks and securities houses who provide investment ideas and execute trades for fund managers (the buy-side).

Series
An expression used in derivatives exchanges. Option contracts on the same underlying with the same strike and expiry.

SETS
Stock Exchange Trading System. The electronic order-driven system for trading securities run by the London Stock Exchange. Buy and sell orders are directly matched. Now extended to international shares as well as top UK shares.

Settlement date
The date when a security is transferred and cash is paid for it. Depending on the market, settlement may be the day after the deal is agreed or a week or more later. The expression '$T + n$' means that settlement is made n business days after the trade date T.

Settlement of differences
With some derivatives contracts there is no physical delivery. The difference between the contract price and the price of the underlying is settled in cash.

Settlement price
The price used by a clearing house to mark-to-market a derivatives contract. Usually an average of the last trades at the end of the trading day.

Short position, short sale, short
Someone who has sold a cash security he or she does not own. Or someone who has sold futures or options without yet having bought contracts to close the position.

SIMEX
Singapore International Monetary Exchange.

Sinking fund
When the issuer sets aside funds to redeem a bond issue or (more commonly) retires a certain amount of the issue each year.

Sovereign
Used in the capital markets to mean a government borrower as opposed to a corporate.

Sovereign risk
The risk that a sovereign borrower might default on a loan or bond issue.

SPAN
Standard Portfolio Analysis of Risk. A system developed on the CME and also used on LIFFE to calculate margins on portfolios of derivatives contracts.

Sparkassen
German savings banks.

Special purpose vehicle (SPV)
A tax-exempt trust company specially set up to implement a securitization. The SPV issues bonds and buys the title to the ownership of the cash flows which will repay the bonds. It manages the payments to the bondholders.

Specialist member
A member firm of the NYSE which manages the order-matching process on a trading post.

Spot foreign exchange rate
The rate for exchanging two currencies in (for major currency pairs) two business days.

Spot interest rate or yield
Zero coupon interest rate or yield.

Spot price
The price of a security for spot delivery. Also known as the 'cash price' although the actual settlement and delivery may take place a day or so after the trade is agreed.

Spread

The difference between two prices or rates. For example, a dealer charges a spread — the difference between his or her bid and offer price. A commercial bank lends money at a margin or spread over its funding rate. The extra yield or return on a corporate bond over the yield on government debt is known as a credit spread since it reflects the additional default risk.

Spread trade

Simultaneously buying and selling to take advantage of anticipated changes in the price difference between two securities or derivatives contracts. Or a trade involving a combination of options. *See*: Bull spread.

Stag

A trader speculating on a new share issue.

Stamp duty

A government tax on share dealings. For a parallel see Dr Johnson's Dictionary entry on Excise: 'A hateful tax levied upon commodities, and adjudged not by the common judges of property, but wretches hired by those to whom Excise is paid'.

Stock exchange or market

An organized and regulated market for trading securities. It can be a physical market located on a trading floor, or based on screens and telephones, or a purely electronic market.

Stock index

An index that tracks the changing price of a typical portfolio of shares. The most commonly quoted index in the UK is the FT-SE 100, an index of 100 top shares. In the US key indices include the Dow Jones Industrial Average and the S&P 500.

Stock index futures

A futures contract on an index such as the FT-SE 100 or the S&P 500. These are 'settlement of differences' contracts — there is no physical delivery of shares. On the main FT-SE 100 futures contract each one index point move in the contract level represents £10 in cash. On the main S&P 500 futures each index point is worth $250.

Stock lending

Holders of shares can make extra money by lending the shares to a borrower for a fee. The lender demands collateral to ensure that the shares are returned.

Stock split

When a company thinks its share price is too unwieldy it issues a number of new shares to replace each existing share. Also known as a bonus or capitalization issue in the UK. It differs from a rights or other new equity issue in that the company is not raising new capital.

Stop-loss order
An order to a broker to close out a position and limit the losses whenever a given price level is reached.

Stop-profit order
An order to a broker to close out a position and take the profits to date whenever a given price level is reached.

Straddle
A combined option strategy which involves simultaneously selling a call and a put (short straddle) or buying a call and a put (long straddle) on the same underlying with the same strike and the same time to expiration.

Straight bond
A bond which pays fixed coupons on fixed dates and has a fixed maturity date. A 'plain vanilla' bond, without non-standard features such as a variable coupon or the right to convert into shares.

Strangle
Like a straddle except the options used in the strategy have different strikes. *See*: Straddle.

Strike price
Another term for the exercise price of an option.

Stripping and strips
Also known as coupon stripping. Separating the principal and the interest payments on a coupon bond and selling off the parts as zero coupon bonds. The resulting zeros may be known as 'strips'.

Structured note
A security usually assembled using derivatives that has non-standard features, e.g. the payments are linked to a commodity price or an equity market, or the difference between interest rates in two currencies, or the change in the credit rating of a bond or loan.

Swap
A binding contract between two parties agreeing to make payments to each other on specified future dates over an agreed time period, where the amount that each has to pay is calculated on a different basis. *See*: Cross-currency swap; Equity swap; Interest rate swap.

Swap curve
A yield curve based on the fixed rates on standard par interest rate swaps. It can be bootstrapped to generate spot rates. *See*: Bootstrapping; Yield curve.

Swaption
An option to enter into an interest rate swap. A payer swaption is an option to pay fixed and receive floating. A receiver swaption is an option to receive fixed and pay floating.

SWIFT
Society for Worldwide Interbank Financial Telecommunications. The interbank payments system based in Brussels.

Syndicate
A group of investment banks combining to underwrite and distribute a new issue of securities, or a group of commercial banks combining to create a syndicated loan.

Syndicated loan
A loan made to a corporation or government by a syndicate of lending banks. Members of the syndicate may allocate a proportion of the deal to a number of 'participating' banks.

Systematic risk
Undiversifiable or market risk.

Systemic risk
The risk that an event such as a bank failure might have a domino effect on the rest of the financial system.

Technical analysis
Analysing the pattern of price movements of an asset to predict future price changes. In the UK also known as chartism.

TED spread
Treasury/Eurodollar spread. The difference between the Eurodollar rate and the rate on US Treasury bills.

Tender
In the UK sometimes used to mean an auction of securities.

Tenor
Time to maturity.

Term (time) deposit or loan
A deposit or loan with a specific maturity.

Term repo
A repo with longer than overnight maturity.

Term structure of interest rates
Spot rates in a given currency for a range of maturities.

Theta
The change in the value of an option as time elapses.

Tick size
The minimum price move allowed in a price quotation.

Tick value
The value of each one tick movement in the quoted price on the whole contract size.

Time value
The difference between an option's premium and its intrinsic value. Time value is related to the probability that the option will make money for its owner (lose money for the seller) and is calculated by models such as Black–Scholes. If an option has no intrinsic value then all the premium is time value.

Time value of money
The basis of discounted cash flow valuation. If interest rates are positive then money today is worth more than money in the future because it can be invested. Money due to be received in the future is therefore worth less today.

Top-down
A style of portfolio management based on firstly making top-level decisions about which classes of assets and which markets to invest in, and only later picking individual securities. *See*: Bottom-up.

Touch
The highest bid and the lowest offer price for a security.

Trade fail
When something goes wrong in the settlement of a trade, e.g. the payment instructions were not carried out properly.

Trader
An individual or an employee of a financial institution who buys and sells securities and runs trading positions.

Tranche
From the French word for 'slice'. In a securitization different tranches of bonds are often sold with different risk/return characteristics to appeal to specific investor groups. *See*: Securitization.

Treasury bill (T-bill)
A short-term negotiable debt security issued and fully backed by a government.

Treasury bond
A longer-term debt security issued and fully backed by a government. US Treasury bonds have maturities between 10 and 30 years when issued. Treasury notes have maturities between one and 10 years.

Triple witching hour
US expression for the day when stock and index options and index futures all expire.

Two-way quotation
A dealer's bid (buy) and offer (ask or sell) price. The difference between the two is the dealer's spread.

Ultra vires
Beyond the legal power. Used when an organization or individual enters into a transaction which they are not legally entitled to conduct.

Underlying
The asset that underlies a derivative product. The value of the derivative is based on the value of the underlying.

Underwriting
The underwriters of a new issue of securities guarantee that the securities will be fully taken up at the issue price. If they cannot find buyers the securities are left with the underwriters. In a larger issue there will be a syndicate of underwriters.

Underwriting risk
The risk that the underwriters will lose money if they are unable to sell securities for more than the price they have guaranteed the issuer.

Universal bank
A banking group that offers a wide variety of products and services globally, including investment and commercial banking. It may also have a retail banking operation, a fund management business and an insurance subsidiary. Sometimes a large banking group that offers a wide range of services but which is focused on one region (e.g. Europe) is called a regional bank.

Unlisted company
A company whose shares are not listed on a major stock market. They may trade over-the-counter or on a market for smaller companies such as the Alternative Investment Market (AIM) in London.

Upside potential
Potential for profits.

Value at Risk (VAR)
A statistical estimate of the maximum loss that can be made on a portfolio of assets to a certain confidence level and over a given time period. For example, if a portfolio of securities is currently worth $1 million and the one-week VAR at the 99% confidence level is $50,000 this means there is only a 1% chance that losses on the portfolio over the course of one week will exceed $50,000.

Value investment
A style of investment that favours relatively 'cheap' shares (with low price/earnings ratios) that are reckoned to be undervalued.

Variation margin
Additional margin paid or received when a derivatives contract is marked-to-market and there is a margin call from the clearing house.

Venture capital
Sometimes used now as a synonym for private equity. More often it means taking a stake in a start-up company or a business in an early growth phase. The venture capitalist often takes a substantial proportion of the equity and plays a 'hands on' role, advising management on the development of the business. *See*: Private equity.

Voice broker
A broker who relays current market bid and offer prices to subscribing clients via a voice-based system rather than electronically.

Volatility
A key component in option pricing. A measure of the variability of the returns on the underlying security. This can be based on historic evidence or future projections. The more volatile the returns on a security the more expensive a standard option on that security will be — the holder of the option has more chance of making money, the seller has more chance of losing money. *See*: Historic volatility; Implied volatility.

Volatility smile
A graph showing the implied volatilities of options on the same underlying for a range of strike prices. It is used to pinpoint the correct volatility to use to price or revalue options. In-, at- and out-of-the-money options often trade on different implied volatilities in the market. In practice the graph is often a skew rather than a smile.

Volatility surface
A three-dimensional graph showing the implied volatilities of options on the same underlying for a range of different strike prices and expiration dates.

Volume weighted average price (VWAP)
The average price at which a share was traded during a given time period, such as one day. Each trading price is weighted by the number of shares traded at that price. Dealers and fund managers use VWAP as a benchmark to see whether or not they have traded close to the market level.

Vostro account
From the Latin for 'your'. A payment account maintained by a bank on behalf of another bank. *See*: Nostro account.

Warrant
A warrant is a long-dated option in the form of a security which can be freely traded, often on a stock exchange. Issuer warrants are issued by a company on its own shares.

Covered warrants are sold by banks and securities houses and are based on another company's shares or on baskets of shares. They may be call or put warrants. Covered warrants are often cash-settled, i.e. the intrinsic value of the option is settled in cash and no physical shares are ever delivered.

Weighted average cost of capital (WACC)
Most companies are funded through a mixture of equity and debt capital. WACC is calculated as the cost of debt times the proportion of debt in the business, plus the cost of equity times the proportion of equity in the business. It is used as a discount rate to establish the present value of a firm's expected future cash flows, and thereby to establish a value for the whole company.

Withholding tax
When a proportion of a coupon or dividend payment is withheld from the investor by the issuer and paid over to the government in tax. Eurobonds are not currently subject to withholding tax.

Working capital
Current assets minus current liabilities.

World Bank
Properly known as the International Bank for Reconstruction and Development.

Writer
The seller of an option.

Yankee bond
A US dollar bond issued inside the US domestic market by a non-US issuer.

Yield
The return on an investment, taking into account the amount invested and the expected future cash flows.

Yield curve
A graph showing the yields on a given class of bonds (e.g. US Treasuries) against time to maturity. A positive or upward-sloping curve occurs when rates on shorter maturity bonds are lower than those on longer maturity bonds. A negative, inverse or downward-sloping curve occurs when short-term yields are higher.

Yield to call
The internal rate of return on a bond assuming that it is held to the first call date and is then called.

Yield to maturity
The total return earned on a bond if it is bought at the current market price and held until maturity with coupons reinvested at a constant rate. The bond's internal rate of return.

Zero cost collar
A collar strategy on which there is zero net premium to pay. The premiums on the calls and puts cancel out.

Zero coupon bond
A bond which does not pay a coupon and which trades at a discount to its par or face value. At maturity the holder of the bond is repaid the face value.

Zero coupon rate (spot rate)
The rate of interest that applies to a specific future date. Specialists in fixed income markets use zero coupon rates to discount cash flows and price instruments because no reinvestment assumptions need be made.

Useful Internet Sites

American Stock Exchange	www.amex.com
Bank for International Settlements	www.bis.org
Bank of Japan	www.boj.or.jp/en
Barclays Capital	www.barclayscapital.com
Bloomberg	www.bloomberg.com
Chicago Board of Trade	www.cbot.com
Chicago Board Options Exchange	www.cboe.com
Chicago Mercantile Exchange	www.cme.com
CIBC World Markets	www.cibcwm.com
Citigroup	www.citigroup.com
Credit Suisse First Boston	www.csfb.com
Deutsche Bank (CIB)	www.db.com
Deutsche Börse	www.deutsche-boerse.com
Dresdner Kleinwort Wasserstein	www.drkw.com
Dun and Bradstreet	www.dnb.com
EBRD	www.edrd.com
Eurex	www.eurexchange.com
Euromoney Publications	www.euromoney.com
Euronext	www.euronext.com
European Central Bank	www.ecb.int
Fannie Mae (FNMA)	www.fanniemae.com
Financial Times	www.ft.com
Fitch	www.fitchibca.com
Freddie Mac (FHLMC)	www.freddiemac.com
Goldman Sachs	www.gs.com
HSBC	www.hsbc.com
International Monetary Fund	www.imf.org
ISMA	www.isma.org
JP Morgan	www.jpmorgan.com
Lehman Brothers	www.lehman.com
LIFFE	www.liffe.com
London Stock Exchange	www.londonstockexchange.com
Merrill Lynch	www.ml.com
Moody's Investor Services	www.moodys.com
Morgan Stanley	www.morganstanley.com
NASDAQ	www.nasdaq.com
New York Stock Exchange	www.nyse.com
Nomura	www.nomura.com
Philadelphia Stock Exchange	www.phlx.com
Reuters	www.reuters.com

Risk Metrics Group	www.riskmetrics.com
Securities & Exchange Commission	www.sec.gov
Securities & Futures Authority	www.fsa.gov.uk/sfa
Standard and Poor's	www.standardandpoors.com
Telerate	www.telerate.com
The Bank of England	www.bankofengland.co.uk
The Economist	www.economist.com
The Royal Bank of Scotland	www.royalbankscot.co.uk
UBS Warburg	www.ubswarburg.com
UK Treasury	www.hm-treasury.gov.uk
US Federal Reserve	www.federalreserve.gov
US Treasury	www.treas.gov
Wall Street Journal	www.info.wsj.com
World Bank	www.worldbank.com

Further Reading

Many books and articles have been written on the capital markets. The following are a few select titles that cover topics raised in the current volume in more detail.

Arditti F.D. *Derivatives*. Harvard Business School Press 1996.
Berstein P.L. *Against the Gods: The Remarkable Story of Risk*. John Wiley & Sons 1996.
Bickerstaffe G. ed. *Mastering Finance*. FT Pitman 1998.
Brearley R.A. and Myers S.C. *Principles of Corporate Finance*. McGraw-Hill 1991.
Choudhry M. *The Bond & Money Markets*. Butterworth-Heinemann 2001.
Cornwell B. *The Equity Risk Premium*. John Wiley & Sons 1999.
Damodaran A. *Investment Valuation*. John Wiley & Sons 1996.
Fabozzi F.J. *Fixed Income Mathematics*. McGraw-Hill 1997.
Hull J.C. *Options, Futures and Other Derivatives*. Fourth edition. Prentice-Hall 2000.
Jarrow R. and Turnbull S. *Derivative Securities*. South-Western College Publishing 1996.
Natenberg S. *Option Volatility & Pricing*. Probus 1994.
Roth P. *Mastering Foreign Exchange & Money Markets*. FT Pitman 1996.
Smithson C.W., Smith C.W. and Sykes Wilford D. *Managing Financial Risk*. Irwin 1995.
Walmsley J. *New Financial Instruments*. John Wiley & Sons 1998.
Walmsley J. *The Foreign Exchange and Money Markets Guide*. Second edition. John Wiley & Sons 2000.

For a highly readable overview of the City of London's recent history try Philip Augar's *The Death of Gentlemanly Capitalism* published by Penguin in 2001. The full story is told in David Kynaston's magnificent series *The City of London* published by Chatto and Windus in four volumes. Volume IV published in 2001 covers the years 1945–2000.

Index